Ravindra Khattree
& Dayanand N. Naik

Applied
Multivariate
Statistics
with
SAS® Software

To the fond memory of my son, Kaushik (R.K.)

To my loving parents (D.N.N.)

iv

Contents

Preface   vii
Commonly Used Notation   xi
About the Authors   xiii

Chapter 1:   Multivariate Analysis Concepts   1

  1.1 Introduction   1
  1.2 Random Vectors, Means, Variances, and Covariances   1
  1.3 Multivariate Normal Distribution   4
  1.4 Sampling from Multivariate Normal Populations   5
  1.5 Some Important Sample Statistics and Their Distributions   8
  1.6 Tests for Multivariate Normality   9
  1.7 Random Vector and Matrix Generation   12
  SAS Code and Output   15

Chapter 2:   Graphical Representation of Multivariate Data   23

  2.1 Introduction   23
  2.2 Scatter Plots   24
  2.3 Profile Plots   26
  2.4 Andrews Function Plots   26
  2.5 Biplot: Plotting Observations and Variables Together   27
  2.6 Q-Q Plots for Assessing Multivariate Normality   30
  2.7 Plots for Detection of Multivariate Outliers   32
  2.8 Bivariate Normal Distribution   33
  2.9 SAS/INSIGHT Software   34
  SAS Code and Output   35

Chapter 3:   Multivariate Regression   67

  3.1 Introduction   67
  3.2 Statistical Background   68
  3.3 Least Squares Estimation   69
  3.4 ANOVA Partitioning   70
  3.5 Testing Hypotheses: Linear Hypotheses   72
  3.6 Simultaneous Confidence Intervals   83
  3.7 Multiple Response Surface Modeling   85
  3.8 General Linear Hypotheses   87
  3.9 Variance and Bias Analyses for Calibration Problems   91
  SAS Code and Output   95

Chapter 4: Multivariate Analysis of Experimental Data 127

       4.1 Introduction **127**
       4.2 Balanced and Unbalanced Data **130**
       4.3 One-Way Classification **134**
       4.4 Two-Way Classification **140**
       4.5 Blocking **144**
       4.6 Fractional Factorial Experiments **146**
       4.7 Analysis of Covariance **149**
       SAS Code and Output **155**

Chapter 5: Analysis of Repeated Measures Data 187

       5.1 Introduction **187**
       5.2 Single Population **188**
       5.3 k Populations **204**
       5.4 Factorial Designs **221**
       5.5 Analysis in the Presence of Covariates **226**
       5.6 Analysis Using Random Coefficient Models **232**
       5.7 The Growth Curve Models **236**
       5.8 Crossover Designs **246**
       SAS Code and Output **253**

References 377
Index 385

Preface

Applied multivariate techniques are routinely used in a variety of disciplines such as agriculture, anthropology, applied statistics, biological sciences, business, chemistry, econometrics, education, engineering, marketing, medicine, psychology, quality control, and sociology. With such a diverse readership, we thought it essential to present multivariate techniques in a general context while at the same time keeping the mathematical and statistical requirements to a bare minimum. We have sincerely attempted to achieve this objective.

Audience

The book was written both as a handy reference for researchers and practitioners and also as a supplementary college text. Researchers and practitioners can also adapt the material for a self-taught tutorial. Students and their instructors in senior undergraduate or beginning graduate classes in applied statistics will find the book useful as an accompanying computational supplement to a more advanced book on applied multivariate statistics. The book can also be adapted for a statistics service course for graduate students from the nonstatistical disciplines.

Approach

Primary emphasis is on statistical methodology as applied to various scientific disciplines. SAS software is used as the crucial computational aid to carry out various intensive calculations which so naturally occur in any typical multivariate analysis application. Discussion in this volume is limited to only the normal theory-based multivariate analysis.

We believe that those who use multivariate methods should not only understand appropriate statistical techniques useful in their particular situation but should also be able to discern the appropriate approach and distinguish it from an approach that *seems* correct but is completely inappropriate in a particular context. Quite often, these differences are subtle, and there are scenarios where the presumably *best approach* may be completely invalid due to one reason or the other. The problem is further compounded by the understandable temptation to take the shortest route by choosing the analysis that can be readily performed using a particular software package, regardless of its appropriateness, over a more appropriate analysis not so readily available. This book attempts to demonstrate this process of discernment, problem definition, selection of an appropriate analysis or a combination of many, while providing both the needed SAS code to achieve these goals and the subsequent interpretation of the SAS output.

This approach largely eliminates the need for two books, one for learning multivariate techniques and another for mastering the software usage. Instead of taking various multivariate procedures in SAS one at a time and demonstrating their potential to solve a large number of different problems, we have chosen to discuss various multivariate situations one by one and then identify the most appropriate SAS analyses for them. Many of these analyses may occasionally result from the combined applications of two or more SAS procedures. All multivariate methods are illustrated by appropriate examples. In most cases, the data sets considered are real and are adapted from the published literature from a variety of disciplines.

Prerequisites

A course in applied statistics dealing with the essentials of the (univariate) experimental designs and regression theory and some familiarity with matrix algebra (just enough to interpret the notationally presented statistical models and linear hypotheses) provide an adequate preparation to read this book. Some familiarity with SAS programming (the DATA step and the basic rules of the SAS language) will also be helpful. See the References for a listing of SAS documentation.

Overview of Chapters

Chapter 1 provides a summary of important multivariate results. In Chapter 2, various graphical methods for the exploratory multivariate analysis are presented. In Chapter 3, a brief review of the multivariate regression models is provided, which is followed by a number of applications. Chapter 4 deals with the analysis of experimental data. Since the underlying theory, though a bit more complex, is essentially parallel to that presented in Chapter 3, we have largely confined our discussion here to modeling and applications in a variety of experimental designs.

Chapter 5, Analysis of Repeated Measures Data, occupies a relatively larger space than other chapters in the book. This emphasis requires some further explanation. The repeated measures data are multivariate in nature but are often analyzed using some of the univariate techniques. Both the univariate and multivariate approaches have their own advantages and shortcomings and both are important in their own rights. Both of these approaches are discussed in this chapter. Complexity of models is inherent in the repeated measures data; variety in terms of models is plentiful, and many of these models are commonly used in different disciplines. As a result, we have decided to provide a careful systematic discussion of some of the most commonly used models with an appropriate explanation of the analyses performed by various SAS procedures. However, our coverage, though extensive, is still by no means, exhaustive.

Finally, in a work of this size, integrating various aspects of statistical methods and data analysis, there are bound to be some errors and gaps. We will greatly appreciate any comments, suggestions or criticisms which will help us improve this work further.

Acknowledgments

A number of people have contributed to this project in a number of ways. Our sincere thanks are due to outside peer reviewers and internal reviewers at SAS Institute for their helpful suggestions. Whole or parts of the manuscript were read by Professors A. M. Kshirsagar, T. K. Nayak, S. D. Peddada, and N. H. Timm. We greatly acknowledge their interest in this project. Special thanks are due to Professor Kshirsagar for a number of discussion sessions at various occasions. Our students Ms. Shobha Prabhala and Ms. Karen Meldrum read parts of an earlier draft of the manuscript. Ms. Raja Vishnubhotla, a local SAS expert at Oakland University, answered our numerous inquiries about SAS. Parts of the book were typed by Ms. Kathy Jegla and Ms. Sujatha Naik. We kindly thank them for their assistance.

People at SAS Institute, especially Mr. David Baggett and Ms. Caroline Brickley, were most helpful and generous with their suggestions and time. We very much appreciate their understanding and their willingness to extend many of the deadlines.

We would also like to acknowledge the Oakland University's Research Foundation for partially supporting some of the travel of R. Khattree and the Old Dominion University for approving the sabbatical of D. N. Naik during Fall 1994. We also thank our two departments in the respective universities for playing the host during our numerous visits to each other's institutions.

Last, but not least, our sincere thanks go to our wives, Nidhi and Sujatha, for allowing us to work during late odd hours and over the weekends. We thank them for their understanding that this book could not have been completed just by working during regular hours.

R. Khattree, Rochester, Michigan

D. N. Naik, Norfolk, Virginia

Commonly Used Notation

$\mathbf{I}_n$, The n by n identity matrix

$\mathbf{1}_n$, The n by 1 vector of unit elements

$\mathbf{O}$, A matrix of appropriate order with all zero entries

λ_i, The ith eigenvalue of the matrix under consideration

$|\mathbf{A}|$, The determinant of the square matrix $\mathbf{A}$

$tr(\mathbf{A})$, The trace of the square matrix $\mathbf{A}$

$\mathbf{A}^{-1}$, The inverse of the matrix $\mathbf{A}$

$\mathbf{A}^{1/2}$, The symmetric square root of the matrix $\mathbf{A}$

$\mathbf{A}^-$, A generalized inverse of the matrix $\mathbf{A}$

$E(\mathbf{y})$, Expected value of a random variable or vector $\mathbf{y}$

$v(\mathbf{y})$, $var(\mathbf{y})$, Variance of a random variable $\mathbf{y}$

$cov(\mathbf{x}, \mathbf{y})$, Covariance *of* random variable (vector) $\mathbf{x}$ *with* random variable (or vector) $\mathbf{y}$

$D(\mathbf{y})$, The variance covariance or the dispersion matrix of $\mathbf{y}$

$N_p(\mu, \Sigma)$, A p-dimensional normal distribution with mean μ and the variance covariance matrix Σ.

$W_p(f, \Sigma)$, A p-dimensional Wishart distribution with f degrees of freedom and parameter Σ (that is, with expected value $f.\Sigma$)

SS&CP Matrix, Matrix of the sums of squares and crossproducts

About the Authors

Ravindra Khattree is a professor of applied statistics at the Oakland University, Rochester, Michigan. He received his graduate training at the Indian Statistical Institute (MS 1980, Diploma in SQC and OR 1980) and the University of Pittsburgh (MS 1985, PhD 1985). He is an author or coauthor of numerous research papers in theoretical and applied statistics in various national and international journals and conference proceedings. His research interests are in multivariate analysis, experimental designs, quality control, repeated measures, and statistical inference. He teaches various graduate and undergraduate courses in these areas. In addition, he regularly consults with industry and academic researchers on various applied statistics problems.

Dayanand N. Naik is an associate professor of statistics at Old Dominion University, Norfolk, Virginia. He received his MS degree in statistics from Karnatak University, India, in 1975 and a PhD degree in statistics from the University of Pittsburgh in 1985. He has several research publications in reputed journals, and he is the thesis advisor of many graduate students. His research and teaching interests are in multivariate analysis, linear models, quality control, regression diagnostics, repeated measures analysis, and growth curve models.

CHAPTER 1: Multivariate Analysis Concepts

1.1 Introduction
1.2 Random Vectors, Means, Variances, and Covariances
1.3 Multivariate Normal Distribution
1.4 Sampling from Multivariate Normal Populations
1.5 Some Important Sample Statistics and Their Distributions
1.6 Tests for Multivariate Normality
1.7 Random Vector and Matrix Generation
    1.7.1   Random Vector Generation from $N_p(\mu, \Sigma)$
    1.7.2   Generation of Wishart Random Matrix

1.1 Introduction

This chapter reviews the underlying multivariate normal theory which is essential for a proper understanding of various multivariate statistical techniques, notation, and nomenclature. The material presented here is meant to be only a refresher and is far from complete.

1.2 Random Vectors, Means, Variances, and Covariances

Suppose $y_1, \ldots, y_p$ are p possibly correlated random variables with respective means (expected values) $\mu_1, \ldots, \mu_p$. Let us arrange these random variables as a column vector denoted by $\mathbf{y}$, that is

$$
\mathbf{y} = \begin{bmatrix} y_1 \\ y_2 \\ \cdot \\ \cdot \\ \cdot \\ y_p \end{bmatrix}
$$

and do the same for $\mu_1, \mu_2, \ldots, \mu_p$ and denote the corresponding vector by μ. Then we say that the vector $\mathbf{y}$ has the mean μ or in notation $E(\mathbf{y}) = \mu$.

Let us denote the covariance between y_i and y_j by σ_{ij}, $i, j = 1, \ldots, p$, that is

$$
\sigma_{ij} = cov(y_i, y_j) = E[(y_i - \mu_i)(y_j - \mu_j)] = E[(y_i - \mu_i)y_j] = E(y_iy_j) - \mu_i\mu_j
$$

and let

$$
\Sigma = (\sigma_{ij}) = \begin{bmatrix} \sigma_{11} & \sigma_{12} & \cdots & \sigma_{1p} \\ \sigma_{21} & \sigma_{22} & \cdots & \sigma_{2p} \\ & & & \\ \sigma_{p1} & \sigma_{p2} & \cdots & \sigma_{pp} \end{bmatrix}.
$$

Since $cov(y_i, y_j) = cov(y_j, y_i)$, we have $\sigma_{ij} = \sigma_{ji}$. Therefore, Σ is symmetric with $(i, j)^{th}$ and $(j, i)^{th}$ elements representing the covariance between y_i and y_j. Further, since $var(y_i) = cov(y_i, y_i) = \sigma_{ii}$, the ith diagonal place of Σ contains the variance of y_i. The matrix Σ is called the dispersion or the variance-covariance matrix of $\mathbf{y}$. In notation, we write this fact as $D(\mathbf{y}) = \Sigma$. Various books follow alternative notations for $D(\mathbf{y})$ such as $cov(\mathbf{y})$ or $var(\mathbf{y})$. However, we adopt the less ambiguous notation of $D(\mathbf{y})$.

Thus,

$$\Sigma = D(\mathbf{y}) = E[(\mathbf{y} - \mu)(\mathbf{y} - \mu)'] = E[(\mathbf{y} - \mu)\mathbf{y}'] = E(\mathbf{y}\mathbf{y}') - \mu\mu',$$

where for any matrix (vector) $\mathbf{A}$, the notation $\mathbf{A}'$ represents its transpose.

Let $\mathbf{u}_{p \times 1}$ and $\mathbf{z}_{q \times 1}$ be two random vectors, with respective means μ_u and μ_z. Then the covariance of $\mathbf{u}$ *with* $\mathbf{z}$ is defined as

$$\Sigma_{uz} = cov(\mathbf{u}, \mathbf{z}) = E[(\mathbf{u} - \mu_u)(\mathbf{z} - \mu_z)'] = E[(\mathbf{u} - \mu_u)\mathbf{z}'] = E(\mathbf{u}\mathbf{z}') - \mu_u\mu_z'.$$

Note that $\Sigma_{uz} = cov(\mathbf{u}, \mathbf{z})$ is *not* the same as $\Sigma_{zu} = cov(\mathbf{z}, \mathbf{u})$, the covariance of $\mathbf{z}$ *with* $\mathbf{u}$. They are, however, related in that

$$\Sigma_{uz} = \Sigma_{zu}'.$$

Notice that for a vector $\mathbf{y}$, $cov(\mathbf{y}, \mathbf{y}) = D(\mathbf{y})$. Thus, when there is no possibility of confusion, we interchangeably use $D(\mathbf{y})$ and $cov(\mathbf{y})(= cov(\mathbf{y}, \mathbf{y}))$ to represent the variance-covariance matrix of $\mathbf{y}$.

A variance-covariance matrix is always positive semidefinite (that is, all its eigenvalues are nonnegative). However, in most of the discussion in this text we encounter the dispersion matrices which are positive definite, a condition stronger than positive semidefiniteness in that all its eigenvalues are strictly positive. Consequently, such dispersion matrices would also admit an inverse. In the subsequent discussion, we assume our dispersion matrix to be positive definite.

Let us partition the vector $\mathbf{y}$ into two subvectors as

$$\mathbf{y} = \begin{bmatrix} \mathbf{y}_1 \\ \mathbf{y}_2 \end{bmatrix} \begin{matrix} p_1 \times 1 \\ (p-p_1) \times 1 \end{matrix}$$

and partition Σ as

$$\Sigma = \begin{bmatrix} \Sigma_{11_{p_1 \times p_1}} & \Sigma_{12_{p_1 \times (p-p_1)}} \\ \Sigma_{21_{(p-p_1) \times p_1}} & \Sigma_{22_{(p-p_1) \times (p-p_1)}} \end{bmatrix}.$$

Then, $E(\mathbf{y}_1) = \mu_1$, $E(\mathbf{y}_2) = \mu_2$, $D(\mathbf{y}_1) = \Sigma_{11}$, $D(\mathbf{y}_2) = \Sigma_{22}$, $cov(\mathbf{y}_1, \mathbf{y}_2) = \Sigma_{12}$, $cov(\mathbf{y}_2, \mathbf{y}_1) = \Sigma_{21}$. We also observe that $\Sigma_{12} = \Sigma_{21}'$.

If ρ_{ij} is the Pearson's *correlation coefficient* between y_i and y_j, defined by

$$\rho_{ij} = \frac{cov(y_i, y_j)}{\sqrt{var(y_i)var(y_j)}} = \frac{\sigma_{ij}}{\sqrt{\sigma_{ii}\sigma_{ij}}},$$

then accordingly, we define the *correlation coefficient matrix* of $\mathbf{y}$ as

$$\mathbf{R} = \begin{bmatrix} \rho_{11} & \rho_{12} & \cdots & \rho_{1p} \\ \rho_{21} & \rho_{22} & \cdots & \rho_{2p} \\ & & & \\ \rho_{p1} & \rho_{p2} & \cdots & \rho_{pp} \end{bmatrix}.$$

It is easy to verify that the correlation coefficient matrix $\mathbf{R}$ is symmetric positive definite, with all the diagonal elements as unity. The matrix $\mathbf{R}$ can be written, in terms of matrix Σ, as

$$\mathbf{R} = [diag(\Sigma)]^{-\frac{1}{2}} \Sigma [diag(\Sigma)]^{-\frac{1}{2}},$$

where $diag(\Sigma)$ is the diagonal matrix obtained by retaining the diagonal elements of Σ and by replacing all the nondiagonal elements by zero.

The probability distribution (density) of a vector $\mathbf{y}$, denoted by $f(\mathbf{y})$, is the same as the joint probability distribution of $y_1, \ldots, y_p$. The marginal distribution $f_1(\mathbf{y}_1)$ of $\mathbf{y}_1 = (y_1, \ldots, y_{p_1})'$, a subvector of $\mathbf{y}$, is obtained by integrating out $\mathbf{y}_2 = (y_{p_1+1}, \ldots, y_p)'$ from the density $f(\mathbf{y})$. The conditional distribution of $\mathbf{y}_2$, when $\mathbf{y}_1$ has been held fixed, is denoted by $g(\mathbf{y}_2|\mathbf{y}_1)$ and is given by

$$g(\mathbf{y}_2|\mathbf{y}_1) = f(\mathbf{y})/f_1(\mathbf{y}_1).$$

An important concept arising from conditional distribution is the *partial correlation coefficient*. If we partition $\mathbf{y}$ as $(\mathbf{y}_1', \mathbf{y}_2')'$ where $\mathbf{y}_1$ is a p_1 by 1 vector and $\mathbf{y}_2$ is a $(p - p_1)$ by 1 vector, then the partial correlation coefficient between two components of $\mathbf{y}_1$, say y_i and y_j, is defined as the Pearson's correlation coefficient between y_i and y_j conditional on $\mathbf{y}_2$ (that is, for a given $\mathbf{y}_2$). If $\Sigma_{11\cdot2} = (a_{ij})$ is the p_1 by p_1 variance-covariance matrix of $\mathbf{y}_1$ given $\mathbf{y}_2$, then the population partial correlation coefficient between y_i and y_j, $i, j = 1, \ldots, p_1$ is given by

$$\rho_{ij \cdot p_1+1, \ldots, p} = a_{ij}/\sqrt{a_{ii}a_{jj}}.$$

The matrix of all partial correlation coefficients $\rho_{ij, p_1+1, \ldots, p}$, $i, j = 1, \ldots, p_1$ is denoted by $\mathbf{R}_{11\cdot2}$. More simply, using the matrix notations, $\mathbf{R}_{11\cdot2}$ can be computed as

$$[diag(\Sigma_{11\cdot2})]^{-\frac{1}{2}} \Sigma_{11\cdot2} [diag(\Sigma_{11\cdot2})]^{-\frac{1}{2}},$$

where $diag(\Sigma_{11\cdot2})$ is a diagonal matrix with respective diagonal entries the same as those in $\Sigma_{11\cdot2}$.

Many times it is of interest to find the correlation coefficients between y_i and y_j, $i, j = 1, \ldots, p$, conditional on all y_k, $k = 1, \ldots, p$, $k \neq i$, $k \neq j$. In this case, the partial correlation between y_i and y_j can be interpreted as the strength of correlation between the two variables after eliminating the effects of all the remaining variables.

In many linear model situations, we would like to examine the overall association of a set of variables with a given variable. This is often done by finding the correlation between the variable and a particular linear combination of other variables. *Multiple correlation* is an index measuring the association between a random variable y_1 and the set of remaining variables represented by a $(p-1)$ by 1 vector $\mathbf{y}_2$. It is defined as the maximum correlation between y_1 and $\mathbf{c}'\mathbf{y}_2$, a linear combination of $\mathbf{y}_2$, where the maximum is taken over all possible nonzero vectors $\mathbf{c}$. This maximum value, representing the multiple correlation coefficient between y_1 and $\mathbf{y}_2$, is given by

$$(\Sigma_{12}\Sigma_{22}^{-1}\Sigma_{21})^{\frac{1}{2}}/\Sigma_{11}^{\frac{1}{2}}$$

where

$$D\begin{bmatrix} y_1 \\ \mathbf{y}_2 \end{bmatrix} = \begin{bmatrix} \Sigma_{11} & \Sigma_{12} \\ \Sigma_{21} & \Sigma_{22} \end{bmatrix},$$

and the maximum is attained for the choice $\mathbf{c} = \Sigma_{22}^{-1}\Sigma_{21}$. The multiple correlation coefficient always lies between zero and one. The square of the multiple correlation coefficient is often used to indicate the power of prediction, or the effect of linear regression, and is often referred to as the *population coefficient of determination.*

The concept of multiple correlation can be extended to the case in which the random variable y_1 is replaced by a random vector. This leads to what are called *canonical correlation coefficients.*

1.3 Multivariate Normal Distribution

A probability distribution that plays a pivotal role in the multivariate analysis is *multivariate normal distribution.* We say that $\mathbf{y}$ has a multivariate normal distribution (with a mean vector μ and the variance-covariance matrix Σ) if its density is given by

$$f(\mathbf{y}) = \frac{1}{(2\pi)^{p/2}|\Sigma|^{1/2}} \cdot \exp(-\frac{1}{2}(\mathbf{y}-\mu)'\Sigma^{-1}(\mathbf{y}-\mu)).$$

In notation, we state this fact as $\mathbf{y} \sim N_p(\mu, \Sigma)$.

Observe that the above density is a straightforward extension of the univariate normal density to which it would reduce when $p = 1$.

Some important properties of the multivariate normal distribution are the following:

- Let $\mathbf{A}_{r\times p}$ be a fixed matrix, then $\mathbf{Ay} \sim N_r(\mathbf{A}\mu, \mathbf{A}\Sigma\mathbf{A}')(r < p)$.
- Let $\mathbf{G}$ be such that $\Sigma^{-1} = \mathbf{GG}'$, then $\mathbf{G}'\mathbf{y} \sim N_p(\mathbf{G}'\mu, I)$ and $\mathbf{G}'(\mathbf{y}-\mu) \sim N_p(\mathbf{0}, I)$.
- Any fixed linear combination of $y_1, \ldots, y_p$, say $\mathbf{c}'\mathbf{y}$, $\mathbf{c} \neq \mathbf{0}$ is also normally distributed. Specifically, $\mathbf{c}'\mathbf{y} \sim N_1(\mathbf{c}'\mu, \mathbf{c}'\Sigma\mathbf{c})$.
- The subvectors $\mathbf{y}_1$ and $\mathbf{y}_2$ are also normally distributed, specifically, $\mathbf{y}_1 \sim N_{p_1}(\mu_1, \Sigma_{11})$ and $\mathbf{y}_2 \sim N_{p-p_1}(\mu_2, \Sigma_{22})$.
- Individual components $y_1, \ldots, y_p$ are all normally distributed. That is, $y_i \sim N_1(\mu_i, \sigma_{ii})$, $i = 1, \ldots, p$.

- The conditional distribution of $\mathbf{y}_1$ given $\mathbf{y}_2$, written as $\mathbf{y}_1|\mathbf{y}_2$, is also normal. Specifically,

$$\mathbf{y}_1|\mathbf{y}_2 \sim N_{p_1}(\mu_1 + \Sigma_{12}\Sigma_{22}^{-1}(\mathbf{y}_2 - \mu_2), \; \Sigma_{11} - \Sigma_{12}\Sigma_{22}^{-1}\Sigma_{21}).$$

Let $\mu_1 + \Sigma_{12}\Sigma_{22}^{-1}(\mathbf{y}_2 - \mu_2) = \mu_1 - \Sigma_{12}\Sigma_{22}^{-1}\mu_2 + \Sigma_{12}\Sigma_{22}^{-1}\mathbf{y}_2 = \mathbf{B_0} + \mathbf{B_1}\mathbf{y}_2$, and $\Sigma_{11.2} = \Sigma_{11} - \Sigma_{12}\Sigma_{22}^{-1}\Sigma_{21}$. The conditional expectation of $\mathbf{y}_1$ for given values of $\mathbf{y}_2$ or the regression function of $\mathbf{y}_1$ on $\mathbf{y}_2$ is $\mathbf{B_0} + \mathbf{B_1}\mathbf{y}_2$, which is linear in $\mathbf{y}_2$. This is a key fact for multivariate multiple linear regression modeling. The matrix $\Sigma_{11.2}$ is usually represented by the variance-covariance matrix of error components in these models. An analogous result (and the interpretation) can be stated for the conditional distribution of $\mathbf{y}_2$ given $\mathbf{y}_1$.

- Let δ be a fixed $p \times 1$ vector, then

$$\mathbf{y} + \delta \sim N_p(\mu + \delta, \Sigma).$$

- The random components $y_1, \ldots, y_p$ are all independent if and only if Σ is a diagonal matrix; that is, all the covariances (or correlations) are zero.
- Let $\mathbf{u}_1$ and $\mathbf{u}_2$ be respectively distributed as $N_p(\mu_{u_1}, \Sigma_{u_1})$ and $N_p(\mu_{u_2}, \Sigma_{u_2})$, then

$$\mathbf{u}_1 \pm \mathbf{u}_2 \sim N_p(\mu_{u_1} \pm \mu_{u_2}, \Sigma_{u_1} + \Sigma_{u_2} \pm (cov(\mathbf{u}_1, \mathbf{u}_2) + cov(\mathbf{u}_2, \mathbf{u}_1))).$$

Note that if $\mathbf{u}_1$ and $\mathbf{u}_2$ were independent, the last two covariance terms would drop out.

There is a vast amount of literature available on the multivariate normal distribution, its properties, and the evaluations of the multivariate normal probabilities. See Tong (1990) for details.

1.4 Sampling from Multivariate Normal Populations

Suppose we have a random sample of size n, say $\mathbf{y}_1, \ldots, \mathbf{y}_n$, from the p dimensional multivariate normal population $N_p(\mu, \Sigma)$. Since $\mathbf{y}_1, \ldots, \mathbf{y}_n$ are independently and identically distributed (*iid*), their sample mean

$$\bar{\mathbf{y}} = \frac{1}{n}[\mathbf{y}_1 + \ldots + \mathbf{y}_n] = \frac{1}{n}\sum_{i=1}^{n}\mathbf{y}_i \tag{1.1}$$

is also normally distributed as $N_p(\mu, \Sigma/n)$. Observe that $\bar{\mathbf{y}}$ has a dispersion matrix which is a $\frac{1}{n}$ multiple of the original population variance-covariance matrix. This result is a straightforward generalization of the corresponding univariate result.

The sample variance of the univariate normal theory is generalized to the sample variance-covariance matrix in the multivariate context. Accordingly chi-square distribution is generalized to a matrix distribution known as the *Wishart distribution*.

The p by p sample variance-covariance matrix is obtained as

$$\mathbf{S} = \frac{1}{n-1} \sum_{i=1}^{n} (\mathbf{y}_i - \bar{\mathbf{y}})(\mathbf{y}_i - \bar{\mathbf{y}})' = \frac{1}{n-1} \{\sum_{i=1}^{n} \mathbf{y}_i \mathbf{y}_i' - n\bar{\mathbf{y}}\bar{\mathbf{y}}'\}. \qquad (1.2)$$

Let

$$\mathbf{Y} = \begin{bmatrix} \mathbf{y}_1' \\ \mathbf{y}_2' \\ \cdot \\ \cdot \\ \cdot \\ \mathbf{y}_n' \end{bmatrix}$$

be the n by p matrix obtained by stacking $\mathbf{y}_1', \ldots, \mathbf{y}_n'$ one below the other. Then, in terms of $\mathbf{Y}$, the sample mean $\bar{\mathbf{y}}$ can be written as

$$\bar{\mathbf{y}} = \frac{1}{n} \mathbf{Y}' \mathbf{1}_n$$

and the sample variance-covariance matrix can be written as

$$\mathbf{S} = \frac{1}{n-1} \{\mathbf{Y}'(\mathbf{I}_n - \frac{1}{n}\mathbf{1}_n\mathbf{1}_n')\mathbf{Y}\} = \frac{1}{n-1} \{\mathbf{Y}'\mathbf{Y} - \frac{1}{n}\mathbf{Y}'\mathbf{1}_n\mathbf{1}_n'\mathbf{Y}\} = \frac{1}{n-1} \{\mathbf{Y}'\mathbf{Y} - n\bar{\mathbf{y}}\bar{\mathbf{y}}'\},$$

where $\mathbf{I}_n$ stands for an n by n identity matrix and $\mathbf{1}_n$ is an n by 1 column vector with all elements as 1.

It is known that $(n-1)\mathbf{S}$ follows a p-dimensional Wishart distribution with $(n-1)$ degrees of freedom and expectation $(n-1)\Sigma$. We denote this as $(n-1)\mathbf{S} \sim W_p(n-1, \Sigma)$. Consequently, $\mathbf{S}$ is an unbiased estimator of Σ (this is always true regardless of the underlying multivariate normality assumption and consequently, without any specific reference to the Wishart distribution).

Note that, in view of the Wishart distribution, the sample variance-covariance matrix possesses certain important properties. Specifically,

- $(n-1)s_{ii}/\sigma_{ii} \sim \chi^2(n-1)$, $i = 1, \ldots, p$.
- Let

$$\mathbf{S} = \begin{bmatrix} \mathbf{S}_{11} & \mathbf{S}_{12} \\ \mathbf{S}_{21} & \mathbf{S}_{22} \end{bmatrix}, \quad \Sigma = \begin{bmatrix} \Sigma_{11} & \Sigma_{12} \\ \Sigma_{21} & \Sigma_{22} \end{bmatrix},$$

$\mathbf{S}_{11.2} = \mathbf{S}_{11} - \mathbf{S}_{12}\mathbf{S}_{22}^{-1}\mathbf{S}_{21}$, $\Sigma_{11.2} = \Sigma_{11} - \Sigma_{12}\Sigma_{22}^{-1}\Sigma_{21}$, $\mathbf{S}_{22.1} = \mathbf{S}_{22} - \mathbf{S}_{21}\mathbf{S}_{11}^{-1}\mathbf{S}_{12}$ and $\Sigma_{22.1} = \Sigma_{22} - \Sigma_{21}\Sigma_{11}^{-1}\Sigma_{12}$, then

(a) $(n-1)\mathbf{S}_{11} \sim W_{p_1}((n-1), \Sigma_{11})$.

(b) $(n-1)\mathbf{S}_{22} \sim W_{p_2}((n-1), \Sigma_{22})$.

(c) $(n-1)\mathbf{S}_{11.2} \sim W_{p_1}((n-p+p_1-1), \Sigma_{11.2})$.

(d) $(n-1)\mathbf{S}_{22.1} \sim W_{p_2}((n-p_1-1), \Sigma_{22.1})$.

(e) $\mathbf{S}_{11}$ and $\mathbf{S}_{22.1}$ are independently distributed.

(f) $\mathbf{S}_{22}$ and $\mathbf{S}_{11.2}$ are independently distributed.

- Let s^{ii} and σ^{ii} be the ith diagonal elements of $\mathbf{S}^{-1}$ and Σ^{-1} respectively, then $(n-1)\sigma^{ii}/s^{ii} \sim \chi^2(n-p)$.

- Let $\mathbf{c} \neq \mathbf{0}$ be an arbitrary but fixed vector, then

$$(n-1)\frac{\mathbf{c}'\mathbf{S}\mathbf{c}}{\mathbf{c}'\Sigma\mathbf{c}} \sim \chi^2(n-1),$$

$$\text{and} \quad (n-1)\frac{\mathbf{c}'\Sigma^{-1}\mathbf{c}}{\mathbf{c}'\mathbf{S}^{-1}\mathbf{c}} \sim \chi^2(n-p).$$

- Let $\mathbf{H}$ be an arbitrary but fixed $k \times p$ matrix $(k \leq p)$, then

$$(n-1)\mathbf{H}\mathbf{S}\mathbf{H}' \sim W_k(n-1, \mathbf{H}\Sigma\mathbf{H}').$$

As a consequence of the above result, if we take $k = p$ and $\mathbf{H} = \mathbf{G}'$ where $\Sigma^{-1} = \mathbf{G}\mathbf{G}'$, then $(n-1)\,\mathbf{S}^* = (n-1)\mathbf{G}'\mathbf{S}\mathbf{G} \sim W_p(n-1, \mathbf{I})$.

In the above discussion, we observed that the Wishart distribution arises naturally in the multivariate normal theory as the distribution of the sample variance-covariance matrix (of course, apart from a scaling by $(n-1)$). Another distribution which is closely related to the Wishart distribution and is useful in various associated hypothesis testing problems is the matrix variate Beta (Type 1) distribution. For example, $\mathbf{A}_1$ and $\mathbf{A}_2$ are two independent random matrices with $\mathbf{A}_1 \sim W_p(f_1, \Sigma)$ and $\mathbf{A}_2 \sim W_p(f_2, \Sigma)$, then $\mathbf{B} = (\mathbf{A}_1 + \mathbf{A}_2)^{-\frac{1}{2}}\mathbf{A}_1(\mathbf{A}_1 + \mathbf{A}_2)^{-\frac{1}{2}}$ follows a matrix variate Beta Type 1 distribution, denoted by $B_p(\frac{n_1-1}{2}, \frac{n_2-1}{2}, \text{Type 1})$. Similarly, $\mathbf{B}^* = \mathbf{A}_2^{-\frac{1}{2}}\mathbf{A}_1\mathbf{A}_2^{-\frac{1}{2}}$ follows $B_p(\frac{n_1-1}{2}, \frac{n_2-1}{2}, \text{Type 2})$, a matrix variate Beta Type 2 (or a matrix variate F apart from a constant) distribution. The matrices $\mathbf{A}_2^{-\frac{1}{2}}$ and $(\mathbf{A}_1 + \mathbf{A}_2)^{-\frac{1}{2}}$ respectively are the symmetric "square root" matrices of $\mathbf{A}_2^{-1}$ and $(\mathbf{A}_1 + \mathbf{A}_2)^{-1}$ in the sense that $\mathbf{A}_2^{-1} = (\mathbf{A}_2)^{-\frac{1}{2}}(\mathbf{A}_2)^{-\frac{1}{2}}$ and $(\mathbf{A}_1 + \mathbf{A}_2)^{-1} = (\mathbf{A}_1 + \mathbf{A}_2)^{-\frac{1}{2}}(\mathbf{A}_1 + \mathbf{A}_2)^{-\frac{1}{2}}$. The eigenvalues of matrices $\mathbf{B}$ and $\mathbf{B}^*$ appear in the expressions of various test statistics needed in hypothesis testing problems in multivariate analysis of variance.

Another important fact about the sample mean $\bar{\mathbf{y}}$ and the sample variance-covariance matrix $\mathbf{S}$ is their statistical independence under the normal sampling theory. This fact plays an important role in constructing the test statistics for certain statistical hypotheses. For details, see Kshirsagar (1972), Timm (1975), or Muirhead (1982).

1.5 Some Important Sample Statistics and Their Distributions

We have already encountered two important sample statistics in the previous section, namely the sample mean vector $\bar{\mathbf{y}}$ in Equation 1.1 and the sample variance-covariance matrix $\mathbf{S}$ in Equation 1.2. These quantities play a pivotal role in defining the test statistics useful in various hypothesis testing problems. The underlying assumption of multivariate normal population is crucial in obtaining the distribution of these test statistics. Therefore, we will assume that the sample $\mathbf{y}_1, \ldots, \mathbf{y}_n$ of size n is obtained from a multivariate population $N_p(\mu, \Sigma)$.

As we have already indicated, $\bar{\mathbf{y}} \sim N_p(\mu, \Sigma/n)$ and $(n-1)\mathbf{S} \sim W_p(n-1, \Sigma)$. Consequently, any linear combination of $\bar{\mathbf{y}}$, say $\mathbf{c}'\bar{\mathbf{y}}$, $\mathbf{c} \neq \mathbf{0}$, follows $N_p(\mathbf{c}'\mu, \mathbf{c}'\Sigma\mathbf{c}/n)$ and the quadratic form $(n-1)\mathbf{c}'\mathbf{S}\mathbf{c}/\mathbf{c}'\Sigma\mathbf{c} \sim \chi^2(n-1)$. Further, it can be shown that $\bar{\mathbf{y}}$ and $\mathbf{S}$ are independently distributed and hence the quantity

$$t = \sqrt{n}\mathbf{c}'(\bar{\mathbf{y}} - \mu)/\sqrt{\mathbf{c}'\mathbf{S}\mathbf{c}}$$

follows a t-distribution with $(n-1)$ degrees of freedom. A useful application of this fact is in the testing problems for certain contrasts or in the testing problems involving a given linear combination of the components of the mean vector.

Often the interest may be in testing a hypothesis if the population has its mean vector equal to a given vector, say μ_0. Since $\bar{\mathbf{y}} \sim N_p(\mu, \Sigma/n)$, it follows that $\mathbf{z} = \sqrt{n}\Sigma^{-\frac{1}{2}}(\bar{\mathbf{y}} - \mu)$ follows $N_p(\mathbf{0}, \mathbf{I})$. This implies that the components of $\mathbf{z}$ are independent and have the standard normal distribution. As a result, if μ is equal to μ_0 the quantity, $z_1^2 + \ldots + z_p^2 = \mathbf{z}'\mathbf{z} = n(\bar{\mathbf{y}} - \mu_0)'\Sigma^{-1}(\bar{\mathbf{y}} - \mu_0)$ follows a chi-square distribution with p degrees of freedom. On the other hand, if μ is not equal to μ_0, then this quantity will not have a chi-square distribution. This observation provides a way of testing the hypothesis that the mean of the normal population is equal to a given vector μ_0. However, the assumption of known Σ is needed to actually perform this test. If Σ is unknown, it seems natural to replace it in $n(\bar{\mathbf{y}} - \mu)'\Sigma^{-1}(\bar{\mathbf{y}} - \mu)$ by its unbiased estimator $\mathbf{S}$, leading to Hotelling's T^2 test statistic defined as

$$T^2 = n(\bar{\mathbf{y}} - \mu_0)'\mathbf{S}^{-1}(\bar{\mathbf{y}} - \mu_0),$$

where we assume that $n \geq p + 1$. This assumption ensures that $\mathbf{S}$ admits an inverse. Under the hypothesis mentioned above, namely $\mu = \mu_0$, the quantity $\frac{n-p}{p(n-1)}T^2$ follows an F distribution with degrees of freedom p and $n - p$.

Assuming normality, the maximum likelihood estimates of μ and Σ are known to be

$$\hat{\mu}_{ml} = \bar{\mathbf{y}}$$

and

$$\hat{\Sigma}_{ml} = \mathbf{S}_n = \frac{1}{n}\mathbf{Y}'(\mathbf{I}_n - \frac{1}{n}\mathbf{1}_n\mathbf{1}_n')\mathbf{Y} = \frac{n-1}{n}\mathbf{S}.$$

While $\hat{\mu}_{ml} = \bar{\mathbf{y}}$ is unbiased for μ, $\hat{\Sigma}_{ml} = \mathbf{S}_n$ is a (negatively) biased estimator of Σ. These quantities are also needed in the process of deriving various maximum likelihood-based tests for the hypothesis testing problems. In general, to test a hypothesis H_0, the likelihood ratio test based on the maximum likelihood estimates is obtained by maximizing the likelihood within the parameter space restricted by H_0 and maximizing it over the entire parameter space (that is, by evaluating the likelihood at $\hat{\mu}_{ml}$ and $\hat{\Sigma}_{ml}$), and then taking the ratio of the two. Thus, the likelihood ratio test statistic can be written as

$$L = \frac{\max_{H_0} f(\mathbf{Y})}{\max_{\text{unrestricted}} f(\mathbf{Y})}.$$

A related test statistic is the Wilks' Λ, which is the $(2/n)^{th}$ power of L. For large n, the quantity $-2\log L$ approximately follows a chi-square distribution, with degrees of freedom ν, which is a function of the sample size n, the number of parameters estimated, and the number of restrictions imposed by the parameters involved under H_0.

A detailed discussion of various likelihood ratio tests in multivariate analysis contexts can be found in Kshirsager (1972), Muirhead (1982) or in Anderson (1984).

1.6 Tests for Multivariate Normality

Before doing any statistical modeling, it is crucial to verify if the data at hand satisfy the underlying distributional assumptions. For most multivariate analyses, it is thus very important that the data indeed follow the multivariate normal, if not exactly at least approximately. If the answer to such a query is affirmative, it can often reduce the task of searching for the procedures which are robust to the departures from multivariate normality. There are many possibilities for departure from multivariate normality and no single procedure is likely to be robust with respect to all such departures from the multivariate normality assumption. Gnanadesikan (1980) and Mardia (1980) provide excellent reviews of various procedures to verify this assumption.

This assumption is often checked by individually testing the univariate normality through various Q-Q plots or some other plots and can at times be very subjective. One of the relatively simpler and mathematically tractable ways to verify the assumption of multivariate normality is by using the tests based on Mardia's *multivariate skewness* and *kurtosis* measures. For any general multivariate distribution we define these respectively as

$$\beta_{1,p} = E\{(\mathbf{y} - \mu)'\Sigma^{-1}(\mathbf{x} - \mu)\}^3,$$

provided that $\mathbf{x}$ is independent of $\mathbf{y}$ but has the same distribution and

$$\beta_{2,p} = E\{(\mathbf{y} - \mu)'\Sigma^{-1}(\mathbf{y} - \mu)\}^2,$$

provided that the expectations in the expressions of $\beta_{1,p}$ and $\beta_{2,p}$ exist. For the multivariate normal distribution, $\beta_{1,p} = 0$ and $\beta_{2,p} = p(p+2)$.

For a sample of size n, the estimates of $\beta_{1,p}$ and $\beta_{2,p}$ can be obtained as

$$\hat{\beta}_{1,p} = \frac{1}{n^2} \sum_{i=1}^{n} \sum_{j=1}^{n} g_{ij}^3$$

$$\hat{\beta}_{2,p} = \frac{1}{n} \sum_{i=1}^{n} g_{ii}^2 = \frac{1}{n} \sum_{i=1}^{n} d_i^4$$

where $g_{ij} = (\mathbf{y}_i - \bar{\mathbf{y}})' \mathbf{S}_n^{-1} (\mathbf{y}_j - \bar{\mathbf{y}})$, and $d_i = \sqrt{g_{ii}}$ is the sample version of the squared *Mahalanobis distance* (Mahalanobis, 1936) between $\mathbf{y}_i$ and (μ which is approximated by) $\bar{\mathbf{y}}$ (Mardia, 1970).

The quantity $\hat{\beta}_{1,p}$ (which is same as the square of sample skewness coefficient when $p = 1$) as well as $\hat{\beta}_{2,p}$ (which is same as sample kurtosis coefficient when $p = 1$) are nonnegative. For the multivariate normal data, we would expect $\hat{\beta}_{1,p}$ to be close to zero. If there is a departure from the spherical symmetry (that is, zero correlation and equal variance), $\hat{\beta}_{2,p}$ will be large. The quantity $\hat{\beta}_{2,p}$ is also useful in indicating the extreme behavior in the squared Mahalanobis distance of the observations from the sample mean. Thus, $\hat{\beta}_{1,p}$ and $\hat{\beta}_{2,p}$ can be utilized to detect the departure from multivariate normality. Mardia (1970) has shown that for large samples, $\kappa_1 = n\hat{\beta}_{1,p}/6$ follows a chi-square distribution with degrees of freedom $p(p+1)(p+2)/6$, and $\kappa_2 = \{\hat{\beta}_{2,p} - p(p+2)\}/\{8p(p+2)/n\}^{\frac{1}{2}}$ follows a standard normal distribution. Thus, we can use the quantities κ_1 and κ_2 to test the null hypothesis of multivariate normality. For small n, see the tables for the critical values for these test statistics given by Mardia (1974). He also recommends (Mardia, Kent, and Bibby 1979, p. 149) that if both the hypotheses are accepted, the normal theory for various tests on the mean vector or the covariance matrix can be used. However, in the presence of nonnormality, the normal theory tests on the mean are sensitive to $\beta_{1,p}$, whereas tests on the covariance matrix are influenced by $\beta_{2,p}$.

It has also been observed that Mardia's multivariate kurtosis can be used as a measure to detect the outliers from the data that are supposedly distributed as the multivariate normal. See Schwager and Margolin (1982), Das and Sinha (1986), and Naik (1989) for details.

For a given data set, the multivariate kurtosis can be computed using the CALIS procedure in SAS/STAT Software. Notice that the quantities reported in the corresponding SAS output are $(\hat{\beta}_{2,p} - p(p+2))$ (shown in Output 1.1 as Mardia's Multivariate Kurtosis) and κ_2 (shown in Output 1.1 as Normalized Multivariate Kurtosis).

Example 1: Testing Multivariate Normality, Cork Data (Rao, 1948)

As an illustration, we consider the cork boring data of Rao (1948) given in Table 1.1, and test the hypothesis that this data set can be considered as a random sample from a multivariate normal population. The data set provided in Table 1.1 consists of the depths of cork boring in four directions (north, east, south, and west) for 28 trees in a block of plantations.

Tree	N E S W	Tree	N E S W
1	72 66 76 77	15	91 79 100 75
2	60 53 66 63	16	56 68 47 50
3	56 57 64 58	17	79 65 70 61
4	41 29 36 38	18	81 80 68 58
5	32 32 35 36	19	78 55 67 60
6	30 35 34 26	20	46 38 37 38
7	39 39 31 27	21	39 35 34 37
8	42 43 31 25	22	32 30 30 32
9	37 40 31 25	23	60 50 67 54
10	33 29 27 36	24	35 37 48 39
11	32 30 34 28	25	39 36 39 31
12	63 45 74 63	26	50 34 37 40
13	54 46 60 52	27	43 37 39 50
14	47 51 52 43	28	48 54 57 43

TABLE 1.1 WEIGHTS OF CORK BORING (IN CENTIGRAMS)
IN FOUR DIRECTIONS FOR 28 TREES

E. S. Pearson had pointed out to C. R. Rao, apparently without any formal statistical testing, that the data are exceedingly asymmetrically distributed. It is therefore of interest to formally test if the data can be assumed to have come from an $N_4(\mu, \Sigma)$.

The SAS statements required to compute the multivariate kurtosis using PROC CALIS are given in Program 1.1. A part of the output giving the value of Mardia's multivariate kurtosis (=-1.0431) and normalized multivariate kurtosis (=-0.3984) is shown as Output 1.1. The output also indicates the observations which are most influential. Although the procedure does not provide the value of multivariate skewness, the PROC IML statements given in Program 1.2 perform all the necessary calculations to compute the multivariate skewness and kurtosis. The results are shown in Output 1.2, which also reports Mardia's test statistics κ_1 and κ_2 described above along with the corresponding p values.

In this program, for the 28 by 4 data matrix $\mathbf{Y}$, we first compute the maximum likelihood estimate of the variance-covariance matrix. This estimate is given by $\mathbf{S}_n = \frac{1}{n}\mathbf{Y}'\mathbf{Q}\mathbf{Y}$, where $\mathbf{Q} = \mathbf{I}_n - \frac{1}{n}\mathbf{1}_n\mathbf{1}_n'$. Also, since the quantities $g_{ij}, i, j = 1, \ldots, n$ needed in the expressions of multivariate skewness and kurtosis are the elements of matrix $\mathbf{G} = \mathbf{Q}\mathbf{Y}\mathbf{S}_n^{-1}\mathbf{Y}'\mathbf{Q}$, we compute the matrix $\mathbf{G}$, using this formula. Their p values are then reported as PVALSKEW and PVALKURT in Output 1.2. The quantities as obtained using PROC CALIS agree with those reported in Mardia, Kent, and Bibby (1979, p. 149).

For this particular data set with its large p values, neither skewness is significantly different from zero, nor is the value of kurtosis significantly different from that for the normal distribution. Consequently, we may assume the normality for testing various hypotheses on the mean vector and the covariance matrix as far as the present data set is concerned. This particular data set is extensively analyzed in the later chapters under the assumption of normality.

Often we are less interested in the multivariate normality of the original data and more interested in the contrasts or any other set of linear combinations of the variables $y_1, \ldots, y_p$. If $\mathbf{C}$ is the corresponding p by r matrix of transformation, then the transformed data can be obtained as $\mathbf{Z} = \mathbf{YC}$. Consequently, the only change in Program 1.2 is to replace the earlier definition of $\mathbf{G}$ by $\mathbf{QYC}(\mathbf{C}'\mathbf{S}_n\mathbf{C})^{-1}\mathbf{C}'\mathbf{Y}'\mathbf{Q}$ and replace p by r in the expressions for κ_1, κ_2 and the degrees of freedom corresponding to κ_1.

Example 1: Testing for Contrasts, Cork Data (continued)

Returning to the cork data, if the interest is in testing if the bark deposit is uniform in all four directions, an appropriate set of transformations would be

$$z_1 = y_1 - y_2 + y_3 - y_4, \quad z_2 = y_3 - y_4, \quad z_3 = y_1 - y_3,$$

where y_1, y_2, y_3, y_4 represent the deposit in four directions listed clockwise and starting from north. The 4 by 3 matrix $\mathbf{C}$ for these transformations will be

$$\mathbf{C} = \begin{bmatrix} 1 & 0 & 1 \\ -1 & 0 & 0 \\ 1 & 1 & -1 \\ -1 & -1 & 0 \end{bmatrix}.$$

It is easy to verify that for these contrasts the assumption of symmetry holds rather more strongly, since the p values corresponding to the skewness are relatively larger. Specifically for these contrasts

$$\hat{\beta}_1 = 1.1770, \qquad \hat{\beta}_2 = 13.5584, \qquad \kappa_1 = 5.4928, \qquad \kappa_2 = -0.6964$$

and the respective p values for skewness and kurtosis tests are 0.8559 and 0.4862. As Rao (1948) points out, this symmetry is not surprising as the contrasts are likely to approximate better to the multivariate normality than the original data. Since one can easily modify the Program 1.1 or Program 1.2 to perform the above analysis on the contrasts z_1, z_2, and z_3, we have not provided the corresponding SAS code or the output.

1.7 Random Vector and Matrix Generation

For various simulation or power studies, it is often necessary to generate a set of random vectors or random matrices. It is therefore of interest to generate these quantities for the probability distributions which arise naturally in the multivariate normal theory. The following sections consider the most common multivariate probability distributions.

1.7.1 Random Vector Generation from $N_p(\mu, \Sigma)$

To generate a random vector from $N_p(\mu, \Sigma)$ use the following steps:

1. Find a matrix $\mathbf{G}$ such that $\Sigma = \mathbf{G}'\mathbf{G}$.
2. Generate p independent standard univariate normal random variables $z_1, \ldots, z_p$ and let $\mathbf{z} = (z_1, \ldots, z_p)'$.
3. Let $\mathbf{y} = \mu + \mathbf{G}'\mathbf{z}$.

The resulting vector $\mathbf{y}$ is an observation from a $N_p(\mu, \Sigma)$ population. To obtain a sample of size n, repeat the above-mentioned steps n times within a loop.

1.7.2 Generation of Wishart Random Matrix

To generate a matrix $\mathbf{A}_1 \sim W_p(f, \Sigma)$, use the following steps:

1. Find a matrix $\mathbf{G}$ such that $\Sigma = \mathbf{G}'\mathbf{G}$.
2. Generate a random sample of size f, say $\mathbf{z}_1, \ldots, \mathbf{z}_f$ from $N_p(\mathbf{0}, \mathbf{I})$. Let $\mathbf{A}_2 = \sum_{i=1}^{f} \mathbf{z}_i \mathbf{z}_i'$.
3. Define $\mathbf{A}_1 = \mathbf{G}'\mathbf{A}_2\mathbf{G}$.

The generation of Beta matrices can easily be done by first generating two independent Wishart matrices with appropriate degrees of freedom and then forming the appropriate products using these matrices as defined in Section 1.4.

Example 2: Random Samples from Normal and Wishart Distributions

In the following example we will illustrate the use of PROC IML for generating the samples from multivariate normal and Wishart distributions respectively. These programs are respectively given as Program 1.3 and Program 1.4. The corresponding outputs have been omitted to save space.

As an example, suppose we want to generate four vectors from $N_3(\mu, \Sigma)$ where

$$\mu' = (1\ 3\ 0)$$

and

$$\Sigma = \begin{bmatrix} 4 & 2 & 1 \\ 2 & 3 & 1 \\ 1 & 1 & 5 \end{bmatrix}.$$

Then save these four vectors as the rows of 4 by 3 matrix $\mathbf{Y}$. It is easy to see that

$$E(\mathbf{Y}) = \begin{bmatrix} \mu' \\ \mu' \\ \mu' \\ \mu' \end{bmatrix} = \mathbf{M},$$

which we call in our program as M. Also, let $\mathbf{G}$ be a matrix such that $\Sigma = \mathbf{G}'\mathbf{G}$. This matrix is obtained using the ROOT function.

We first generate a 4 by 3 random matrix $\mathbf{Z}$, with all its entries distributed as $N(0,1)$. To do this, we use the normal random number generator (NORMAL) repeated for all the entries of $\mathbf{Z}$, through the REPEAT function. Consequently, if we define $\mathbf{Y} = \mathbf{ZG} + \mathbf{M}$, then the ith row of $\mathbf{Y}$, say $\mathbf{y}_i'$, can be written in terms of the ith row of $\mathbf{Z}$, say $\mathbf{z}_i$, as

$$\mathbf{y}_i' = \mathbf{z}_i'\mathbf{G} + \mu'$$

or when written as a column vector

$$\mathbf{y}_i = \mathbf{G}'\mathbf{z}_i + \mu.$$

Consequently, $\mathbf{y}_i$, $i = 1, \ldots, n(= 4 \text{ here})$ are normally distributed with the mean $E(\mathbf{y}_i) = \mathbf{G}'E(\mathbf{z}_i) + \mu = \mu$ and the variance covariance matrix $D(\mathbf{y}_i) = \mathbf{G}'D(\mathbf{z}_i)\mathbf{G} + 0 = \mathbf{G}'\mathbf{IG} = \mathbf{G}'\mathbf{G} = \Sigma$.

Program 1.4 illustrates the generation of $n = 4$ Wishart matrices from $W_p(f, \Sigma)$ with $f = 7$, $p = 3$, and Σ as given in the previous program. After obtaining the matrix $\mathbf{G}$, as earlier, we generate a 7 by 3 matrix $\mathbf{T}$, for which all the elements are distributed as the standard normal. Consequently, the matrix $\mathbf{W} = \mathbf{G}'\mathbf{T}'\mathbf{TG}$, (written as $\mathbf{x}'\mathbf{x}$, where $\mathbf{x} = \mathbf{TU}$) follows $W_3(7, \Sigma)$ distribution. We have used the DO loop to repeat the process $n = 4$ times to obtain four such matrices.

These programs can be easily modified to generate the Beta matrices of either Type 1 or Type 2, as the generation of such matrices essentially amounts to generating the pairs of Wishart matrices with appropriate degrees of freedom and then combining them as per their definitions.

More efficient algorithms, especially for f large relative to p are available in the literature. One such convenient method based on Bartlett's decomposition can be found in Smith and Hocking (1972). Certain other methods are briefly summarized in Kennedy and Gentle (1980, p. 231).

```
/* Program 1.1 */

options ls=78 ps=45 nodate nonumber;
data cork;
infile 'cork.dat' firstobs = 1;
input north east south west;

proc calis  data = cork  kurtosis ;
title1 j=l "Output 1.1";
title2 "Computation of Mardia's Kurtosis" ;

lineqs
north = e1 ,
east = e2 ,
south = e3 ,
west = e4  ;

std
e1=eps1, e2=eps2, e3=eps3, e4=eps4 ;

cov
e1=eps1, e2=eps2, e3=eps3, e4=eps4 ;

run ;
```

Output 1.1
Computation of Mardia's Kurtosis

Covariance Structure Analysis: Maximum Likelihood Estimation

	28 Observations	Model Terms	1
	4 Variables	Model Matrices	4
	10 Informations	Parameters	4

VARIABLE	Mean	Std Dev	Skewness	Kurtosis
NORTH	50.53571429	17.04130525	0.8553723415	-.1766560957
EAST	46.17857143	14.83003352	0.8800270196	-.0736595992
SOUTH	49.67857143	18.70839299	0.7986972209	0.0167549222
WEST	45.17857143	15.03342836	0.4671334889	-.6904229162

Mardia's Multivariate Kurtosis . . . .   -1.0431
Relative Multivariate Kurtosis 0.9565
Normalized Multivariate Kurtosis . . . . . .   -0.3984
Mardia Based Kappa (Browne, 1982). . . . . . .   -0.0435
Mean Scaled Univariate Kurtosis . . . .   -0.0770
Adjusted Mean Scaled Univariate Kurtosis . . .   -0.0770

Observation numbers with largest contribution to kurtosis

	16	15	18	1	19
	35.3336	24.0781	21.0472	14.6781	11.6791

Vector of Initial Estimates

EPS1	1	1.00000	Matrix Entry: _PHI_[1:1]
EPS2	2	1.00000	Matrix Entry: _PHI_[2:2]
EPS3	3	1.00000	Matrix Entry: _PHI_[3:3]
EPS4	4	1.00000	Matrix Entry: _PHI_[4:4]

```
/* cork.dat */

72  66  76   77
60  53  66   63
56  57  64   58
41  29  36   38
32  32  35   36
30  35  34   26
39  39  31   27
42  43  31   25
37  40  31   25
33  29  27   36
32  30  34   28
63  45  74   63
54  46  60   52
47  51  52   43
91  79  100  75
56  68  47   50
79  65  70   61
81  80  68   58
78  55  67   60
46  38  37   38
39  35  34   37
32  30  30   32
60  50  67   54
35  37  48   39
39  36  39   31
50  34  37   40
43  37  39   50
48  54  57   43
```

/* Cork Boring Data: Source: C.R.Rao (1948). Reproduced with
permission of the Biometrika Trustees. */

17

```
/* Program 1.2 */

title 'Output 1.2';
options ls = 76 nodate nonumber;

/* In this program we are testing for the multivariate normality
of C. R. Rao's cork data using the Mardia's skewness and kurtosis
measures*/

proc iml ;
y ={
72 66 76 77,
60 53 66 63,
56 57 64 58,
41 29 36 38,
32 32 35 36,
30 35 34 26,
39 39 31 27,
42 43 31 25,
37 40 31 25,
33 29 27 36,
32 30 34 28,
63 45 74 63,
54 46 60 52,
47 51 52 43,
91 79 100 75,
56 68 47 50,
79 65 70 61,
81 80 68 58,
78 55 67 60,
46 38 37 38,
39 35 34 37,
32 30 30 32,
60 50 67 54,
35 37 48 39,
39 36 39 31,
50 34 37 40,
43 37 39 50,
48 54 57 43} ;

/* Here we determine the number of data points and the dimension
of the vector. dfchi is the degrees of freedom for the chi square
approximation of Multivariate skewness. */

n = nrow(y) ;
p = ncol(y) ;
dfchi = p*(p+1)*(p+2)/6 ;

/* q is projection matrix. s is the maximum likelihood estimate
of the variance covariance matrix. g_matrix is n by n the matrix
of g(i,j) elements. beta1hat and beta2hat are respectively the
Mardia's sample skewness and kurtosis measures. Kappa1 and kappa2
are the test statistics based on skewness and kurtosis to test
for normality and pvalskew and pvalkurt are corresponding p
values. */

q = i(n) - (1/n)*j(n,n,1) ;
s = (1/(n))*y'*q*y ; s_inv = inv(s) ;
g_matrix = q*y*s_inv*y'*q ;
```

```
/* Program 1.2 continued */

beta1hat = (  sum(g_matrix#g_matrix#g_matrix)  )/(n*n)  ;
beta2hat =trace(  g_matrix#g_matrix  )/n ;

kappa1 = n*beta1hat/6 ;
kappa2 = (beta2hat - p*(p+2) ) /sqrt(8*p*(p+2)/n) ;

pvalskew = 1 - probchi(kappa1,dfchi) ;
pvalkurt = 2*( 1 - probnorm(abs(kappa2))  ) ;
print s ;
print s_inv ;

print beta1hat ;
print kappa1 ;
print pvalskew ;

print beta2hat ;
print kappa2 ;
print pvalkurt ;
run;
```

```
            S
280.03444  215.76148  278.13648  218.19005
215.76148  212.07526  220.87883  165.25383
278.13648  220.87883  337.50383  250.27168
218.19005  165.25383  250.27168   217.9324
```

```
      S_INV
 0.0332462  -0.016361  -0.008139  -0.011533
-0.016361   0.0228758  -0.005199  0.0050046
-0.008139  -0.005199   0.0276698  -0.019685
-0.011533   0.0050046  -0.019685  0.0349464
```

BETA1HAT
4.4763816

KAPPA1
20.889781

PVALSKEW
0.4036454

BETA2HAT
22.95687

KAPPA2
-0.398352

PVALKURT
0.6903709

```
/* Program 1.3 */

title 'Output 1.3: Multivariate Normal Sample';
/*Generate n random vector from a p dimensional population with
mean mu and the covariance matrix sigma   */

options ls = 76 nodate nonumber;
proc iml ;
seed = 549065467 ;
n = 4 ;
sigma = { 4 2 1,
          2 3 1,
          1 1 5 };


mu = {1, 3, 0};
p = nrow(sigma);
m = repeat(mu',n,1) ;
g =inv(root(sigma)) ;
z =normal(repeat(seed,n,p)) ;
y = z*g + m ;
print y ;
run;
```

```
/* Program 1.4 */

title 'Output 1.4: Wishart Random Matrix';
/*Generate n  p by p Wishart matrices with degrees of freedom f */

options ls=76 nodate nonumber;
proc iml;
n = 4 ;
f = 7 ;
seed = 4509049 ;
sigma = {4 2 1,
         2 3 1,
         1 1 5 } ;
g = inv( root(sigma) );
p = nrow(sigma) ;
do i = 1 to n ;
t = normal(repeat(seed,f,p)) ;
x = t*g ;
w = x'*x ;
print w ;
end ;
run;
```

CHAPTER 2: Graphical Representation of Multivariate Data

2.1 Introduction
2.2 Scatter Plots
    2.2.1 Two-Dimensional Scatter Plot
    2.2.2 Three-Dimensional Scatter Plot
    2.2.3 Scatter Plot Matrix
2.3 Profile Plots
2.4 Andrews Function Plots
2.5 Biplot: Plotting Observations and Variables Together
2.6 Q-Q Plots for Assessing Multivariate Normality
2.7 Plots for Detection of Multivariate Outliers
2.8 Bivariate Normal Distribution
    2.8.1 Probability Density Function Plotting
    2.8.2 Contour Plot of Density
2.9 SAS/INSIGHT Software
    2.9.1 Summary of Features

2.1 Introduction

Graphical techniques have become an integral part of any data analysis, especially now due to a tremendous increase in the accessibility to computing facilities. In general it is easy to use graphical methods for data with one, two, or even three variables. However, for multivariate data in dimensions higher than three, data reduction to two or three variables is needed before it is possible to plot them. Several methods to represent multivariate data are available in the literature. This chapter covers four of these methods in Sections 2.2 through 2.5. It may be mentioned that Section 2.5 may require a slightly higher level of familiarity with matrix decompositions and may be skipped at first reading. See Friendly (1991) for details on various other graphical methods.

Multivariate normal distribution is a basis for most of the testing of hypotheses theory in multivariate analysis. Often graphical methods are used to assess the multivariate normality and to detect multivariate outliers. These methods are covered in Sections 2.6 and 2.7 respectively.

The *probability density function* of a bivariate normal distribution and the contours of the probability density function drawn graphically give information about the magnitude of the variances and correlation between the two variables. Section 2.8 discusses these graphs briefly. SAS/INSIGHT software, an interactive tool for graphical data analysis, is briefly discussed at the end of the chapter.

For illustration purposes, we have confined ourselves to the data set from Rao (1948). This data set, given in Table 1.1, consists of weights of cork boring taken from the north (N), east (E), south (S), and west (W) directions of the trunks of 28 trees in a block of plantations.

2.2 Scatter Plots

Scatter plots are among the most basic and useful of graphical representation techniques. A scatter plot of two sets of variables is simply a two-dimensional representation of the points in a plane to show the relationship between two variables. The scatter plots are most useful in identifying the type of relationship (linear or nonlinear) between two sets of variables. Further, if the relationship is linear they help determine the negative or positive relationship between the two variables. This section uses various SAS procedures to plot scatter plots in two and three dimensions. When there are more than two variables, scatter plots of two variables at a time are displayed in a matrix of plots.

2.2.1 Two-Dimensional Scatter Plot

Two-dimensional scatter plots can be drawn using the SAS PLOT procedure. The SAS code shown in Program 2.1 produces two scatter plots. The first plots the data corresponding to the directions of north (N) and east (E), and the second plots the contrasts of the directions north (N) and south (S) (Y1=N-S) against those of the directions east (E) and west (W) (Y2=E-W). These are shown in Output 2.1. The statement PLOT Y1*Y2 in the program plots the variable Y1 versus variable Y2. That is, the variable listed first in the PLOT statement is plotted on the vertical axis and the other variable is plotted on the horizontal axis. The code

```
proc plot;
plot y1*y2;
```

uses the default symbols A, B, etc., in the plot, as shown in Output 2.1. A statement of the form

PLOT Y1*Y2='CHAR';

can be used to specify a plotting symbol where 'CHAR' stands for the user-specified symbols (such as * or +). If several points fall in the same location, a note is printed indicating the number of hidden observations. The appropriate size of the plot can be determined by the PAGESIZE= and LINESIZE= options.

In a scatter plot, if the points follow an increasing straight line pattern then there may be a positive correlation between the two variables. This pattern indicates that as one variable increases the other increases also. On the other hand, if the points follow a decreasing straight line pattern then there may be a negative correlation indicating that one variable may be decreasing as the other variable is increasing. If the points are randomly scattered in the plane then there may be only a weak or no correlation between the two variables. The first scatter plot in Output 2.1 indicates that there is a positive correlation between the weights of cork boring in the directions of north and east. On the other hand, the second scatter plot in Output 2.1 suggests the possibility of a weak or no correlation between the two contrasts, N-S and E-W.

2.2.2 Three-Dimensional Scatter Plot

A three-dimensional scatter plot is needed to simultaneously display the relationships between three variables. It can be a useful plot to visually determine any groups or clusters that might exist in the data set. The SCATTER statement in the G3D procedure can be used to draw a three-dimensional scatter plot. The code given in Program 2.2 produces a scatter plot of the variables N, E, and S by taking the variables N and S on the horizontal plane and E on the axis perpendicular to the plane as displayed in Output 2.2. Notice the SCATTER statement in Program 2.2 that plots the values of variables N and S on the horizontal plane and those of E on the axis perpendicular to that plane. The options J=L and J=R in the FOOTNOTE and TITLE statements indicate that the footnote or the title should be written on the left and on the right side of the page, respectively.

As in the two-dimensional scatter plot, if the points follow a pattern in the space then there may be correlations between any two or all three variables. If the points are scattered in the space then there is a weak or no correlation between any of the three variables. For example, the scatter plot of the three variables N, S, and E indicates that the points have an increasing pattern not only in the horizontal plane but also in the perpendicular direction. This seems to indicate that there is a correlation between the variables (N,S), between (S,E), and between (N,E).

Program 2.3 generates a three-dimensional scatter plot for the three contrasts C1=N-E-W+S, C2=N-S, and C3=E-W shown in Output 2.3. This scatter plot seems to show weak or no correlation among the three contrasts.

2.2.3 Scatter Plot Matrix

For multivariate data with p variables, $x_1, ..., x_p$, a scatter plot of each pair of variables can be displayed in a p by p matrix of scatter plots. In this matrix the scatter plot of two different variables x_i and x_j is in the $(i, j)^{th}$ position of the matrix. The diagonal positions are usually used for writing descriptive comments. The scatter plot matrix is a useful way of representing multivariate data on a single two-dimensional display. It simultaneously identifies the relationships between various variables.

A macro for drawing a scatter plot matrix is given in Friendly (1991). Scatter plot matrices can also be drawn very easily using SAS/INSIGHT software. See Section 2.9.1 for a brief description of the software. Program 2.4 produces the 4 by 4 scatter plot matrix presented in Output 2.4. The plot indicates that there is a positive correlation between every pair of variables in the four directions. The correlation seems to be strongest between the variables S and W, but weakest between the variables E and W.

It may sometimes be cumbersome to represent all the variables on a matrix plot, especially if the number of variables is large. In order to visually extract the maximum information possible from these plots it may be necessary to restrict the choice to a moderate number of variables (say 5 or 6) at a time.

2.3 Profile Plots

One of the simplest ways of representing p-dimensional measurements is by using profile plots. These plots are the polygonal representations of p-dimensional observation vectors. Each p-dimensional observation vector is represented by p points with the vertical coordinate of each point proportional to the value of the corresponding variable. The successive points are joined using straight line segments. The resulting curve is called the *profile* of that observation. These plots can be very helpful in identifying clusters of the observations and outliers. More details about these plots can be found in Hartigan (1975). Many times it may be more meaningful to plot the standardized variables in order to have a uniform scale for each variable. The standardization of variables can easily be achieved using the STANDARD procedure. See the *SAS Procedures Guide, Version 6, Third Edition* for details on PROC STANDARD.

Program 2.5 produces a profile plot, as shown in Output 2.5. In the program, the features of PROC TRANSPOSE have been utilized for data manipulation. The new variable DIRECTN (one of the 28 variables corresponding to 28 trees) placed in the first column is used in the PLOT statement to plot the tree profiles for each of the four directions. An alternative set of SAS code for drawing the profiles, using the ARRAY statement instead of PROC TRANSPOSE, is commented out in Program 2.5. By removing the comment delimiters, here as well as in all the programs to come, it is possible to use alternative methods. In Output 2.5 the profile plot of the fifteenth tree (denoted by the letter M) stands out. This tree may possibly be an outlier. An examination of the data indicates that this tree has bark deposit measurements that are unusually large in magnitude compared to the rest. The profile plots also seem to indicate that there is a cluster of 12 to 14 trees, with relatively smaller measurements.

Plotting the profiles of sample mean vectors for different groups helps one to see whether the profiles may be parallel. These profile plots serve as convenient graphical tools to explore the data before any sophisticated multivariate statistical analysis techniques, like profile analysis (see Section 5.3.2), are applied to a data set.

2.4 Andrews Function Plots

Andrews (1972) suggests an innovative method to pictorially display the multivariate data as curves. This pictorial representation can sometimes be very helpful in visually grouping similar objects together and in searching for any striking dissimilarities between the objects or the groups of the objects on which the multivariate data are collected.

Andrews' approach consists of representing a p-dimensional vector $\mathbf{x}'_i = (x_{i1}, ..., x_{ip})$ corresponding to the ith individual ($i = 1, ..., n$) by a function $f_{\mathbf{x}_i}(t)$ of a single variable t. Andrews suggested the function $f_{\mathbf{x}_i}(t)$ to be the Fourier series expansion

$$f_{\mathbf{x}_i}(t) = x_{i1}/\sqrt{2} + x_{i2}sin(t) + x_{i3}cos(t) + x_{i4}sin(2t) + x_{i5}cos(2t) + ...$$

For $i = 1, ..., n$ we have respective functions $f_{\mathbf{x}_1}(t), ..., f_{\mathbf{x}_n}(t)$, which are drawn for various values of t in the range $(-\pi, \pi)$. These plots preserve the distances between the two vector valued observations. That is, for any two vectors $\mathbf{x}_i$ and $\mathbf{x}_j$

$$\frac{1}{\pi} \int_{-\pi}^{\pi} [f_{\mathbf{x}_i}(t) - f_{\mathbf{x}_j}(t)]^2 dt = \sum_{k=1}^{p} (x_{ik} - x_{jk})^2.$$

Thus the observations that are far apart in p-dimensional space plot as curves with large distances between them. These plots, therefore, can be used to detect the clusters and the outliers within the data set. Program 2.6 draws Andrews function plots for the cork data. For each observation $\mathbf{x}_i$, the values of the function $f_{\mathbf{x}_i}(t)$ are generated for various values of t between $-\pi$ and π at the steps of $2\pi/100 = \pi/50$ units. These are denoted by the variable Z in Program 2.6. The OUTPUT statement writes the values of the function for each value of t in the SAS data set ANDREWS. A two-dimensional plot of Z versus t is obtained by using PROC GPLOT. Output 2.6 is the result of this program.

An examination of the Andrews plot indicates that the fifteenth tree (M) again stands out from the rest. As noted in the profile plot from the last section, this tree may be an outlier. As earlier, there is also a group of 12 to 14 trees that are clumped together.

An Andrews function plot of an observational vector may be affected by the ordering of the elements of that vector. Since low frequencies are more readily seen than high frequencies, it may be useful to take the most important meaningful variable as the first component of the vector, the second most important variable as the second component, and so on.

2.5 Biplot: Plotting Observations and Variables Together

Introduced by Gabriel (1971), a biplot is a graphical representation of a data matrix by means of two sets of markers representing its rows and columns respectively. These can be very helpful for the visual examination of the data for any striking patterns or peculiarities as well as for any influential observations.

Suppose we have a set of n observations on p variables. A biplot describes the relationships among the p variables and the n observations. It is based on the fact that any n by p matrix $\mathbf{Y}$ of rank r can be expressed as

$$\mathbf{Y} = \mathbf{GH}', \tag{2.1}$$

where $\mathbf{G}$ and $\mathbf{H}$ respectively are n by r and p by r matrices of rank r. Each y_{ij} the $(i,j)^{th}$ element of $\mathbf{Y}$ is thus expressed as $y_{ij} = \mathbf{g}_i'\mathbf{h}_j$, where $\mathbf{g}_i'$ is the ith row of $\mathbf{G}$ and $\mathbf{h}_j$ is the jth column of $\mathbf{H}'$. Thus each element y_{ij} of $\mathbf{Y}$ is represented by two r-dimensional vectors, $\mathbf{g}_i'$, corresponding to the ith row and $\mathbf{h}_j$, corresponding to the jth column of the matrix $\mathbf{Y}$.

When the rank of the data matrix $\mathbf{Y}$ is $r = 2$, the vectors $\mathbf{g}_i$ and $\mathbf{h}_j$ are all of size 2 by 1. Therefore, the $n + p$ points, $\mathbf{g}_1, ..., \mathbf{g}_n$ and $\mathbf{h}_1, ..., \mathbf{h}_p$ can be plotted on the plane to get the biplot. The same procedure can be adopted if $r = 3$, and in that case the corresponding biplot will be in a three-dimensional space. For the data matrix $\mathbf{Y}$ with the rank $r > 3$, an approximation matrix of the lower rank, say of rank 2 or 3, can be constructed, and it can be used for plotting the biplot yielding an approximate biplot for $\mathbf{Y}$.

To obtain meaningful properties for the vectors $\mathbf{g}_i$ and $\mathbf{h}_j$ Gabriel (1971) suggests that the *singular value decomposition* (SVD) (Rao, 1973, p. 42) of the data matrix be used for the representation (Equation 2.1). That is, write $\mathbf{Y}$ as

$$\mathbf{Y} = \mathbf{U}\mathbf{\Lambda}\mathbf{V}' = \sum_{i=1}^{r} \lambda_i \mathbf{u}_i \mathbf{v}_i',$$

where $\mathbf{\Lambda}$ is r by r diagonal matrix with positive diagonal elements $\lambda_1 \geq \lambda_2 \geq ... \geq \lambda_r > 0$, $\mathbf{U}$, an n by r matrix with columns $\mathbf{u}_1, ..., \mathbf{u}_r$, is such that $\mathbf{U}'\mathbf{U} = \mathbf{I}_r$ and $\mathbf{V}$, a p by r matrix with columns $\mathbf{v}_1, ..., \mathbf{v}_r$, is such that $\mathbf{V}'\mathbf{V} = \mathbf{I}_r$. The values $\lambda_1, ..., \lambda_r$ are called the singular values of $\mathbf{Y}$. In fact, $\lambda_1^2, ..., \lambda_r^2$ are the nonzero eigenvalues of the matrix $\mathbf{Y}\mathbf{Y}'$ or $\mathbf{Y}'\mathbf{Y}$, the vectors $\mathbf{u}_1, ..., \mathbf{u}_r$ are the corresponding eigenvectors of $\mathbf{Y}\mathbf{Y}'$, and $\mathbf{v}_1, ..., \mathbf{v}_r$ are those corresponding to $\mathbf{Y}'\mathbf{Y}$.

For the rest of the discussions in this section suppose that the data matrix $\mathbf{Y}$ is already centered to have zero column means. Then $\lambda_1^2, ..., \lambda_r^2$ respectively represent the portion of the total variation accounted for by the dimensions $1, ..., r$. If an approximation of dimension two is used for $\mathbf{Y}$, that is, if

$$\mathbf{Y} \approx \lambda_1 \mathbf{u}_1 \mathbf{v}_1' + \lambda_2 \mathbf{u}_2 \mathbf{v}_2', \tag{2.2}$$

then we get an approximate biplot for $\mathbf{Y}$ and the corresponding goodness of fit is measured by

$$\eta = \frac{\lambda_1^2 + \lambda_2^2}{\sum_{i=1}^{r} \lambda_i^2}.$$

If the actual dimension of $\mathbf{Y}$ is 2, then $\eta = 1$. If $r \geq 3$, $\eta < 1$. Thus if η is near one, the biplot will give a good approximation of the biplot of $\mathbf{Y}$.

From Equation 2.2 several choices for the coordinates of the biplot are possible.

a.

$$\mathbf{g}_i' = (\sqrt{\lambda_1} u_{1i}, \sqrt{\lambda_2} u_{2i}), i = 1, ..., n,$$
$$\mathbf{h}_j' = (\sqrt{\lambda_1} v_{1j}, \sqrt{\lambda_2} v_{2j}), j = 1, ..., p.$$

This is the most useful representation of the data. It is used to represent the relationships between observations and the relationship between the variables with equal importance. This is also the same as the principal components representation of the data. The $\mathbf{g}_i$'s are same as the principal component scores and the $\mathbf{h}_j$'s are the principal component weights (see the PRINCOMP procedure in *SAS/STAT User's Guide, Version 6, Fourth Edition, Volume 2*).

b.

$$\mathbf{g}'_i = (u_{1i}, u_{2i}), i = 1, ..., n,$$
$$\mathbf{h}'_j = (\lambda_1 v_{1j}, \lambda_2 v_{2j}), j = 1, ..., p.$$

This is used to represent the relationships among variables more prominently than the relationship among observations. Also, this leads to some interesting interpretations. For example, the distance between any two $\mathbf{g}_i$'s, say $\mathbf{g}_i$ and $\mathbf{g}_{i'}$, approximates the squared Mahalanobis distance between the observation vectors (that is, the ith and the i'^{th} rows of the data matrix $\mathbf{Y}$). Further, the angle (cosine of the angle) between any two $\mathbf{h}_j$'s, say $\mathbf{h}_j$ and $\mathbf{h}_{j'}$, approximates the angle between the corresponding columns of the data matrix $\mathbf{Y}$ (approximates to the correlation between variables y_j and $y_{j'}$).

c.

$$\mathbf{g}'_i = (\lambda_1 u_{1i}, \lambda_2 u_{2i}), i = 1, ..., n,$$
$$\mathbf{h}'_j = (v_{1j}, v_{2j}), j = 1, ..., p.$$

This representation is used to focus on the relationships between the observations more closely than the relationship between the variables. In this representation the usual Euclidean distance between $\mathbf{g}_i$ and $\mathbf{g}_{i'}$ approximates the Euclidean distance between the ith and the i'^{th} rows of the data matrix $\mathbf{Y}$.

The macro BIPLOT in Friendly (1991) is designed to draw a biplot of any of the above three types **(a)**, **(b)**, or **(c)**. For completeness' sake we have given this macro with some minor notational changes in Program 2.7. The program is used to draw a biplot of cork boring data using choice **(a)**, as shown in Output 2.7. It gives the biplot coordinates and the plot using PROC GPLOT.

The first two dimensions together account for more than 96% of the variation in the data. Dimension 1 (the horizontal axis) in Output 2.7 is interpreted as overall magnitude (weighted average), corrected for the mean, of an observation vector corresponding to a tree. This is so since the coefficients of the linear combination of the variables that are used to form the value corresponding to Dimension 1 are all positive and are approximately of the same magnitude (see the first coordinates of the four variables). Hence the trees whose corresponding values fall at the right in the positive direction have an overall larger magnitude. For example, the fifteenth tree (T15) seems to have the largest weighted average after correcting for the mean. The trees T1 and T18 have the next largest averages. There is a group of trees (as noted previously) that have smaller weighted averages than the overall mean and are clustered together. Dimension 2 (the vertical axis) represents a contrast between the cork boring by direction, that is, the contrast N+E-S-W. This is so since the second coordinates of the four variables have positive signs for north and east directions, but negative signs for south and west directions. The trees T12 and T18 seem to have the greatest difference in the cork boring in those directions.

The vectors in the biplot represent various variables (four directions in the present example). The cosines of the angles between these vectors indicate the degree of correlations between the variables. Variables corresponding to the pair of vectors with small angles between them are highly positively correlated. Variables corresponding to the vectors at right angles are uncorrelated, and those with angles more than 90° are negatively correlated. An examination of these vectors in the biplot indicates that the correlation between the measurements in the directions of west and south is the highest followed by between south and north, and then between west and north. The weakest correlation is observed between the measurements in the east and west directions.

2.6 Q-Q Plots for Assessing Multivariate Normality

We present a simple method of assessing multivariate normality using a Q-Q plot. A Q-Q plot is a quantile-quantile comparison of two distributions either or both of which may be empirical or theoretical. When we compare the probability distributions of two random variables, the Q-Q plot will result in a straight line if the two variables are linearly related. These plots are especially good for discriminating in the tail areas of the distributions since the quantiles change more rapidly there and hence the larger distances will occur between consecutive quantiles.

To assess multivariate normality, Q-Q plots are used rather indirectly. Since for multivariate normal data certain quantiles (as described below) approximately follow a chi-square distribution, the empirical quantiles obtained from the data are therefore plotted against the theoretical quantiles of certain chi-square distributions. The details are described below. For some other graphical and numerical methods for assessing or testing for multivariate normality see Gnanadesikan (1980).

Let $\mathbf{x}_i, i = 1, ..., n$, be a random sample presumably from a multivariate normal distribution $N_p(\mu, \Sigma)$. Then $\mathbf{z}_i = \Sigma^{-1/2}(x_i - \mu)$, $i = 1, ..., n$ are iid $N_p(0, I)$ and hence

$$\delta_i^2 = \mathbf{z}_i'\mathbf{z}_i = (\mathbf{x}_i - \mu)'\Sigma^{-1}(\mathbf{x}_i - \mu), i = 1, ..., n,$$

follows a chi-square distribution with p degrees of freedom. The quantity δ_i^2 is the squared Mahalanobis distance (Mahalanobis, 1936) between $\mathbf{x}_i$ and its expectation μ. If the observations, $\mathbf{x}_i$'s, are indeed from an $N_p(\mu, \Sigma)$ then the distances (the sample versions of squared Mahalanobis distances)

$$d_i^2 = (\mathbf{x}_i - \bar{\mathbf{x}})'\mathbf{S}^{-1}(\mathbf{x}_i - \bar{\mathbf{x}}), i = 1, ..., n,$$

where $\bar{\mathbf{x}} = \frac{1}{n}\sum_{i=1}^{n}\mathbf{x}_i$ and $\mathbf{S} = \frac{1}{n-1}\sum_{i=1}^{n}(\mathbf{x}_i - \bar{\mathbf{x}})(\mathbf{x}_i - \bar{\mathbf{x}})'$ will approximately be distributed as a chi-square on p degrees of freedom. Hence the suggestion is to plot ordered d_i^2 values against the quantiles of chi-square distribution on p degrees of freedom. If the assumed normality holds, then the plot should approximately resemble a straight line passing through the origin at a 45° angle with the horizontal axis.

An efficient program using PROC IML to plot the above Q-Q plot is provided by Friendly (1991). Program 2.8 uses PROC PRINCOMP to compute d_i^2, and then produces the Q-Q plot shown in Output 2.8.

In order to explain the computations performed in Program 2.8, let $u_1, ..., u_p$ be the p sample principal components with estimated means $\bar{u}_1, ..., \bar{u}_p$ and the estimated variances $l_1, ..., l_p$ respectively. Then for each $i = 1, ..., n$ the standardized variables $(u_{ij} - \bar{u}_j)/\sqrt{l_j}$, $j = 1, ..., p$ approximately follow independent standard normal distributions. This yields the approximate distribution of

$$d_i^2 = (\mathbf{x}_i - \bar{\mathbf{x}})'\mathbf{S}^{-1}(\mathbf{x}_i - \bar{\mathbf{x}}) = \sum_{j=1}^{p}(\frac{u_{ij} - \bar{u}_j}{\sqrt{l_j}})^2,$$

$i = 1, ..., n$ as a chi-square on p degrees of freedom. The values of d_i^2 can be easily computed using the right-most expression in the equation given above. In SAS/STAT software, they can be achieved using the STD option (to standardize the principal components) in PROC PRINCOMP statement and then the SAS function USS to compute their (uncorrected) sums of squares. The automatic variable $\_N\_$ created by SAS is used in the process of computing the probabilities at which the quantiles of the chi-square variable (on p=4 degrees of freedom) are generated. The function CINV computes these quantiles for the given probabilities. For this program these probability values are chosen as $(i - 0.5)/28$, i=1,...,28 and these are specified as $(\_N\_ - 0.5)/TOTN$ within the function CINV.

This program can also be slightly improved to plot the points on a 45^0 angle line passing through the origin on the same graph using the OVERLAY option in the PLOT command. These points are denoted by a plus sign $(+)$ in Output 2.9. In addition, it is possible to avoid counting the number of observations and explicitly specifying the number of observations as TOTN=28.0, by using PROC MEANS. Program 2.9 and Output 2.9 show the modified program output.

Alternatively, the QQPLOT statement in the CAPABILITY procedure of SAS/QC software can be used to draw a Q-Q plot. Alternatively, use the PROBPLOT statement to draw a percentile plot. Details about these can be found in *SAS/QC Software: Reference, Version 6, First Edition*. SAS codes for these are given in Program 2.8 and are commented out.

Examination of the plots in Outputs 2.8 and 2.9 indicates that most of the points are around the 45° angle line passing through the origin. Hence it can be assumed that the observations are coming from a multivariate normal population. This is not surprising since the test for multivariate normality for the data described in Chapter 1 also resulted in the acceptance of multivariate normality assumption.

2.7 Plots for Detection of Multivariate Outliers

The plots explained in the previous section can also be used to detect possible outliers in the multivariate data. If one or more points fall outside the majority of the points on the Q-Q plot, then those points are suspected to be outliers. However, it is known that the statistics $\bar{\mathbf{x}}$ and $\mathbf{S}$ are both sensitive to the presence of outliers. Hence the squared Mahalanobis distance d_i^2 calculated using the formula $d_i^2 = (\mathbf{x}_i - \bar{\mathbf{x}})' \mathbf{S}^{-1} (\mathbf{x}_i - \bar{\mathbf{x}})$ may not indicate $\mathbf{x}_i$ to be an outlier even when it actually is. An alternative is to use other more robust estimators of μ and Σ in place of $\bar{\mathbf{x}}$ and $\mathbf{S}$ to compute d_i^2. One such procedure is to use $\bar{\mathbf{x}}_{(i)}$ and $\mathbf{S}_{(i)}$ in place of $\bar{\mathbf{x}}$ and $\mathbf{S}$ in the definition of d_i^2 , where $\bar{\mathbf{x}}_{(i)}$ and $\mathbf{S}_{(i)}$ are the values of sample mean vector and the sample variance covariance matrix without using the ith observation vector. Thus for every $i = 1, ..., n$ we compute the robust squared distances

$$D_i^2 = (\mathbf{x}_i - \bar{\mathbf{x}}_{(i)})' \mathbf{S}_{(i)}^{-1} (\mathbf{x}_i - \bar{\mathbf{x}}_{(i)}).$$

To get a Q-Q plot similar to that in the previous section, plot the values of D_i^2 against the quantiles of chi-square distribution with p degrees of freedom. Fortunately, the quantities d_i^2 and D_i^2 are functionally related. Hence, Program 2.8 can be suitably modified, as shown in Program 2.10, by adding a few additional commands to compute D_i^2 from d_i^2 using this relationship which is given by

$$D_i^2 = \left(\frac{n}{n-1}\right)^2 \frac{(n-2)\frac{d_i^2}{n-1}}{1 - \left(\frac{n}{n-1}\right)\frac{d_i^2}{n-1}}.$$

The plot is presented as Output 2.10. The plot indicates that there is definitely one point, and possibly more, that stands out from the rest. The points that stand separate are those with high robust distance. As shown by the RDSQ values presented in Output 2.10, the highest distance turns out to be for observation 16 (not 15 as we may have expected). The squared distance D_{16}^2 for this observation is 17.32 which is considerably larger compared to the corresponding chi-square value of 11.93. Observation 15 with a D_i^2 value of 13.73, observation 18 with 12.77, and observation 1 with 10.76 also stand apart from the majority of the data vectors. As we have previously seen, observation 15 is different from the rest because of the magnitudes of its individual components. A closer look at observation 16 reveals that this particular tree is unique in the sense that its measurement in the direction of south is unusually low compared to those in the other directions. This phenomenon is markedly different from the majority of the trees for which the measurement in the direction of south is higher. See the profile plot in Output 2.5. Hence the sixteenth tree may be classified as an outlier. Trees 15, 18, and 1 may be classified as outliers also.

Detection of outliers from a set of multivariate data is a difficult problem. Some numerical measures for outlier detection are given in Chapter 1. Rao (1964) suggested a method for detection of outliers using a distance measure based on the last few principal components.

2.8 Bivariate Normal Distribution

One of the most commonly used distributions in multivariate data analysis is multivariate normal distribution. This distribution has been briefly discussed in Chapter 1. The p-variate normal distribution with $p=2$ is often referred to as a *bivariate normal distribution*. For a bivariate normal distribution, it is possible to present much of the information about the distribution very effectively in a graph. In this section we consider a bivariate normal distribution and give plots for its probability density function (pdf) as well as its contours. Contours of a function on the higher dimension are the graphs of the projections of the function on a plane at the fixed values of the function. In the present context, these plots can help us visualize the shape of the pdf of the multivariate normal distribution by examining its various bivariate marginal pdfs and their contour plots.

2.8.1 Probability Density Function Plotting

The pdf of a p-variate normal distribution with mean vector μ is given by

$$f(\mathbf{x}) = \frac{1}{(2\pi)^{p/2}|\Sigma|^{1/2}} exp\{-\frac{1}{2}(\mathbf{x} - \mu)'\Sigma^{-1}(\mathbf{x} - \mu)\},$$

where Σ is the dispersion (variance-covariance) matrix of the p by 1 vector $\mathbf{x}$. When $p = 2$, the mean vector of $\mathbf{x} = (x_1, x_2)'$ is $\mu = (\mu_1, \mu_2)$ and the dispersion matrix is a 2 by 2 matrix

$$\Sigma = \begin{bmatrix} \sigma_1^2 & \rho\sigma_1\sigma_2 \\ \rho\sigma_1\sigma_2 & \sigma_2^2 \end{bmatrix},$$

where $\sigma_1^2 = var(x_1)$, $\sigma_2^2 = var(x_2)$ and ρ is the correlation coefficient between x_1 and x_2. In Program 2.11 we use PROC G3D to plot the pdf of the bivariate normal distribution for specific values of $\mu_1 = 0.0$, $\mu_2 = 0.0$, $\sigma_1^2 = 2.0$, $\sigma_2^2 = 1.0$, and $\rho = 0.5$. The KEEP statement in the program saves the variables that are listed in that statement. Alternatively, a DROP statement could be used to drop the variables not needed by listing them after the DROP command. The output of Program 2.11 is shown in Output 2.11.

An examination of the pdf plot in Output 2.11 shows the effect of the variance of x_1 being larger than that of x_2. Further, the effect of positive correlation between these two variables can be seen from the shape of the density surface which is concentrated along the line $x_1 = x_2$ in the horizontal plane.

2.8.2 Contour Plot of Density

The contour plots of a bivariate probability density function show the degrees of association between the two random variables. For the same data as in Program 2.11 we draw the contours of the pdf using the GCONTOUR procedure. Adding a few more SAS statements to Program 2.11 we have Program 2.12 which achieves the desired objective. The output is shown in Output 2.12. The LEVELS option in the PLOT statement of the program is used to specify the fixed values of the pdf for which the contours are to be drawn. These values should be the plausible values of the function and hence should be between zero and the maximum possible value of the pdf. Noting that the maximum value of the pdf of a bivariate normal distribution corresponds to $x_1 = \mu_1$ and $x_2 = \mu_2$, we can determine the maximum value that can be given in the LEVELS option, for the given values of σ_1^2, σ_2^2, and ρ. For example, the maximum value of the pdf is $\frac{1}{2\pi\sqrt{(1.5)}}$ for the choices $\mu_1 = \mu_2 = 0$, $\sigma_1^2 = 2.0$, $\sigma_2^2 = 1.0$, and $\rho = 0.5$.

The contours of a bivariate probability density function have the following interpretations.

- For a zero correlation between the variables and equal variances, the contours are circles centered at (μ_1, μ_2).
- For zero correlation and the variance of x_1 greater than that of x_2, the contours are ellipses whose major axes are parallel to the horizontal axis (if the variance of x_2 is greater than that of x_1 then the major axis will be parallel to vertical axis).
- If the correlation between the variables is nonzero, then the contours are ellipses.
- Additionally if the two variances are equal then for any contour, the major axis is at an angle (with the horizontal axis) whose cosine is same as the correlation coefficient between the two variables.

The contours in Output 2.12 indicate the positive correlation between the two variables x_1 and x_2.

2.9 SAS/INSIGHT Software

SAS/INSIGHT software is an interactive tool for data exploration and analysis. Use it to explore data through a variety of interactive graphs and analyses linked across multiple windows. In addition, use it to analyze univariate distributions, investigate multivariate distributions, and fit explanatory models using analysis of variance, regression, and the generalized linear model. The following summary of features is adapted from the *SAS/INSIGHT User's Guide, Version 6, First Edition* published by SAS Institute.

2.9.1 Summary of Features

SAS/INSIGHT software offers a comprehensive set of graphical tools. For example, it can rotate data in three-dimensional plots; create Q-Q (quantile-quantile) plots; fit curves including polynomial, kernel density estimates, and smoothing spline curves; and create residual and leverage plots. Because it is a part of the SAS System, SAS/INSIGHT software can explore results from any SAS procedure.

The statements given in Program 2.4 invoke SAS/INSIGHT software. Once SAS/INSIGHT is invoked, there are several options for extensive data analysis to choose from just by clicking the button on the mouse. The scatter plot matrix given in Output 2.4 was obtained using SAS/INSIGHT.

```
/* Program 2.1*/

title1 j=1 'Output 2.1';
options ls=64 ps=40 nodate nonumber;
data cork;
infile 'cork.dat';
input n e s w;
/* n:north,e:east,s:south,w:west*/
y1=n-s;
y2=e-w;

title2 'Two Dimensional Scatter Plot ';
title3 'Cork Boring Data: Source C.R.Rao (1948)';
proc plot data=cork;
plot n*e;
label n='Direction: North'
        e='Direction: East';
 run;

title2 'Two Dimensional Scatter Plot ';
title3 'Cork Boring Data: Source C.R.Rao (1948)';
proc plot data=cork;
plot y1*y2;
label y1='Contrast: North-South'
      y2='Contrast: East-West';
 run;
```

Output 2.1
Two Dimensional Scatter Plot
Cork Boring Data: Source C.R.Rao (1948)

Plot of N*E.   Legend: A = 1 obs, B = 2 obs, etc.

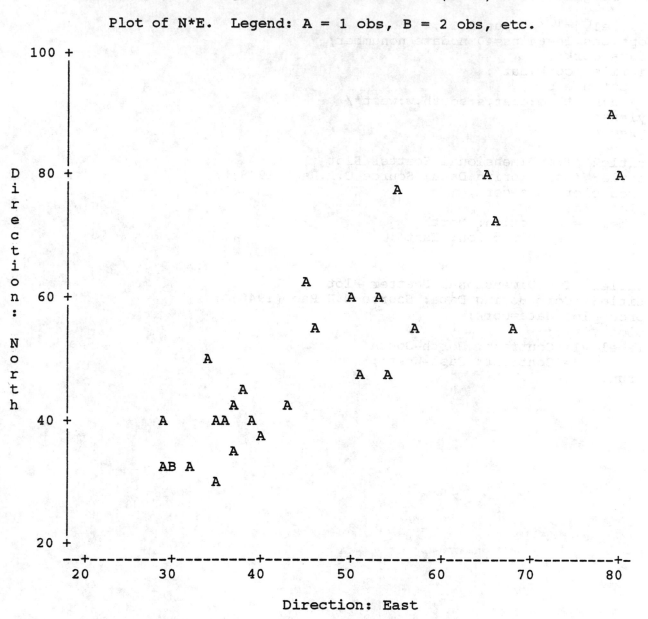

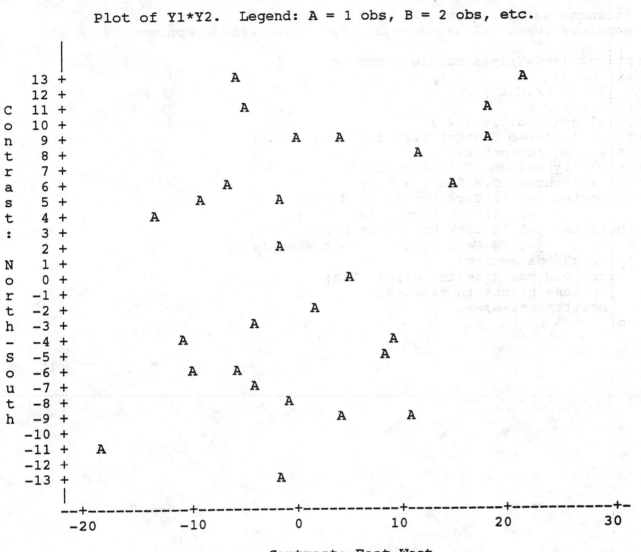

Output 2.1
Two Dimensional Scatter Plot
Cork Boring Data: Source C.R.Rao (1948)

Plot of Y1*Y2.   Legend: A = 1 obs, B = 2 obs, etc.

```
/* Program 2.2 */

 filename gsasfile "prog22.graph";
 goptions reset=all gaccess=gsasfile   autofeed dev=pslmono;

options ls=64 ps=45 nodate nonumber;
data cork;
infile 'cork.dat';
input n e s w;
title1 j=l 'Output 2.2';
title1 'Three-D Scatter Plot for Cork Data';
title2 j=l 'Output 2.2';
title3 'by weight of cork boring';
title4 'Source: C.R.Rao (1948)';
 footnote1 j=l 'N:Cork boring in North'
           j=r 'E:Cork boring in East';
 footnote2 j=l 'S:Cork boring in South'
           j=r 'W:West boring is not shown';
  proc g3d data=cork;
   goptions horigin=1in vorigin=2in;
   goptions hsize=6in vsize=8in;
    scatter n*s=e;
run;
```

Three–D Scatter Plot for Cork Data

Output 2.2

by weight of cork boring
Source: C.R.Rao (1948)

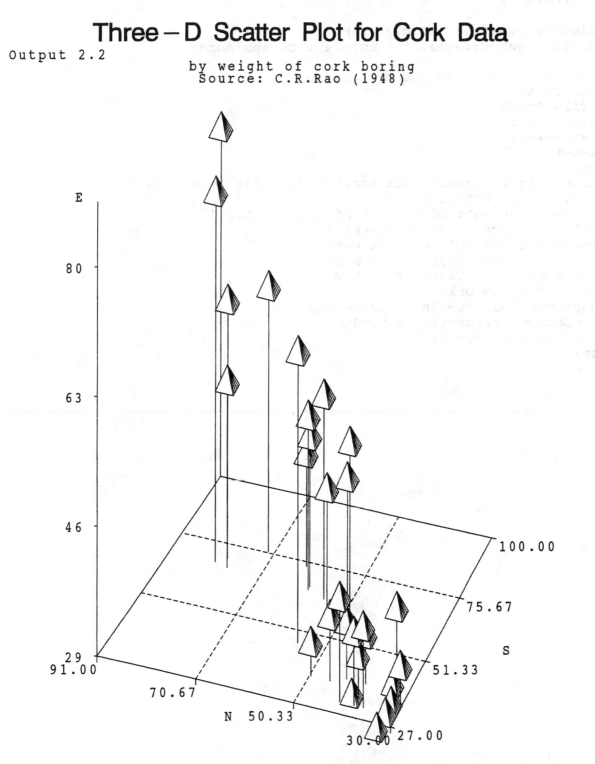

N:Cork boring in North   E:Cork boring in East
S:Cork boring in South   W:West boring is not shown

```
/* Program 2.3*/

filename gsasfile "prog23.graph";
goptions gaccess=gsasfile autofeed dev=pslmono;

options ls=64 ps=45 nodate nonumber;
data cork;
infile 'cork.dat';
input n e s w;
c1=n-e-w+s;
c2=n-s;
c3=e-w;
title1 'Three-Dimensional Scatter Plot for Cork Data';
 title2 j=l 'Output 2.3';
title3 'Contrasts of weights of cork boring';
title4 'Source: C.R.Rao (1948)';
 footnote1 j=l 'C1:Contrast N-E-W+S'
           j=r 'C2:Contrast N-S';
 footnote2 j=r 'C3:Contrast E-W';
proc g3d data=cork;
 goptions horigin=1in vorigin=2in;
   goptions hsize=6in vsize=8in;
   scatter c1*c2=c3;
run;
```

Three−Dimensional Scatter Plot for Cork Data

Output 2.3

Contrasts of weights of cork boring
Source: C.R.Rao (1948)

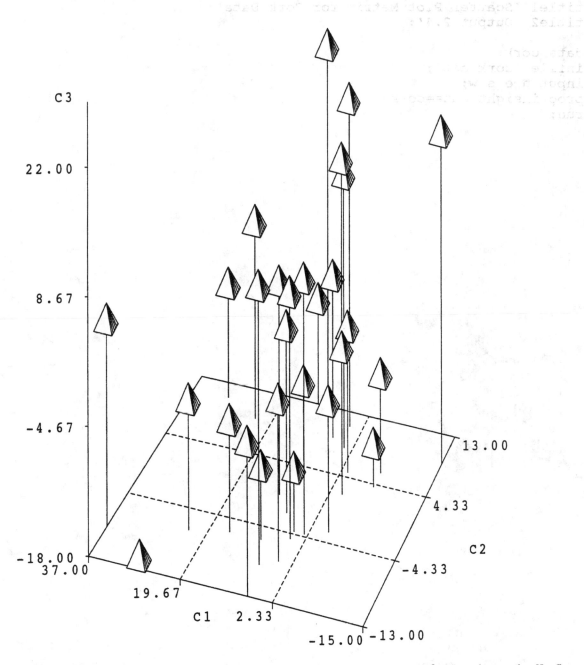

C1:Contrast N−E−W+S

C2:Contrast N−S
C3:Contrast E−W

```
/* Program 2.4 */

  filename gsasfile "prog24.graph";
  goptions reset=all gaccess=gsasfile autofeed dev=pslmono;
  goptions horigin=1in vorigin=2in;
  goptions hsize=6in vsize=8in;
  options ls=64 ps=40 nodate nonumber;

title1 'Scatter Plot Matrix for Cork Data';
title2 'Output 2.4';

data cork;
infile 'cork.dat';
input n e s w;
proc insight data=cork;
run;
```

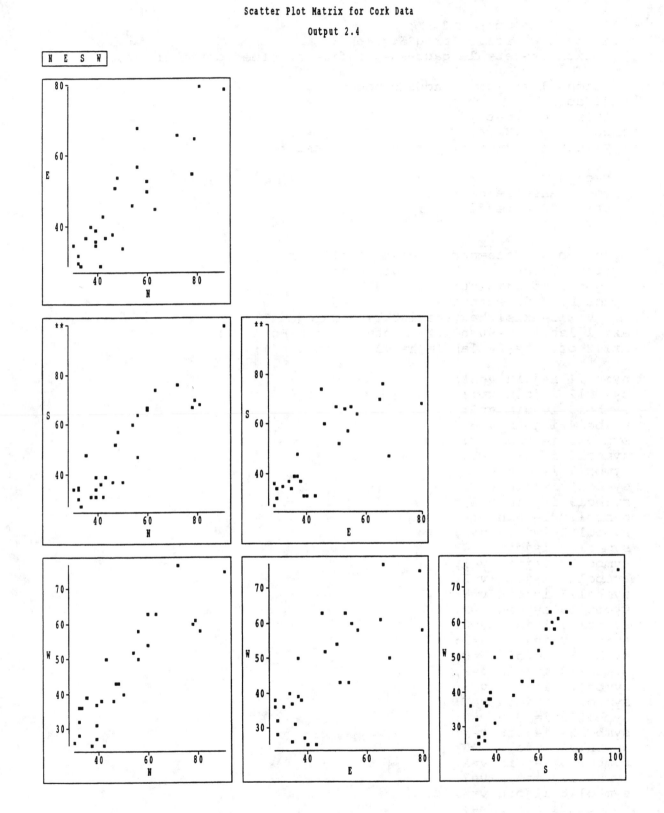

```
/* Program 2.5 */

 title1 j=l 'Output 2.5';
 filename gsasfile "prog25.graph";
 goptions reset=all gaccess=gsasfile autofeed dev=pslmono;

 options ls=64 ps=45 nodate nonumber;
data cork;
infile 'cork.dat';
input y1 y2 y3 y4;
/*y1=north, y2=east, y3=south, y4=west */

 tree=_n_;
 proc transpose data=cork
 out=cork2 name=directn;
   by tree;

 proc gplot data=cork2(rename=(col1=bore));
 goptions horigin=1in vorigin=2in;
   goptions hsize=6in vsize=8in;
 plot bore*directn=tree/
    vaxis=axis1 haxis=axis2 legend=legend1;
axis1 label=(a=90 h=1.2 'Depth of Cork Boring');
axis2 offset=(2) label=(h=1.2 'Direction');

symbol1 i=join v=star;
symbol2 i=join v=+;
symbol3 i=join v=A;
symbol4 i=join v=B;
symbol5 i=join v=C;
symbol6 i=join v=D;
symbol7 i=join v=E;
symbol8 i=join v=F;
symbol9 i=join v=G;
symbol10 i=join v=H;
symbol11 i=join v=I;
symbol12 i=join v=J;
symbol13 i=join v=K;
symbol14 i=join v=L;
symbol15 i=join v=M;
symbol16 i=join v=N;
symbol17 i=join v=O;
symbol18 i=join v=P;
symbol19 i=join v=Q;
symbol20 i=join v=R;
symbol21 i=join v=S;
symbol22 i=join v=T;
symbol23 i=join v=U;
symbol24 i=join v=V;
symbol25 i=join v=W;
symbol26 i=join v=X;
symbol27 i=join v=Y;
symbol28 i=join v=Z;
   legend1 across=4;
title1 'Profiles of Cork Data';
title2 j=l 'Output 2.5';
title3 'Source: C.R.Rao (1948)';
```

```
/* Program 2.5 continued */

/*
data plot;
set cork;
array y{4} y1 y2 y3 y4;
do directn=1 to 4;
bore =y(directn);
output;
end;
drop y1 y2 y3 y4;
proc gplot data=plot;
 goptions horigin=1in vorigin=2in;
    goptions hsize=6in vsize=8in;
plot bore*directn=tree/
   vaxis=axis1 haxis=axis2 legend=legend1;
axis1 label=(a=90 h=1.2 'Depth of Cork Boring');
 axis2 offset=(2) label=(h=1.2 'Direction');

symbol1  i=join v=star;
symbol2  i=join v=+;
symbol3  i=join v=A;
symbol4  i=join v=B;
symbol5  i=join v=C;
symbol6  i=join v=D;
symbol7  i=join v=E;
symbol8  i=join v=F;
symbol9  i=join v=G;
symbol10 i=join v=H;
symbol11 i=join v=I;
symbol12 i=join v=J;
symbol13 i=join v=K;
symbol14 i=join v=L;
symbol15 i=join v=M;
symbol16 i=join v=N;
symbol17 i=join v=O;
symbol18 i=join v=P;
symbol19 i=join v=Q;
symbol20 i=join v=R;
symbol21 i=join v=S;
symbol22 i=join v=T;
symbol23 i=join v=U;
symbol24 i=join v=V;
symbol25 i=join v=W;
symbol26 i=join v=X;
symbol27 i=join v=Y;
symbol28 i=join v=Z;
   legend1 across=4;
title1 'Profiles of Cork Data';
title2 j=l 'Output 2.5';
title3 'Source: C.R.Rao (1948)';
*/
run;
```

Profiles of Cork Data

Source: C.R.Rao (1948)

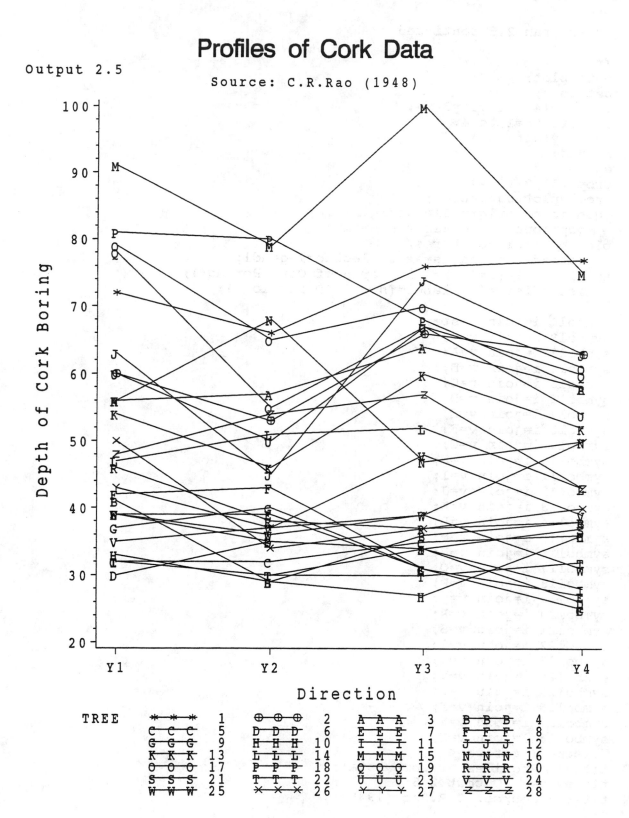

```
/* Program 2.6 */

 filename gsasfile "prog26.graph";
 goptions reset=all gaccess=gsasfile autofeed dev=pslmono;

options ls=64 ps=40 nodate nonumber;
title1 'Andrews Function Plot for Cork Data';
 title2 j=l 'Output 2.6';
data andrews;
infile 'cork.dat';
input y1-y4;
tree=_n_;
pi=3.14159265;
s=1/sqrt(2);
 inc=2*pi/100;
 do t=-pi to pi by inc;
 z=s*y1+sin(t)*y2+cos(t)*y3+sin(2*t)*y4;
  output;
    end;
*symbol1 c=black i=join v=plus;
symbol1 i=join v=star;
symbol2 i=join v=+;
symbol3 i=join v=A;
symbol4 i=join v=B;
symbol5 i=join v=C;
symbol6 i=join v=D;
symbol7 i=join v=E;
symbol8 i=join v=F;
symbol9 i=join v=G;
symbol10 i=join v=H;
symbol11 i=join v=I;
symbol12 i=join v=J;
symbol13 i=join v=K;
symbol14 i=join v=L;
symbol15 i=join v=M;
symbol16 i=join v=N;
symbol17 i=join v=O;
symbol18 i=join v=P;
symbol19 i=join v=Q;
symbol20 i=join v=R;
symbol21 i=join v=S;
symbol22 i=join v=T;
symbol23 i=join v=U;
symbol24 i=join v=V;
symbol25 i=join v=W;
symbol26 i=join v=X;
symbol27 i=join v=Y;
symbol28 i=join v=Z;

  proc gplot data=andrews;
 goptions horigin=1in vorigin=2in;
   goptions hsize=6in vsize=8in;
   plot z*t=tree/vaxis=axis1 haxis=axis2;
   axis1 label=(a=90 h=1.5 f=duplex 'f(t)');
    axis2 label=(h=1.5 f=duplex 't')offset=(2);
run;
```

Andrews Function Plot for Cork Data

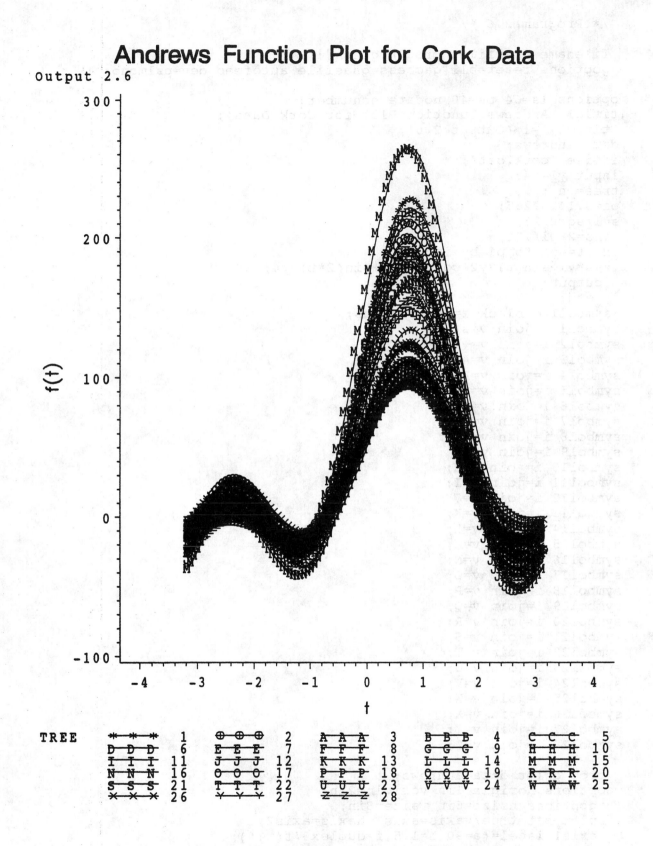

TREE	* * *	1	⊕ ⊕ ⊕	2	A A A	3	B B B	4	C C C	5
	D D D	6	E E E	7	F F F	8	G G G	9	H H H	10
	I I I	11	J J J	12	K K K	13	L L L	14	M M M	15
	N N N	16	O O O	17	P P P	18	Q Q Q	19	R R R	20
	S S S	21	T T T	22	U U U	23	V V V	24	W W W	25
	X X X	26	Y Y Y	27	Z Z Z	28				

```
/* Program 2.7*/

options ls=64 ps=45 nodate nonumber;
data cork;
infile 'newcork.dat';
input tree$ north east south west;
%include biplot; /* Include the macro "biplot.sas" */
%biplot( data = cork,
         var = North East South West,
          id = TREE, factype=SYM, std =STD  );

filename gsasfile "prog27.graph";
 goptions reset=all gaccess=gsasfile autofeed dev=pslmono;

 proc gplot data=biplot;
      plot dim2 * dim1  /anno=bianno frame
                         href=0 vref=0 lvref=3 lhref=3
                         vaxis=axis2 haxis=axis1
                         vminor=1 hminor=1;

axis1 length=6 in order=(-2 to 2 by .5)
         offset=(2)
         label = (h=1.3 'Dimension 1');
   axis2 length=6 in order =(-2 to 2 by .5)
         offset=(2)
         label=(h=1.3 a=90 r=0  'Dimension 2');
   symbol v=none;
title1 h=1.5 f=duplex  'Biplot of Cork Data ';
title2 j=l 'Output 2.7';
   title3 h=1.3   f=duplex
          'Observations are points, Variables are vectors';
run;
```

49

```
/* Program 2.7 continued; page 1 of biplot.sas */

/* This macro named as "biplot.sas", is called by
                                   Program 2.7 */
%macro BIPLOT(
        data=_LAST_,
        var =_NUMERIC_,
         id = ID,
        dim = 2,
    factype=SYM,
      scale=1,
        out=BIPLOT,
      anno=BIANNO,
        std=MEAN,
      pplot=YES);

%let factype=%upcase(&factype);
        %if &factype=GH  %then %let p=0;
%else  %if &factype=SYM %then %let p=.5;
%else  %if &factype=JK  %then %let p=1;
%else %do;
   %put  BIPLOT:  FACTYPE must be GH,SYM, or JK."&factype"
is not valid.;
   %goto done;
   %end;


Proc IML;
Start BIPLOT(Y,ID,VARS,OUT,power,scale);
   N = nrow(Y);
   P = ncol(Y);
   %if &std = NONE
%then Y = Y - Y[:] %str(;);   /*remove grand mean */
%else Y = Y - J(N,1,1)*Y[:,] %str(;); /*remove column means*/
   %if &std = STD %then  %do;
       S = sqrt(Y[##,] / (N-1));
       Y = Y * diag (1/S);
   %end;


*_ _  Singular value decomposition:
        Y is expressed as U diag(Q) V prime
        Q contains singular values in descending order;
   call svd(u,q,v,y);

   reset fw=8 noname;
   percent = 100*q##2 / q[##];
*__ cumulate by multiplying by lower triangular matrix of 1s;

   j = nrow(q);
   tri = (1:j)' * repeat(1,1,j) >= repeat(1,j,1)*(1:j);
   cum = tri*percent;
   Print "Singular values and variance accounted for",,
           q        [colname={'Singular Values'} format=9.4]
           percent [colname={'Percent'} format=8.2]
           cum      [colname={'cum % '} format = 8.2];

     d = &dim;
*__extract first d columns of U & V,and first d elements of Q;

     U=U[,1:d];
     V=V[,1:d];
     Q=Q[1:d];
```

```
/* Program 2.7 continued; page 2 of biplot.sas */

*__ scale the vectors by QL ,QR;

QL= diag(Q ## power);
QR= diag(Q ## (1-power));
A = U * QL;
B = V * QR # scale;
OUT=A // B;

*__ Create observation labels;
id = id // vars';
type = repeat({"OBS "},n,1) //  repeat({"VAR "},p,1);
 id  = concat(type,id);

factype = {"GH" "Symmetric" "JK"}[1+2#power];
print "Biplot Factor Type",factype;
cvar = concat(shape({"DIM"},1,d),char(1:d,1.));
print "Biplot coordinates",
        out[rowname=id colname=cvar];
%if &pplot = YES %then
call pgraf(out,substr(id,5),'Dimension 1','Dimension 2','Biplot');
;
create &out from out[rowname=id colname=cvar];
append from out[rowname=id];
finish;

use &data;
read all var{&var} into y[colname=vars rowname=&id];
power=&p;
scale=&scale;
run biplot(y,&id,vars,out,power,scale);
quit;

/*__ split id into _type_ and _Name_*/

data &out;
    set &out;
    drop id;
    length _type_  $3 _name_ $16;
    _type_ = scan(id,1);
    _name_ = scan(id,2);

/*Annotate  observation labels and variable vectors */
data &anno;
set &out;
length function text $8;
xsys='2';
ysys='2';
text=_name_;

if _type_='OBS' then do;
    color = 'BLACK';
    x = dim1;
    y = dim2;
    position='5';
    function='LABEL       ';
        output;
    end;
```

```
            /* Program 2.7 continued; page 3 of biplot.sas */

    if _type_ ='VAR' then do;        /*Draw  line from*/
       color='RED        ';
       x=0; y=0;                 /*the origin to*/
       function ='MOVE';
          output;
       x=dim1;y=dim2;      /* the variable point*/
       function ='DRAW';
           output;
       if dim1>=0
           then position ='6';    /*left justify*/
           else position ='2';  /*right justify*/
       function='LABEL;
    output;    /* variable name */
       end;

    %done:
    %mend BIPLOT;
    run;
```

The SAS System

Singular values and variance accounted for

Singular Values	Percent	cum %
9.8547	89.92	89.92
2.6169	6.34	96.26
1.4707	2.00	98.27
1.3687	1.73	100.00

Biplot Factor Type
Symmetric

Biplot coordinates

		DIM1	DIM2
OBS	T1	0.973778	-0.26912
OBS	T2	0.490221	-0.31383
OBS	T3	0.423518	-0.07012
OBS	T4	-0.46332	-0.28677
OBS	T5	-0.54788	-0.17694
OBS	T6	-0.6499	0.149762
OBS	T7	-0.53787	0.32465
OBS	T8	-0.4888	0.51141
OBS	T9	-0.56768	0.393327
OBS	T10	-0.63869	-0.18796
OBS	T11	-0.66159	-0.04571
OBS	T12	0.50511	-0.63311
OBS	T13	0.192446	-0.24976
OBS	T14	0.013386	0.163816
OBS	T15	1.476734	0.03805
OBS	T16	0.306205	0.632152
OBS	T17	0.809711	0.160337
OBS	T18	0.935508	0.734152
OBS	T19	0.659912	-0.10836
OBS	T20	-0.31355	0.011575
OBS	T21	-0.44802	-0.06281
OBS	T22	-0.65406	-0.09832
OBS	T23	0.372905	-0.21109
OBS	T24	-0.32323	-0.20306
OBS	T25	-0.45761	0.05773
OBS	T26	-0.29577	-0.14301
OBS	T27	-0.2088	-0.33082
OBS	T28	0.097333	0.213838
VAR	NORTH	1.603826	0.204998
VAR	EAST	1.51622	1.230219
VAR	SOUTH	1.595599	-0.48638
VAR	WEST	1.561282	-0.90822

Biplot of Cork Data
Observations are points, Variables are vectors

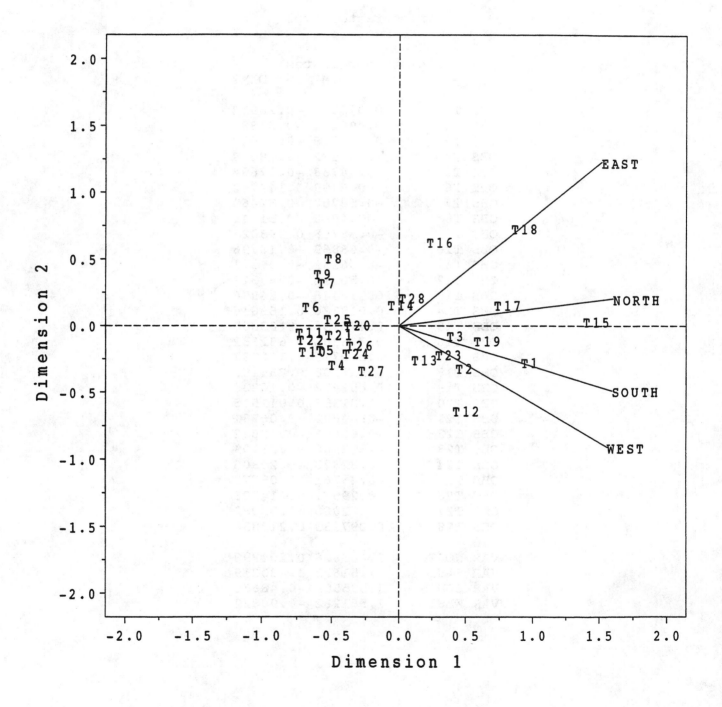

```
/* newcork.dat */

/* In Cork Boring Data of C.R.Rao (1948) the trees have
   have been numbered as T1-T28 */

T1  72 66  76  77
T2  60 53  66  63
T3  56 57  64  58
T4  41 29  36  38
T5  32 32  35  36
T6  30 35  34  26
T7  39 39  31  27
T8  42 43  31  25
T9  37 40  31  25
T10 33 29  27  36
T11 32 30  34  28
T12 63 45  74  63
T13 54 46  60  52
T14 47 51  52  43
T15 91 79 100  75
T16 56 68  47  50
T17 79 65  70  61
T18 81 80  68  58
T19 78 55  67  60
T20 46 38  37  38
T21 39 35  34  37
T22 32 30  30  32
T23 60 50  67  54
T24 35 37  48  39
T25 39 36  39  31
T26 50 34  37  40
T27 43 37  39  50
T28 48 54  57  43
```

```
/* Program 2.8*/

title1 j=l 'Output 2.8';
options ls=64 ps=45 nodate nonumber;
data a;
infile 'cork.dat';
input y1-y4;
totn=28.0;   /* totn is the number of observations */

proc princomp data=a cov std out=b noprint;
var y1-y4;
data qq;
set b;
dsq=uss(of prin1-prin4);

/*
data qq;
set qq;
ndsq=dsq/2;
proc capability noprint;
qqplot ndsq/gamma(alpha=2);
probplot ndsq/gamma(alpha=2);
run;
*/

proc sort;
by dsq;
data qq;
set qq;
chisq=cinv(((_n_-.5)/ totn),4);
proc plot;
plot dsq*chisq='*';
title2 'Q-Q Plot for Assessing Normality';
label dsq='Mahalanobis D Square'
      chisq='Chi-Square Quantile';
run;
```

Output 2.8
Q-Q Plot for Assessing Normality

Plot of DSQ*CHISQ.   Symbol used is '*'.

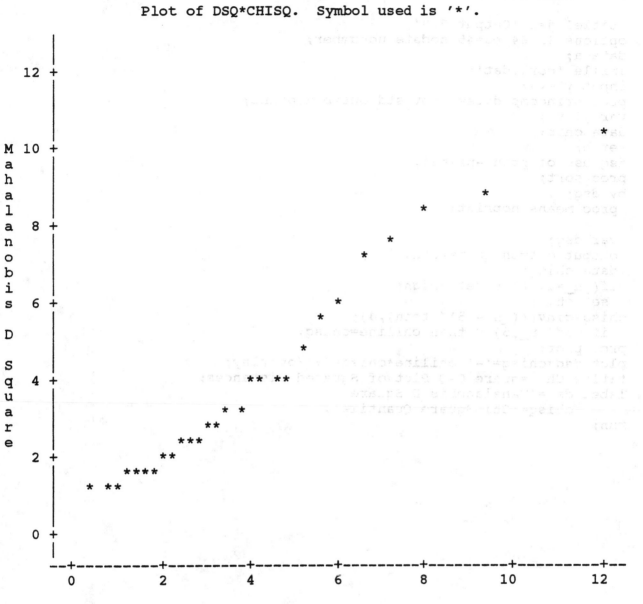

Chi-Square Quantile

```
/* Program 2.9 */

 title1 j=1 'Output 2.9';
options ls=64 ps=45 nodate nonumber;
data a;
infile 'cork.dat';
input y1-y4;
proc princomp data=a cov std out=b noprint;
var y1-y4;
data chiq;
set b;
dsq=uss(of prin1-prin4);
proc sort;
by dsq;
 proc means noprint;

 var dsq;
 output out=chiqn n=totn;
 data chiqq;
 if(_n_=1) then set chiqn;
   set chiq;
chisq=cinv(((_n_-.5)/ totn),4);
   if mod(_n_,5)=0 then chiline=chisq;
proc plot;
plot dsq*chisq='-' chiline*chisq='+'/overlay;
title2 Chi-square Q-Q Plot of Squared Distances;
label dsq='Mahalanobis D Square'
      chisq='Chi-Square Quantile';
run;
```

Output 2.9
Chi-square Q-Q Plot of Squared Distances

Plot of DSQ*CHISQ.　　Symbol used is '–'.
Plot of CHILINE*CHISQ.　Symbol used is '+'.

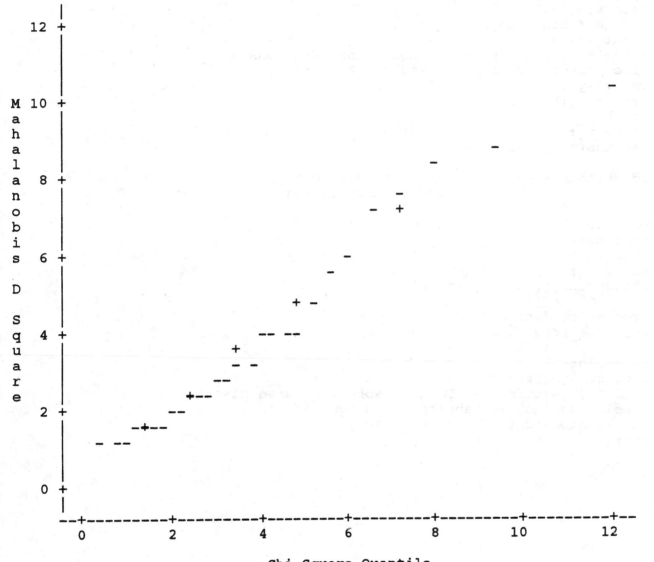

NOTE: 23 obs had missing values.

```
/* Program 2.10 */

title1 j=l 'Output 2.10';
options ls=64 ps=45 nodate nonumber;
data a;
infile 'cork.dat';
input y1-y4;
totn=28.0; /* totn is the no. of observations*/
proc princomp data=a cov std out=b noprint;
var y1-y4;
data chiq;
set b;
tree=_n_;
dsq=uss(of prin1-prin4);

rdsq=(totn/(totn-1))**2*(((totn-2)*dsq/totn)/
              (1-(totn*dsq/(totn-1)**2))));

proc sort;
by rdsq;
data chiq;
set chiq;
chisq=cinv(((_n_-.5)/ totn),4);

proc print data=chiq;
var tree rdsq chisq;

proc plot;
plot rdsq*chisq='*';
title2 Chi-square Q-Q Plot of Robust Squared Distances;
label rdsq='Robust Mahalanobis D Square'
      chisq='Chi-Square Quantile';
run;
```

OBS	TREE	RDSQ	CHISQ
1	13	1.1061	0.4041
2	21	1.1321	0.7390
3	22	1.4472	0.9939
4	20	1.5165	1.2188
5	25	1.7561	1.4282
6	14	1.8060	1.6290
7	5	1.8669	1.8253
8	11	2.2808	2.0197
9	23	2.2940	2.2142
10	7	2.4152	2.4106
11	2	2.7735	2.6103
12	4	2.7877	2.8148
13	3	3.0261	3.0255
14	9	3.1341	3.2440
15	6	3.4746	3.4720
16	10	3.7941	3.7117
17	28	4.4528	3.9654
18	24	4.5990	4.2361
19	17	4.8254	4.5276
20	8	4.8794	4.8450
21	26	5.6789	5.1951
22	27	6.8230	5.5875
23	12	7.6034	6.0366
24	19	9.7945	6.5654
25	1	10.7571	7.2140
26	18	12.7730	8.0633
27	15	13.7286	9.3204
28	16	17.3191	11.9329

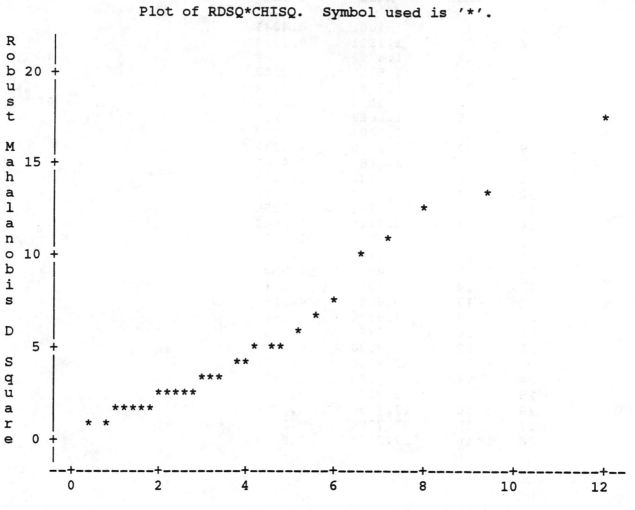

Output 2.10
Chi-square Q-Q Plot of Robust Squared Distances

Plot of RDSQ*CHISQ.   Symbol used is '*'.

Chi-Square Quantile

```
/* Program 2.11 */

filename gsasfile "prog211.graph";
 goptions reset=all gaccess=gsasfile  autofeed dev=pslmono;
 options ls=64 ps=45 nodate nonumber;

title1 'PDF of Bivariate Normal Distribution';
title2 j=l 'Output 2.11';
title3 'Mu_1=0, Mu_2=0, Sigma_1^2=2, Sigma_2^2=1 and Rho=0.5';
 data normal;
mu_1=0.0;
mu_2=0.0;
vx1=2;
vx2=1;
rho=.5;
keep x1 x2 z;
label z='Density';
con=1/(2*3.141592654*sqrt(vx1*vx2*(1-rho*rho)));
do x1=-4 to 4 by 0.3;
do x2=-3 to 3 by 0.10;
zx1=(x1-mu_1)/sqrt(vx1);
zx2=(x2-mu_2)/sqrt(vx2);
hx=zx1**2+zx2**2-2*rho*zx1*zx2;
z=con*exp(-hx/(2*(1-rho**2)));
if z>.001 then output;
end;
end;
proc g3d data=normal;
 goptions horigin=1in vorigin=2in;
   goptions hsize=6in vsize=8in;
  plot x2*x1=z;
*plot x2*x1=z/ rotate=30;
 run;
```

PDF of Bivariate Normal Distribution

Mu_1=0, Mu_2=0, Sigma_1^2=2, Sigma_2^2=1 and Rho=0.5

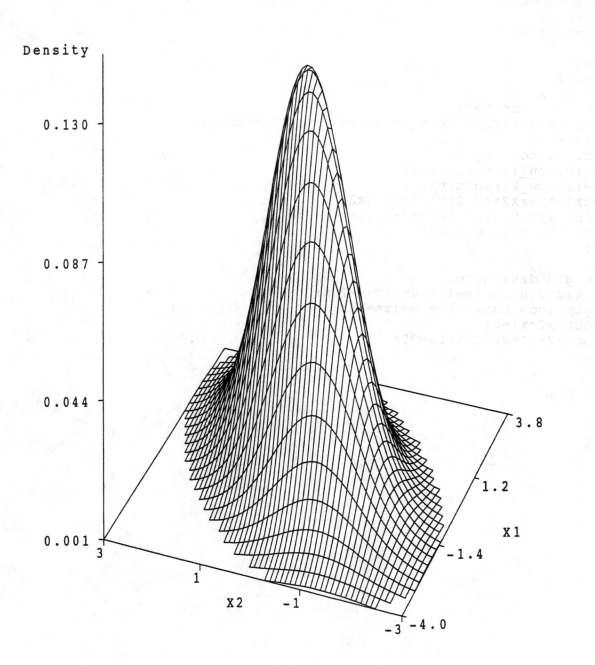

```
/* Program 2.12 */

filename gsasfile "prog212.graph";
 goptions reset=all gaccess=gsasfile  autofeed dev=pslmono;

 options ls=64 ps=45 nodate nonumber;
title1 'Contours of Bivariate Normal Distribution';
title2 j=l 'Output 2.12';
title3 'Mu_1=0, Mu_2=0, Sigma_1^2=2, Sigma_2^2=1 and Rho=0.5';
 data normal;
vx1=2;
vx2=1;
rho=.5;
keep x1 x2 z;
label z='Density';
con=1/(2*3.141592654*sqrt(vx1*vx2*(1-rho*rho)));
do x1=-4 to 4 by 0.3;
do x2=-3 to 3 by 0.10;
zx1=x1/sqrt(vx1);
zx2=x2/sqrt(vx2);
hx=zx1**2+zx2**2-2*rho*zx1*zx2;
z=con*exp(-hx/(2*(1-rho**2)));
if z>.001 then output;
end;
end;
proc gcontour data=normal;
 goptions horigin=1in vorigin=2in;
   goptions hsize=6in vsize=8in;
plot x2*x1=z/
  levels=.02 .03 .04 .05 .06 .07 .08;
run;
```

Contours of Bivariate Normal Distribution

Mu_1=0, Mu_2=0, Sigma_1^2=2, Sigma_2^2=1 and Rho=0.5

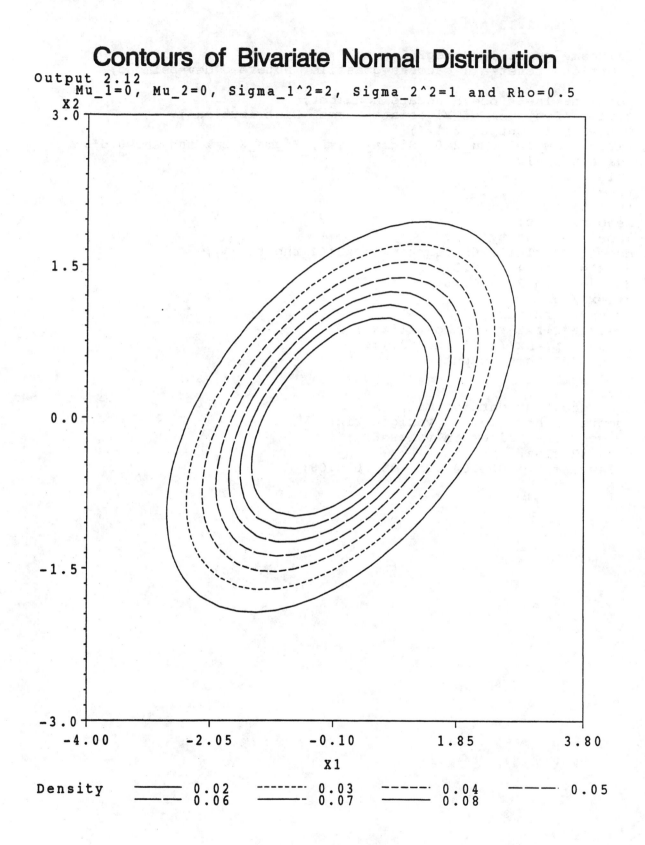

Density ——— 0.02 ------- 0.03 --- --- 0.04 —— —— 0.05
         —— —— 0.06 —— — 0.07 ——— 0.08

CHAPTER 3: Multivariate Regression

3.1 Introduction
3.2 Statistical Background
3.3 Least Squares Estimation
3.4 ANOVA Partitioning
3.5 Testing Hypotheses: Linear Hypotheses
    3.5.1 Multivariate Tests
    3.5.2 Stepdown Analysis
3.6 Simultaneous Confidence Intervals
3.7 Multiple Response Surface Modeling
3.8 General Linear Hypotheses
3.9 Variance and Bias Analyses for Calibration Problems

3.1 Introduction

Regression analysis primarily deals with the issues related to estimating or predicting the expected value of the dependent or response variable using the known values of one or more independent or predictor variables. Usually a model is postulated relating the response variable to the predictor variables with certain unknown coefficients. A model that is linear in these coefficients is often referred to as a *linear regression model* or simply a linear model.

The multivariate linear regression model is a natural generalization of a (univariate) linear regression model. That is, two or more possibly correlated dependent variables are simultaneously modeled as the linear functions of the same set of predictor variables. For reasons of mathematical convenience in developing an appropriate theory, it is required that the particular model for each response variable be in exactly the same functional form. For example, if y_1 and y_2 are the response variables and x_1 and x_2 are the predictors, then the univariate models $y_1 = a_0 + a_1 x_1 + a_2 x_2 + \epsilon_1$ and $y_2 = b_0 + b_1 x_1 + b_2 x_2 + \epsilon_2$ have the same functional forms, whereas the models $y_1 = a_0 + a_1 x_1 + a_2 x_2 + \epsilon_1$ and $y_2 = b_0 + b_1 x_1 + \epsilon_2$ do not. It is possible to argue that the last model (for y_2) has the same functional form as the choice $b_2 = 0$. However, this suggests that b_2 is completely known and hence its estimation is irrelevant. But multivariate regression theory assumes that all the coefficients in the model are unknown and are to be estimated.

In the univariate regression models, we assume that there are n observations available on a response variable y as well as on predictors $x_1, ..., x_k$. If these n data values on y are stored in an n by 1 column vector $\mathbf{y}$ and values on x_i, $i = 1, ..., k$ are stacked, in the same order, in an n by 1 vector $\mathbf{x}_i$ then the complete linear model for the data can be expressed as the linear relation between these column vectors

$$\mathbf{y} = \beta_0 \mathbf{1}_n + \beta_1 \mathbf{x}_1 + ... + \beta_k \mathbf{x}_k + \epsilon.$$

In multivariate situations, that is, when there are two or more response variables, the functional form of the linear model for each of these response variables is assumed to be the same as above. However, each model will have a different set of unknown coefficients $\beta_0, \ldots, \beta_k$ and a different error vector.

3.2 Statistical Background

A multivariate linear model in p (possibly correlated) response variables $y_1, \ldots, y_p$ and k independent or predictor variables $x_1, \ldots, x_k$ is represented by a system of p univariate linear models

$$\left.\begin{array}{l} \mathbf{y}_1 = \beta_{01}\mathbf{1}_n + \beta_{11}\mathbf{x}_1 + \beta_{21}\mathbf{x}_2 + \ldots + \beta_{k1}\mathbf{x}_k + \epsilon_1 \\ \mathbf{y}_2 = \beta_{02}\mathbf{1}_n + \beta_{12}\mathbf{x}_1 + \beta_{22}\mathbf{x}_2 + \ldots + \beta_{k2}\mathbf{x}_k + \epsilon_2 \\ \vdots \\ \mathbf{y}_p = \beta_{0p}\mathbf{1}_n + \beta_{1p}\mathbf{x}_1 + \beta_{2p}\mathbf{x}_2 + \ldots + \beta_{kp}\mathbf{x}_k + \epsilon_p \end{array}\right\}, \tag{3.1}$$

where $\mathbf{y}_i$, $\mathbf{x}_i$, and ϵ_i are all n by 1 vectors. The vectors $\mathbf{y}_i$ and $\mathbf{x}_i$ are respectively the data vectors on the variables y_i and x_i. These equations can compactly be represented using matrix notation as

$$\mathbf{Y} = \mathbf{XB} + \mathcal{E}, \tag{3.2}$$

where

$$\mathbf{Y}_{n \times p} = (\mathbf{y}_1 : \mathbf{y}_2 : \ldots : \mathbf{y}_p),$$
$$\mathbf{X}_{n \times (k+1)} = (\mathbf{1}_n : \mathbf{x}_1 : \mathbf{x}_2 : \ldots : \mathbf{x}_k),$$
$$\mathbf{B} = \begin{bmatrix} \beta_{01} & \beta_{02} & \ldots & \beta_{0p} \\ \beta_{11} & \beta_{12} & \ldots & \beta_{1p} \\ . \\ . \\ \beta_{k1} & \beta_{k2} & \ldots & \beta_{kp} \end{bmatrix}$$

and $\mathcal{E} = (\epsilon_1 : \epsilon_2 : \ldots : \epsilon_p)$. The vector $\mathbf{1}_n$ here represents an n by 1 column vector with all elements as unity. Assume that $n > (k+1)$.

In case we wish to deal with a model without an intercept term, we could still write the corresponding model as in Equation 3.2 by omitting the first columns of the respective matrices $\mathbf{X}$ and β defined above. The only additional change would be to replace $k+1$ by k in what follows.

A typical equation in Equation 3.1, say the ith one,

$$\mathbf{y}_i = \beta_{0i}\mathbf{1}_n + \beta_{1i}\mathbf{x}_1 + \ldots + \beta_{ki}\mathbf{x}_k + \epsilon_i$$

represents a univariate regression model, which can be written as $\mathbf{y}_i = \mathbf{X}\beta_i + \epsilon_i$ with $\beta_i = (\beta_{0i}, \beta_{1i}, \ldots, \beta_{ki})'$ and hence could be analyzed independently of the other regression models in Equation 3.1. However, since the response variables may themselves be correlated with each other, this dependence should also be taken into account when drawing the statistical conclusions using the inferential methods. This suggests the need for using the model in Equation 3.2, where the collection of all the dependent variables is analyzed as a single data set.

Analogous to the univariate setup, each ϵ_i is assumed to be distributed with zero mean and the variance-covariance matrix $D(\epsilon_i) = \sigma_{ii}\mathbf{I}_n$, where $\mathbf{I}_n$ is an n by n identity matrix. However, to incorporate the dependence between the response variables, it is assumed that for $i, j = 1, \ldots, p$, $cov(\mathbf{y}_i, \mathbf{y}_j|\mathbf{X}) = cov(\epsilon_i, \epsilon_j) = \sigma_{ij}\mathbf{I}_n$. In other words, while the ith column of $\mathcal{E}$ has the variance-covariance matrix $\sigma_{ii}\mathbf{I}_n$, a typical row of $\mathcal{E}$ has that as $\Sigma = (\sigma_{ij})$, a symmetric p by p matrix that is assumed to be positive definite.

As in the univariate linear regression setup, assume that the regression matrix $\mathbf{X}$ is of full rank, thereby implying that $Rank(\mathbf{X}'\mathbf{X}) = Rank(\mathbf{X}) = k+1$. This, in turn, ensures the existence of the inverse of $\mathbf{X}'\mathbf{X}$. If $\mathbf{X}$ is not of full rank, $(\mathbf{X}'\mathbf{X})^-$, a *generalized inverse* of $\mathbf{X}'\mathbf{X}$, will replace $(\mathbf{X}'\mathbf{X})^{-1}$ in most situations. However, extra care is needed in interpreting the results of the data analysis in such instances.

An assumption of multivariate normality for error vectors is needed for hypothesis testing problems and construction of confidence regions, even though it is not needed for the linear estimation problems. Most of the resulting exact and approximate statistical tests for the multivariate linear regression models are the consequences of this assumption.

3.3 Least Squares Estimation

A natural criterion to obtain some meaningful estimators of $\mathbf{B}$ is to minimize $\sum_{i=1}^p \epsilon_i'\epsilon_i = \sum_{i=1}^p (\mathbf{y}_i - \mathbf{X}\beta_i)'(\mathbf{y}_i - \mathbf{X}\beta_i)$ with respect to the matrix $\mathbf{B} = (\beta_1 : \beta_2 : \ldots : \beta_p)$. The criterion is the same as that of minimizing $tr(\mathbf{Y} - \mathbf{XB})'(\mathbf{Y} - \mathbf{XB})$, the *trace* of the p by p matrix $(\mathbf{Y} - \mathbf{XB})'(\mathbf{Y} - \mathbf{XB})$, resulting in the system of normal equations

$$(\mathbf{X}'\mathbf{X})\mathbf{B} = \mathbf{X}'\mathbf{Y} \tag{3.3}$$

and yielding

$$\hat{\mathbf{B}} = (\mathbf{X}'\mathbf{X})^{-1}\mathbf{X}'\mathbf{Y} \tag{3.4}$$

as the least squares estimator of matrix $\mathbf{B}$. It means that $\hat{\beta}_i$, the ith column of $\hat{\mathbf{B}}$, which estimates β_i, the ith column of $\mathbf{B}$, is given by

$$\hat{\beta}_i = (\mathbf{X}'\mathbf{X})^{-1}\mathbf{X}'\mathbf{y}_i, \ i = 1, \ldots, p.$$

It is easy to observe that $\hat{\mathbf{B}}$ given by Equation 3.4 is unbiased for $\mathbf{B}$, that is, $E(\hat{\mathbf{B}}) = \mathbf{B}$. Further, $cov(\hat{\beta}_i, \hat{\beta}_j) = \sigma_{ij}(\mathbf{X}'\mathbf{X})^{-1}$ for all $i, j = 1, \ldots, p$. In addition, under the assumption of the model in Equation 3.2, $\hat{\mathbf{B}}$ is the Best Linear Unbiased Estimator (BLUE) of $\mathbf{B}$ in the sense that it has the smallest total variance among all linear unbiased estimators. By *total variance* we mean the sum of the variances of all elements of the matrix used as the estimator.

When the matrix $\mathbf{X}$ is not of full rank, a least squares solution to the system of normal equations, Equation 3.3, is given by

$$\hat{\mathbf{B}}^{(g)} = (\mathbf{X}'\mathbf{X})^{-}\mathbf{X}'\mathbf{Y} \qquad (3.5)$$

and

$$\hat{\beta}_i^{(g)} = (\mathbf{X}'\mathbf{X})^{-}\mathbf{X}'\mathbf{y}_i, \, i = 1, \dots, p.$$

The matrix $\hat{\mathbf{B}}^{(g)}$ defined in Equation 3.5

- is not unique,
- depends on the particular choice of the generalized inverse used, and
- merely represents one of the many solutions to a *singular* system of normal equations.

In that sense, $\hat{\mathbf{B}}^{(g)}$ is really not an estimator and one or more components of $\hat{\mathbf{B}}^{(g)}$ may be biased for their counterparts in $\mathbf{B}$. However, as indicated in Searle (1971), certain linear functions of $\mathbf{B}$ can still be uniquely estimated. Such functions are called the *estimable functions*. Specifically, as shown by Bose (1951), and Searle (1971), a linear function $\mathbf{c}'\mathbf{B}$, where $\mathbf{c} \neq \mathbf{0}$ is a nonrandom $(k+1)$ by 1 vector, is *estimable* if and only if

$$(\mathbf{X}'\mathbf{X})(\mathbf{X}'\mathbf{X})^{-}\mathbf{c} = \mathbf{c}.$$

Accordingly, a linear hypothesis on the regression parameters will be a "testable hypothesis" if it involves only the estimable functions of $\mathbf{B}$.

3.4 ANOVA Partitioning

In the multivariate context, the role of the total sum of squares is played by the p by p positive definite matrix of (corrected) total sums of squares and crossproducts (SS&CP) defined as

$$\mathbf{T} = \mathbf{Y}'\mathbf{Y} - \frac{1}{n}\mathbf{Y}'\mathbf{1}_n\mathbf{1}_n'\mathbf{Y} = \mathbf{Y}'(\mathbf{I}_n - \frac{1}{n}\mathbf{1}_n\mathbf{1}_n')\mathbf{Y}. \qquad (3.6)$$

Apart from the dividing factor, a typical element of the matrix in Equation 3.6, say the one corresponding to the ith row and j^{th} column, is the same as the sample covariance between the ith and j^{th} dependent variables. Consequently, the diagonal elements of $\mathbf{T}$ are the (corrected) total sums of squares for the respective dependent variables.

Assuming that $Rank(\mathbf{X}) = k + 1$, this matrix can be partitioned as the sum of the two p by p positive definite matrices

$$\mathbf{T} = \mathbf{R} + \mathbf{E},$$

where

$$\mathbf{R} = \mathbf{Y}'[\mathbf{X}(\mathbf{X}'\mathbf{X})^{-1}\mathbf{X}' - \frac{1}{n}\mathbf{1}_n\mathbf{1}'_n]\mathbf{Y} = \mathbf{Y}'\mathbf{X}\hat{\mathbf{B}} - \frac{1}{n}\mathbf{Y}'\mathbf{1}_n\mathbf{1}'_n\mathbf{Y}, \qquad (3.7)$$

$$\mathbf{E} = \mathbf{Y}'[\mathbf{I} - \mathbf{X}(\mathbf{X}'\mathbf{X})^{-1}\mathbf{X}']\mathbf{Y} = \mathbf{Y}'\mathbf{Y} - \mathbf{Y}'\mathbf{X}(\mathbf{X}'\mathbf{X})^{-1}\mathbf{X}'\mathbf{Y}$$

$$= \mathbf{Y}'\mathbf{Y} - \mathbf{Y}'\mathbf{X}\hat{\mathbf{B}} = (\mathbf{Y} - \hat{\mathbf{Y}})'(\mathbf{Y} - \hat{\mathbf{Y}}), \qquad (3.8)$$

and $\hat{\mathbf{Y}} = \mathbf{X}\hat{\mathbf{B}}$ is the matrix of the predicted values of matrix $\mathbf{Y}$. The matrix $\mathbf{R}$ represents the matrix of model or regression sums of squares and crossproducts and the matrix $\mathbf{E}$ represents that corresponding to error. Note that the diagonal elements of these matrices respectively represent the usual regression and error sums of squares for the corresponding dependent variables in the univariate linear regression setup.

Table 3.1 summarizes the partitioning explained above, along with a similar partitioning for the degrees of freedom (DF).

Source	DF	SS & CP Matrix	E(SS & CP)
Regression	k	$\mathbf{R}$	$k\Sigma + \mathbf{B}'\mathbf{X}'(\mathbf{I}_n - \frac{1}{n}\mathbf{1}\mathbf{1}')\mathbf{X}\mathbf{B}$
Error	$n-k-1$	$\mathbf{E}$	$(n-k-1)\Sigma$
Corrected Total	$n-1$	$\mathbf{T}$	

TABLE 3.1 MULTIVARIATE ANALYSIS OF VARIANCE (MANOVA) TABLE

An unbiased estimator of Σ is given by

$$\hat{\Sigma} = \mathbf{E}/(n-k-1). \qquad (3.9)$$

When $\mathbf{X}$ is not of full rank, $(\mathbf{X}'\mathbf{X})^{-1}$ is replaced by $(\mathbf{X}'\mathbf{X})^-$, a generalized inverse of $\mathbf{X}'\mathbf{X}$ in the formulas in Equations 3.7 and 3.8, but the matrices $\mathbf{R}$, $\mathbf{E}$ and $\hat{\mathbf{Y}}$ are invariant of the choice of a particular generalized inverse and remain the same regardless of which generalized inverse is used. However, in this case the unbiased estimator of Σ is given by $\mathbf{E}/(n - Rank(X))$, which differs from Equation 3.9 in its denominator.

Depending on the rank of $\mathbf{R}$, the matrix $\mathbf{R}$ can further be partitioned into two or more positive definite matrices. This fact is useful in developing the tests for various linear hypotheses on $\mathbf{B}$. If needed, for example, as in the lack-of-fit analysis, a further partitioning of matrix $\mathbf{E}$ is also possible.

The matrix $\mathbf{R}$, of regression sums of squares and crossproducts, measures the effect of the part of the model involving the independent variables. By contrast, $\mathbf{E}$, the error sums of squares and product matrix, measures the effect due to random error or the variation not explained by the independent variables. Further partitioning of $\mathbf{R}$ and $\mathbf{E}$ can also be given certain similar interpretations.

In univariate regression models, the coefficient of determination R^2, which is the ratio of regression sum of squares to total sum of squares, is taken as an index to measure the adequacy of the fitted model. Analogously, in the present context, it is possible to define

$$|\mathbf{R}|/|\mathbf{R} + \mathbf{E}|$$

and

$$tr[\mathbf{R}(\mathbf{R} + \mathbf{E})^{-1}]$$

as two possible generalizations of R^2. In the hypothesis testing context, the latter measure is often referred to as *Pillai's trace statistic*. These indices can be interpreted in essentially the same way as the univariate coefficient of determination R^2.

Another useful measure of the strength of the relationship or the adequacy of the model can be defined as $1 - |\mathbf{E}|/|\mathbf{R} + \mathbf{E}| = 1 - \Lambda$, where $\Lambda = |\mathbf{E}|/|\mathbf{R} + \mathbf{E}|$ is called the *Wilks' ratio*. However, this index of association is strongly biased. Jobson (1992) provides two modifications of $1 - \Lambda$, one of which has considerably less bias while another provided by Tatsuoka (1988) is approximately unbiased. As the value of Λ is produced by several SAS procedures, these two measures are easily computable using the formulas given in Jobson (1992).

3.5 Testing Hypotheses: Linear Hypotheses

One important aspect of statistical inference is testing the hypothesis of interest. In the context of multivariate linear models, the hypotheses may be on the functions of

- matrix $\mathbf{B}$ only,
- matrix Σ only, or
- matrices $\mathbf{B}$ and Σ both.

In this section, we will confine the discussion to the hypothesis on the functions of $\mathbf{B}$ only. Some of the hypotheses involving the matrix Σ are discussed in Chapter 5.

A hypothesis on $\mathbf{B}$ may be of interest in a variety of situations. It may be needed in the context of data reduction, to test the redundancy of certain variables, or in connection with model reduction schemes as in the process of selecting variables. Of course a number of hypotheses are important in their own right, e.g., when a comparison of two or more populations is needed.

Most of the hypotheses of interest on $\mathbf{B}$ can be expressed as the general linear hypothesis

$$H_0 : \mathbf{LB} = \mathbf{D} \text{ vs. } H_1 : \mathbf{LB} \neq \mathbf{D} \tag{3.10}$$

with known full row rank matrix $\mathbf{L}$ of order r by $(k + 1)$ and known $\mathbf{D}$. The matrix $\mathbf{D}$ is usually a zero matrix for most linear hypotheses; in the cases when $\mathbf{D}$ is not a zero matrix, a suitable transformation of data on dependent variables would provide an equivalent linear hypothesis with zero matrix on the right-hand side in terms of the reparameterization of $\mathbf{B}$, as indicated below.

Since $\mathbf{L}$ is of full row rank, $\mathbf{LL'}$ admits the inverse. Consequently, by subtracting $\mathbf{XL'(LL')}^{-1}\mathbf{D}$ from both sides of Equation 3.2, we have,

$$\mathbf{Y} - \mathbf{XL'(LL')}^{-1}\mathbf{D} = \mathbf{X}(\mathbf{B} - \mathbf{L'(LL')}^{-1}\mathbf{D}) + \mathcal{E}$$

or equivalently

$$\mathbf{Y}^* = \mathbf{X}\mathbf{\Gamma} + \mathcal{E},$$

where $\mathbf{Y}^* = \mathbf{Y} - \mathbf{XL}'(\mathbf{LL}')^{-1}\mathbf{D}$, $\mathbf{\Gamma} = \mathbf{B} - \mathbf{L}'(\mathbf{LL}')^{-1}\mathbf{D}$, and the hypothesis in Equation 3.10 can be equivalently written as

$$H_0 : \mathbf{L}\mathbf{\Gamma} = \mathbf{0} \text{ vs. } H_1 : \mathbf{L}\mathbf{\Gamma} \neq \mathbf{0}.$$

Hence, it is enough to consider the hypotheses of type

$$H_0 : \mathbf{LB} = \mathbf{0} \text{ vs. } H_1 : \mathbf{LB} \neq \mathbf{0} \tag{3.11}$$

for the discussion that follows.

Note: Statistical analysis in Sections 3.5.1 and 3.5.2 assume multivariate normality for the rows of $\mathcal{E}$.

3.5.1 Multivariate Tests

To test the null hypothesis in Equation 3.11, various test criteria based on the eigenvalues of certain matrices which may be the functions of $\mathbf{L}$ and $\hat{\mathbf{B}}$ are available. Specifically, let

$$\mathbf{H} = \hat{\mathbf{B}}'\mathbf{L}'[\mathbf{L}(\mathbf{X}'\mathbf{X})^{-1}\mathbf{L}']^{-1}\mathbf{L}\hat{\mathbf{B}}, \tag{3.12}$$

and define $\lambda_1 \geq \lambda_2 \geq \ldots \geq \lambda_p \geq 0$ as the ordered eigenvalues of $\mathbf{E}^{-1}\mathbf{H}$. As $\mathbf{E}$ is assumed to be positive definite, the existence of $\mathbf{E}^{-1}$ is ensured. Various test statistics for the hypothesis in Equation 3.11 are given below.

Wilks' Λ Criterion

$$\Lambda = |(\mathbf{H} + \mathbf{E})^{-1}\mathbf{E}| = |\mathbf{E}^{-1}\mathbf{H} + \mathbf{I}|^{-1} = \Pi_{i=1}^{p}(1 + \lambda_i)^{-1} \tag{3.13}$$

Pillai's Trace Criterion (Bartlett-Nanda-Pillai's Trace)

$$V = tr[(\mathbf{H} + \mathbf{E})^{-1}\mathbf{H}] = \sum_{i=1}^{p} \lambda_i/(1 + \lambda_i) \tag{3.14}$$

Hotelling-Lawley Trace Criterion (Bartlett-Hotelling-Lawley Trace)

$$U = tr(\mathbf{E}^{-1}\mathbf{H}) = \sum_{i=1}^{p} \lambda_i \tag{3.15}$$

Roy's Maximum Root Criterion

$$\lambda_{\max} = \max(\lambda_1, \lambda_2, \ldots, \lambda_p) = \lambda_1. \tag{3.16}$$

For tables of critical values for these test statistics, see Pillai (1960). However, approximations to F statistics are summarized in Table 3.2.

Criterion	F	Approx. Dist. of F Under H_0
$Wilks(\Lambda)$	$\frac{gt-2u}{rr_t}\frac{1-\Lambda^{1/t}}{\Lambda^{1/t}}$	$F(rr_t, gt-2u)$
$Pillai\ (V)$	$\frac{2m_2+s+1}{2m_1+s+1}\frac{V}{s-V}$	$F(s(2m_1+s+1), s(2m_2+s+1))$
$Hotelling-Lawley\ (U)$	$\frac{2(sm_2+1)}{s^2(2m_1+s+1)}U$	$F(s(2m_1+s+1), 2(sm_2+1))$
$Roy\ (\lambda_{max})$	$\frac{n-k-h+r-1}{h}\lambda_{max}$	$F(h, n-k-h+r-1)^*$

TABLE 3.2 F APPROXIMATIONS FOR VARIOUS TESTS

* *This F statistic is an upper bound on the F statistic that provides a lower bound on the assumed level of significance.*

Various quantities used in Table 3.2 are defined below.

$$r_t = \text{Rank}\ (\mathbf{H} + \mathbf{E})$$
$$r = \text{Rank}\ (\mathbf{L})$$
$$s = \min\ (r, r_t)$$
$$h = \max\ (r, r_t)$$
$$m_1 = [|r - r_t| - 1]/2$$
$$m_2 = (n - k - r_t - 2)/2$$
$$g = (n - k - 1) - \frac{(r_t - r + 1)}{2}$$
$$u = (rr_t - 2)/4$$
$$t = \begin{cases} \sqrt{(r^2 r_t^2 - 4)/(r_t^2 + r^2 - 5)} & \text{if } (r_t^2 + r^2 - 5) > 0 \\ 1 & \text{otherwise} \end{cases}.$$

The following table adapted from Rao (1973, p. 555) (*Copyright 1973, John Wiley & Sons, Inc. Reprinted by permission of John Wiley & Sons, Inc.*) shows that in certain special cases a transformation of Wilks' Λ to F statistic is exact:

Values of r and p	*F*	*Exact F Under H_0*
$r = 1$ for any p	$\frac{n-k+r-p-1}{p}\frac{1-\Lambda}{\Lambda}$	$F(p, n-k+r-p-1)$
$r = 2$ for any p	$\frac{n-k+r-p-2}{p}\frac{1-\sqrt{\Lambda}}{\sqrt{\Lambda}}$	$F(2p, 2(n-k+r-p-2))$
$p = 1$ for any r	$\frac{n-k-1}{r}\frac{1-\Lambda}{\Lambda}$	$F(r, n-k-1)$
$p = 2$ for any r	$\frac{n-k-1}{r}\frac{1-\sqrt{\Lambda}}{\sqrt{\Lambda}}$	$F(2r, 2(n-k-1))$

TABLE 3.3 THE EXACT F IN SPECIAL CASES

Two considerably more accurate approximations than those given in Table 3.2 of the distribution of Wilks' Λ are suggested by Gupta and Richards (1983). The simpler of the two approximates the distribution of $-ln(\Lambda)$ by a chi-square distribution. Specifically,

$$Pr[-ln(\Lambda) < u] = Pr[\chi^2_{pd_{\mathbf{H}}} < u/\zeta]$$

where,

$$\begin{aligned}
\zeta &= [2(d_{\mathbf{E}} - p + 1)]^{-1} + [d_{\mathbf{E}} + d_{\mathbf{H}} - 2]^{-1}, \\
d_{\mathbf{E}} &= \text{degrees of freedom of } \mathbf{E}, \\
d_{\mathbf{H}} &= \text{degrees of freedom of } \mathbf{H}
\end{aligned}$$

and $\chi^2_{pd_{\mathbf{H}}}$ is a chi-square random variable with degrees of freedom $pd_{\mathbf{H}}$. The value of Λ is readily available in the SAS output and $d_{\mathbf{H}}$ and $d_{\mathbf{E}}$ can be calculated from the appropriate partitioning of the total SS&CP matrix. Therefore, the approximate probabilities corresponding to the Wilks' Λ statistic can be more accurately calculated via this approximation.

In general, none of the tests based on the criteria defined in Equations 3.13 through 3.16 is uniformly best. Giri (1977, p. 219) provides a review of various optimality properties of these tests. Based on the power studies by Pillai and Jayachandran (1967, 1968), the following general recommendations can be made (Seber, 1984, p. 415, Muirhead, 1982, p. 484).

- For $p = 2$ and for small departures from H_0 or for large deviations from H_0 with the two nonzero eigenvalues of $\mathbf{HE}^{-1}$ nearly equal, Pillai's test is superior to Wilks' Λ which in turn is better than Hotelling-Lawley's U.
- For $p = 2$ and for large departures from H_0 and when the two nonzero eigenvalues of $\mathbf{HE}^{-1}$ are very different, the order of preference given above is reversed.

- For general p, and for small departures from H_0, the order of preference is the same as that in the first item above.

Asymptotically, all the three tests are equivalent. Specifically, as $n \to \infty$, and under H_0, $\{n - k - \frac{1}{2}(p - r + 3)\} ln \, \Lambda$, $(n - k - 1)U$, and $(n - k - 1)V$ are all asymptotically distributed as central chi-square distributions with degrees of freedom pr. When $p = 1$, these tests and also Roy's $\lambda_{\max}$ test are all identical.

The four multivariate tests described above are available as options in the GLM procedure as well as in the REG procedure. Both of these perform various aspects of multivariate regression analysis. However, on occasion, one may be superior to the other in achieving certain specific tasks. PROC GLM is more general in that it can be used for analyzing the regression as well as the experimental design models and can also be applied with little effort to situations involving the blocking effects or *covariables*. In contrast, PROC REG is more convenient for regression analysis and provides certain options for specialized analyses in the regression context. In the examples that follow, we will utilize both choices depending on the context as well as the convenience and we occasionally also comment on the specific differences as well as their relative merits.

Example 1: Hotelling T^2 Test for Cork Data (Rao, 1948)

The cork data in Rao (1948) presented in Table 1.1 consist of the weights of cork borings from the north, east, south, and west directions of the trunks for 28 trees. The problem is to test whether the bark deposit varies, in thickness and hence in weight, in the four directions. We therefore set up the null hypothesis as "the bark deposit is uniform along all four directions". The multivariate tests illustrated above will be described for this null hypothesis. If we denote the 28 by 1 column vectors of bark deposits in four directions by $\mathbf{y}_1$, $\mathbf{y}_2$, $\mathbf{y}_3$ and $\mathbf{y}_4$ respectively, then, with $\mathbf{Y} = (\mathbf{y}_1 : \mathbf{y}_2 : \mathbf{y}_3 : \mathbf{y}_4)$, we have the model

$$(\mathbf{y}_1 : \mathbf{y}_2 : \mathbf{y}_3 : \mathbf{y}_4) = (\mu_1 \mathbf{1} : \mu_2 \mathbf{1} : \mu_3 \mathbf{1} : \mu_4 \mathbf{1}) + (\epsilon_1 : \epsilon_2 : \epsilon_3 : \epsilon_4),$$
$$\text{i.e. } \mathbf{Y} = \mathbf{1B} + \mathcal{E},$$

where $\mathbf{B} = (\mu_1 : \mu_2 : \mu_3 : \mu_4)$ is a 1 by 4 matrix of mean bark deposit in four directions. The null hypothesis $\mu_1 = \mu_2 = \mu_3 = \mu_4$ can be presented as

$$H_0 : \begin{cases} \mu_1 - \mu_2 = 0 \\ \mu_1 - \mu_3 = 0 \\ \mu_1 - \mu_4 = 0. \end{cases}$$

If we accordingly define three variables

$$DNE = y_1 - y_2 \text{ (difference between north and east measurements)}$$
$$DNS = y_1 - y_3 \text{ (difference between north and south measurements)}$$

and
$$DNW = y_1 - y_4 \text{ (difference between north and west measurements)}$$

then under H_0, the three variables defined above have zero means. Since there are no independent variables, the linear model in the three variables has the matrix of regression coefficients, say $\mathbf{B}_d$, consisting of only one row of intercepts, and our null hypothesis is equivalent to testing the hypothesis that $\mathbf{B}_d = \mathbf{0}$. This hypothesis can be tested by performing multivariate significance tests on the model with only intercept and no independent variables. The SAS code given in Program 3.1 performs these tests, as explained in the following paragraphs.

First, within the data set named Cork.Dat we create three new variables DNE, DNS, and DNW as defined in Program 3.1. The NOUNI option suppresses the univariate analysis of individual variables. Finally, the statement

```
manova h=intercept;
```

performs multivariate hypothesis testing, when the hypothesis of interest is on the intercept vector.

In Output 3.1 note that since the model has only an intercept vector and no other independent variables, the matrix $\mathbf{E}^{-1}\mathbf{H}$ is of rank 1. Consequently, only the first eigenvalue is nonzero and is 0.7682. The four test statistics Λ, V, U and $\lambda_{\max}$ are reported next. All four tests are equivalent in this case, and lead to the same observed value of the F statistic. With $n = 28$, $k = 0$, $p = 3$, and $r = 1$, the observed value of exact F statistic is given by $F = \frac{n-k+r-p-1}{p}(\frac{1-\Lambda}{\Lambda}) = 6.4019$ (see Table 3.3). It follows an F distribution with (3, 25) degrees of freedom, leading to the p value of 0.0023. Consequently, in view of small p value, we reject the null hypothesis of the uniform cork deposits in the four directions.

The value of Hotelling's T^2 can be easily obtained from the value of Wilks' Λ. Specifically,

$$T^2 = (n-1)\left(\frac{1-\Lambda}{\Lambda}\right),$$

which is equal to 20.7420 for this particular data set.

There is another way of testing the same hypothesis, yet without directly creating the data on the differences, that is to use the SAS M= specification. These alternative statements are given in Program 3.2.

Program 3.2 attempts to directly fit the model $\mathbf{Y} = \mathbf{XB} + \mathcal{E}$ with $\mathbf{X} = \mathbf{1}_n$, an n by 1 column vector of ones. Through the MANOVA statement, we specify the null hypothesis of interest; the intercepts of the variables indicated in the M=specification are zero. In the M= specification, we essentially define the variables DNE, DNS, and DNW from Program 3.1, but without any such explicit assignment. This, in turn, defines a matrix

$$\mathbf{M} = \begin{bmatrix} -1 & 1 & 0 & 0 \\ -1 & 0 & 1 & 0 \\ -1 & 0 & 0 & 1 \end{bmatrix}, \text{ and with } \mathbf{L} = \mathbf{I} = 1, \text{ the hypothesis of interest is written as}$$

$H_0 : \mathbf{LBM} = \mathbf{0}$, the general linear hypothesis which is further described in Section 3.6. The corresponding SAS code is

```
proc glm;
model y1 y2 y3 y4= /nouni;
manova h=intercept m=y2-y1,
                    y3-y1,
                    y4-y1
mnames=d1 d2 d3;
```

Thus in the M= specification, three variables earlier denoted by DNE, DNS, and DNW respectively are defined and are subsequently named $D1$, $D2$, and $D3$ using the MNAMES= specification. The NOUNI option on the MODEL statement suppresses the output corresponding to the univariate models in $y1$, $y2$, $y3$, and $y4$. Output 3.2 first prints the **M** matrix indicated above and then produces the output which is essentially identical to Output 3.1. An alternative to the M= specification indicated above is to explicitly specify the **M** matrix column by column. That is, by specifying

```
m = (-1 -1 -1,
      1  0  0,
      0  1  0,
      0  0  1);
```

Since the specification is by columns, the representation above resembles $\mathbf{M}'$ and not $\mathbf{M}$. The resulting output and the corresponding interpretations are essentially same as those for Output 3.1.

Example 2: Multivariate Regression for Fish Data (Srivastava and Carter, 1983)

The data for the illustration of multivariate regression are taken from Srivastava and Carter (1983). This toxicity study was conducted to determine the effect of copper on fish mortality. Twenty-five tanks of twenty trout were given various doses (DOSE) of copper in mg. per liter. The average weight of the fish (WT) was also recorded and used as one of the covariables. The proportions of dead fish after 8, 14, 24, 36, and 48 hours were recorded and an arcsine transformation was used to obtain the transformed variables y_i, $i = 1, \ldots, 5$. Such a transformation was used to stabilize the variances. Further, in keeping with the standard practice in many dose response studies, the various doses were converted into logarithmic scale. This transformation in turn made the spacing between the various levels more uniform.

The problems of interest are to

• fit a multivariate model expressing y_i as the linear functions of weights and the natural logarithm of the dose, which are to be treated as the independent variables,

- test the significance of the dose as a variable,
- test the significance of the fish weight as a variable, and
- test the overall significance of the model.

The SAS statements presented in Program 3.3 are used to obtain the appropriate output presented as Output 3.3. Only selected parts of output are presented.

After reading the raw data on proportions $p_1, \ldots, p_5$, we obtain the variables $y_1, \ldots, y_5$ by defining

$$y_i = \sin^{-1}\{\sqrt{p_i}\}, \quad i = 1, \ldots, 5.$$

This is done in the DATA step. We denote the natural logarithm of dose by $X1$ and the weight of the fish by $X2$. In PROC GLM, the MODEL statement fits the model

$$\mathbf{Y}_{25 \times 5} = \mathbf{X}_{25 \times 3}\mathbf{B}_{3 \times 5} + \mathcal{E}_{25 \times 5},$$

where $\mathbf{B} = \begin{bmatrix} \beta_0 \\ \beta_1 \\ \beta_2 \end{bmatrix}$. To test the significance of the model, we have the null hypothesis

$H_0 : \begin{bmatrix} \beta_1 \\ \beta_2 \end{bmatrix} = \mathbf{0}$. Assuming the multivariate normality of the error, this null hypothesis can be tested using Wilks' Λ test. This test statistic cannot be computed using PROC GLM. However, we will describe its computation later using PROC REG. The statement

```
manova h=x1 x2;
```

is used to test the other two hypotheses of interest, namely $H_0 : \beta_1 = 0$ and $H_0 : \beta_2 = 0$. The options PRINTE and PRINTH are used to print the error sums of squares and products matrix $\mathbf{E}$ and the appropriate $\mathbf{H}$ matrix corresponding to the desired hypothesis.

Output 3.3 first presents the error sums of squares and crossproducts matrix $\mathbf{E}$. The sums of squares due to error in the case of individual variables y_i can be obtained as the diagonal elements of this matrix. The output then presents the analysis corresponding to variable $X1$, the natural logarithm of the variable DOSE. By default, Type III sums of squares and crossproducts are used and hence these are adjusted for the other variable X2 which represents the initial weight of the fish. However, for most regression situations, the Type II sums of squares and crossproducts are most meaningful. Various types of sums of squares are discussed in some detail in Chapter 4 and in relatively greater detail in *SAS/STAT User's Guide, Version 6, Fourth Edition.*

All four multivariate tests (all of which are exact in this case) indicate that the variable $X1$ does indeed have a very significant effect on the variables $Y1, \ldots, Y5$. At the same time, a similar test for $X2$ shows that initial weight does not significantly contribute to the death rate. Thus, the null hypothesis corresponding to the significance of dose is rejected while that corresponding to significance of weight is accepted. It may be pointed out that the data analyzed here represent repeated measurements. See Chapter 5 for extensive analysis of repeated measures data.

The PROC GLM code in Program 3.3 does not provide any test for $\begin{bmatrix} \beta_1 \\ \beta_2 \end{bmatrix} = \mathbf{0}$. However, the test can be completed by using the MTEST statement in PROC REG. Specifically, for the null hypothesis of the type indicated above, that is, those on all the regression coefficients, the corresponding MTEST statement should include all the independent variables separated by commas. If the intercept is also one of the parameters in the null hypothesis, it is specified using the keyword INTERCEPT in the MTEST statement. In our case the SAS code is

```
proc reg;
model y1 y2 y3 y4 y5=x1 x2;
mtest x1, x2/print;
```

The PRINT option prints the corresponding $\mathbf{H}$ matrix and the error SS&CP matrix $\mathbf{E}$. The output contains the value of Wilks' Λ as well as the other three statistics. For our data set, the p value in each case is quite small, and consequently the null hypothesis can be rejected. Hence we conclude that the death rate does indeed depend on the average weight or the dose or both.

The MTEST statement in PROC REG can also be used to test the individual hypotheses on X1 and X2. The corresponding SAS statements are

```
mtest x1/print;
mtest x2/print;
```

Thus, it is possible to use the MTEST statement in PROC REG as an alternative to the MANOVA statement in PROC GLM. In addition using MTEST is a useful way of performing *partial tests*, the multivariate versions of univariate partial F tests, on the subsets of independent variables; that task is not easy to accomplish with PROC GLM. To perform a partial test, list these independent variables and separate them by commas in the MTEST statement. On the other hand, unlike PROC GLM, PROC REG does not provide any facility to suppress the accompanying univariate analyses, and hence its use may not always be an optimal way of performing multivariate analysis of the data.

The MTEST statement is also useful for a variety of other multivariate null hypotheses. For example, null hypotheses stating any interrelationships between independent variables can be included as equations in the MTEST statement. For example, a hypothesis of the form $H_0 : \beta_1 - \beta_2 = c_0$, where c_0 is a specified constant, can be tested using the statement

```
mtest x1-x2=c0/print;
```

The dependent variables can also be included in the MTEST statement. It is a very useful feature for situations where two or more univariate regression models are to be compared. We will address these issues in Section 3.8.

A few comments may be made about the possible alternative approaches to the analysis presented here for the fish data. The actual raw data deal with the counts, namely the number of dead fish, and are multinomial in nature. The normality was obtained by applying the variance stabilizing transformation which in general may or may not stabilize the correlations between the variables. Although for this particular data set the transformation works well, there may be some extreme cases with 0% and 100% mortalities that cannot be transformed to normality. In such instances, it is advisable to use the iterative reweighted least square analysis. However, this topic is beyond the scope of the present work and therefore we will not pursue this analysis here.

3.5.2 Stepdown Analysis

Another test for linear hypotheses which is especially useful when there is a certain order in the response variables due to some physical interpretation of such ordering is based on what is commonly referred to as *stepdown analysis*. To perform the analysis, let the physically meaningful ordering for consideration among the dependent variables, for a particular situation, be $y_1, y_2, \ldots, y_p$. The essential idea behind this procedure is to sequentially perform univariate tests on the univariate models associated with dependent variables, $\mathbf{y}_j$ conditional on (that is, fixing), $\mathbf{y}_1, \mathbf{y}_2, \ldots, \mathbf{y}_{j-1}$. As a result, the hypotheses in Equation 3.11

$$H_0 : \mathbf{LB} = \mathbf{0} \text{ vs. } H_1 : \mathbf{LB} \neq \mathbf{0}$$

can be written in terms of the intersection and union of univariate subhypotheses H_{i1}, $H_{i2}, \ldots, H_{ip}$, $i = 0$ or 1 as

$$H_0 = \bigcap_{j=1}^{p} H_{0j} \text{ and } H_1 = \bigcup_{j=1}^{p} H_{1j}.$$

Thus, the null hypothesis H_0 is accepted if and only if all $H_{0j} : \mathbf{L}\eta_j = \mathbf{0}$, $j = 1, \ldots, p$ are accepted and is rejected if at any stage a rejection occurs. The hypothesis H_{0j} is the null hypothesis on parameters η_j of the jth model $E(\mathbf{y}_j) = \mathbf{X}\eta_j + \gamma_1 \mathbf{y}_1 + \ldots + \gamma_{p-1} \mathbf{y}_{p-1}$. That is, the model which corresponds to $\mathbf{y}_j$, conditional on $\mathbf{y}_1, \ldots, \mathbf{y}_{j-1}$. By definition, if $j = 1$, it is unconditional. Further, H_{0j} can be reduced to $\mathbf{L}\beta_j = \mathbf{0}$ assuming that $H_{01}, \ldots, H_{0,j-1}$ have been accepted at previous stages. This is so since in this case $\mathbf{L}\eta_j = \mathbf{0}$ implies $\mathbf{L}\beta_j = \mathbf{0}$. The F statistic, F_j for testing H_{0j}, conditional on $\mathbf{y}_1, \ldots, \mathbf{y}_{j-1}$ follows an $F(r, n - k - j)$ distribution when H_{0j} is true. As before, $r = Rank(\mathbf{L})$. Further, $F_1, \ldots, F_k$ are all independently distributed of each other, since the conditional distributions are the same as the unconditional ones. We therefore test H_0 at the significance level α by sequentially testing $H_{01}, \ldots, H_{0p}$ using $\alpha_1, \ldots, \alpha_p$ as the levels of significance, where

$$P[\bigcap_{j=1}^{p}(F_j < F_{\alpha_j}(r, n - k - j))] = \Pi_{j=1}^{p}(1 - \alpha_j) = 1 - \alpha.$$

Thus the stepdown analysis can be easily implemented using successive univariate regression models by including at every stage all the dependent variables previously tested in the list of independent variables. Note that at any particular stage, except the first one, the matrix $\mathbf{L}$ has to be augmented by additional zero columns corresponding to the dependent variables added to the set of independent variables. The levels of significance $\alpha_1, \ldots, \alpha_p$ are to be chosen so as to satisfy $(1-\alpha_1)(1-\alpha_2)\ldots(1-\alpha_p) = (1-\alpha)$. For example, choosing α_j to be equal to, say, α^* leads to $\alpha^* = 1 - (1 - \alpha)^{1/p}$.

Example 3: Stepdown Analysis for Fish Data (Srivastava and Carter, 1983)

We again consider the fish data, given in Srivastava and Carter (1983). As shown in Example 2, the original proportions of dead fish after 8, 14, 24, 36, and 48 hours are transformed into new variables y_1 through y_5 respectively using the arcsine transformation. Since there is a definite natural ordering among the dependent variables $y_1, \ldots, y_5$ (through time), stepdown analysis is a meaningful possibility. Following the natural time ordering, we perform stepwise tests on y_j conditional on all y_i, $i < j$. If the problem is to see the significance of the effects of $x_1 = \log_e(\text{DOSE})$ and $x_2 = $ average weight, on $y_1, \ldots, y_5$, then the null hypothesis H_0 of no significant effect of either x_1 or x_2 on $y_1, \ldots, y_5$, can be written as

$$H_0 = H_{01} \bigcap H_{02} \bigcap H_{03} \bigcap H_{04} \bigcap H_{05},$$

where

H_{01} : x_1 and x_2 do not have any effect on y_1,

H_{02} : x_1 and x_2 do not have any effect on y_2 given y_1,

H_{03} : x_1 and x_2 do not have any effect on y_3 given y_1 and y_2,

H_{04} : x_1 and x_2 do not have any effect on y_4 given y_1, y_2 and y_3,

and

H_{05} : x_1 and x_2 do not have any effect on y_5 given y_1, y_2, y_3 and y_4.

We test all five null hypotheses listed above in the natural time order. If the total level of significance is desired to be $\alpha = 0.05$, then for any individual null hypothesis, the significance level, assuming it to be the same for all subhypotheses, will be $\alpha^* = 1-(1-0.05)^{1/5} \cong .010$. Since at the jth stage all y_i, $i < j$ are conditioned, they would appear in the right side of the model as independent variables (or *covariates*) along with x_1 and x_2. For example, to test the hypothesis, say H_{03}, the corresponding SAS statements are

```
proc reg;
model y3 = x1 x2 y1 y2;
test x1 = 0.0, x2=0.0;
```

and the MODEL statement in the above SAS code corresponds to the univariate linear model

$$\mathbf{y}_3 = \beta_0 + \beta_1\mathbf{x}_1 + \beta_2\mathbf{x}_2 + \gamma_1\mathbf{y}_1 + \gamma_2\mathbf{y}_2 + \epsilon_3.$$

The TEST statement tests the null hypothesis

$$H_{03} : \beta_1 = \beta_2 = 0$$

in the presence of the conditioned variables y_1 and y_2 as the other independent variables in the model. A complete SAS program, which specifically tests the statistical significance of $x_1 = \log_e(\text{DOSE})$ and of $x_2 = $ average weight using the stepdown analysis, is given in Program 3.4. The rejection of H_0 is attained as soon as any subhypothesis H_{0j} is rejected at the desired significance level $\alpha^*(\simeq .010)$. In view of the very small p value, which is 0.0001 (see Output 3.4), for the very first model (for y_1) we reject the null hypothesis H_0 and conclude that the fish death rates do indeed depend on either dose or weight of the fish or both.

3.6 Simultaneous Confidence Intervals

If $H_0 : \mathbf{LB} = \mathbf{0}$ is rejected, it may be of interest to provide the confidence intervals for the individual components of $\mathbf{LB}$ (or $\mathbf{B}$ if $\mathbf{L} = \mathbf{I}_{k+1}$) or the linear functions of these components. Under the assumption of the full rank of $\mathbf{X}$, a set of simultaneous confidence intervals for the linear combinations of the type $\mathbf{c}'\mathbf{LBd}$ corresponding to the linear hypothesis $H_0 : \mathbf{LB} = \mathbf{0}$ can be constructed.

Noting that $H_0^{(\mathbf{c},\mathbf{d})} : \mathbf{c}'\mathbf{LBd} = 0$ is true for all $\mathbf{c}$ and $\mathbf{d}$ if and only if H_0 is true, we can write H_0 as the intersection of all such $H_0^{(\mathbf{c},\mathbf{d})} : \mathbf{c}'\mathbf{LBd} = \mathbf{0}$. Testing of $H_0^{(\mathbf{c},\mathbf{d})} : \mathbf{c}'\mathbf{LBd} = \mathbf{0}$ can be done using the appropriate F test. Let the corresponding F statistic be $F^{(\mathbf{c},\mathbf{d})}$ and let F_α be the cutoff point. Then, H_0 is accepted if and only if all $H_0^{(\mathbf{c},\mathbf{d})}$ are accepted, that is, if and only if $\max_{\mathbf{c},\mathbf{d}} F^{(\mathbf{c},\mathbf{d})} \leq F_\alpha$. In fact, the $\max_{\mathbf{c},\mathbf{d}} F^{(\mathbf{c},\mathbf{d})}$ is equal to $(n - k - 1)\lambda_{\max}$, where $\lambda_{\max}$ is the Roy's largest root test statistic corresponding to H_0 indicated above. Thus $100(1 - \alpha)\%$ simultaneous confidence intervals for all linear combinations $\mathbf{c}'\mathbf{LBd}$ are given by

$$\mathbf{c}'\mathbf{L}\hat{\mathbf{B}}\mathbf{d} \pm \{\lambda_\alpha \mathbf{c}'\mathbf{L}(\mathbf{X}'\mathbf{X})^{-1}\mathbf{L}'\mathbf{c} \cdot \mathbf{d}'\mathbf{Ed}\}^{1/2},$$

where $\mathbf{E}$ is the error sums of squares and product matrix and λ_α, the cutoff point for $\lambda_{\max}$, is such that $P[\lambda_{\max} \leq \lambda_\alpha] = 1 - \alpha$.

The tables for the cutoff points λ_α are available in Pillai (1960). Alternatively, the F approximation for λ_{max} reported in Table 3.2 can be used. For the Program 3.5, we follow the latter alternative. Thus the $(1 - \alpha)100\%$ cutoff point λ_α can be approximated by

$$\lambda_\alpha = \frac{h}{n - k - h + r - 1} F_\alpha(h, n - k - h + r - 1). \tag{3.17}$$

The calculations of the confidence intervals for a choice of $\mathbf{c}$ and $\mathbf{d}$ are illustrated in the following example using the IML procedure (see Program 3.5). Note that the matrices $\hat{\mathbf{B}}$, $(\mathbf{X}'\mathbf{X})^{-1}$ and $\mathbf{E}$ are available as the outputs of PROC REG or PROC GLM. Selected parts of the output of Program 3.5 are shown in Output 3.5.

Example 4: Confidence Intervals for Bark Deposits in Cork Data (Rao, 1948)

Chapter 1 states that the interest in these data is in discovering if the bark deposit is uniform in all the four directions. Also, recall that an appropriate set of transformations of variables to do this would be

$$z_1 = y_1 - y_2 + y_3 - y_4, \quad z_2 = y_3 - y_4, \quad z_3 = y_1 - y_3.$$

To construct the $(1-\alpha)100\%$ simultaneous confidence intervals on the corresponding means $\mu_1 - \mu_2 + \mu_3 - \mu_4$, $\mu_3 - \mu_4$ and $\mu_1 - \mu_3$, we write each of these means as $\mathbf{c'LBd}$ with the respective choices of $\mathbf{d}$ as the columns of

$$\begin{bmatrix} 1 & 0 & 1 \\ -1 & 0 & 0 \\ 1 & 1 & -1 \\ -1 & -1 & 0 \end{bmatrix}$$

and with $\mathbf{c} = 1$, $\mathbf{L} = 1$, and $\mathbf{B} = (\mu_1 \ \mu_2 \ \mu_3 \ \mu_4)$.

In Program 3.5 the matrices $\mathbf{c}$, $\mathbf{d}$, $\mathbf{L}$ and matrices $\hat{\mathbf{B}}$, $\mathbf{X'X}$ (both obtained from the output of PROC REG) and the matrix $\mathbf{E}$ (obtained from the output of PROC GLM) are explicitly specified.

In the present context,

$r_t = Rank(\mathbf{H} + \mathbf{E}) = p = 4$,
$r = Rank(\mathbf{L}) = Rank([1]) = 1$,
$n = 28$,
$k = 0$,
$s = min(r, r_t) = 1$,
$h = max(r, r_t) = 4$,
$m_1 = (|r - r_t| - 1)/2 = 1$ and
$m_2 = (n - k - r_t - 2)/2 = 11$.

As a result $\frac{n-k-h+r-1}{h}\lambda_{max} = 6\lambda_{max}$ follows an exact $F(4, 24)$ distribution (since $s{=}1$) $F(h, n - k - h + r - 1)$. If $\alpha = 0.05$, then using Equation 3.17 we can compute the 95% cutoff point $\lambda_{0.05}$ as $\frac{1}{6}F_{0.05}(4, 24) = 0.4627$.

In the PROC IML code given in Program 3.5 it is necessary only to specify r_t, r, n, k and α explicitly. The rest of the parameters and the (approximate) value of λ_{α} are computed by the program.

Output 3.5, resulting from the PROC IML code given in Program 3.5, shows that three confidence intervals are (1.2787, 16.4356), (-0.5398, 9.5398) and (-4.4672, 6.1815) respectively.

Hotelling's T^2 offers another choice of simultaneous confidence intervals. See Johnson and Wichern (1992, p. 191) for further details. These simultaneous confidence intervals have the drawback of being too wide. However, if the interest is in only a few specific linear combinations, it is possible to provide corresponding confidence intervals, which are shorter, using Bonferroni's inequality. These confidence intervals are based on the usual Student's t test for the associated univariate linear hypothesis. For instance, if $c_i'LBd_i$, $i = 1, \ldots, g$ are the g linear functions of interest, then $100(1 - \alpha)\%$ Bonferroni's intervals are

$$c_i'\hat{L}Bd_i \pm t_{n-k-1}(\alpha_i/2)\sqrt{(c_i'L(X'X)^{-1}L'c_i)(d_i'Ed_i)}, \quad i = 1, \ldots, g,$$

where $\alpha_1 + \ldots + \alpha_g = \alpha$ and $t_\nu(\delta)$ is the $100(1-\delta)\%$ upper cutoff point from a t-distribution with ν degrees of freedom. Note that in order to compute these intervals the IML procedure as shown in Program 3.5 can be used with $\lambda_d^{1/2}$ replaced by $t_{n-k-1}(\alpha_i/2)$, for $i = 1, \ldots, g$ respectively. The corresponding statements have been included in Program 3.5 with $\alpha_i = \alpha/3$ but have been commented out. To obtain the Bonferroni intervals replace these statements with those corresponding to simultaneous confidence intervals.

3.7 Multiple Response Surface Modeling

Response surface modeling is essentially a regression analysis problem. In situations where data are collected on a number of response (dependent) variables under the controlled levels of process or recipe (independent) variables, these responses are correlated. However, as it often happens, the levels of process or recipe variables optimum for one dependent variable may not be optimum for others. Therefore it is important to investigate response variables simultaneously and not individually or independently of one another, in order to also account for interrelationships. Consequently, the "best model" search for the individual response variables may not be meaningful. What is desired is a best *set* of models for these responses. A way to do this would be to simultaneously fit multivariate regression models and statistically test the significance of various terms corresponding to independent variables using the multivariate methods. This can be done by the repeated use of the MTEST statement in PROC REG.

Example 5: Quality Improvement of Mullet Flesh (Tseo et al., 1983)

Tseo, Deng, Cornell, Khuri, and Schmidt (1983) considered a study of quality improvement of minced mullet flesh where three process variables, namely washing temperature (TEMP), washing time (TIME), and washing ratio (WRATIO) were varied in a controlled manner in a designed experiment. The four responses, springiness (SPRNESS) in mm, TBA number (TBA), cooking loss (COOKLOSS) in % and whiteness index (WHITNESS) were observed for all 17 experiments. For the analysis, all the variables are standardized to have zero means. The standardization of independent variables was carried out to have the levels of the three variables as $+1$ and -1 in the 2^3 full factorial part of the design. To do so, we define

$$X1 = \frac{TEMP - 33}{7}, \quad X2 = \frac{TIME - 5.5}{2.7}, \quad X3 = \frac{WRATIO - 22.5}{4.5}.$$

The four response variables are standardized to have sample variances equal to 1. The standardized variables are respectively denoted by $Y1$, $Y2$, $Y3$, and $Y4$. The multiple response surfaces are fitted for $Y1$, $Y2$, $Y3$, and $Y4$ as functions of $X1$, $X2$, and $X3$.

Interest is to simultaneously fit models which contain effects only up to the second degree in $X1$, $X2$, and $X3$ and up to two variable interactions. For that, we first obtain the values for the variables $X1$, $X2$, and $X3$ as indicated above and their respective interactions defined as $X1X2 = X1 * X2$, $X1X3 = X1 * X3$, $X2X3 = X2 * X3$ and the quadratic effects $X1SQ = X1 * X1$, $X2SQ = X2 * X2$ and $X3SQ = X3 * X3$, within the DATA step for the data set WASH. The values for variables $Y1, \ldots, Y4$ are obtained by using PROC STANDARD where the options MEAN = 0 and STD = 1 are used to set the respective sample means at zero and respective sample standard deviations at unity for these variables which are listed in the VAR statement. Output is stored in the data set WASH2. We perform the multivariate regression analysis on WASH2 to obtain the appropriate response surfaces by performing the various significance tests.

A complete second order model would involve a total of nine terms, namely $X1$, $X2$, $X3$, $X1X2$, $X1X3$, $X2X3$, $X1SQ$, $X2SQ$, and $X3SQ$, apart from the intercept. We will confine our discussion to only three specific hypotheses

$H_0^{(1)}$: The multivariate model contains only the linear terms plus an intercept vector.

$H_0^{(2)}$: The multivariate model is quadratic without any interaction terms.

$H_0^{(3)}$: The multivariate model has only linear, two-variable interaction terms and an intercept vector but no quadratic terms.

The three null hypotheses stated above can respectively be tested using the following three MTEST statements:

```
linear:   mtest x1sq, x2sq, x3sq, x1x2, x1x3, x2x3/print;
noquad:   mtest x1x2, x1x3, x2x3/print;
nointctn: mtest x1sq, x2sq, x3sq/print;
```

The names LINEAR, NOQUAD and NOINTCTN before the colon (:) in the respective three statements are used only for labeling purposes and are optional. The SAS code and resulting output are presented in Program 3.6 and Output 3.6.

The output resulting from the MTEST statements indicated above shows that the null hypothesis $H_0^{(1)}$ is probably not true. The p value corresponding to Wilks' Λ is 0.0107. Except for Pillai's trace test, all the other multivariate tests result in small p values. Thus at least some of the quadratic and/or interaction terms may be important and may need to be included in the model. Also, it may be of interest to test the hypotheses $H_0^{(2)}$ and $H_0^{(3)}$ (among many others) which exclusively test for the absence of quadratic effects and the absence of two-variable interaction effects respectively. As Output 3.6 shows, in view of small p values corresponding to all multivariate tests except the Pillai's trace statistic,

$H_0^{(2)}$ is rejected leading to the conclusion that there are at least some quadratic effects present. The null hypothesis $H_0^{(3)}$ is, however, accepted and hence, we may probably drop all the two-variable interaction terms from the model. As a result, the equations of the four estimated response surfaces, obtained from the output corresponding to univariate analyses, (not shown), are

$$\hat{Y}1 = 0.5831 - 0.7187 * X1 - 0.0073 * X2 + 0.0667 * X3 - 0.7569 * X1SQ$$
$$+ 0.0099 * X2SQ + 0.0227 * X3SQ,$$

$$\hat{Y}2 = -0.8297 - 0.6071 * X1 - 0.0186 * X2 - 0.1314 * X3 + 0.8736 * X1SQ$$
$$+ 0.0510 * X2SQ + 0.1065 * X3SQ,$$

$$\hat{Y}3 = -1.1671 + 0.1854 * X1 - 0.0025 * X2 - 0.2660 * X3 + 0.856 * X1SQ$$
$$+ 0.2044 * X2SQ + 0.3904 * X3SQ,$$

$$\hat{Y}4 = 0.2979 - 0.4684 * X1 + 0.1212 * X2 + 0.0516 * X3 - 0.6040 * X1SQ$$
$$+ 0.1275 * X2SQ + 0.1075 * X3SQ.$$

Note that even the terms $X2$, $X3$, $X2SQ$, and $X3SQ$ can also be dropped, leaving the four quadratic response surfaces as functions of the variable $X1$, that is temperature only. In that sense, the four responses appear to be robust with respect to washing time and washing ratio.

3.8 General Linear Hypotheses

Sometimes our interest may be in comparing the regression coefficients from the models corresponding to different variables. For example, in a multivariate linear model with two response variables, it may be interesting to test if the intercepts, means, or some other regression coefficients are equal in the respective models corresponding to these two response variables. Such a hypothesis cannot be expressed in the form of Equation 3.11. This hypothesis can, however, be formulated as a general linear hypothesis which can be written as

$$H_0 : \mathbf{LBM} = \mathbf{0} \text{ vs. } H_1 : \mathbf{LBM} \neq \mathbf{0},$$

where r by $(k + 1)$ matrix $\mathbf{L}$ is, as earlier, of rank r and the p by s matrix $\mathbf{M}$ is of rank s. These two matrices have different roles to play and need to be chosen carefully depending on the particular hypothesis to be tested. Specifically, the premultiplied matrix $\mathbf{L}$ is used to obtain a linear function of the regression coefficients within the individual models while the postmultiplied matrix $\mathbf{M}$ does the same for the coefficients from different models but corresponding to the same set of regressors or independent variables. In other words, the matrix $\mathbf{L}$ provides a means of comparing of coefficients within models, whereas the matrix $\mathbf{M}$ offers a way for "between models" comparisons of regression coefficients. As a result, the simultaneous pre- and postmultiplication to **B** by **L** and **M** respectively provides a method for defining a general linear hypothesis involving various coefficients of **B**. For example, let $\mathbf{B} = (\beta_{ij})$, that is, β_{ij} is the regression coefficient of the ith independent variable in the jth model (that is, the model for j^{th} dependent variable). Suppose we want to test the hypothesis that the difference between the coefficients of first and second independent variables is the same for the two univariate models involving the first two dependent variables. In other words, the null hypothesis to be tested is $\beta_{11} - \beta_{21} = \beta_{12} - \beta_{22}$, i.e., $H_0 : (\beta_{11} - \beta_{21}) - (\beta_{12} - \beta_{22}) = 0$. This equation in matrix notation is written as $\mathbf{LBM} = \mathbf{0}$ with

$$\mathbf{L} = (0 \quad 1 \quad -1 \quad 0 \quad \dots \quad 0)$$

and

$$\mathbf{M} = \begin{bmatrix} 1 \\ -1 \\ 0 \\ . \\ . \\ . \\ 0 \end{bmatrix}.$$

These types of general linear hypotheses occur frequently in the studies of growth curves, repeated measures, and crossover designed data. Chapter 5 covers various examples of these data.

Example 6: Spatial Uniformity in Semiconductor Processes (Guo and Sachs, 1993)

Guo and Sachs (1993) presented a case study that attempted to model and optimize the spatial uniformity of the product output characteristics at different locations in a batch of products. This example empirically modeled these responses using the multiple response surfaces and interpreted the problem of testing the spatial uniformity as a problem of general linear hypothesis testing.

The independent variables under consideration are two flow rates denoted by $X1$ and $X2$ and the resulting dependent variables are the deposition rates at three measurement sites. We denote these by $Y1$, $Y2$, and $Y3$ respectively. We are interested in the spatial uniformity, that is, we want to achieve a uniformity between the values of $Y1$, $Y2$, and $Y3$ for the given levels of two flow rates.

This example fits the multivariate regression model for $Y1$, $Y2$, and $Y3$ in terms of $X1$ and $X2$. Assume that there is no interaction between $X1$ and $X2$ and that the effects of $X1$ and $X2$ are both linear. The individual models can be obtained by using the SAS statements

```
proc reg;
model y1 y2 y3 = x1 x2;
```

given as part of Program 3.7. Output 3.7, which corresponds to Program 3.7, provides the estimates (collected from three separate univariate analysis) of regression coefficients:

$$\hat{\mathbf{B}} = \begin{bmatrix} 29.8449 & 34.0764 & 41.3942 \\ 0.2940 & 0.2048 & 0.1346 \\ 0.1175 & 0.1378 & 0.0355 \end{bmatrix}$$

and hence the three models are

$$\hat{Y}1 = 29.8449 + 0.2940X1 + 0.1175X2,$$

$$\hat{Y}2 = 34.0764 + 0.2048X1 + 0.1378X2,$$

$$\hat{Y}3 = 41.3942 + 0.1346X1 + 0.0355X2.$$

In the ideal case of complete spatial uniformity, we would expect the models for $Y1$, $Y2$, and $Y3$ to be identical. We construct an appropriate null hypothesis from this interpretation of spatial uniformity.

Let

$$\mathbf{B} = \begin{bmatrix} \beta_{01} & \beta_{02} & \beta_{03} \\ \beta_{11} & \beta_{12} & \beta_{13} \\ \beta_{21} & \beta_{22} & \beta_{23} \end{bmatrix}.$$

Then the columns of $\mathbf{B}$ represent the regression coefficients in the models for $Y1$, $Y2$, and $Y3$ respectively. Thus the complete spatial uniformity amounts to testing the hypothesis that the three columns of $\mathbf{B}$ are identical, that is, our null hypothesis is

$$H_0: \quad \beta_{01} = \beta_{02} = \beta_{03},$$
$$\beta_{11} = \beta_{12} = \beta_{13},$$
$$\beta_{21} = \beta_{22} = \beta_{23};$$

or,

$$H_0: \quad \beta_{01} - \beta_{02} = 0, \quad \beta_{02} - \beta_{03} = 0,$$
$$\beta_{11} - \beta_{12} = 0, \quad \beta_{12} - \beta_{13} = 0,$$
$$\beta_{21} - \beta_{22} = 0, \quad \beta_{22} - \beta_{23} = 0;$$

or,

$$H_0: \quad \begin{bmatrix} \beta_{01} & \beta_{02} & \beta_{03} \\ \beta_{11} & \beta_{12} & \beta_{13} \\ \beta_{21} & \beta_{22} & \beta_{23} \end{bmatrix} \begin{bmatrix} 1 & 0 \\ -1 & 1 \\ 0 & -1 \end{bmatrix} = \begin{bmatrix} 0 & 0 \\ 0 & 0 \\ 0 & 0 \end{bmatrix};$$

or,

$$H_0: \mathbf{LBM} = 0$$

$$\text{with } \mathbf{L} = \mathbf{I}_3 \text{ and } \mathbf{M} = \begin{bmatrix} 1 & 0 \\ -1 & 1 \\ 0 & -1 \end{bmatrix}.$$

To test this null hypothesis, we use the MTEST statement in PROC REG. An alternative could be to use the CONTRAST and MANOVA statements in PROC GLM, but since that is applicable only for designed experiments and not otherwise, we do not make this choice here. Chapters 4 and 5 elaborate on this approach. The approach using the MTEST statement is general and applicable for all regression modeling problems even when the data are collected from undesigned experiments.

If H_0 is true, then the coefficients of the three models are identical. And hence the means (expected values) of $Y1 - Y2$ and $Y2 - Y3$ would both be zero. Therefore, in order to test H_0 we could simultaneously test the three linear hypotheses. Specifically, the null hypotheses are that the intercepts, as well as the coefficients of $X1$ and $X2$ in the models for these two variables, are all zero. This can be done using the MTEST statement after the MODEL statement. Models without intercepts can be fitted by using the NOINT option in the MODEL statement.

Consequently, to test H_0 : $\mathbf{LBM} = \mathbf{0}$ with the choice of $\mathbf{L}$ and $\mathbf{M}$ indicated above, we use the following SAS statements:

```
proc reg;
model y1 y2 y3 = x1 x2;
mtest y1-y2, y2-y3, intercept, x1, x2/print;
```

Note that the MTEST statement performs the four multivariate tests on variables $Y1 - Y2$ and $Y2 - Y3$. An alternative yet equivalent approach would have been to define $Z1 = Y1 - Y2$ and $Z2 = Y2 - Y3$ early in the DATA step after INPUT statement as shown below:

```
data semicond;
input x1 x2 y1 y2 y3;
z1=y1-y2;
z2=y2-y3;
```

and then use the MODEL and MTEST statements

```
model z1 z2 = x1 x2;
mtest intercept, x1, x2/print;
```

We do not need to include variables $Z1$ and $Z2$ in the MTEST statement given above. They are included by default since, if the list in the MTEST statement does not include any dependent variable, SAS automatically includes the variables being analyzed and listed on the left side of the MODEL statement. In Program 3.7 we have, however, used the MTEST statement to avoid creating two extra variables $Z1$ and $Z2$. The PRINT option in MTEST statement prints the corresponding $\mathbf{H}$ and $\mathbf{E}$ matrices for variables $Y1 - Y2$ and $Y2 - Y3$.

The first part of Output 3.7 presents the results of multivariate tests. The error $SS\&CP$ matrix $\mathbf{E}$ and the hypothesis $SS\&CP$ matrix $\mathbf{H}$ are given first and are then followed by four multivariate tests. All of the four multivariate tests reject the null hypothesis, for example, the value of Wilks' Λ is 0.0088, which is quite small. It leads to the observed value of an (exact) $F\,(6,10)$ test statistic of 16.0644, and a p value of 0.0001. In view of this extremely small p value, there is sufficient evidence to reject H_0 and conclude the lack of spatial uniformity.

Having rejected the null hypothesis of equality of all regression coefficients including the intercepts in the three models, we may want to test if the three models differ only in their intercepts and if the respective coefficients of $X1$ and $X2$ are the same in the models for $Y1$, $Y2$ and $Y3$. Therefore, we exclude the keyword INTERCEPT in the MTEST statement. The appropriate MODEL and MTEST statements are

```
model y1 y2 y3 =x1 x2;
mtest y1-y2, y2-y3, x1, x2/print;
```

Of course, as earlier, $Y1 - Y2$ and $Y2 - Y3$ can be removed from the list in the MTEST statement if $Z1 = Y1 - Y2$ and $Z2 = Y2 - Y3$ have already been defined in the DATA step and if the variables $Z1$ and $Z2$ are analyzed in the MODEL statement. The resulting multivariate outputs would be identical. These are presented in the latter part of Output 3.7. As in the previous case, the null hypothesis in the present case is also rejected by all four multivariate tests leading us to believe that the deposition rates Y1, Y2, and Y3 at the three different measurement sites depend differently on the two flow rates X1 and X2.

3.9 Variance and Bias Analyses for Calibration Problems

This last section presents an application of the multivariate analysis of variance techniques to test for equality of variances in several measuring devices. The approach is taken from Christensen and Blackwood (1993). Such calibration problems occur frequently in assessing the relative measurement quality of various instruments or of a particular instrument at various times.

Suppose $y_{ij}\ i = 1, \ldots, n, \ j = 1, \ldots, q$ are the measurements for a random sample of n items distributed around their respective true values, each measured by q instruments or at q different laboratories. If α_j is the fixed bias of the jth instrument and ϵ_{ij} are the independent random errors with zero mean and variance σ_j^2, then the problem of testing the equality of the error variances, namely

$$H_0 : \sigma_1^2 = \sigma_2^2 = \ldots = \sigma_q^2,$$

can be reduced to a MANOVA problem with the test based on the multivariate regression coefficients.

Let us define, for each of n items, $\bar{y}_i = \frac{1}{q}\sum_{j=1}^{q} y_{ij}$ as the average measurement and $\tilde{y}_{ij} = y_{ij} - \bar{y}_i$ as the deviation of each measurement from $\bar{y}_i$. Then the testing problem stated above is equivalent to testing

$$H_0 : \beta_{11} = \beta_{12} = \ldots = \beta_{1,q-1} = 0$$

in the multivariate linear model

$$\tilde{y}_{ij} = \beta_{0j} + \beta_{1j}\bar{y}_i + \epsilon_{ij},$$

$j = 1, ..., (q-1); i = 1, ..., n$. The above model in matrix form is written as

$$
\begin{bmatrix}
\tilde{y}_{11} & \cdots & \tilde{y}_{1,q-1} \\
\tilde{y}_{21} & \cdots & \tilde{y}_{2,q-1} \\
\cdot & & \\
\cdot & & \\
\cdot & & \\
\tilde{y}_{n1} & \cdots & \tilde{y}_{n,q-1}
\end{bmatrix}
=
\begin{bmatrix}
1 & \bar{y}_1 \\
1 & \bar{y}_2 \\
\cdot & \cdot \\
\cdot & \cdot \\
\cdot & \cdot \\
1 & \bar{y}_n
\end{bmatrix}
\begin{bmatrix}
\beta_{01} & \beta_{02} & \cdots & \beta_{0,q-1} \\
\beta_{11} & \beta_{12} & \cdots & \beta_{1,q-1}
\end{bmatrix}
+
\begin{bmatrix}
\epsilon_{11} & \cdots & \epsilon_{1\,q-1} \\
\epsilon_{21} & \cdots & \epsilon_{2\,q-1} \\
\cdot & & \\
\cdot & & \\
\cdot & & \\
\epsilon_{n1} & \cdots & \epsilon_{n\,q-1}
\end{bmatrix}
$$

or

$$\mathbf{Y} = \mathbf{XB} + \mathcal{E}$$

and our null hypothesis is that the vector of the slope parameters for the $(q-1)$ variables is equal to zero. This is one of the standard null hypotheses that can be easily tested using PROC GLM or PROC REG.

In the above discussion, $\tilde{y}_{iq}, i = 1, \ldots, n$ have not been included in the model. In general, any other set, $\tilde{y}_{ij}, i = 1, \ldots, n$ could have been dropped instead. Although the data thus created would differ, the resulting test statistics and hence also the conclusions are invariant of any such choice.

Example 7: Equality of Variances in Calibration of Thermocouples (Christensen and Blackwood, 1993)

Christensen and Blackwood (1993) described a study in which 64 measurements on a high temperature furnace were taken by each of five thermocouples that had been bound together and inserted in the furnace. The objective is to test if all five thermocouples have the same precision. In other words, in this example we want to test the hypothesis of the equality of the variances for the five thermocouples.

The data and the corresponding SAS code for analysis are presented in Program 3.8. From the five temperature variables TC1 through TC5 corresponding to these thermocouples and their average $TCBAR = (TC1 + TC2 + \ldots + TC5)/5$ the variables Y1TILDA through Y5TILDA are defined by taking the differences from their mean TCBAR. For these data, since $q = 5$, we only need to take $q - 1 = 4$ of these five variables as the response variables to fit a multivariate regression model with TCBAR as the independent variable.

Choose any four of these five as the response variable. As mentioned previously, the values of the test statistics and the corresponding P values are unaffected by any such choice.

Testing the hypothesis of equality of variances of TC1 through TC5 is equivalent to testing that in the corresponding multivariate linear model; the slope parameters corresponding to independent variable TCBAR are all zero. This hypothesis is tested by using the SAS code

```
proc glm;
model y2tilda y3tilda y4tilda y5tilda = tcbar/nouni;
manova h = tcbar/printe printh;
```

or alternatively by using

```
proc reg;
model y2tilda y3tilda y4tilda y5tilda = tcbar;
EqualVar:  mtest tcbar/print;
```

The latter choice is included in Program 3.8, and the output is presented in Output 3.8. All the multivariate tests are exact in this case and are also equivalent. Corresponding to the observed value of $F(4, 59)$ as 3.6449, the p value is equal to .0101 leading to the rejection of the null hypothesis of equality of the five variances. The next step may be to determine the equality of various variances in subgroups. The slope coefficients for regressing Y2TILDA through Y5TILDA on TCBAR respectively, obtained from the corresponding outputs of univariate analysis, (not shown), are 0.1288, 0.0242, -0.0697, and -0.0808. Because the five response variables sum to zero in this model the sum of all five coefficients (corresponding to Y1TILDA through Y5TILDA) equals zero. Thus the slope coefficient for regressing Y1TILDA on TCBAR is -0.0025. Further, the smaller regression coefficients correspond to smaller variances. Hence the five variances can be ordered as

$$\sigma_5^2, \sigma_4^2, \ \sigma_1^2, \ \sigma_3^2, \ \sigma_2^2.$$

Using the Student-Newman-Keuls test Christensen and Blackwood (1993) summarized the grouping as given below.

$$\left[\sigma_5^2, \sigma_4^2, \ \left(\sigma_1^2\right], \ \sigma_3^2, \ \sigma_2^2\right).$$

See Christensen and Blackwood (1993) for further details.

Another problem of interest in calibration is to test for the equality of both the device variances σ_i^2 and biases α_i^2, $i = 1, \ldots, q$. Christensen and Blackwood (1993) showed that with $\tilde{y}_{ij} = y_{ij} - \bar{y}_i$, $j = 1, \ldots, q - 1$ as defined earlier, the null hypothesis of equality of variances and equality of biases is equivalent to testing

$$H_0 : \quad \beta_{01} = \beta_{02} = \ldots = \beta_{0,q-1} = 0,$$
$$\beta_{11} = \beta_{12} = \ldots = \beta_{1,q-1} = 0.$$

in the linear model $\tilde{y}_{ij} = \beta_{0j} + \beta_{1j}\overline{y}_i + \epsilon_{ij}$, $j = 1, \ldots, q-1$; $i = 1, \ldots, n$. Thus the hypothesis is on slope coefficients as well as the intercepts. To test this null hypothesis using SAS, we can, as earlier, use the MTEST statement in PROC REG. The SAS code for this is given at the end of Program 3.8. All four multivariate tests lead to very small p values, for example, the Wilks' Λ results in the observed value of exact $F(8, 118)$ as 3484.124, leading to a p value of 0.0001. Consequently, we conclude that for at least two thermocouples either the variances, or the biases, or both of the temperatures are unequal. For further discussion of analysis involving biases and variances, see Christensen and Blackwood (1993).

Finally, note that the inference in multivariate regression can be sensitive to the assumption of multivariate normality as well as the presence of outliers. We have briefly indicated some of the approaches to these problems in Chapters 1 and 2. It is a good practice to apply these checks before performing the formal multivariate analysis described in this chapter. Some of the test statistics in a normal MANOVA are more sensitive to nonnormality than others. In general, if the data are not strictly normal, Pillai's test is the most robust of the MANOVA tests with adequate power and therefore is especially recommended for such situations.

```
/* Program 3.1 */

  option ls=76 ps=45 nodate nonumber;

data cork;
infile 'cork.dat' firstobs = 1 ;
input north east south west;
y1=north;
y2=east;
y3=south;
y4=west;

/* Hotelling's T-square by creating the differences*/
data cork;
set cork;
dne=y1-y2;
dns=y1-y3;
dnw=y1-y4;
proc glm data=cork;
 model dne dns dnw= /nouni;
 manova h=intercept;
title1 ' Output 3.1 ';
title2 ' Cork Bore Data: C. R. Rao (1948)' ;
run;
```

General Linear Models Procedure
Multivariate Analysis of Variance

Characteristic Roots and Vectors of: E Inverse * H, where
H = Type III SS&CP Matrix for INTERCEPT   E = Error SS&CP Matrix

Characteristic Root	Percent	Characteristic Vector V'EV=1	
		DNE DNW	DNS
0.76822288	100.00	0.01256587 0.02243791	-0.01086704
0.00000000	0.00	-0.00378101 -0.00088456	0.02474866
0.00000000	0.00	-0.02093912 0.01870549	-0.01046880

Manova Test Criteria and Exact F Statistics for
the Hypothesis of no Overall INTERCEPT Effect
H = Type III SS&CP Matrix for INTERCEPT   E = Error SS&CP Matrix

S=1   M=0.5   N=11.5

Statistic	Value	F	Num DF	Den DF	Pr > F
Wilks' Lambda	0.56553956	6.4019	3	25	0.0023
Pillai's Trace	0.43446044	6.4019	3	25	0.0023
Hotelling-Lawley Trace	0.76822288	6.4019	3	25	0.0023
Roy's Greatest Root	0.76822288	6.4019	3	25	0.0023

```
/* Program 3.2 */

option ls=76 ps=45 nodate nonumber;

data cork;
infile 'cork.dat' firstobs=1;
input north east south west;
y1=north;
y2=east;
y3=south;
y4=west;

/* Hotelling's T**2 using m statement*/
proc glm data=cork;
model y1 y2 y3 y4= /nouni;
manova h=intercept
m=y2-y1, y3-y1,y4-y1
mnames=d1 d2 d3;
title1 ' Output 3.2 ' ;
title2 ' Use of M statement for Cork Bore Data:
C. R. Rao (1948) ' ;
/* Testing for equality of bark contents in the opposite
direction, that is, South-North and West-East.*/

/*
proc glm data=cork;
model y1 y2 y3 y4= /nouni;
manova h=intercept
m=y3-y1, y4-y2
 mnames=dy3y1 dy4y2;
*/
run ;
```

Output 3.2
Use of M statement for Cork Bore Data: C. R. Rao (1948)

General Linear Models Procedure
Multivariate Analysis of Variance

M Matrix Describing Transformed Variables

	Y1	Y2	Y3	Y4
D1	-1	1	0	0
D2	-1	0	1	0
D3	-1	0	0	1

Use of M statement for Cork Bore Data: C. R. Rao (1948)

General Linear Models Procedure
Multivariate Analysis of Variance

Characteristic Roots and Vectors of: E Inverse * H, where
H = Type III SS&CP Matrix for INTERCEPT   E = Error SS&CP Matrix

Variables have been transformed by the M Matrix

Characteristic Root	Percent	Characteristic Vector V'EV=1	
		D1 D3	D2
0.76822288	100.00	0.01256587 0.02243791	-0.01086704
0.00000000	0.00	-0.00378101 -0.00088456	0.02474866
0.00000000	0.00	-0.02093912 0.01870549	-0.01046880

Manova Test Criteria and Exact F Statistics for
the Hypothesis of no Overall INTERCEPT Effect
on the variables defined by the M Matrix Transformation
H = Type III SS&CP Matrix for INTERCEPT   E = Error SS&CP Matrix

S=1   M=0.5   N=11.5

Statistic	Value	F	Num DF	Den DF	Pr > F
Wilks' Lambda	0.56553956	6.4019	3	25	0.0023
Pillai's Trace	0.43446044	6.4019	3	25	0.0023
Hotelling-Lawley Trace	0.76822288	6.4019	3	25	0.0023
Roy's Greatest Root	0.76822288	6.4019	3	25	0.0023

```
/* Program 3.3 */

option ls=76 ps=45 nodate nonumber;
title1 ' Output 3.3 ' ;
data fish;
infile 'fish.dat' firstobs = 1;
input p1 p2 p3 p4 p5 dose wt @@;
y1=arsin(sqrt(p1));
y2=arsin(sqrt(p2));
y3=arsin(sqrt(p3));
y4=arsin(sqrt(p4));
y5=arsin(sqrt(p5));
x1=log(dose);
x2=wt;
 proc print data=fish;
 var y1 y2 y3 y4 y5 x1 x2;
 proc print data=fish;
 var p1 p2 p3 p4 p5 dose x2;
title2 'Transformed Fish Data: Srivastava & Carter
(1983, p. 143)';

 proc glm data=fish;
 model y1 y2 y3 y4 y5=x1 x2/nouni;
 manova h=x1 x2/printe printh;

/*
mtest option of proc reg can be used instead of manova
option of proc glm to get the same results;
*/

 proc reg data=fish;
 model y1 y2 y3 y4 y5=x1 x2;
 Model: mtest x1, x2/print;

 Onlyx1: mtest x1/print;
 Onlyx2: mtest x2/print;

run;
```

OBS	Y1	Y2	Y3	Y4	Y5	X1	X2
1	0.00000	0.00000	0.52360	0.52360	0.52360	5.59842	0.6695
2	0.00000	0.32175	0.57964	0.57964	0.57964	6.01616	0.6405
3	0.00000	0.78540	1.04720	1.24905	1.24905	6.41346	0.7290
4	0.39770	0.93774	1.57080	1.57080	1.57080	6.84588	0.7700
5	0.73531	1.57080	1.57080	1.57080	1.57080	7.27932	0.5655
6	0.00000	0.22551	0.46365	0.46365	0.46365	5.59842	0.7820
7	0.22551	0.32175	0.57964	0.57964	0.57964	6.01616	0.8120
8	0.22551	0.73531	1.34528	1.57080	1.57080	6.41346	0.8215
9	0.32175	0.99116	1.57080	1.57080	1.57080	6.84588	0.8690
10	0.46365	1.17310	1.57080	1.57080	1.57080	7.27932	0.8395
11	0.00000	0.00000	0.00000	0.00000	0.22551	5.59842	0.8615
12	0.00000	0.22551	0.39770	0.52360	0.57964	6.01616	0.9045
13	0.00000	0.39770	1.34528	1.34528	1.34528	6.41346	1.0280
14	0.00000	0.83548	1.34528	1.57080	1.57080	6.84588	1.0445
15	0.32175	1.17310	1.57080	1.57080	1.57080	7.27932	1.0455
16	0.00000	0.00000	0.00000	0.22551	0.32175	5.59842	0.6195
17	0.00000	0.22551	0.39770	0.46365	0.52360	6.01616	0.5305
18	0.32175	0.73531	1.34528	1.34528	1.34528	6.41346	0.5970
19	0.32175	0.99116	1.57080	1.57080	1.57080	6.84588	0.6385
20	0.63305	1.34528	1.57080	1.57080	1.57080	7.27932	0.6645
21	0.00000	0.22551	0.46365	0.46365	0.46365	5.59842	0.5685
22	0.00000	0.00000	0.39770	0.52360	0.52360	6.01616	0.6040
23	0.00000	0.68472	1.24905	1.57080	1.57080	6.41346	0.6325
24	0.22551	0.93774	1.57080	1.57080	1.57080	6.84588	0.6845
25	0.57964	1.17310	1.57080	1.57080	1.57080	7.27932	0.7230

Transformed Fish Data: Srivastava & Carter (1983, p. 143)

OBS	P1	P2	P3	P4	P5	DOSE	X2
1	0.00	0.00	0.25	0.25	0.25	270	0.6695
2	0.00	0.10	0.30	0.30	0.30	410	0.6405
3	0.00	0.50	0.75	0.90	0.90	610	0.7290
4	0.15	0.65	1.00	1.00	1.00	940	0.7700
5	0.45	1.00	1.00	1.00	1.00	1450	0.5655
6	0.00	0.05	0.20	0.20	0.20	270	0.7820
7	0.05	0.10	0.30	0.30	0.30	410	0.8120
8	0.05	0.45	0.95	1.00	1.00	610	0.8215
9	0.10	0.70	1.00	1.00	1.00	940	0.8690
10	0.20	0.85	1.00	1.00	1.00	1450	0.8395
11	0.00	0.00	0.00	0.00	0.05	270	0.8615
12	0.00	0.05	0.15	0.25	0.30	410	0.9045
13	0.00	0.15	0.95	0.95	0.95	610	1.0280
14	0.00	0.55	0.95	1.00	1.00	940	1.0445
15	0.10	0.85	1.00	1.00	1.00	1450	1.0455
16	0.00	0.00	0.00	0.05	0.10	270	0.6195
17	0.00	0.05	0.15	0.20	0.25	410	0.5305
18	0.10	0.45	0.95	0.95	0.95	610	0.5970
19	0.10	0.70	1.00	1.00	1.00	940	0.6385
20	0.35	0.95	1.00	1.00	1.00	1450	0.6645
21	0.00	0.05	0.20	0.20	0.20	270	0.5685
22	0.00	0.00	0.15	0.25	0.25	410	0.6040
23	0.00	0.40	0.90	1.00	1.00	610	0.6325
24	0.05	0.65	1.00	1.00	1.00	940	0.6845
25	0.30	0.85	1.00	1.00	1.00	1450	0.7230

General Linear Models Procedure

Number of observations in data set = 25

E = Error SS&CP Matrix

	Y1	Y2	Y3	Y4	Y5
Y1	0.3521207721	0.1323723295	-0.081582595	-0.238505417	-0.211550264
Y2	0.1323723295	0.3986006993	0.2479046457	0.2352986084	0.2252678955
Y3	-0.081582595	0.2479046457	1.2273557756	1.2221331781	1.0891872222
Y4	-0.238505417	0.2352986084	1.2221331781	1.4505775203	1.3142693993
Y5	-0.211550264	0.2252678955	1.0891872222	1.3142693993	1.2243378999

Transformed Fish Data: Srivastava & Carter (1983, p. 143)

General Linear Models Procedure
Multivariate Analysis of Variance

H = Type III SS&CP Matrix for X1

	Y1	Y2	Y3	Y4	Y5
Y1	0.9444331687	2.1396606906	2.4004527379	2.3189700315	2.2097384417
Y2	2.1396606906	4.8475085618	5.4383460192	5.2537428628	5.0062732199
Y3	2.4004527379	5.4383460192	6.1011975631	5.8940940938	5.6164616708
Y4	2.3189700315	5.2537428628	5.8940940938	5.6940206946	5.4258124278
Y5	2.2097384417	5.0062732199	5.6164616708	5.4258124278	5.1702377073

Characteristic Roots and Vectors of: E Inverse * H, where
H = Type III SS&CP Matrix for X1   E = Error SS&CP Matrix

Characteristic Root	Percent	Characteristic Vector V'EV=1	
		Y1	Y2
		Y3	Y4
		Y5	
14.2472850	100.00	0.55171485	1.04785724
		0.06215532	−0.11654144
		0.46436590	
0.0000000	0.00	−0.31734319	−0.24878068
		0.72475369	−5.81185638
		5.68836531	
0.0000000	0.00	1.31612722	−0.65966844
		−2.38942315	2.54603108
		0.00000000	
0.0000000	0.00	0.43144422	−1.25612329
		0.94990722	0.00000000
		0.00000000	
0.0000000	0.00	−1.78764520	0.78905568
		0.00000000	0.00000000
		0.00000000	

Transformed Fish Data: Srivastava & Carter (1983, p. 143)

General Linear Models Procedure
Multivariate Analysis of Variance

Manova Test Criteria and Exact F Statistics for
the Hypothesis of no Overall X1 Effect
H = Type III SS&CP Matrix for X1   E = Error SS&CP Matrix

S=1   M=1.5   N=8

Statistic	Value	F	Num DF	Den DF	Pr > F
Wilks' Lambda	0.06558545	51.2902	5	18	0.0001
Pillai's Trace	0.93441455	51.2902	5	18	0.0001
Hotelling-Lawley Trace	14.24728504	51.2902	5	18	0.0001
Roy's Greatest Root	14.24728504	51.2902	5	18	0.0001

H = Type III SS&CP Matrix for X2

	Y1	Y2	Y3	Y4	Y5
Y1	0.0976730369	0.0792504059	-0.01314736	-0.020670718	-0.032603961
Y2	0.0792504059	0.0643025654	-0.010667567	-0.016771904	-0.026454355
Y3	-0.01314736	-0.010667567	0.0017697113	0.0027823991	0.0043886832
Y4	-0.020670718	-0.016771904	0.0027823991	0.0043745806	0.0069000341
Y5	-0.032603961	-0.026454355	0.0043886832	0.0069000341	0.0108834365

Characteristic Roots and Vectors of: E Inverse * H, where
H = Type III SS&CP Matrix for X2   E = Error SS&CP Matrix

Characteristic Root	Percent	Characteristic Vector V'EV=1	
		Y1	Y2
		Y3	Y4
		Y5	
0.52693756	100.00	1.54528621	0.54470517
		-1.23989398	3.77134305
		-2.89593127	

Transformed Fish Data: Srivastava & Carter (1983, p. 143)

General Linear Models Procedure
Multivariate Analysis of Variance

Characteristic Roots and Vectors of: E Inverse * H, where
H = Type III SS&CP Matrix for X2   E = Error SS&CP Matrix

Characteristic Root	Percent	Characteristic Vector	V'EV=1
		Y1	Y2
		Y3	Y4
		Y5	
0.00000000	0.00	0.70777693	−0.73863887
		0.90830216	0.30892057
		−0.23721330	
0.00000000	0.00	0.88973917	−0.71121690
		−2.13333142	1.69536789
		0.72207496	
0.00000000	0.00	−1.15517657	1.56318576
		0.08060993	−0.81221542
		0.82145754	
0.00000000	0.00	0.71005629	−0.06199478
		0.46994370	−4.73509285
		4.78897304	

Manova Test Criteria and Exact F Statistics for
the Hypothesis of no Overall X2 Effect
H = Type III SS&CP Matrix for X2   E = Error SS&CP Matrix

Transformed Fish Data: Srivastava & Carter (1983, p. 143)

General Linear Models Procedure
Multivariate Analysis of Variance

S=1   M=1.5   N=8

Statistic	Value	F	Num DF	Den DF	Pr > F
Wilks' Lambda	0.65490563	1.8970	5	18	0.1449
Pillai's Trace	0.34509437	1.8970	5	18	0.1449
Hotelling-Lawley Trace	0.52693756	1.8970	5	18	0.1449
Roy's Greatest Root	0.52693756	1.8970	5	18	0.1449

Transformed Fish Data: Srivastava & Carter (1983, p. 143)

Multivariate Test: MODEL

E, the Error Matrix

```
 0.3521207721    0.1323723295   -0.081582595   -0.238505417   -0.211550264
 0.1323723295    0.3986006993    0.2479046457    0.2352986084    0.2252678955
-0.081582595     0.2479046457    1.2273557756    1.2221331781    1.0891872222
-0.238505417     0.2352986084    1.2221331781    1.4505775203    1.3142693993
-0.211550264     0.2252678955    1.0891872222    1.3142693993    1.2243378999
```


H, the Hypothesis Matrix

```
 0.9538786705    2.1157383555    2.3410489485    2.2590396342    2.1485124778
 2.1157383555    4.9080959325    5.58879619      5.4055267572    5.1613383564
 2.3410489485    5.58879619      6.4747944636    6.2710028881    6.0015184245
 2.2590396342    5.4055267572    6.2710028881    6.0742707424    5.8142826656
 2.1485124778    5.1613383564    6.0015184245    5.8142826656    5.567105838
```

Multivariate Statistics and F Approximations

S=2   M=1   N=8

Statistic	Value	F	Num DF	Den DF	Pr > F
Wilks' Lambda	0.04668792	13.0610	10	36	0.0001
Pillai's Trace	1.21319964	5.8594	10	38	0.0001
Hotelling-Lawley Trace	14.85233102	25.2490	10	34	0.0001
Roy's Greatest Root	14.46757522	54.9768	5	19	0.0001

NOTE: F Statistic for Roy's Greatest Root is an upper bound.
NOTE: F Statistic for Wilks' Lambda is exact.

```
/* fish.dat */

0 0. .25 .25 .25 270 .6695
0. .10 .30 .30 .30 410 .6405
0. .5 .75 .9 .9 610 .729
.15 .65 1.0 1.0 1.0 940 .77
.45 1. 1. 1. 1. 1450 .5655
0. .05 .20 .20 .2 270 .782
.05 .1 .3 .3 .3 410 .812
.05 .45 .95 1. 1. 610 .8215
.1 .7 1. 1. 1. 940 .869
.2 .85 1. 1. 1. 1450 .8395
0. 0. 0. 0. .05 270 .8615
0. .05 .15 .25 .30 410 .9045
0. .15 .95 .95 .95 610 1.028
0. .55 .95 1. 1. 940 1.0445
.1 .85 1. 1. 1. 1450 1.0455
0. 0. 0. .05 .10 270 .6195
0. .05 .15 .20 .25 410 .5305
.1 .45 .95 .95 .95 610 .597
.1 .7 1 1 1 940 .6385
.35 .95 1. 1. 1. 1450 .6645
0 .05 .20 .20 .20 270 .5685
0 0 .15 .25 .25 410 .604
0 .4 .9 1. 1. 610 .6325
.05 .65 1 1. 1. 940 .6845
.3 .85 1. 1. 1. 1450 .723

/* Source: Srivastava and Carter (1983, p. 143). */
```

```
/* Program 3.4 */

/* Data is from Srivastava and Carter, 1983, p. 143*/

options ls=76 ps=45 nodate nonumber;
data fish;
infile 'fish.dat';

input p1 p2 p3 p4 p5 dose wt @@;
y1=arsin(sqrt(p1));
y2=arsin(sqrt(p2));
y3=arsin(sqrt(p3));
y4=arsin(sqrt(p4));
y5=arsin(sqrt(p5));
x1=log(dose);
x2=wt;

title1 'Output 3.4 ';
title2 ' Stepown Analysis';
/*This does the calculations for Stepdown Analysis*/

proc reg data=fish;
model y1=x1 x2;
fishwt: test x2=0.0;
fmodel: test x1=0.0,x2=0.0;
proc reg data=fish;
model y2=x1 x2 y1;
fishwt: test x2=0.0;
fmodel: test x1=0.0,x2=0.0;
proc reg data=fish;
model y3=x1 x2 y1 y2;
fishwt: test x2=0.0;
fmodel: test x1=0.0,x2=0.0;
proc reg data=fish;
model y4=x1 x2 y1 y2 y3;
fishwt: test x2=0.0;
fmodel: test x1=0.0,x2=0.0;
proc reg data=fish;
model y5=x1 x2 y1 y2 y3 y4;
fishwt: test x2=0.0;
fmodel: test x1=0.0,x2=0.0;
run;
```

Model: MODEL1
Dependent Variable: Y1

Analysis of Variance

Source	DF	Sum of Squares	Mean Square	F Value	Prob>F
Model	2	0.95388	0.47694	29.798	0.0001
Error	22	0.35212	0.01601		
C Total	24	1.30600			

Root MSE	0.12651	R-square	0.7304	
Dep Mean	0.19092	Adj R-sq	0.7059	
C.V.	66.26628			

Parameter Estimates

Variable	DF	Parameter Estimate	Standard Error	T for H0: Parameter=0	Prob > |T|
INTERCEP	1	-1.651099	0.28363283	-5.821	0.0001
X1	1	0.336405	0.04379362	7.682	0.0001
X2	1	-0.430791	0.17438706	-2.470	0.0217

```
/* Program 3.5 */

options ls=76 ps=45 nodate nonumber;
title 'Output 3.5';
   proc iml;
   alpha = .05 ;
   n=28;
 /* Calulations for simultraneous confidence intervals
    are shown below.
    r_t =Rank (H+E)=p=4, Rank(L)=1, k=0
    df of error matrix = dferror = 27
    s = min(r, r_t) = 1, h=max(r,r_t)=4
    m1 = .5(|r-r_t| - 1) = 1
    m2 = .5(n-k-r_t-2) = 11.
    lambda  = [h/(n-k-h+r-1)]F(alpha,h, n-k-h+r-1)
      */
  r_t=4;
  r=1;
  k=0;
    s = min(r, r_t);
    h=max(r,r_t);
    m1 = .5*(abs(r-r_t) - 1);
    m2 = .5*(n-k-r_t-2);
   lambda  = (h/(n-k-h+r-1))*finv(1-alpha,h,n-k-h+r-1);
   cutoff = sqrt(lambda);
 /*For Bonferroni intervals the cut off point will be
computed as follows:
dferror = 27 ; * dferror=n-1;
g=3.0; * g is the no. of comparisons;
     cutoff = tinv(1-alpha/2*g,dferror)/sqrt(n);
   */
   xpx= {28};
   e = {7840.9643 6041.3214 7787.8214 6109.3214,
        6041.3214 5938.1071 6184.6071 4627.1071,
        7787.8214 6184.6071 9450.1071 7007.6071,
        6109.3214 4627.1071 7007.6071 6102.1071};
bhat = {50.535714 46.178571 49.678571 45.178571};
l = {1} ;
c={1};
d1={1,-1,1,-1};
d2={0,0,1,-1};
d3={1,0,-1,0};
 clbhatd1=c'*l*bhat*d1;
 clbhatd2=c'*l*bhat*d2;
 clbhatd3=c'*l*bhat*d3;
cwidth1=cutoff*sqrt((c'*l*(inv(xpx))*l'*c)*(d1'*e*d1));
cwidth2=cutoff*sqrt((c'*l*(inv(xpx))*l'*c)*(d2'*e*d2));
cwidth3=cutoff*sqrt((c'*l*(inv(xpx))*l'*c)*(d3'*e*d3));
cl11=clbhatd1-cwidth1;
cl12=clbhatd1+cwidth1;
cl21=clbhatd2-cwidth2;
cl22=clbhatd2+cwidth2;
cl31=clbhatd3-cwidth3;
cl32=clbhatd3+cwidth3;
print 'Simultaneous Confidence Intervals';
print 'For first contrast: (' cl11', '  cl12 ')';
print 'For second contrast:(' cl21', ' cl22 ')';
print 'For third contrast: (' cl31', ' cl32 ')';
run;
```

Simultaneous Confidence Intervals

```
                          CL11          CL12
For first contrast: ( 1.2786666 ,  16.435619 )


                          CL21          CL22
For second contrast:( -0.539816 ,  9.5398157 )


                          CL31          CL32
For third contrast: ( -4.467176 ,  6.1814617 )
```

```
/* Program 3.6 */

option ls=76 ps=45 nodate nonumber;

data wash;
input temp time wratio sprness tba cookloss whitness ;
x1 = (temp - 33)/7.0 ;
x2 = (time - 5.5)/2.7 ;
x3 = (wratio-22.5)/4.5 ;
x1sq =x1*x1;
x2sq = x2*x2;
x3sq = x3*x3;
x1x2 = x1*x2;
x1x3 = x1*x3;
x2x3 = x2*x3;
y1= sprness;
y2= tba;
y3 = cookloss;
y4= whitness ;
lines;
26.0  2.8   18.0   1.83 29.31 29.50 50.36
40.0  2.8   18.0   1.73 39.32 19.40 48.16
26.0  8.2   18.0   1.85 25.16 25.70 50.72
40.0  8.2   18.0   1.67 40.81 27.10 49.69
26.0  2.8   27.0   1.86 29.82 21.40 50.09
40.0  2.8   27.0   1.77 32.20 24.00 50.61
26.0  8.2   27.0   1.88 22.01 19.60 50.36
40.0  8.2   27.0   1.66 40.02 25.10 50.42
21.2  5.5   22.5   1.81 33.00 24.20 29.31
44.8  5.5   22.5   1.37 51.59 30.60 50.67
33.0  1.0   22.5   1.85 20.35 20.90 48.75
33.0 10.0   22.5   1.92 20.53 18.90 52.70
33.0  5.5   14.9   1.88 23.85 23.00 50.19
33.0  5.5   30.1   1.90 20.16 21.20 50.86
33.0  5.5   22.5   1.89 21.72 18.50 50.84
33.0  5.5   22.5   1.88 21.21 18.60 50.93
33.0  5.5   22.5   1.87 21.55 16.80 50.98
;
/* Source: Tseo et al. (1983).  Reprinted by permission of the
   Institute of Food Technologists. */

proc standard data=wash mean=0 std=1 out=wash2 ;
var  y1 y2 y3 y4 ;

proc reg data = wash2;
model y1 y2 y3 y4 = x1 x2 x3 x1sq x2sq x3sq
                       x1x2 x1x3 x2x3 ;
Linear : mtest x1sq, x2sq, x3sq, x1x2, x1x3,
                       x2x3/print canprint;
Noquad: mtest x1sq, x2sq, x3sq/print;
Nointctn: mtest x1x2,x1x3,x2x3/print;
title1 'Output 3.6';
title2 'Quality Improvement in Mullet Flesh
                       (Tseo et al., 1983)';

proc reg data = wash2;
model y1 y2 y3 y4 = x1 x2 x3 x1sq x2sq x3sq ;
run;
```

Quality Improvement in Mullet Flesh (Tseo et al., 1983)

Multivariate Test: LINEAR

E, the Error Matrix

0.8657014633	0.0034272456	−0.815101433	−1.634723273
0.0034272456	0.661373219	−0.17637356	0.6463179546
−0.815101433	−0.17637356	1.9374527491	2.2687768511
−1.634723273	0.6463179546	2.2687768511	6.765404456

H, the Hypothesis Matrix

8.0041171357	−8.822976865	−7.893007279	6.5980348245
−8.822976865	10.054652572	9.1165224684	−7.103378577
−7.893007279	9.1165224684	12.622482263	−5.15027833
6.5980348245	−7.103378577	−5.15027833	5.9966106878

Multivariate Statistics and F Approximations

S=4   M=0.5   N=1

Statistic	Value	F	Num DF	Den DF	Pr > F
Wilks' Lambda	0.00181192	3.2280	24	15.16437	0.0107
Pillai's Trace	2.00152769	1.1685	24	28	0.3436
Hotelling-Lawley Trace	88.26169966	9.1939	24	10	0.0004
Roy's Greatest Root	83.82687288	97.7980	6	7	0.0001

NOTE: F Statistic for Roy's Greatest Root is an upper bound.

Quality Improvement in Mullet Flesh (Tseo et al., 1983)

Multivariate Test: NOQUAD

E, the Error Matrix

0.8657014633	0.0034272456	−0.815101433	−1.634723273
0.0034272456	0.661373219	−0.17637356	0.6463179546
−0.815101433	−0.17637356	1.9374527491	2.2687768511
−1.634723273	0.6463179546	2.2687768511	6.765404456

H, the Hypothesis Matrix

7.6803011193	−8.382833817	−7.134947069	6.6287026452
−8.382833817	9.3528485931	8.4300829636	−7.078088833
−7.134947069	8.4300829636	8.6640951737	−5.644015041
6.6287026452	−7.078088833	−5.644015041	5.9121733755

Multivariate Statistics and F Approximations

S=3   M=0   N=1

Statistic	Value	F	Num DF	Den DF	Pr > F
Wilks' Lambda	0.00415372	6.2945	12	10.87451	0.0024
Pillai's Trace	1.65942848	1.8568	12	18	0.1141
Hotelling-Lawley Trace	81.05601060	18.0124	12	8	0.0002
Roy's Greatest Root	79.06246846	118.5937	4	6	0.0001

NOTE: F Statistic for Roy's Greatest Root is an upper bound.

Quality Improvement in Mullet Flesh (Tseo et al., 1983)

Multivariate Test: NOINTCTN

E, the Error Matrix

0.8657014633	0.0034272456	−0.815101433	−1.634723273
0.0034272456	0.661373219	−0.17637356	0.6463179546
−0.815101433	−0.17637356	1.9374527491	2.2687768511
−1.634723273	0.6463179546	2.2687768511	6.765404456

H, the Hypothesis Matrix

0.3238160164	−0.440143047	−0.758060209	−0.030667821
−0.440143047	0.7018039785	0.6864395048	−0.025289745
−0.758060209	0.6864395048	3.9583870894	0.4937367103
−0.030667821	−0.025289745	0.4937367103	0.0844373123

Multivariate Statistics and F Approximations

S=3   M=0   N=1

Statistic	Value	F	Num DF	Den DF	Pr > F
Wilks' Lambda	0.06157390	1.6927	12	10.87451	0.1973
Pillai's Trace	1.44339590	1.3909	12	18	0.2558
Hotelling-Lawley Trace	7.20568905	1.6013	12	8	0.2566
Roy's Greatest Root	5.86997985	8.8050	4	6	0.0110

NOTE: F Statistic for Roy's Greatest Root is an upper bound.

```
/* Program 3.7 */

option ls=76 ps=45 nodate nonumber;

data semicond;
input x1 x2 y1 y2 y3;
z1=y1-y2;z2=y2-y3;
lines;
46 22 45.994 46.296 48.589
56 22 48.843 48.731 49.681
66 22 51.555 50.544 50.908
46 32 47.647 47.846 48.519
56 32 50.208 49.930 50.072
66 32 52.931 52.387 51.505
46 42 47.641 49.488 48.947
56 42 51.365 51.365 50.642
66 42 54.436 52.985 51.716
;
/* Source: Guo and Sachs (1993).  Reprinted by permission of the
   Institute of Electrical and Electronics Engineers, Inc.
   Copyright 1993 IEEE. */

proc reg data = semicond ;
model y1 y2 y3 =  x1 x2 ;
AllCoef: mtest y1-y2,y2-y3,intercept,x1,x2/print;
title1 ' Output 3.7 ';
title2 'Spatial Uniformity in Semiconductor Processes
                                    (Guo and Sachs, 1993)' ;

proc reg data = semicond ;
model y1 y2 y3 = x1 x2 ;
X1andX2: mtest y1-y2,y2-y3,x1,x2/print;
run;
```

117

Model: MODEL1
Dependent Variable: Y1

Analysis of Variance

Source	DF	Sum of Squares	Mean Square	F Value	Prob>F
Model	2	60.14535	30.07268	201.946	0.0001
Error	6	0.89348	0.14891		
C Total	8	61.03883			

Root MSE	0.38589	R-square	0.9854	
Dep Mean	50.06889	Adj R-sq	0.9805	
C.V.	0.77073			

Parameter Estimates

Variable	DF	Parameter Estimate	Standard Error	T for H0: Parameter=0	Prob > |T|
INTERCEP	1	29.844889	1.02421553	29.139	0.0001
X1	1	0.294000	0.01575405	18.662	0.0001
X2	1	0.117500	0.01575405	7.458	0.0003

Spatial Uniformity in Semiconductor Processes (Guo and Sachs, 1993)

Dependent Variable: Y2

Analysis of Variance

Source	DF	Sum of Squares	Mean Square	F Value	Prob>F
Model	2	36.54818	18.27409	251.850	0.0001
Error	6	0.43536	0.07256		
C Total	8	36.98354			

Root MSE	0.26937	R-square	0.9882
Dep Mean	49.95244	Adj R-sq	0.9843
C.V.	0.53925		

Parameter Estimates

Variable	DF	Parameter Estimate	Standard Error	T for H0: Parameter=0	Prob > |T|
INTERCEP	1	34.076444	0.71494183	47.663	0.0001
X1	1	0.204767	0.01099694	18.620	0.0001
X2	1	0.137783	0.01099694	12.529	0.0001

Spatial Uniformity in Semiconductor Processes (Guo and Sachs, 1993)

Dependent Variable: Y3

Analysis of Variance

Source	DF	Sum of Squares	Mean Square	F Value	Prob>F
Model	2	11.61893	5.80947	183.301	0.0001
Error	6	0.19016	0.03169		
C Total	8	11.80910			

Root MSE	0.17803	R-square	0.9839	
Dep Mean	50.06433	Adj R-sq	0.9785	
C.V.	0.35560			

Parameter Estimates

Variable	DF	Parameter Estimate	Standard Error	T for H0: Parameter=0	Prob > |T|
INTERCEP	1	41.394200	0.47250828	87.605	0.0001
X1	1	0.134567	0.00726792	18.515	0.0001
X2	1	0.035450	0.00726792	4.878	0.0028

Spatial Uniformity in Semiconductor Processes (Guo and Sachs, 1993)

Multivariate Test: ALLCOEF

E, the Error Matrix

```
 1.9090653889      -0.761418778
-0.761418778        0.6168702222
```

H, the Hypothesis Matrix

```
5.1464346111       2.3958517778
2.3958517778       9.3527627778
```

Multivariate Statistics and F Approximations

S=2   M=0   N=1.5

Statistic	Value	F	Num DF	Den DF	Pr > F
Wilks' Lambda	0.00883542	16.0644	6	10	0.0001
Pillai's Trace	1.61764114	8.4614	6	12	0.0010
Hotelling-Lawley Trace	41.27570857	27.5171	6	8	0.0001
Roy's Greatest Root	39.47971908	78.9594	3	6	0.0001

NOTE: F Statistic for Roy's Greatest Root is an upper bound.
NOTE: F Statistic for Wilks' Lambda is exact.

Spatial Uniformity in Semiconductor Processes (Guo and Sachs, 1993)

Multivariate Test: X1ANDX2

E, the Error Matrix

```
 1.9090653889      -0.761418778
-0.761418778       0.6168702222
```

H, the Hypothesis Matrix

```
5.0244008333       2.5131113333
2.5131113333       9.2400906667
```

Multivariate Statistics and F Approximations

S=2   M=-0.5   N=1.5

Statistic	Value	F	Num DF	Den DF	Pr > F
Wilks' Lambda	0.00915958	23.6217	4	10	0.0001
Pillai's Trace	1.60532546	12.2024	4	12	0.0003
Hotelling-Lawley Trace	41.08869970	41.0887	4	8	0.0001
Roy's Greatest Root	39.38536205	118.1561	2	6	0.0001

NOTE: F Statistic for Roy's Greatest Root is an upper bound.
NOTE: F Statistic for Wilks' Lambda is exact.

```
/*Program 3.8 */

option ls=76 ps=45 nodate nonumber;

/* Testing the precisions of five thermocouples
   Source : Christensen and Blackwood(1993),
Technometrics, 35, 411-420.
*/
title1 'Output 3.8';
title2 'Testing the Precisions of Five Thermocouples' ;
title3 'Data from Christensen and Blackwood(1993),
                         Technometrics, 35, 411-420';

data calib ;
input  tc1  tc2  tc3  tc4  tc5  @@ ;
tcbar = (tc1+tc2+tc3+tc4+tc5)/5 ;
y1tilda = tc1 - tcbar ;
y2tilda = tc2 - tcbar ;
y3tilda = tc3 - tcbar ;
y4tilda = tc4 - tcbar ;
y5tilda = tc5 - tcbar ;
lines ;
326.06   321.92 326.03 323.59    322.84
326.09 322.00 326.06 323.63    322.92
326.07   321.98 326.03 323.62    322.88
326.08 321.99 326.06 323.64    322.91
326.05   321.96 326.02 323.64    322.89
326.05 321.96 326.02 323.60    322.89
326.03   321.94 326.01 323.62    322.87
326.08 321.86 326.01 323.64    322.89
326.00   321.85 325.99 323.58    322.85
326.16 322.05 326.13 323.70    322.98
326.00   321.90 325.97 323.55    322.84
326.20 322.12 326.20 323.76    323.03
325.97   321.89 325.95 323.55    322.82
326.20 322.10 326.18 323.74    323.02
326.07   321.99 326.04 323.66    322.93
326.11 322.02 326.08 323.66    322.93
326.00   321.91 325.98 323.57    322.82
326.20 322.11 326.16 323.75    323.03
326.13   322.04 326.12 323.70    322.95
326.12 322.03 326.08 323.68    322.95
326.14   322.04 326.11 323.69    322.94
326.15 322.05 326.12 323.70    322.97
326.07   321.96 326.03 323.62    322.89
326.11 322.00 326.08 323.66    322.93
326.07   321.97 326.03 323.62    322.89
326.13 322.02 326.07 323.67    323.02
326.01   321.92 325.99 323.58    322.85
326.22 322.25 326.19 323.77    323.03
326.08   321.97 326.05 323.63    322.90
326.16 322.06 326.12 323.70    322.97
325.99   321.91 325.96 323.55    322.81
326.14 322.03 326.11 323.68    322.93
325.97   321.86 325.94 323.51    322.80
326.17 322.06 326.14 323.70    322.99
326.02   321.93 325.99 323.58    322.84
326.14 322.04 326.11 323.71    322.96
326.03   321.93 325.98 323.59    322.86
326.10 321.99 326.08 323.66    322.91
326.02   321.91 325.98 323.56    322.93
```

```
/* Program 3.8 continued */

326.15 322.04 326.13 323.69   322.96
326.10  322.00 326.03 323.64    322.91
326.05 321.96 326.02 323.63   322.88
326.07  321.96 326.04 323.61    322.88
326.00 321.90 325.97 323.57   322.84
326.07  321.98 326.04 323.62    322.89
325.96 321.86 325.90 323.51   322.80
326.08  321.98 326.05 323.63    322.88
326.09 321.99 326.06 323.65   322.92
326.06  321.96 326.01 323.61    322.86
326.11 322.01 326.00 323.65   322.93
326.10  321.99 326.06 323.65    322.90
326.12 322.02 326.07 323.67   322.94
326.05  322.11 326.02 323.62    322.87
326.03 321.95 326.00 323.60   322.87
326.07  321.98 326.05 323.62    322.89
326.14 321.95 326.01 323.62   322.89
326.09  322.00 326.06 323.65    322.91
326.04 321.93 326.01 323.60   322.87
326.17  322.08 326.14 323.72    322.99
326.10 321.88 326.07 323.65   322.92
326.02  321.95 326.00 323.59    322.86
326.11 322.02 326.08 323.67   322.94
326.07  321.96 326.04 323.65    322.90
326.07 321.98 326.03 323.62   322.89
;
```

```
/*
proc glm data = calib ;
model  y2tilda y3tilda y4tilda y5tilda = tcbar /nouni;
manova h = tcbar/printe printh;proc glm data = calib ;
*/

proc reg data = calib ;
model  y2tilda y3tilda y4tilda y5tilda = tcbar;
EqualVar:mtest tcbar/print;

proc reg data = calib ;
model  y2tilda y3tilda y4tilda y5tilda = tcbar;
Bias_Var:mtest intercept, tcbar/print;

run;
```

Testing the Precisions of Five Thermocouples
Data from Christensen and Blackwood(1993), Technometrics, 35, 411-420

Multivariate Test: EQUALVAR

E, the Error Matrix

```
 0.0475701116     -0.011049524     -0.009544794     -0.013674773
-0.011049524       0.0129013449     0.0015628105     -0.003486742
-0.009544794       0.0015628105     0.0075360191     -0.0005665
-0.013674773      -0.003486742     -0.0005665        0.0173898899
```

H, the Hypothesis Matrix

```
 0.0036643259      0.0006892739    -0.001983269      -0.002297977
 0.0006892739      0.0001296551    -0.000373061      -0.000432258
-0.001983269      -0.000373061      0.0010734184      0.00124375
-0.002297977      -0.000432258      0.00124375        0.0014411101
```

Multivariate Statistics and Exact F Statistics

S=1   M=1   N=28.5

Statistic	Value	F	Num DF	Den DF	Pr > F
Wilks' Lambda	0.80185427	3.6449	4	59	0.0101
Pillai's Trace	0.19814573	3.6449	4	59	0.0101
Hotelling-Lawley Trace	0.24710940	3.6449	4	59	0.0101
Roy's Greatest Root	0.24710940	3.6449	4	59	0.0101

Output 3.8
Testing the Precisions of Five Thermocouples
Data from Christensen and Blackwood(1993), Technometrics, 35, 411-420

Multivariate Test: BIAS_VAR

E, the Error Matrix

0.0475701116	-0.011049524	-0.009544794	-0.013674773
-0.011049524	0.0129013449	0.0015628105	-0.003486742
-0.009544794	0.0015628105	0.0075360191	-0.0005665
-0.013674773	-0.003486742	-0.0005665	0.0173898899

H, the Hypothesis Matrix

295.33648078	-263.4663775	67.96997654	168.39596614
-263.4663775	235.03968978	-60.63831058	-150.2289007
67.96997654	-60.63831058	15.645075922	38.758738355
168.39596614	-150.2289007	38.758738355	96.021841751

Multivariate Statistics and F Approximations

S=2   M=0.5   N=28.5

Statistic	Value	F	Num DF	Den DF	Pr > F
Wilks' Lambda	0.00001777	3484.124	8	118	0.0001
Pillai's Trace	1.14862594	20.2372	8	120	0.0001
Hotelling-Lawley Trace	47904.335344	347306.4	8	116	0.0001
Roy's Greatest Root	47904.160743	718562.4	4	60	0.0001

NOTE: F Statistic for Roy's Greatest Root is an upper bound.
NOTE: F Statistic for Wilks' Lambda is exact.

CHAPTER 4: Multivariate Analysis of Experimental Data

4.1 Introduction
4.2 Balanced and Unbalanced Data
4.3 One-Way Classification
4.4 Two-Way Classification
4.5 Blocking
4.6 Fractional Factorial Experiments
4.7 Analysis of Covariance

4.1 Introduction

In the previous chapter, we considered the multivariate linear regression model

$$\mathbf{Y} = \mathbf{XB} + \mathcal{E}. \tag{4.1}$$

In the model, the

- n by p matrix $\mathbf{Y}$ contains the random observations on p dependent variables,
- $k + 1$ by p matrix $\mathbf{B}$ is the matrix of unknown parameters,
- n by p matrix $\mathcal{E}$ is the matrix of random errors such that each row of $\mathcal{E}$ is a p variate normal vector with mean vector zero and variance-covariance matrix Σ. The matrix Σ is assumed to be a p by p positive definite matrix.
- n by $k + 1$ matrix $\mathbf{X}$ was assumed to be of full rank, that is, $Rank(\mathbf{X}) = k + 1$.

There are, however, situations especially those involving the analysis of classical experimental designs where the assumption $Rank(\mathbf{X}) = k + 1$ cannot be made. This in turn requires certain suitable modifications in the estimation and testing procedures. In fact, following the same sequence of development as in the previous chapter, a generalized theory has been developed, which contains the results of the previous chapter as the special "full rank" case.

Let us assume that $Rank(\mathbf{X}) = r < k + 1$. It was pointed out in Chapter 3 that in this case, the solution to the normal equations in Equation 3.3 is not unique. If $(\mathbf{X}'\mathbf{X})^-$ is a generalized inverse of $\mathbf{X}'\mathbf{X}$, then correspondingly a least square solution is given by

$$\hat{\mathbf{B}}^{(g)} = (\mathbf{X}'\mathbf{X})^-\mathbf{X}'\mathbf{Y},$$

which will depend on the particular choice of the generalized inverse. As a result, the matrix $\mathbf{B}$ is not (uniquely) estimable. The following example illustrates this case.

*Example 1: Checking Estimability, Jackson's Laboratories Comparison Data
(Jackson, 1991)*

Jackson (1991) considered a situation where samples were tested in three different laboratories using two different methods. Each of the laboratories received four samples and each of the samples was divided into subsamples to be tested by these two methods. As a result, the observations on the subsamples arising out of the same sample are correlated leading to the data as the four bivariate vector observations per laboratory. The data are shown in Table 4.1.

Laboratory	Method 1	Method 2
1	10.1	10.5
	9.3	9.5
	9.7	10.0
	10.9	11.4
2	10.0	9.8
	9.5	9.7
	9.7	9.8
	10.8	10.7
3	11.3	10.1
	10.7	9.8
	10.8	10.1
	10.5	9.6

TABLE 4.1 LABORATORY DATA: J. E. JACKSON (1991)

Let $\mathbf{y}_{ij}$ be the 2 by 1 vector of observation on the jth sample sent to the ith laboratory, $j = 1, .., 4; i = 1, 2, 3$. If we assume that $\mathbf{y}_{ij}$ has a bivariate normal distribution $N_2\left(\begin{bmatrix} \mu_1 + \tau_{i1} \\ \mu_2 + \tau_{i2} \end{bmatrix}, \Sigma\right)$, where Σ represents the variance covariance matrix of two subsample observations, then we can write our model as

$$(y_{ij1}, y_{ij2}) = (\mu + \tau_{i1}, \mu + \tau_{i2}) + (\epsilon_{ij1}, \epsilon_{ij2}),$$
$$i = 1, 2, 3, \; j = 1, .., 4.$$

Stacking these equations one below the other for $j = 1, .., 4$ and (then for) $i = 1, 2, 3$, leads

to

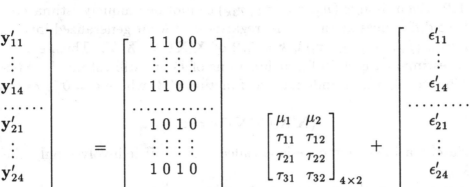

where $\epsilon_{ij} = \begin{pmatrix} \epsilon_{ij1} \\ \epsilon_{ij2} \end{pmatrix}$ represents the sample-to-sample variation. The model represented by the set of equations given above is in the form of Equation 4.1, with

$$X = \begin{bmatrix} 1_4 & 0 & 0 \\ 1_{12} & 0 & 1_4 & 0 \\ & 0 & 0 & 1_4 \end{bmatrix},$$

where 1_q represents a q by 1 vector of unit elements. Since all the elements of X are either zero or one, with zero representing the absence and one representing the presence of the particular parameter in the individual equation, this can be considered as a situation where the regression is performed on the dummy variables. It is easy to see that since the last three columns of the matrix X above add to the first column, the first column is linearly dependent on the last three columns. A similar statement can be made about the linear dependence of any other columns on the remaining three. As a result, the matrix X is not of full column rank. In fact, $Rank\,(X) = 3$, as the last three columns of X form a linearly independent set of vectors. Now as $Rank\,(X'X) = Rank\,(X) = 3$, the 4 by 4 matrix $X'X$ is singular, thereby not admitting the inverse $(X'X)^{-1}$. Therefore the least squares system of linear equations corresponding to Equation 4.1,

$$X'XB = X'Y$$

do not admit a unique solution $\hat{B}$. As a result, for $k = 1, 2$, $(\mu_k, \tau_{1k}, \tau_{2k}, \tau_{3k})$ *cannot* be uniquely estimated.

If we want to estimate the mean measurement for each of the two methods, then the quantities of interest are $\nu_{ik} = \mu_k + \tau_{ik}$, $i = 1, 2, 3$, $k = 1, 2$. We may also be interested in comparing the laboratories, that is, in estimating the differences between the true means for the three laboratories, namely $\nu_{1k} - \nu_{2k} = \tau_{1k} - \tau_{2k}$, $\nu_{1k} - \nu_{3k} = \tau_{1k} - \tau_{3k}$ and $\nu_{2k} - \nu_{3k} =$

$\tau_{2k} - \tau_{3k}$, $k = 1, 2$. Even though $(\mu_k, \tau_{1k}, \tau_{2k}, \tau_{3k})$ cannot be uniquely estimated, the unique estimates of these differences are available, regardless of what generalized inverse is used to obtain the solution $(\hat{\mu}_k, \hat{\tau}_{1k}, \hat{\tau}_{2k}, \hat{\tau}_{3k})$, $k = 1, 2$ of $\mathbf{X}'\mathbf{X}\mathbf{B} = \mathbf{X}'\mathbf{Y}$. Thus, even though the matrix $\mathbf{B}$ is not estimable, certain linear functions of $\mathbf{B}$ are still estimable. Specifically, as mentioned in Chapter 3, a nonrandom linear function $\mathbf{c}'\mathbf{B}$, where $\mathbf{c} \neq \mathbf{0}$ is *estimable* if and only if

$$(\mathbf{X}'\mathbf{X})(\mathbf{X}'\mathbf{X})^{-}\mathbf{c} = \mathbf{c}. \tag{4.2}$$

Quite appropriately, a linear hypothesis is called *testable* if it involves only the estimable functions of $\mathbf{B}$.

For the first laboratory, the vector of mean measurements for each of the two methods (ν_{11}, ν_{12}) is given by

$$(\nu_{11}, \nu_{12}) = (\mu_1 + \tau_{11}, \mu_2 + \tau_{12}) = (1\ 1\ 0\ 0) \begin{bmatrix} \mu_1 & \mu_2 \\ \tau_{11} & \tau_{12} \\ \tau_{21} & \tau_{22} \\ \tau_{31} & \tau_{32} \end{bmatrix} = \mathbf{c}'\mathbf{B},$$

with $\mathbf{c}' = (1\ 1\ 0\ 0)$. The choices of respective $\mathbf{c}'$ vectors for the other two laboratory means are obtained in the same way. These are $(1\ 0\ 1\ 0)$ and $(1\ 0\ 0\ 1)$. Similarly, for the differences between the laboratory means the three choices of $\mathbf{c}$ are

$$\mathbf{c}' = (0\ 1\ -1\ 0), \quad (0\ 1\ 0\ -1), \quad \text{and} \quad (0\ 0\ 1\ -1).$$

It can be theoretically shown (Searle, 1971) that all the above choices of $\mathbf{c}$ satisfy Equation 4.2 and hence all the laboratory means and their pairwise differences are estimable. It is equivalent to saying that all of the above choices of $\mathbf{c}'$ can be expressed as the linear function of the rows of $\mathbf{X}$. That this is true in our example is easily verified by the visual examination of the rows of our matrix $\mathbf{X}$. The actual rank of the matrix $\mathbf{X}$ would depend on the particular design and the particular statistical model. For a one-way classification model with k groups, the rank of $\mathbf{X}_{n \times (k+1)}$ is k. This deficiency in rank of $\mathbf{X}$ affects the tests for the statistical significance in many ways. First of all, such tests can be performed only for the testable linear hypotheses. That given, all the univariate and multivariate tests can still be adopted after making a simple yet important modification. When the hypothesis is linear, the quantity $r = Rank(\mathbf{X})$ replaces $(k+1)$ in most formulas of Chapter 3.

4.2 Balanced and Unbalanced Data

When the design is balanced in the sense that each group has the same number of measurements or certain orthogonality conditions are met (Searle, 1971), the analysis is relatively much simpler with respect to the computations as well as interpretations. In this case for a given response variable, the (univariate) ANOVA partitioning of the corrected total sums of squares into various sources of variation specified by the model is unique. This simplicity is unfortunately lost as soon as the underlying design becomes unbalanced. The partitioning of the corrected total sums of squares is no longer unique in that it depends on the model and the various submodels of it as specified by the order in which various sums of squares are extracted. For example, suppose we have an unbalanced (univariate) two-way classification design with interaction, for which the statistical model is

$$y_{ijk} = \mu + \alpha_i + \beta_j + (\alpha\beta)_{ij} + \epsilon_{ijk}$$
$$i = 1,\dots,a; \ j = 1,\dots,b; \ k = 1,\dots, n_{ij}.$$

Denoting the main effects as A and B and the interaction effect as AB, the corrected model sum of squares $R(A, B, AB|\mu)$ can be partitioned in the following two alternative ways:

$$R(A, B, AB|\mu) = R(A|\mu) + R(B|\mu, A) + R(AB|\mu, A, B) \qquad (4.3)$$

or

$$R(A, B, AB|\mu) = R(B|\mu) + R(A|\mu, B) + R(AB|\mu, A, B), \qquad (4.4)$$

where $R(A|\mu)$ is the sum of squares due to A after correcting for μ, and $R(B|\mu, A)$ is the sum of squares due to B after correcting for μ and the variable A (i.e., after discounting the effect of A). Other quantities are similarly defined. Unless the design is balanced, $R(B|\mu, A) \neq R(B|\mu)$ and $R(A|\mu, B) \neq R(A|\mu)$. The complexity increases further for the higher order unbalanced designs. As a result, SAS computes the four types of sums of squares, commonly referred to as Type I through Type IV sums of squares. A brief summary of these four sums of squares, from Littell, Freund and Spector (1991) follows.

- The Type I sums of squares represent a partitioning of the model sum of squares into component sums of squares due to each variable or interaction as it is added sequentially to the model in the order prescribed by the MODEL statement. They are often referred to as sequential sums of squares. In view of their dependence on the order prescribed the corresponding partitioning of the model sum of squares is not unique. For example, for a three-way classification model with all possible interactions in variables A, B, and C the MODEL statement

```
model y = a b c a*b a*c b*c a*b*c/ss1 ss2 ss3 ss4;
```

results in the Type I sum of squares (generated by the use of option SS1) for, say, A*C as the one which is adjusted for all the previous terms in the model: A, B, C, and A*B.

- The Type II sums of squares for a particular variable represent the increase in the model sum of squares. This increase is due to adding the particular variable or interaction to a model that already contains all the other variables *and* interactions in the MODEL statement which do not *notationally* contain the particular variable or interaction. For example, for the MODEL statement given above, the Type II sums of squares for A*C represents the increase in the model sum of squares by adding A*C while A, B, C, A*B, and B*C have already been included in the model. The three-factor interaction is not included in this because the notational symbol A*B*C contains the symbol A*C. Type II sums of squares do not depend on the order in which the variables and interactions are listed in the MODEL statement. In general, Type II sums of squares for various variables and interactions do not add up to the model sum of squares. Type II sums of squares are commonly called partial sums of squares.

- The Type III sums of squares are also a kind of partial sums of squares. They differ from Type II sums of squares in that a particular sum of squares represents increase in the model sum of squares due to adding the particular variable or interaction to a model that contains all the other variables and interactions listed in the MODEL statement. For example, for the MODEL statement given above the Type III sums of squares for A*C represents the increase in the model sum of squares by adding A*C while all the remaining terms in the right-hand side of the MODEL statement, A, B, C, A*B, B*C, and A*B*C, have already been included in the model. As in the case of Type II, Type III sums of squares also do not depend on the order in which the variables and interactions are listed in the MODEL statement. Further, in general Type III sums of squares for various variables and interactions do not add up to the model sum of squares.

- The Type IV sums of squares were designed primarily for situations where there are empty cells. Unfortunately, they can be discussed only in the general framework of estimable functions and their constructions. For cross-classified unbalanced data, these are not unique when there are empty cells in that they depend on the way the data may have been arranged. When there are no empty cells, Type IV sums of squares are identical to Type III sums of squares. For details, see the *SAS/STAT User's Guide, Version 6, Fourth Edition*, Littell, Freund and Spector (1991), and Milliken and Johnson (1991).

For multivariate analysis purposes, when the data are multivariate in nature we analogously define the sums of squares and crossproducts (SS&CP) matrices rather than just the sums of squares. The partitioning that is essentially similar to ANOVA partitioning, called in the literature MANOVA partitioning (M for multivariate), can be done for the corrected total SS&CP matrix. As is true in the univariate case, we will encounter problems related to the nonuniqueness of this partitioning for the unbalanced data. Needless to say, the interpretations similar to those mentioned in the references given above can be assigned to various types of analyses to help in choosing the appropriate MANOVA partitioning and/or analysis.

Based on Milliken and Johnson (1991) we make the following recommendations for two-way classification models. For most higher order models, a straightforward modification of these recommendations will be applicable, in most situations.

- Type III SS&CP matrices are appropriate when the interest is in comparing the effects of the experimental variables. The corresponding null hypotheses are equivalent to the hypotheses tested in the balanced classifications. Specifically, the hypotheses being tested are

$$i. \quad \alpha_i + b^{-1} \sum_{j=1}^{b} (\alpha\beta)_{ij} \quad \text{are all equal, } i = 1, \ldots, a.$$

$$ii. \quad \beta_j + a^{-1} \sum_{i=1}^{a} (\alpha\beta)_{ij} \quad \text{are all equal, } j = 1, \ldots, b.$$

$$iii. \quad (\alpha\beta)_{i'j'} - b^{-1} \sum_{j=1}^{b} (\alpha\beta)_{i'j} - a^{-1} \sum_{i=1}^{a} (\alpha\beta)_{ij'} + (ab)^{-1} \sum_{i=1}^{a} \sum_{j=1}^{b} (\alpha\beta)_{ij} = 0$$

$$\text{for all } i' = 1, \ldots, a; \; j' = 1, \ldots, b.$$

- For model-building purposes such as in response surface modeling, where we want to predict the responses, Type I and/or Type II SS&CP is desirable. Usually, since the terms are to be added sequentially in the process of model building, Type I analysis may be more appropriate.

- In survey designs and observational studies such as in sociology, where the data are collected "passively," rather than "actively" generated under a designed experiment, the number of observations per cell will be approximately proportional to the actual relative frequencies of these cells in the reference population. As a result, the weighted averages with observed cell sizes as weights may be of interest in the course of analyzing the data. In this case, it is advisable to attempt and carefully interpret the two possible sequential analyses using Type I SS&CP leading to the partitioning given by Equations 4.3 and 4.4. Of course, the three-way or other higher order cross-classified designs would require several sequential analyses.

Remember that underlying any test statistic or significant effect as shown in any computer output, there is a specific statement in the null hypothesis which is being tested. In the case of designed experiments, the cell sizes are determined by the experimenter or by certain circumstances which are beyond the control of the experimenter. The effects, significant or not, are the characteristics of the reference population and in no way should be a function of the design parameters such as the cell sizes. It makes no intuitive sense that a null hypothesis would involve these parameters of the particular design. It is, therefore, very important that any appropriate null hypothesis is *a priori* identified before declaring an effect significant or nonsignificant rather than retroactively identifying what the hypothesis is, corresponding to a significant or nonsignificant p value associated with a particular test statistic. In fact, in the case of highly unbalanced designs, the SS&CP matrices for the *notationally same* effects (in the computer output) under Type I, II, or III analyses may correspond to very different null hypotheses. Not surprisingly, one often obtains mutually conflicting conclusions from these analyses. Of course, the best solution to this problem is to construct a design which is as balanced as possible.

The issues related to which of the three sums of squares is appropriate have been the subject of considerable discussion for the past several years. See Goodnight (1976) and Searle (1987). These issues do not seem to have subsided or been adequately settled or clarified as evident from the recent contributions to this topic. See Dallal (1992), De Long (1994), Goldstein (1994) and Searle (1994). It is thus inevitable not to find a consensus on various modes of analyses considered in the specific examples in this book. Wherever possible, we attempt to intuitively justify the type of analysis chosen, while at the same time deliberately avoiding the complex notational and mathematical representations of the underlying hypotheses.

Type IV analysis is appropriate in the case of missing observations when, for certain cells, the cell frequency is zero. In this case, none of the Type I, II, or III analyses may be entirely satisfactory, and may be difficult to interpret. The Type IV hypotheses are constructed to have balance in the cell mean coefficients in such cases. As a result, meaningful interpretations can be assigned to the underlying hypotheses being tested by these SS&CP matrices. For designs with missing observations, PROC GLM automatically generates certain Type IV hypotheses which can be identified by examining the list of estimable functions generated by SAS under the given design. Unfortunately, the resulting hypotheses being tested may themselves depend on the numbering of the variables. Consequently, the very same set of treatments in the same data set, if renumbered or reordered, may result in a different set of Type IV SS&CP matrices. See Milliken and Johnson (1991) for an especially readable discussion in which the authors devote an entire chapter to these and other related issues, of course in an univariate setting.

The preceding discussion about the unbalanced designs pertains only to the cases where there are an unequal number of observations per cell or where balancedness conditions (Searle, 1971) on the cell sizes are not satisfied. Imbalance may also occur in cases when, for some observations or experiments, the data are available only on some of the response variables and not available on the others. This situation, although quite common in practice, cannot be handled in the standard multivariate analysis of variance setup. As a result, for any multivariate analysis procedure, observations with missing values for one or more response variables are automatically deleted by SAS before any analysis.

4.3 One-Way Classification

In the previous section, we considered an interlaboratory study where four bivariate observations corresponding to two different methods were made in three different laboratories. The purpose of the study was to compare the three laboratories and decide if these laboratories provide, on the average, the same bivariate measurements. The three groups or classes of interest were three laboratories, which define a categorical variable (or factor) with three levels represented by these laboratories. In general, a one-way classification model can be defined for a variable with a levels or groups. If we denote by $\mathbf{y}_{ij}$, the p by 1 vector of responses on the jth unit of the ith group, then we can write

$$\mathbf{y}_{ij} = \mu + \tau_i + \epsilon_{ij}, \ j = 1, \ldots, n_i; \ i = 1, \ldots, a,$$

where ϵ_{ij} is the p by 1 random vector corresponding to error, and is assumed to have a zero vector as the mean and the variance-covariance matrix Σ. The surplus or slack effect of the ith group is represented by the p by 1 vector τ_i and the p by 1 vector μ is the overall mean. The n_i is the number of observations in the ith group. If $n_1 = \ldots = n_a$, then the design is balanced. A usual assumption, though not crucial but only convenient, is to take $\sum_{i=1}^{a} n_i \tau_i = 0$. In fact, any other linear restriction on $\tau_1, \ldots, \tau_a$ can be used instead so long as it provides an additional equation which is linearly independent of the system of normal equations given in Equation 3.3. The purpose of making such an assumption is to devise a convenient method to find an appropriate generalized inverse of $\mathbf{X'X}$, where $\mathbf{X}$ is the corresponding design matrix when the above model is represented as a multivariate linear model given in Equation 3.1. In fact, PROC GLM makes the alternative assumption of $\tau_a = 0$ rather than the traditional assumption of $\Sigma_{i=1}^{a} n_i \tau_i = 0$ adopted by various multivariate analysis and experimental design books.

As mentioned earlier, since the choice of the generalized inverse is immaterial when estimating an estimable linear function or performing a testable linear hypothesis, what linear restriction is placed on τ_i does not affect the subsequent analysis in any way. Since for a one-way classification model $Rank\,(\mathbf{X}_{n \times (a+1)}) = a$, the rank of $\mathbf{X}$ is short only by one. As a result, only one linear restriction on τ_i is needed. For the higher order classifications, the number of linearly independent restrictions needed is equal to the rank deficiency of $\mathbf{X}$.

To test the multivariate null hypothesis of no differences in the group means, that is, $H_0 : \tau_1 = \tau_2 = \ldots = \tau_a$, it is possible to use any of the four multivariate tests described in Chapter 3, after making the appropriate modifications in the degrees of freedom. Specifically, the quantity $(a+1)$ (which was $(k+1)$ in the notation of Chapter 3), which was the rank of $\mathbf{X}$ in the full rank model of Chapter 3, would be replaced by a, the actual rank of the matrix $\mathbf{X}$.

Example 1: Hypothesis Testing, Laboratories Comparison Data (continued)

We return to the Jackson's (1991) data as presented in Table 4.1. The objective of simultaneously comparing the three laboratories translates to the bivariate null hypothesis,

$$H_0 : \quad \tau_1 = \tau_2 = \tau_3$$

against the alternative

$$H_1 : \quad \text{At least two } \tau_i \text{ are different from each other.}$$

The null hypothesis is testable, as seen earlier, and the four different multivariate tests, namely Wilks' Λ, Pillai's trace, Hotelling-Lawley's trace, and Roy's maximum root test, are available to test H_0. Further, the design is balanced with no missing values and hence the four types of analyses are equivalent, all resulting in identical SS&CP matrices (in fact, for one-way classification, this is true even for unbalanced data). The SAS code to do this analysis is presented in Program 4.1.

The independent variable which defines the classification is denoted by LAB and the two methods specified as METHOD1 and METHOD2 are the dependent variables. We perform the analysis using PROC GLM. The MANOVA statement performs multivariate analysis. It is important that the variable LAB is specified in the CLASS statement. This enables SAS to create the appropriate **X** matrix. We could have used any other numeric or nonnumeric coding for the values taken by the class variable LAB, since classification variables can be either character or numeric.

To test the null hypothesis, it suffices to indicate the variable LAB as H=LAB in the MANOVA statement. The PRINTE and PRINTH options enable us to print the SS&CP matrices corresponding to the error and the null hypothesis H_0. We could have also specified the type of SS&CP matrices to be used in the analysis in the MODEL statement but since the four types of analyses are identical in this case, it is not necessary to specify one type over another. As a result, SAS uses the default, Type III analysis.

For the present data set, the number of data points $n = 12$ and the number of dependent variables $p = 2$. The null hypothesis can be written as

$$H_0 : \begin{bmatrix} 0 & 1 & -1 & 0 \\ 0 & 1 & 0 & -1 \end{bmatrix} \begin{bmatrix} \mu \\ \tau_1 \\ \tau_2 \\ \tau_3 \end{bmatrix} = 0 \quad \text{or} \quad \mathbf{LB = 0}$$

and since the left-most matrix in H_0, that is **L**, has rank 2, the value of $r = Rank(\mathbf{L}) = 2$ (see Table 3.2). The four test statistics corresponding to the null hypothesis are shown in Output 4.1. Recall that according to Table 3.3, the transformation of Wilks' Λ to F statistic is exact, since $p = 2$ here. As a result,

$$F = \left(\frac{n - k - 1}{r} \right) \cdot \left(\frac{1 - \sqrt{\Lambda}}{\sqrt{\Lambda}} \right) = \left(\frac{12 - 3 - 1}{2} \right) \left(\frac{1 - \sqrt{\Lambda}}{\sqrt{\Lambda}} \right) = \frac{8}{2} \left(\frac{1 - \sqrt{\Lambda}}{\sqrt{\Lambda}} \right)$$

follows an F (4, 16) distribution. Corresponding to the observed value of F = 11.1299 with df (4,16), the p value is 0.0002. Consequently, we conclude that there is sufficient evidence against H_0 and that there is a significant difference between the laboratories. We reach essentially the same conclusions under the other three test criteria. The output also presents the corresponding SS&CP matrices for error and the hypothesis as results of PRINTE and PRINTH options in the the MANOVA statement. These were respectively denoted by **E** and **H** in the previous chapter.

Example 2: An Unbalanced One-Way Classification, Diabetic Patients Study Data (Crowder and Hand, 1990)

Crowder and Hand (1990, p. 8) provided this example of unbalanced data. Two groups of subjects, an eight-member normal control group and a six-member group of diabetic patients without complications, were to be compared as part of a medical experiment. The subjects performed a small physical task, and the measurements were recorded on each of the subjects during various subsequent time points. The data in Table 4.2 are these measurements after one minute, five minutes, and ten minutes after performing the task. The question of interest concerns differences between the two groups. In other words, we want to investigate if the two groups differ from each other in their abilities to perform the specified physical task.

		Time		
	Subject	1	5	10
Group 1	1	7.6	8.7	7.0
	2	10.1	8.9	8.6
	3	11.2	9.5	9.4
	4	10.8	11.5	11.4
	5	3.9	4.1	3.7
	6	6.7	7.3	6.6
	7	2.2	2.5	2.4
	8	2.1	2.0	2.0
Group 2	9	8.5	5.6	8.4
	10	7.5	5.0	9.5
	11	12.9	13.6	15.3
	12	8.8	7.9	7.3
	13	5.5	6.4	6.4
	14	3.2	3.4	3.2

TABLE 4.2 EFFECT OF A PHYSICAL TASK ON HOSPITAL PATIENTS: CROWDER AND HAND (1990, p. 8)

This one-way classification data has GROUP as the CLASS variable. On each of the 14 subjects, a trivariate vector of data representing the three measurements at one, five, and ten minutes after performing the physical task, is available. If the respective population mean vectors for the two groups on these measurements are represented as $\mu^{(1)} = \mu + \tau_1$ and $\mu^{(2)} = \mu + \tau_2$, then the matrix $\mathbf{B}$ of regression coefficients can be written as

$$\mathbf{B}_{3 \times 3} = \begin{bmatrix} \mu' \\ \tau_1' \\ \tau_2' \end{bmatrix}.$$

To test the equality of the treatment effects (that is, the two groups' abilities to complete the specified physical task) between the two groups for all the three time points, the null hypothesis is

$$H_0: \quad [0\ 1\ -1] \begin{bmatrix} \mu_1 & \mu_2 & \mu_3 \\ \tau_{11} & \tau_{12} & \tau_{13} \\ \tau_{21} & \tau_{22} & \tau_{23} \end{bmatrix} = \mathbf{0}$$

that is,

$$H_0: \mathbf{LB} = \mathbf{0},$$

which can be tested as in Example 1. However, in the present context a more realistic hypothesis may be to test that the amount of change in measurements from one minute to five minutes is equal for the two groups and that the change between the five minutes and ten minutes is equal for the two groups. These can be represented as

$$H_0: \quad [0\ 1\ -1] \begin{bmatrix} \mu_1 & \mu_2 & \mu_3 \\ \tau_{11} & \tau_{12} & \tau_{13} \\ \tau_{21} & \tau_{22} & \tau_{23} \end{bmatrix} \begin{bmatrix} 1 & 0 \\ -1 & 1 \\ 0 & -1 \end{bmatrix} = \mathbf{0}$$

or,

$$H_0: \mathbf{LBM} = \mathbf{0} \tag{4.5}$$

with $\mathbf{L} = (0\ 1\ -1)$, and $\mathbf{M} = \begin{bmatrix} 1 & 0 \\ -1 & 1 \\ 0 & -1 \end{bmatrix}$.

The above representation deserves some further explanation. Let us first premultiply $\mathbf{B}$ to $\mathbf{M}$, resulting in

$$\mathbf{BM} = \begin{bmatrix} \mu_1 - \mu_2 & \mu_2 - \mu_3 \\ \tau_{11} - \tau_{12} & \tau_{12} - \tau_{13} \\ \tau_{21} - \tau_{22} & \tau_{22} - \tau_{23} \end{bmatrix}.$$

The entries in the first row of the above matrix represent the successive differences in the intercept or the overall mean for the three time points. The second row represents the successive treatment differences for Group 1 and the third row represents the same for Group 2. Since we want to compare these differences for the two groups, this is accomplished by premultiplying $\mathbf{BM}$ by $\mathbf{L} = (0\ 1\ -1)$ and equating the product to zero. This results in the simplification of $H_0: \mathbf{LBM} = \mathbf{0}$ to

$$H_0: \begin{bmatrix} (\tau_{11}-\tau_{12}) & - & (\tau_{21}-\tau_{22}) \\ (\tau_{12}-\tau_{13}) & - & (\tau_{22}-\tau_{23}) \end{bmatrix}' = \begin{bmatrix} 0 \\ 0 \end{bmatrix}'.$$

The choices of either $\mathbf{L}$ or $\mathbf{M}$ indicated here are not unique. For example, $\mathbf{L} = (0\ -1\ 1)$ and $\mathbf{M} = \begin{bmatrix} 1 & 1 \\ -1 & 0 \\ 0 & -1 \end{bmatrix}$ are the other equally legitimate choices for $\mathbf{L}$ and $\mathbf{M}$. The tests for the hypotheses of the type $H_0: \mathbf{LBM} = \mathbf{0}$ were described in Chapter 3. In SAS, this objective is attained by specifying the $\mathbf{M}$ matrix in the MANOVA statement. SAS automatically identifies the corresponding $\mathbf{L}$ matrix from the specification H = GROUP.

The **M** matrix can be specified using one of the two different yet equivalent ways. We can either explicitly specify all the entries of **M** in the M= specification of the MANOVA statement as

$$m = (1 \ -1 \ 0,$$
$$0 \ 1 \ -1);$$

or ask SAS to create it so as to correspond to the measurement differences of interest. The latter is achieved by using the algebraic statements which, in the present context, are

```
m = min1 - min5,
    min5 - min10;
```

where MIN1, MIN5, and MIN10 were the names assigned in Program 4.2 to the measurements at 1, 5, and 10 minutes after performing the physical task. It may also be pointed out that when using the former choice, the assignment is column after column separated by commas. Similarly, when the respective columns are written in different lines of the program, the matrix in the SAS code may visually resemble **M'** and not **M**. In Program 4.2, we have used the latter alternative.

Suppose, in addition, that we are also interested in testing the null hypothesis that the changes with respect to time in the levels of overall means (intercepts) are zero. This amounts to testing $H_0 : \mu_1 = \mu_2 = \mu_3$ or

$$H_0 : \quad \begin{bmatrix} \mu_1 - \mu_2 \\ \mu_2 - \mu_3 \end{bmatrix} = \mathbf{0}. \tag{4.6}$$

With the choice of **M** the same as earlier and **L** = (1 0 0), this hypothesis also reduces to the form $H_0 : \mathbf{LBM} = \mathbf{0}$. As earlier, the corresponding **M** will be specified through the M= specification of the MANOVA statement. However, the choice of **L** in this case is specified by indicating H = INTERCEPT.

The null hypotheses in Equations 4.5 and 4.6 are tested using Program 4.2. Output 4.2 presents portions of the resulting output. We use the default Type III analysis since all the four types of analyses are identical in this case.

In both the cases, since **L** is a nonzero row vector, it is of rank 1. Consequently, all four multivariate test criteria lead to an exact and identical F test statistic. For the hypothesis in Equation 4.5, the p value corresponding to the test statistic is 0.0979, which indicates that there is some evidence, though it is not very strong, against the null hypothesis. However, with respect to the null hypothesis in Equation 4.6, there is not enough evidence to reject H_0 (p value=0.4709) and hence we conclude that levels of overall mean are the same for the three periods.

Certain other ways of analyzing repeated measures data are discussed in Chapter 5.

4.4 Two-Way Classification

In one-way classification models, the interest is in comparing the treatment effects which correspond to a single variable. When there are two variables, say A and B, various treatments are obtained by combining the various levels of variable A with those of variable B. If A is at a different levels and B is at b levels, then assuming that all possible levels of A can be attempted with those of B, the experiment consists of ab treatment combinations. In such a case, we say that A and B are *crossed* with each other, and the design is often referred to as a two-way classification. If each ab treatment is tried an equal numbers of times, then the resulting design is balanced. Such designs usually lead to a simpler analysis in that the corrected total SS&CP matrix has a unique partitioning: the SS&CP matrices corresponding to variables A and B, the interaction AB, and the error. In fact, this same uniqueness of partitioning can be ensured if r_{ij}, the number of observations in the $(i, j)^{th}$ cell, that is, corresponding to the ith level of variable A and the jth level of variable B, $i = 1, \ldots, a$, $j = 1, \ldots, b$ is such that

$$r_{ij} = \frac{r_i . r_{.j}}{r_{..}},$$

where

$$r_{i.} = \sum_{j=1}^{b} r_{ij}, \quad r_{.j} = \sum_{i=1}^{a} r_{ij}, \quad \text{and} \quad r_{..} = \sum_{i=1}^{a} r_{i.} = \sum_{j=1}^{b} r_{.j}.$$

Example 3: A Balanced Two-Way Classification, Weight Loss in Mice (Morrison, 1976)

Morrison (1976, p. 190) presented a two-way classification study to compare the loss in weights of male and female mice under three different drugs. Four mice of each sex were randomly assigned to each of the three drugs and weight losses were measured at the end of the first and second weeks. The resulting bivariate data correspond to a balanced two-way classification with interaction:

$$\mathbf{y}_{ijk} = \mu + \alpha_i + \beta_j + (\alpha\beta)_{ij} + \epsilon_{ijk}$$
$$i = 1, 2, \quad j = 1, 2, 3, \quad k = 1, 2, 3, 4,$$

where suffix i indicates the particular level of variable SEX, and j indicates the particular level of variable DRUG.

The purpose in this example is to test the significance of the effects of SEX, the effects of DRUG, and their interaction. Program 4.3 provides the needed SAS code. The output is presented as Output 4.3.

The MANOVA statement in the program asks for the individual multivariate testing for the variables SEX, DRUG, and the interaction SEX*DRUG. The PRINTE and PRINTH options are used to print the resulting SS&CP matrices corresponding to the error and the particular hypotheses in each of the three tests.

We discuss the test for the interaction first. Note that the same SS&CP matrix $\mathbf{E}$ for error will be used for the tests for main effects as well, unless the model is modified. Here

$$\mathbf{E} = \begin{bmatrix} 94.5 & 76.5 \\ 76.5 & 114.0 \end{bmatrix}.$$

The SS&CP matrix corresponding to the hypothesis of no interaction is

$$\mathbf{H}_{int} = \begin{bmatrix} 14.3333 & 21.3333 \\ 21.3333 & 32.3333 \end{bmatrix}.$$

As a result, Wilks' Λ is computed as $\Lambda_{int} = \frac{|\mathbf{E}|}{|\mathbf{E}+\mathbf{H}_{int}|} = 0.7744$. From Table 3.3, $F_{int} = \frac{17}{2}\{\frac{1-\sqrt{0.7744}}{\sqrt{0.7744}}\} = 1.1593$ is the observed value from an F(4, 34) distribution. As the corresponding p value $= 0.3459$ is quite large, we accept the hypothesis of no interaction between the variables SEX and DRUG. Other test statistics were calculated using the corresponding formulas, and their respective p values also support this conclusion. As a result, it may be assumed that an additive model for SEX and DRUG is valid.

In the absence of possible interaction, we may want to perform tests of significance on the main variables. A similar calculation provides for variable SEX: $\Lambda_{sex} = 0.9925$, $F_{sex} = 0.0639$ with $df = (2, 17)$ (p value $= 0.9383$) and for variable DRUG: $\Lambda_{drug} = 0.1686$, $F_{drug} = 12.1991$ with $df = (4, 34)$ (p value $= 0.0001$). As a result, we conclude that the variable DRUG has a significant effect on weight loss, but the sex of the rats does not play any important role, that is, rats of either sex lost weight in the same way.

When the design is not balanced, the partitioning of corrected total SS&CP is not unique. This issue has already been addressed in Section 4.2. As mentioned earlier, for most comparison purposes, when the variables are being treated as categorical, and the purpose is merely to compare or identify treatment effects, Type III analysis can be adopted. However, for model-building purposes, where we are implicitly performing a selection of variables analyses to obtain an appropriate model, the analysis using the sequential sums of squares and crossproducts (Type I) may be appropriate.

The following example with unbalanced data provides an illustration.

Example 4: Optimization of Uniformity and Selectivity in Etching Process

In manufacturing in the integrated circuit industry, the process must etch layers uniformly across the wafers. This study investigated whether pressure (PRESS) and power (POWER) are the two main explanatory variables which considerably affect various response variables. The list of response variables includes the uniformity of the etching of the two layers (UNIF1 and UNIF2) and the selectivity (SELECT), which is defined as the ratio of the etch rates of the two layers. The problems in this example are first to see the effects of PRESS and POWER on the response variables indicated above and second to fit a model for the three response variables in terms of the variables PRESS and POWER and possibly their interaction. Observations at each of two levels of POWER (240 and 290 watts) and three levels of PRESS (90, 110 and 130 torr) were made with a total of 15 observations leading to an unbalanced design. Three different response variables were observed in each of these 15 experiments. The data are shown as part of Program 4.4. For each of the fifteen experiments, as the three responses have resulted from the same experiment and are taken on the same wafer, they will be correlated and hence the three separate univariate analyses may give misleading results. It seems logical to perform a multivariate analysis of variance to draw meaningful results. In addition, since we also want to find a suitable choice of the levels of POWER and PRESS, to optimize the three responses, we also want to find suitable regression models for the uniformity of the two etches and the selectivity. Here a Type I analysis seems more appropriate than Type III; the three analyses are not going to be identical since the design under consideration is not balanced.

It is possible that the variable PRESS may be more influential than the variable POWER. This possibility indicates that, in the right-hand side of MODEL statement, PRESS should precede POWER and their interaction. To obtain a Type I analysis, we use the following sequential SS&CP partitioning. See Equations 4.3 and 4.4 for notations.

$$R(PRESS, POWER, PRESS*POWER|INTERCEPT)$$
$$= R(PRESS|INTERCEPT) + R(POWER|INTERCEPT, PRESS)$$
$$+ R(PRESS*POWER|INTERCEPT, PRESS, POWER).$$

In Program 4.4, we ask for all the three types of analyses, namely Types I, II, and III. The appropriate SS&CP matrices computed by the statement:

```
manova h = press power press*power/printe printh;
```

for various hypotheses are indicated below. We have used the same notations as in Equations 4.3 and 4.4, with the understanding that the corresponding values are SS&CP matrices and not just the sums of squares.

$Type I$: $R(PRESS|INTERCEPT)$, $R(POWER|INTERCEPT, PRESS)$,
$R(PRESS*POWER|INTERCEPT, PRESS, POWER)$, Error SS&CP.

$Type II$: $R(PRESS|INTERCEPT, POWER)$, $R(POWER|INTERCEPT, PRESS)$,
$R(PRESS*POWER|INTERCEPT, PRESS, POWER)$, Error SS&CP.

$Type III$: $R(PRESS|INTERCEPT, POWER, PRESS*POWER)$,
$R(POWER|INTERCEPT, PRESS \, PRESS*POWER)$,
$R(PRESS*POWER|INTERCEPT, PRESS, POWER)$, Error SS&CP.

The results of Program 4.4 appear in Output 4.4. Since PRESS may play a more important role than POWER, and hence if possible should be included in the model when fitting a response surface, we examine the Type I analysis next. We first consider the interaction term for testing. It is so because a significant interaction causes the main effect tests to be meaningless. After discounting for the effects of PRESS and POWER, we find that the interaction PRESS*POWER is not significant. The p value for Wilks' Λ is 0.3605. The other multivariate tests also provide comparable p values and similar conclusions. We therefore look sequentially at the statistical significance of the main effect PRESS and then POWER after discounting for PRESS.

The analysis shows that the variable PRESS is highly significant with the corresponding calculated value of $F(3, 7)=264.6643$ under all four criteria. These tests are all equivalent for PRESS but not for POWER and PRESS*POWER. This is so since the rank of the corresponding $\mathbf{L}$ matrix is 1 for PRESS whereas it is 2 for the other two hypotheses. The corresponding p values are all very small. For POWER, significance is observed but only marginally. For example, corresponding to Wilks' test the p value is 0.0477. Note that the test for the variable POWER was performed after discounting for the effect of PRESS. As a result, we conclude that the variable POWER also has some effect on the response variables. It may be pointed out that these conclusions are further supported by Type II as well as Type III analyses outputs, which are not included here.

Since our present goal is to predict the optimum combination of PRESS and POWER, both of which are the continuous variables, we obtain the appropriate response surface models by examining the importance of various terms in the model. We thus transform PRESS and POWER as $x_1 = (PRESS - 265)/25$ and $x_2 = (POWER - 110)/20$. Since PRESS is at two levels and POWER at three, only the following terms can be included in the model:

$$X1 = x_1, \; X2 = x_2, \; X2SQ = x_2^2, \; X1X2 = x_1 x_2, \text{ and } X1X2SQ = x_1 x_2^2.$$

However, since we have already found the interaction PRESS*POWER to be nonsignificant, we may not want to include the terms $x_1 x_2$ and $x_1 x_2^2$ in the model. As a result, for the three response variables we simultaneously fit three models with x_1, x_2, and x_2^2 as the independent variables. As earlier, we rely primarily on the Type I analysis, with the sequence of the terms as specified. Since in regression modeling the quadratic effect x_2^2 is treated as a new variable and not as a function of x_2, the Type I and Type II SS&CP matrices and the corresponding test statistics for x_2^2 are identical.

Output 4.4 shows the result of testing various hypotheses under Type I analysis. All four multivariate tests are equivalent in this case. In view of the small p value ($=0.0001$) for the tests on x_1 (PRESS), it is important. Even after discounting the effect of PRESS, the variable POWER represented by x_2 is also significant with p value $= 0.0092$. The quadratic effect of POWER, however, is not significant as evident from the large p value ($=0.6231$) for x_2^2. Note that a significant effect obtained through a multivariate analysis does not necessarily imply that the effect is significant for each response variable. The conclusions drawn from a univariate analysis for an individual response variable may or may not be in complete agreement with those derived by performing a multivariate analysis of all the response variables collectively. This is true also in the present example where it can be verified in univariate significance testing that none of the three variables x_1, x_2, and x_2^2 appear to have any significant effect on selectivity.

4.5 Blocking

In order to remove the additional variability in the data due to other external sources, blocking is often desired. Likewise, if the external variability is present due to two independent sources or in two orthogonal directions, two-way blocking using the Latin square design is often used. If the data are available for all the cells in the Latin square, the orthogonality of the two blocking variables and the treatment is automatically accomplished. Hence the Type I, II, III, and IV analyses are identical. A problem, however, occurs if the data are not available for certain cells or the blocks are of unequal size. The question in that case is, which analysis is appropriate? As the treatments are to be compared only after eliminating the effects due to blocking variables, the Type I analysis is clearly the appropriate choice with the treatment variables listed after the blocking variables (in an appropriate sequence) in the MODEL statement of PROC GLM. As an illustration, see the following example, where data are collected under a Latin square design setup for all the cells except two.

Example 5: Experiments in Blocks, Comparison of Corn Varieties
(Srivastava and Carter, 1983)

We consider a part of the data from Srivastava and Carter (1983, p. 107), where a certain area of land was used for testing four varieties of corn represented by four levels of the variable VARIETY. Due to the slope of the land, differences from north to south (NS) and from east to west (EW) were possible. As a result, the experiment was conducted using a Latin square design with the corresponding layout given in Table 4.3.

Note that for our analysis the experiments corresponding to A_3B_2 and A_4B_4 are not included in Table 4.3, so the design is unbalanced. For each experiment, two characteristics, namely the height of the plant (HEIGHT) and the yield (YIELD), were measured. Thus, the additive bivariate model ($p = 2$) containing the variable VARIETY as well as the two blocking variables NS and EW will be fitted for the response variables HEIGHT and YIELD.

As indicated earlier, sequential MANOVA partitioning (Type I) is used to adjust the treatment SS&CP matrix for the block effects. The corresponding MODEL statement is

```
model height yield = ew ns variety/ss1;
```

An alternative is to use the SS3 option instead of SS1 to get all the SS&CP matrices adjusted for all the remaining terms in the right side of the MODEL statement. However, if in the MODEL statement given above, VARIETY was specified before NS and EW, then SS3 and not SS1 would be the correct option since under the SS1 option, the SS&CP matrix for variety would be adjusted only for the intercept.

				East	-	*West*	
				A1	A2	A3	A4
		B1	Variety	C2	C3	C4	C1
			Height	65	68	67	68
			Yield	24	21	26	27
		B2	Variety	C3	C2	–	C3
			Height	66	63	–	67
			Yield	20	23	–	24
North – South		B3	Variety	C1	C4	C2	C3
			Height	65	67	64	63
			Yield	24	25	19	20
		B4	Variety	C4	C1	C3	–
			Height	65	64	64	–
			Yield	26	25	25	–

TABLE 4.3 DATA ON CORN YIELD AND PLANT HEIGHT

Therefore, since the MODEL statement in Program 4.5 lists VARIETY first, we have chosen the Type III analysis and specified the SS3 option. The multivariate tests based on Type III analysis (that is, after adjusting for the two directions in the Latin squares, in this case) are presented as Output 4.5. Based on any of the four multivariate tests, there does not appear to be significant difference between the four varieties; the p value for Wilks' Λ is 0.2638. If there were indeed a significant difference, it would also have been interesting to perform the pairwise comparisons of the four varieties. This can be done using the CONTRAST statement. For instance, if we wanted to compare the varieties C_2 and C_4, then the corresponding SAS statement, which should follow the MODEL statement but must precede the MANOVA statement, is

```
contrast 'c2 vs.  c4' variety 0 1 0 -1;
```

For the optional phrase $c2$ versus $c4$ enclosed by single quotation marks (' '), we could have used any other alternative identifier appropriately indicating the type of contrast.

Since the pairwise comparisons are not meaningful in the present context of nonsignificant effect on VARIETY, we do not pursue this analysis further for this example.

4.6 Fractional Factorial Experiments

As the number of variables in an experiment increases, so does the total number of all possible combinations or treatments obtained by combining various levels of these variables. As a result, the number of experiments needed to obtain data on the corresponding full factorial design may soon become overwhelming. One way to reduce the total number of experiments is to carefully choose the combinations of variable levels, so that the information on all main effects and certain important lower order interactions can still be extracted from these experiments. This, of course, requires assuming the absence of certain interactions. Also it is necessary to choose the design carefully to ensure that various important interactions which are expected to be significant can still be estimated. When the effects of two variables or interactions on a response variable cannot be distinguished from one another they are said to be *confounded*. In general, it is best to avoid confounding important variables or interactions. In fact, the confounding scheme of the design plays an important role in the choice of fractions of factorial experiments. These are often termed *fractional factorial experiments*.

There is a vast amount of literature available on the construction and analysis of the fractional factorial experiments. John (1971) and Montgomery (1991) provide excellent discussions at different mathematical levels, the latter being more accessible to nonmathematical audiences. However, only univariate analysis is considered in both of these references. As for construction, SAS/QC software provides a number of design generation choices including fractional factorial designs through PROC FACTEX. Also available are certain SAS macros to generate more advanced designs in the same reference. See *SAS/QC Software, Version 6, First Edition*, for details.

The multivariate nature of the data in response variables does not play any role in the choice of fractional factorial designs or on the confounding scheme. In fact, these issues relate only to the independent variables and are usually decided prior to the experimentation. However, a multivariate analysis of various response variables may be more appropriate due to possible correlations between various response variables. The standard multivariate tests can be performed as described earlier. For various main effects and interactions use either PROC GLM or PROC REG. The latter is appropriate when all the independent variables are continuous, or the variables are categorical, when they are only at two levels. Since fractional factorial designs are balanced designs, PROC ANOVA is also applicable, when we are only interested in comparison and the significance or nonsignificance of various variables and interactions and not in modeling.

It should also be noted that multivariate analysis may sometimes be restrictive in that it tests that a given variable or interaction is significant or nonsignificant collectively for all the response variables. As a result, it is possible to miss the very strong effect of a particular variable or interaction on one response variable simply because it did not significantly affect the other response variables. It is therefore advisable that various univariate analyses accompany the multivariate results to ensure that the two results do not drastically contradict each other.

Example 6: A 2^{8-3} Fractional Factorial Experiment, Modeling of a Chemical Process (Daniel and Riblett, 1954)

Daniel and Riblett (1954) described a chemical experiment with eight variables, A to H, in 32 runs. Two response variables under consideration were catalyst activity (ACTIVT) and selectivity (SELECTVT). The experiment was run as a one-eighth fraction of a full factorial (that is, a 2^{8-3} fractional factorial design) with all the variables at two levels: $+1$ and -1. The design allowed the estimation and testing of all the main effects and the following two variable interactions: AB, AC, AD, AE, AF, AG, AH, BG, BH, CE, CF, CG, CH, DG, DH, EG, EH, FG, FH, and GH. All other interactions were assumed to be nonexistent.

The purpose of the analysis was to first identify important main variables and interactions using the statistical tests, then estimate their effects and finally obtain a bivariate regression model for the catalyst activity and selectivity.

The data corresponding to this study are presented in Program 4.6. This example also illustrates the use of PROC REG as an occasionally more efficient alternative to PROC GLM. PROC REG is especially helpful here since for two-level fractional factorial experiments, the computation of various effects can be easily achieved through the estimation of certain regression coefficients as we shall see later.

For two variables, say A and B, each at two levels, denoted by $+1$ and -1, interaction can be represented by their ordinary algebraic product $A * B$. We can correspondingly create the values of the new independent variables representing various interactions by simply multiplying the columns of the values (coded as ± 1) of appropriate main variables. In Program 4.6, variables AB, AC, etc., are defined using this rule only. Having done that, we fit the models for the variables ACTIVT and SELECTVT using all the main variables and interactions indicated earlier, as the independent variables. Since these variables are being treated as continuous and not categorical, we can use PROC REG. All the main variables and interactions are defined as continuous variables which take values $+1$ and -1 for this data set. The estimated regression coefficients are saved in the output file EST1. Next the MODEL statement is specified for the two dependent variables ACTIVT and SELECTVT. Since the underlying design is a fractional factorial and hence balanced, all three types of analyses are identical. We have thus used the default choice of Type III SS. Also, since the effects are orthogonal (fractional factorial designs are always orthogonal), dropping a particular interaction or main variable term from the model would not alter the estimated regression coefficients of other terms in the reduced model.

In order to test the joint effect of a set of independent variables or an individual independent variable on the response variables, we use the MTEST statement. We first test if the bivariate model with only main variables as independent variables is adequate. To do so we include the list of all the independent variables (separated by commas) corresponding to the two variable interactions in the MTEST statement. The label ONLYMAIN is used to indicate that under the null hypothesis stated by MTEST, the reduced model contains only the main effects. The hypothesis in the MTEST statement can also be specified as an equation or a set of equations. For example, an alternative way to write the MTEST statement is

```
onlymain:  mtest ab=0, ac=0, ad=0, ae=0, af=0, ag=0,
           ah=0, bg=0, bh=0, ce=0, cf=0, cg=0, ch=0,
           dg=0, dh=0, eg=0, eh=0, fg=0, fh=0, gh=0;
```

The remaining MTEST statements in Program 4.6 are used to individually test the hypotheses on the particular interactions. The four multivariate tests for these individual tests are equivalent as well as exact. See Table 3.3.

Selected parts of the output are presented as Output 4.6. The null hypothesis, all the two-variable interactions are zero, is accepted by all four multivariate tests. For instance, the p value corresponding to Wilks' Λ is 0.8258. Similarly, all the individual null hypotheses for the interactions are also accepted at a 5% level of significance. In the output, we show the values of various (equivalent) test statistics and the corresponding p values ($=0.7824$) for $H_0 : AG = 0$ only.

We also want to compute the effects for various main variables. Since all the variables are at two levels and the design is orthogonal, the computation of effects is especially simple. In this case, the effect of a particular variable (or interaction, if it exists) is nothing but twice the estimated value of the corresponding regression coefficient. Since all the regression coefficients of the two models corresponding to two response variables, namely ACTIVT and SELECTVT, have been output in a data set EST1, we define a new data set EFFECTS, where effects for various main variables and the interactions are computed. For example, the regression coefficient of the variable A in the model for ACTIVT is 0.01719; correspondingly, the effect of A is $2 \times (0.01719) = 0.03438$ as shown in the output.

An alternative way to compute the values of various effects would have been to use PROC GLM, treat all the main variables as classification variables, and use the ESTIMATE statement. For example, the corresponding statement for the effect of A is

```
estimate 'factor a' a 1 -1;
```

It would, however, require that the variable A be declared as a classification variable, thereby not permitting direct computation of the regression coefficients.

It is also possible to identify significant effects using the stepdown analysis discussed in Chapter 3. Roy, Gnanadesikan, and Srivastava (1971) point out that in the context of the present data set, it is known that the response variable ACTIVT is observable with greater precision than the response variable SELECTVT. As a result, we decided that ACTIVT is more important than SELECTVT and there is a natural ordering between the two variables. Thus the overall bivariate null hypothesis of no treatment effect can be tested by first considering the hypothesis of no treatment effect on the response ACTIVT marginally. Then we can consider the hypothesis of no treatment effect on the response variable SELECTVT conditional on ACTIVT (that is, on SELECTVT after adjusting for the covariate ACTIVT). Since any effect is merely a multiple of corresponding regression coefficients for this design, we can directly apply a stepdown analysis on these regression coefficients only.

For illustration, we consider only the main factor model by assuming that all the interactions are negligible and hence our regression model contains only the main variables. In the stepdown analysis (see Chapter 3), the overall null hypothesis is accepted if and only if the corresponding hypotheses at all the stages are accepted. We will therefore reject the overall null hypothesis if it is rejected at either the first stage (that is, in the model for ACTIVT) or the second stage (that is, in the model for SELECTVT, with ACTIVT as a covariate) or at both the stages. As a result, an occurrence of a small p value at either of the two stages leads to the rejection of the overall null hypothesis. Of course, the individual levels of significance, α_1 and α_2 for the two hypotheses, should be appropriately decided. See Section 3.5.2.

The corresponding two models are fitted by using the last three lines of Program 4.6. As shown in Output 4.6, in the first model (for the variable ACTIVT), the effects E and G have small p values and hence are statistically significant. In the model for SELECTVT adjusted for the covariate ACTIVT, we observe that A, C, E, and F are statistically significant at a 5% level of significance. Consequently, we conclude that all the effects except B, D, and H are significant.

In the above example, we have seen how univariate analysis of covariance can be used in the analysis to adjust one response variable for the other and to test a multivariate hypothesis. However, keep in mind that situations exist in which genuine covariates are available as the independent variables. In such situations any comparison of various variables needs to be done after adjusting for the effects of these covariates.

4.7 Analysis of Covariance

When we want to compare various treatments, but the responses are affected by not only the particular treatments but also by certain other variables termed covariates or concomitant variables, we need to modify the analysis to account for these covariates and eliminate their effects. In other words, to make a fair comparison of various treatments, the data on the response variables need to be made comparable by first adjusting for the covariates. These situations commonly occur in social, biological, medical, physical, and other sciences.

For analyzing these data we utilize the following model

$$\mathbf{Y} = \mathbf{XB} + \mathbf{Z\Gamma} + \mathcal{E}, \tag{4.7}$$

where the matrices $\mathbf{Y}$ and $\mathcal{E}$ are defined as before. The term $\mathbf{XB}$ represents the design part of the model with a rank of the n by $k+1$ matrix $\mathbf{X}$ equal to r. The n by q matrix $\mathbf{Z}$ is the matrix of data on the covariates with $Rank(\mathbf{Z}) = q$, and the q by p matrix Γ is the matrix of unknown parameters representing the regression of $\mathbf{Y}$ on $\mathbf{Z}$. Hence the term $\mathbf{Z\Gamma}$ in the model in Equation 4.7 represents the covariate part of the model. First we want to test the significance of some or all covariates in $\mathbf{Z}$ by testing the corresponding rows of Γ to be zero and second to test the linear hypotheses about $\mathbf{B}$, after adjusting for the effects of the variables $\mathbf{Z}$, to answer the usual questions discussed in the earlier sections. We rewrite Equation 4.7 in the standard linear model form as

$$\mathbf{Y} = (\mathbf{X}\ \mathbf{Z}) \begin{bmatrix} \mathbf{B} \\ \Gamma \end{bmatrix} + \mathbf{U} = \mathbf{W}\Phi + \mathbf{U}.$$

Then using the usual least squares principle, the least square solutions for Γ and $\mathbf{B}$ respectively are

$$\hat{\Gamma} = (\mathbf{Z}'\mathbf{Q}\mathbf{Z})^-\mathbf{Z}'\mathbf{Q}\mathbf{Y}$$

and

$$\hat{\mathbf{B}} = (\mathbf{X}'\mathbf{X})^-\mathbf{X}'(\mathbf{Y} - \mathbf{Z}\hat{\Gamma}),$$

where $\mathbf{Q} = \mathbf{I} - \mathbf{X}(\mathbf{X}'\mathbf{X})^-\mathbf{X}'$.

Now for the first test $H_0^{(a)} : \Gamma = \mathbf{0}$, that is, covariates have no effect on the response variables, we use the matrices

$$\mathbf{H} = \mathbf{Y}'\mathbf{Q}\mathbf{Z}(\mathbf{Z}'\mathbf{Q}\mathbf{Z})^-\mathbf{Z}'\mathbf{Q}\mathbf{Y} = \hat{\Gamma}'\mathbf{Z}'\mathbf{Q}\mathbf{Y}$$

and

$$\mathbf{E} = \mathbf{Y}'\mathbf{Q}\mathbf{Y} - \hat{\Gamma}'\mathbf{Z}'\mathbf{Q}\mathbf{Y}.$$

When H_{01} is true, then assuming $n > q + r$, $\mathbf{H}$ and $\mathbf{E}$ are independently distributed as $W_p(q, \Sigma)$ and $W_p(n - q - r, \Sigma)$ respectively. Using these matrices the usual multivariate tests can be used to test $H_0^{(a)}$. Next, for the second test $H_0^{(b)} : \mathbf{AB} = \mathbf{0}$, the same $\mathbf{E}$ matrix is used and the matrix $\mathbf{H}$ is determined using the model

$$\mathbf{Y} = \mathbf{W}\Phi + \mathbf{U}.$$

Since $H_0^{(b)} : \mathbf{AB} = \mathbf{0}$ can be written as $\mathbf{A}_1\Phi = \mathbf{0}$ with $\mathbf{A}_1 = (\mathbf{A} : \mathbf{0})$, the $\mathbf{H}$ matrix for $H_0^{(b)}$ is same as that for $\mathbf{A}_1\Phi = \mathbf{0}$. We use PROC GLM to test these hypotheses, as is illustrated in the next example.

Example 7: Comparisons in the Presence of Covariates, A Flammability Study

Consider a situation where the interest is in comparing the effects of various types of foams and fabrics used in carpets on carpet flammability. Three types of foams, namely A, B, and C, and three types of fabric materials denoted by X, Y, and Z were used, leading to nine possible compositions for the carpets. Two specimens of equal size (by volume) were taken and separately subjected to flame under identical temperature, pressure, and space. The heat releases at 5, 10, and 15 minutes (HR5, HR10, and HR15) were observed in each experiment. The experiment was designed to determine the most heat-resistant foam and fabric after determining if there were any significant differences between various types of foams and fabrics. The problem appears to fit in the multivariate two-way classification setup.

One important issue, however, needs to be addressed. Although the specimens are all supposedly of the same volume, the amount of heat release relates more to the weight of the specimens than to the volume. Due to different densities for various types of foams and fabrics, the equality of volumes does not necessarily imply the equality of weights of all these specimens. As a result, for a fair comparison, the values of heat releases need to be adjusted for the differing weights of the various specimens.

These fictitious data inspired by an actual experiment are presented as part of Program 4.7. A two-way classification model with interaction in the classification variables FOAM and FABRIC is fitted for the response variables, HR5, HR10, and HR15. The weight of the specimen (WT) is taken as the covariate.

Even though the design appears to be balanced in the variables FOAM and FABRIC, the balancedness is lost due to the presence of the covariate WT as it changes from specimen to specimen. The various types of SS&CP matrices are therefore not identical and a careful analysis of the data is needed.

Since the effects and the SS&CP matrices of the FOAM, FABRIC, and FOAM*FABRIC are all to be adjusted for WT, a sequential partitioning of the total SS&CP matrix is appropriate with the WT listed first in the corresponding MODEL statement. The partitioning results in all the subsequent SS&CP matrices adjusted at least for this covariate. As far as the other two variables are concerned, there does not appear to be any reason to prefer one over the other. If we want a Type I analysis, we should examine the output resulting from two possible orders in the MODEL statement, namely

```
model hr5 hr10 hr15 = wt foam fabric foam*fabric/ss1;
```

and

```
model hr5 hr10 hr15 = wt fabric foam foam*fabric/ss1;
```

hoping for consistency in the conclusions. We have, however, chosen to limit our output for the first of these statements.

An examination of Output 4.7 reveals that the interaction FOAM*FABRIC is highly significant under all of the four test criteria. In view of this, it makes sense to conduct various pairwise comparisons for the nine treatments to decide which treatments are similar and which are not. This unfortunately requires as many as 36 pairwise comparisons; in general it is not advisable to perform too many tests since in a large number of pairwise tests, some are likely to appear to be significant just by chance. Based on the least square cell means computed by the LSMEANS statement, it appears that the treatments (A, Z) and (C, X) are comparable with relatively low values for heat release at various time points. The output from the LSMEANS statement is not shown to save space. Suppose we want to see if these two preferred treatments are significantly different from each other. Such a comparison can be made using the CONTRAST statement. Note that the CONTRAST statement should always appear before a MANOVA statement.

In order to identify an appropriate CONTRAST statement, it is helpful to write down the two-way classification model (the covariate term in the model can be ignored for this purpose) for the 1 by 3 response vector HR

$$HR_{ijk} = INTERCEPT + FOAM_i + FABRIC_j$$
$$+ (FOAM * FABRIC)_{ij} + ERROR_{ijk},$$

where $i = A, B, C$, $j = X, Y, Z$ and $k = 1, 2$.

Our interest is in the contrast $E(HR_{AZk} - HR_{CXk})$, where E indicates the expected value. Dropping the replication suffix $'k'$ for convenience, this can be written as

$$(INTERCEPT - INTERCEPT)$$
$$+ (FOAM_A - FOAM_C) + (FABRIC_Z - FABRIC_X)$$
$$+ ((FOAM_A * FABRIC_Z) - (FOAM_C * FABRIC_X))$$

$$= 0 \times INTERCEPT + (1\ 0\ -1) \begin{bmatrix} FOAM_A \\ FOAM_B \\ FOAM_C \end{bmatrix} + (-1\ 0\ 1) \begin{bmatrix} FABRIC_X \\ FABRIC_Y \\ FABRIC_Z \end{bmatrix}$$

$$+ (0\ 0\ 1\ :\ 0\ 0\ 0\ :\ -1\ 0\ 0) \begin{bmatrix} FOAM_A * FABRIC_X \\ FOAM_A * FABRIC_Y \\ FOAM_A * FABRIC_Z \\ FOAM_B * FABRIC_X \\ FOAM_B * FABRIC_Y \\ FOAM_B * FABRIC_Z \\ FOAM_C * FABRIC_X \\ FOAM_C * FABRIC_Y \\ FOAM_C * FABRIC_Z \end{bmatrix}.$$

The above representation indicates that in order to get the contrast between treatments (A, Z) and (C, X),

- the coefficient for intercept is zero,
- the vector of coefficients for the vector of foams $(A, B, C)'$ is $(1\ 0\ -1)'$,
- the vector of fabrics $(X, Y, Z)'$ is $(-1\ 0\ 1)'$,
- the vector of coefficients for the 9 by 1 vector of interactions

$$((A * X), (A * Y), (A * Z), (B * X), (B * Y), (B * Z),$$
$$(C * X), (C * Y), (C * Z))'$$

is obtained by respectively putting 1 and -1 at the places corresponding to $(A * Z)$ and $(C * X)$ and zeros elsewhere.

All of this is specified in the CONTRAST statement as

```
contrast 'label' intercept 0 foam 1 0 -1 fabric -1 0 1
                 foam*fabric 0 0 1 0 0 0 -1 0 0;
```

The name (A, Z) versus (C, X) enclosed within single quotation marks (' ') in Program 4.7 is used as the label. A label is required in the CONTRAST statement.

For the desired contrast, it is possible to use any of the four multivariate tests. In the present case, since the rank of underlying **L** matrix is one (there is only a single contrast) all four tests are identical and exact. The corresponding observed value of the $F(3, 6)$ test statistic is 0.5982 leading to a p value of 0.6392. Hence the null hypothesis of no overall difference between (A, Z) and (C, X) treatments *cannot* be rejected.

Although it is not quite relevant in the present context (because of highly significant interaction), if the interest were to compare the effect of Foam A with that of Foam B, the CONTRAST statement in simplified form can be written as

```
contrast 'label' foam 1 -1 0;
```

It is so, since in this case the coefficients of INTERCEPT, the vector of FABRIC, and the vector of FOAM*FABRIC all have zero coefficients and hence need not be explicitly specified in the CONTRAST statement.

Note that in the data presented here, the heat releases at various time points the repeated measures on the same specimen. Further analysis may be possible using various other repeated measures techniques. We address some of these techniques in the next chapter.

Remember that all the analyses presented in this chapter assume the equality of the variance-covariance matrices of the rows of matrix $\mathcal{E}$. If in a multiway classification, this assumption of the homogeneity of the variance-covariance matrix is not satisfied, the analysis presented here may not be appropriate. We therefore strongly recommend that some appropriate tests for the homogeneity of the variance-covariance matrices be applied to the data prior to performing any multivariate analysis of variance. The equality of variance-covariance matrices can be tested using PROC DISCRIM. See *SAS/STAT User's Guide, Version 6, Fourth Edition, Volume 1*, for details.

```
/* Program  4.1 */

options ls = 78 ps=45 nodate nonumber;

*Data From Edward Jackson(1991, p. 301) ;
data jack ;
input lab method1 method2 ;
lines ;
1 10.1 10.5
1 9.3 9.5
1 9.7 10.0
1 10.9 11.4
2 10.0 9.8
2 9.5 9.7
2 9.7 9.8
2 10.8 10.7
3 11.3 10.1
3 10.7 9.8
3 10.8 10.1
3 10.5 9.6
;
/* Source: Jackson (1991, p. 301). Principal Components.  Copyright
   1991 John Wiley & Sons, Inc.  Reprinted by permission of
   John Wiley & Sons, Inc. */

Title1 'Output 4.1' ;
title2 'Data from Jackson (1991, p. 301): One Way MANOVA' ;
proc glm data = jack ;
class lab ;
model method1 method2 = lab/nouni;
manova h = lab/printe printh ;

/*
proc glm data = jack ;
class lab ;
model method1 method2 = lab/nouni;
contrast 'Test: lab eff.' lab 1 -1  0,
                          lab 1  0 -1;
manova /printe printh ;
*/
run;
```

General Linear Models Procedure
Class Level Information

Class	Levels	Values
LAB	3	1 2 3

Number of observations in data set = 12

E = Error SS&CP Matrix

	METHOD1	METHOD2
METHOD1	2.7275	2.63
METHOD2	2.63	2.81

Output 4.1
Data from Jackson (1991, p. 301): One Way MANOVA

General Linear Models Procedure
Multivariate Analysis of Variance

H = Type III SS&CP Matrix for LAB

	METHOD1	METHOD2
METHOD1	1.815	-0.605
METHOD2	-0.605	0.4466666667

Characteristic Roots and Vectors of: E Inverse * H, where
H = Type III SS&CP Matrix for LAB   E = Error SS&CP Matrix

Characteristic Root	Percent	Characteristic Vector V'EV=1	
		METHOD1	METHOD2
12.6651590	99.63	-1.93040411	1.86294560
0.0469779	0.37	0.18266371	0.42293426

Manova Test Criteria and F Approximations for
the Hypothesis of no Overall LAB Effect
H = Type III SS&CP Matrix for LAB   E = Error SS&CP Matrix

S=2   M=-0.5   N=3

Statistic	Value	F	Num DF	Den DF	Pr > F
Wilks' Lambda	0.06989527	11.1299	4	16	0.0002
Pillai's Trace	0.97169119	4.2522	4	18	0.0135
Hotelling-Lawley Trace	12.71213692	22.2462	4	14	0.0001
Roy's Greatest Root	12.66515903	56.9932	2	9	0.0001

NOTE: F Statistic for Roy's Greatest Root is an upper bound.
NOTE: F Statistic for Wilks' Lambda is exact.

```
/* Program 4.2 */
options ls=78 ps=45 nonumber nodate;

* Data from Crowder and Hand (1990, p. 8) on effect of
                                        physical task;
* Values are the repeated measures on 14 subjects
                            during 1, 5 and 10 minutes;
data phytask ;
input group min1 min5 min10 ;
lines ;
1 7.6   8.7   7.0
1 10.1  8.9   8.6
1 11.2  9.5   9.4
1 10.8  11.5  11.4
1 3.9   4.1   3.7
1 6.7   7.3   6.6
1 2.2   2.5   2.4
1 2.1   2.0   2.0
2 8.5   5.6   8.4
2 7.5   5.0   9.5
2 12.9  13.6  15.3
2 8.8   7.9   7.3
2 5.5   6.4   6.4
2 3.2   3.4   3.2
;
/* Source: Crowder and Hand (1990, p. 8). */

title1 ' Output 4.2 ' ;
title2 'Data from Crowder and Hand (1990): Unbalanced
                            One Way MANOVA' ;

proc glm data = phytask ;
class group ;
model min1 min5 min10 = group/nouni ;
manova h = group m = min1-min5 ,
            min5-min10/printe printh ;

manova h = intercept m = min1-min5 ,
            min5-min10/printe printh ;
run;
```

Data from Crowder and Hand (1990): Unbalanced One Way MANOVA

General Linear Models Procedure
Multivariate Analysis of Variance

M Matrix Describing Transformed Variables

	MIN1	MIN5	MIN10
MVAR1	1	-1	0
MVAR2	0	1	-1

E = Error SS&CP Matrix

	MVAR1	MVAR2
MVAR1	19.96375	-13.5125
MVAR2	-13.5125	22.388333333

General Linear Models Procedure
Multivariate Analysis of Variance

H = Type III SS&CP Matrix for GROUP

	MVAR1	MVAR2
MVAR1	1.8648214286	-4.530357143
MVAR2	-4.530357143	11.005952381

Characteristic Roots and Vectors of: E Inverse * H, where
H = Type III SS&CP Matrix for GROUP   E = Error SS&CP Matrix

Variables have been transformed by the M Matrix

Characteristic Root	Percent	Characteristic Vector V'EV=1	
		MVAR1	MVAR2
0.52592493	100.00	0.07435204	0.24920432
0.00000000	0.00	0.28135067	0.11581179

Manova Test Criteria and Exact F Statistics for
the Hypothesis of no Overall GROUP Effect
on the variables defined by the M Matrix Transformation
H = Type III SS&CP Matrix for GROUP   E = Error SS&CP Matrix

S=1   M=0   N=4.5

Statistic	Value	F	Num DF	Den DF	Pr > F
Wilks' Lambda	0.65534023	2.8926	2	11	0.0979
Pillai's Trace	0.34465977	2.8926	2	11	0.0979
Hotelling-Lawley Trace	0.52592493	2.8926	2	11	0.0979
Roy's Greatest Root	0.52592493	2.8926	2	11	0.0979

Output 4.2
Data from Crowder and Hand (1990): Unbalanced One Way MANOVA

General Linear Models Procedure
Multivariate Analysis of Variance

H = Type III SS&CP Matrix for INTERCEPT

	MVAR1	MVAR2
MVAR1	1.9933928571	-2.461785714
MVAR2	-2.461785714	3.0402380952

Characteristic Roots and Vectors of: E Inverse * H, where
H = Type III SS&CP Matrix for INTERCEPT   E = Error SS&CP Matrix

Variables have been transformed by the M Matrix

Characteristic Root	Percent	Characteristic Vector V'EV=1	
		MVAR1	MVAR2
0.14674099	100.00	0.07947781	-0.15533995
0.00000000	0.00	0.27994589	0.22668185

Manova Test Criteria and Exact F Statistics for
the Hypothesis of no Overall INTERCEPT Effect
on the variables defined by the M Matrix Transformation
H = Type III SS&CP Matrix for INTERCEPT   E = Error SS&CP Matrix

S=1   M=0   N=4.5

Statistic	Value	F	Num DF	Den DF	Pr > F
Wilks' Lambda	0.87203650	0.8071	2	11	0.4709
Pillai's Trace	0.12796350	0.8071	2	11	0.4709
Hotelling-Lawley Trace	0.14674099	0.8071	2	11	0.4709
Roy's Greatest Root	0.14674099	0.8071	2	11	0.4709

```
/* Program 4.3 */

options ls=78 ps=45 nodate nonumber;
* Data on Weight loss in mice. Morrison(1976);

data wtloss ;
input sex $ drug $  week1 week2 ;
lines;
male    a  5  6
male    a  5  4
male    a  9  9
male    a  7  6
male    b  7  6
male    b  7  7
male    b  9 12
male    b  6  8
male    c 21 15
male    c 14 11
male    c 17 12
male    c 12 10
female a  7 10
female a  6  6
female a  9  7
female a  8 10
female b 10 13
female b  8  7
female b  7  6
female b  6  9
female c 16 12
female c 14  9
female c 14  8
female c 10  5
;
/* Source: Morrison (1976, p. 190). Multivariate Statistical
   Methods, McGraw-Hill, Inc.  Reproduced with permission
   of  McGraw-Hill, Inc. */

proc glm data = wtloss ;
class sex drug ;
model week1 week2= sex|drug/nouni ;
*model week1 week2= sex drug sex*drug/nouni ;
manova h = sex drug sex*drug/printe printh ;
title1 'Output 4.3';
title2 'Data on Weight Loss in Mice: Morrison
                                (1976, p. 190)' ;

run;
```

Data on Weight Loss in Mice: Morrison (1976, p. 190)

General Linear Models Procedure
Class Level Information

Class	Levels	Values
SEX	2	female male
DRUG	3	a b c

Number of observations in data set = 24

E = Error SS&CP Matrix

	WEEK1	WEEK2
WEEK1	94.5	76.5
WEEK2	76.5	114

Output 4.3
Data on Weight Loss in Mice: Morrison (1976, p. 190)

General Linear Models Procedure
Multivariate Analysis of Variance

H = Type III SS&CP Matrix for SEX

	WEEK1	WEEK2
WEEK1	0.6666666667	0.6666666667
WEEK2	0.6666666667	0.6666666667

Characteristic Roots and Vectors of: E Inverse * H, where
H = Type III SS&CP Matrix for SEX   E = Error SS&CP Matrix

Characteristic Root	Percent	Characteristic Vector V'EV=1	
		WEEK1	WEEK2
0.00751918	100.00	0.07175780	0.03444374
0.00000000	0.00	-0.13423121	0.13423121

Manova Test Criteria and Exact F Statistics for
the Hypothesis of no Overall SEX Effect
H = Type III SS&CP Matrix for SEX   E = Error SS&CP Matrix

S=1   M=0   N=7.5

Statistic	Value	F	Num DF	Den DF	Pr > F
Wilks' Lambda	0.99253694	0.0639	2	17	0.9383
Pillai's Trace	0.00746306	0.0639	2	17	0.9383
Hotelling-Lawley Trace	0.00751918	0.0639	2	17	0.9383
Roy's Greatest Root	0.00751918	0.0639	2	17	0.9383

Data on Weight Loss in Mice: Morrison (1976, p. 190)

General Linear Models Procedure
Multivariate Analysis of Variance

H = Type III SS&CP Matrix for DRUG

	WEEK1	WEEK2
WEEK1	301	97.5
WEEK2	97.5	36.333333333

Characteristic Roots and Vectors of: E Inverse * H, where
H = Type III SS&CP Matrix for DRUG   E = Error SS&CP Matrix

Characteristic Root	Percent	Characteristic Vector V'EV=1	
		WEEK1	WEEK2
4.57602675	98.63	0.14784109	−0.07693601
0.06350991	1.37	−0.03619684	0.11526161

Manova Test Criteria and F Approximations for
the Hypothesis of no Overall DRUG Effect
H = Type III SS&CP Matrix for DRUG   E = Error SS&CP Matrix

S=2   M=−0.5   N=7.5

Statistic	Value	F	Num DF	Den DF	Pr > F
Wilks' Lambda	0.16862952	12.1991	4	34	0.0001
Pillai's Trace	0.88037810	7.0769	4	36	0.0003
Hotelling-Lawley Trace	4.63953666	18.5581	4	32	0.0001
Roy's Greatest Root	4.57602675	41.1842	2	18	0.0001

NOTE: F Statistic for Roy's Greatest Root is an upper bound.
NOTE: F Statistic for Wilks' Lambda is exact.

General Linear Models Procedure
Multivariate Analysis of Variance

H = Type III SS&CP Matrix for SEX*DRUG

	WEEK1	WEEK2
WEEK1	14.333333333	21.333333333
WEEK2	21.333333333	32.333333333

Characteristic Roots and Vectors of: E Inverse * H, where
H = Type III SS&CP Matrix for SEX*DRUG   E = Error SS&CP Matrix

Characteristic Root	Percent	Characteristic Vector V'EV=1	
		WEEK1	WEEK2
0.28372273	97.94	-0.00284433	0.09555092
0.00596889	2.06	-0.15218117	0.10037136

Manova Test Criteria and F Approximations for
the Hypothesis of no Overall SEX*DRUG Effect
H = Type III SS&CP Matrix for SEX*DRUG   E = Error SS&CP Matrix

S=2   M=-0.5   N=7.5

Statistic	Value	F	Num DF	Den DF	Pr > F
Wilks' Lambda	0.77436234	1.1593	4	34	0.3459
Pillai's Trace	0.22694905	1.1520	4	36	0.3481
Hotelling-Lawley Trace	0.28969161	1.1588	4	32	0.3473
Roy's Greatest Root	0.28372273	2.5535	2	18	0.1056

NOTE: F Statistic for Roy's Greatest Root is an upper bound.
NOTE: F Statistic for Wilks' Lambda is exact.

```
/* Program 4.4 */

options ls=78 ps=45 nodate nonumber;

* Data for unbalanced two way classification ;
data etch;
input press power etch1 etch2 unif1 unif2 ;
select = etch1/etch2 ;
x1 = (press-265)/25 ;
x2 = (power-110)/20 ;
x2sq = x2*x2 ;
lines ;
240   90   793 300 13.2 25.1
240   90   830 372 15.1 24.6
240   90   843 389 14.2 25.7
240  110  1075 400 15.8 25.9
240  110  1102 410 14.9 25.1
240  130  1060 397 15.3 24.9
240  130  1049 427 14.7 23.8
290   90   973 350  7.4 18.3
290   90   998 373  8.3 17.7
290  110   940 365  8.0 16.9
290  110   935 365  7.1 17.2
290  110   953 342  8.9 17.4
290  110   928 340  7.3 16.6
290  130  1020 402  8.6 16.3
290  130  1034 409  7.5 15.5
;
title1 'Output 4.4';
title2 'Unbalanced Two way Classification: MANOVA' ;
title3 'Effect of Pressure and Power on Etch
                     Uniformity and Selectivity' ;
proc glm data = etch ;
class press power ;
model select unif1 unif2 press power press*power/ss1 nouni ;
manova h = press power press*power/printe printh ;

proc glm data = etch ;
class press power ;
model select unif1 unif2=press power press*power/ss2 nouni ;
manova h = press power press*power/printe printh ;

proc glm data = etch ;
class press power ;
model select unif1 unif2=press power press*power/ss3 nouni ;
manova h = press power press*power/printe printh ;

proc glm data = etch ;
model select unif1 unif2  = x1 x2 x2sq /ss1 nouni;
manova h = x1 x2 x2sq /printe printh ;

/* proc glm data = etch ;
model select unif1 unif2  = x1 x2 x2sq /ss2 nouni;
manova h = x1 x2 x2sq /printe printh ;

proc glm data = etch ;
model select unif1 unif2  = x1 x2 x2sq /ss3 nouni;
manova h = x1 x2 x2sq /printe printh ; */
run;
```

Unbalanced Two way Classification: MANOVA
Effect of Pressure and Power on Etch Uniformity and Selectivity

General Linear Models Procedure
Class Level Information

Class	Levels	Values
PRESS	2	240 290
POWER	3	90 110 130

Number of observations in data set = 15

E = Error SS&CP Matrix

	SELECT	UNIF1	UNIF2
SELECT	0.1994753941	-0.222508225	0.1134897068
UNIF1	-0.222508225	5.3891666667	0.8908333333
UNIF2	0.1134897068	0.8908333333	2.3991666667

Unbalanced Two way Classification: MANOVA
Effect of Pressure and Power on Etch Uniformity and Selectivity

General Linear Models Procedure
Multivariate Analysis of Variance

Partial Correlation Coefficients from the Error SS&CP Matrix / Prob > |r|

DF = 9	SELECT	UNIF1	UNIF2
SELECT	1.000000	-0.214605	0.164052
	0.0001	0.5516	0.6506
UNIF1	-0.214605	1.000000	0.247745
	0.5516	0.0001	0.4901
UNIF2	0.164052	0.247745	1.000000
	0.6506	0.4901	0.0001

General Linear Models Procedure
Multivariate Analysis of Variance

H = Type I SS&CP Matrix for PRESS

	SELECT	UNIF1	UNIF2
SELECT	0.0737146599	-3.596295771	-4.210822998
UNIF1	-3.596295771	175.45144048	205.43220238
UNIF2	-4.210822998	205.43220238	240.5360119

Characteristic Roots and Vectors of: E Inverse * H, where
H = Type I SS&CP Matrix for PRESS   E = Error SS&CP Matrix

Characteristic Root	Percent	Characteristic Vector V'EV=1		
		SELECT	UNIF1	UNIF2
113.427574	100.00	-0.31952750	0.12225917	0.57669319
0.000000	0.00	-0.50377877	-0.44243375	0.36904585
0.000000	0.00	2.27851364	0.04670357	0.00000000

Manova Test Criteria and Exact F Statistics for
the Hypothesis of no Overall PRESS Effect
H = Type I SS&CP Matrix for PRESS   E = Error SS&CP Matrix

S=1   M=0.5   N=2.5

Statistic	Value	F	Num DF	Den DF	Pr > F
Wilks' Lambda	0.00873915	264.6643	3	7	0.0001
Pillai's Trace	0.99126085	264.6643	3	7	0.0001
Hotelling-Lawley Trace	113.42757414	264.6643	3	7	0.0001
Roy's Greatest Root	113.42757414	264.6643	3	7	0.0001

Unbalanced Two way Classification: MANOVA
Effect of Pressure and Power on Etch Uniformity and Selectivity

General Linear Models Procedure
Multivariate Analysis of Variance

H = Type I SS&CP Matrix for POWER

	SELECT	UNIF1	UNIF2
SELECT	0.0567261552	0.1685855434	0.0282871709
UNIF1	0.1685855434	1.0145721024	-1.41912062
UNIF2	0.0282871709	-1.41912062	4.4140195418

Characteristic Roots and Vectors of: E Inverse * H, where
H = Type I SS&CP Matrix for POWER   E = Error SS&CP Matrix

Characteristic Root	Percent	Characteristic Vector V'EV=1		
		SELECT	UNIF1	UNIF2
2.51322871	85.48	-0.77345829	-0.23846242	0.66291206
0.42682517	14.52	1.97461468	0.22283088	0.13001362
0.00000000	0.00	-1.02478018	0.32612610	0.11141781

Manova Test Criteria and F Approximations for
the Hypothesis of no Overall POWER Effect
H = Type I SS&CP Matrix for POWER   E = Error SS&CP Matrix

S=2   M=0   N=2.5

Statistic	Value	F	Num DF	Den DF	Pr > F
Wilks' Lambda	0.19949077	2.8908	6	14	0.0477
Pillai's Trace	1.01450483	2.7452	6	16	0.0498
Hotelling-Lawley Trace	2.94005389	2.9401	6	12	0.0529
Roy's Greatest Root	2.51322871	6.7019	3	8	0.0142

NOTE: F Statistic for Roy's Greatest Root is an upper bound.
NOTE: F Statistic for Wilks' Lambda is exact.

Output 4.4
Unbalanced Two way Classification: MANOVA
Effect of Pressure and Power on Etch Uniformity and Selectivity

General Linear Models Procedure
Multivariate Analysis of Variance

H = Type I SS&CP Matrix for PRESS*POWER

	SELECT	UNIF1	UNIF2
SELECT	0.1317292294	0.308715428	0.4298967168
UNIF1	0.308715428	0.9221540881	1.0227515723
UNIF2	0.4298967168	1.0227515723	1.4041352201

Characteristic Roots and Vectors of: E Inverse * H, where
H = Type I SS&CP Matrix for PRESS*POWER   E = Error SS&CP Matrix

Characteristic Root	Percent	Characteristic Vector V'EV=1		
		SELECT	UNIF1	UNIF2
1.22333918	97.37	1.65041640	0.16545030	0.30654610
0.03310349	2.63	-0.12317091	0.42867099	-0.28179245
0.00000000	0.00	-1.67584901	-0.04175566	0.54350012

Manova Test Criteria and F Approximations for
the Hypothesis of no Overall PRESS*POWER Effect
H = Type I SS&CP Matrix for PRESS*POWER   E = Error SS&CP Matrix

$S=2$ $M=0$ $N=2.5$

Statistic	Value	F	Num DF	Den DF	Pr > F
Wilks' Lambda	0.43536193	1.2030	6	14	0.3605
Pillai's Trace	0.58226883	1.0952	6	16	0.4068
Hotelling-Lawley Trace	1.25644267	1.2564	6	12	0.3457
Roy's Greatest Root	1.22333918	3.2622	3	8	0.0805

NOTE: F Statistic for Roy's Greatest Root is an upper bound.
NOTE: F Statistic for Wilks' Lambda is exact.

```
/* Program 4.5 */

*Data on Corn yield and plant height.
                    Srivastava and Carter(1983, p. 109) ;
* Design used is a Latin Square Design. ;

options ls=78 ps=45 nodate nonumber;

data corn1 ;
input ew  $ ns $ variety  $ height yield ;
lines ;
a1 b1 c2 65 24
a1 b2 c3 66 20
a1 b3 c1 65 24
a1 b4 c4 65 26
a2 b1 c3 68 21
a2 b2 c2 63 23
a2 b3 c4 67 25
a2 b4 c1 64 25
a3 b1 c4 67 26
a3 b3 c2 64 19
a3 b4 c3 64 25
a4 b1 c1 68 27
a4 b2 c4 67 24
a4 b3 c3 63 20
;
/* Source: Srivastava and Carter (1983, p. 109). */

title1 'Output 4.5';
title2
"Latin Square Design: Corn Yield and Plant Height:
                    Srivastava & Carter (1983)" ;

proc glm data = corn1 ;
class ew ns variety ;
model height yield = variety ew ns/ss3 nouni ;
manova h =variety/printe printh ;

run;
```

Latin Square Design: Corn Yield and Plant Height: Srivastava & Carter (1983)

General Linear Models Procedure
Multivariate Analysis of Variance

H = Type III SS&CP Matrix for VARIETY

	HEIGHT	YIELD
HEIGHT	14.8875	13.7875
YIELD	13.7875	34.9875

Characteristic Roots and Vectors of: E Inverse * H, where
H = Type III SS&CP Matrix for VARIETY   E = Error SS&CP Matrix

Characteristic Root	Percent	Characteristic Vector V'EV=1	
		HEIGHT	YIELD
3.52250883	84.78	0.26228827	0.18315263
0.63249011	15.22	-0.23355367	0.14981097

Manova Test Criteria and F Approximations for
the Hypothesis of no Overall VARIETY Effect
H = Type III SS&CP Matrix for VARIETY   E = Error SS&CP Matrix

S=2   M=0   N=0.5

Statistic	Value	F	Num DF	Den DF	Pr > F
Wilks' Lambda	0.13544720	1.7172	6	6	0.2638
Pillai's Trace	1.16632266	1.8653	6	8	0.2033
Hotelling-Lawley Trace	4.15499895	1.3850	6	4	0.3925
Roy's Greatest Root	3.52250883	4.6967	3	4	0.0846

NOTE: F Statistic for Roy's Greatest Root is an upper bound.
NOTE: F Statistic for Wilks' Lambda is exact.

```
/* Program 4.6 */

options ls = 70 ps=45 nodate nonumber;

/*
Ref: Analysis and Design of certain quantitative
                        multiresponse experiments;
by S. N. Roy, R. Gnanadesikan and J. N. Srivastava p. 53.

Independent Variables:        Dependent Variables:
A: Air Injection              Y1: Density
B: Nozzle Teperature          Y2: Seive (%)
C: Crutcher Amps              Y3: Moisture (%)
D: Inlet Air teperature       Y4: Rate (Bins/hour)
E: Tower Air flow             Y5: Tailings (#/hour times .01)
F: Number of baffles          Y6: Stickiness
G: Nozzle Pressure            Y7: Free Moisture
*/

data actselct ;
input a b c d e f g h  activt selectvt  ;
ab = a*b;
ac = a*c;
ad = a*d;
ae = a*e;
af = a*f;
ag = a*g;
ah = a*h;
bg = b*g;
bh = b*h;
ce = c*e;
cf = c*f;
cg = c*g;
ch = c*h;
dg = d*g;
dh = d*h;
eg = e*g;
eh = e*h;
fg = f*g;
fh = f*h;
gh = g*h;

lines ;
1  1  1  1  1  1  1 -1 4.99 92.2
1  1  1  1  1  1 -1  1 5.00 93.9
1  1  1  1 -1 -1  1  1 5.61 94.6
1  1  1  1 -1 -1 -1 -1 4.76 95.1
1  1 -1 -1  1  1  1  1 5.23 91.8
1  1 -1 -1  1  1 -1 -1 4.77 94.1
1  1 -1 -1 -1 -1  1 -1 4.99 95.4
1  1 -1 -1 -1 -1 -1  1 5.17 93.4
1 -1  1 -1  1 -1  1  1 4.90 94.1
1 -1  1 -1  1 -1 -1 -1 4.90 93.2
1 -1  1 -1 -1  1  1 -1 5.24 92.8
1 -1  1 -1 -1  1 -1  1 4.95 93.8
1 -1 -1  1  1 -1  1 -1 4.96 91.6
1 -1 -1  1  1 -1 -1  1 5.03 92.3
1 -1 -1  1 -1  1  1  1 5.14 90.6
1 -1 -1  1 -1  1 -1 -1 5.05 93.4
```

```
/* Program 4.6 continued */

-1   1   1  -1   1  -1   1  -1 4.97 93.1
-1   1   1  -1   1  -1  -1   1 4.83 93.3
-1   1   1  -1  -1   1   1   1 5.27 92.0
-1   1   1  -1  -1   1  -1  -1 5.20 92.5
-1   1  -1   1   1  -1   1   1 5.34 91.9
-1   1  -1   1   1  -1  -1  -1 5.00 92.1
-1   1  -1   1  -1   1   1  -1 5.28 91.9
-1   1  -1   1  -1   1  -1   1 4.93 93.7
-1  -1   1   1   1   1   1   1 4.91 91.0
-1  -1   1   1   1   1  -1  -1 4.71 92.9
-1  -1   1   1  -1  -1   1  -1 4.99 94.8
-1  -1   1   1  -1  -1  -1   1 4.91 94.1
-1  -1  -1  -1   1   1   1  -1 4.86 91.7
-1  -1  -1  -1   1   1  -1   1 4.65 89.4
-1  -1  -1  -1  -1  -1   1   1 5.24 92.8
-1  -1  -1  -1  -1  -1  -1  -1 5.05 93.7
;
/* Source: Daniel and Riblett (1954).  Reprinted with
   permission from American Chemical Society. Copyright 1954,
   American Chemical Society. */

title1 'Output 4.6';
title2
' Data from Daniel & Riblett (1954) and illustrated
                              by Gnanadesikan et al.';

proc reg outest = est1  data = actselct ;
model activt selectvt = a b c d e f g h ab ac ad ae af
        ag ah bg bh ce cf cg ch dg dh eg eh fg fh gh ;

onlymain: mtest ab, ac, ad, ae, af, ag, ah, bg, bh,
        ce, cf, cg, ch, dg, dh, eg, eh, fg, fh, gh ;

ag_eq_0: mtest ag;

/*
ab_eq_0: mtest ab ;
ac_eq_0: mtest ac ;
ad_eq_0: mtest ad ;
ae_eq_0: mtest ae ;
af_eq_0: mtest af ;
ah_eq_0: mtest ah ;
bg_eq_0: mtest bg ;
bh_eq_0: mtest bh ;
ce_eq_0: mtest ce ;
cf_eq_0: mtest cf ;
cg_eq_0: mtest cg ;
ch_eq_0: mtest ch ;
dg_eq_0: mtest dg ;
dh_eq_0: mtest dh ;
eg_eq_0: mtest eg ;
eh_eq_0: mtest eh ;
fg_eq_0: mtest fg ;
fh_eq_0: mtest fh ;
gh_eq_0: mtest gh ;
*/
```

```
/* Program 4.6 continued */

data effects;
set est1 ;
eff_a=2*a;
eff_b=2*b;
eff_c=2*c;
eff_d=2*d;
eff_e=2*e;
eff_f=2*f;
eff_g=2*g;
eff_h=2*h;
eff_ab=2*ab;
eff_ac=2*ac;
eff_ad=2*ad;
eff_ae=2*ae;
eff_af=2*af;
eff_ag=2*ag;
eff_ah=2*ah ;
eff_bg=2*bg ;
eff_bh=2*bh ;
eff_ce=2*ce ;
eff_cf=2*cf ;
eff_cg=2*cg ;
eff_ch=2*ch ;
eff_dg=2*dg ;
eff_dh=2*dh ;
eff_eg=2*eg ;
eff_eh=2*eh ;
eff_fg=2*fg ;
eff_fh=2*fh ;
eff_gh=2*gh ;

proc print data = effects ;
var _depvar_ eff_a eff_b eff_c eff_d eff_e eff_f
                                       eff_g eff_h ;

title2 'effects for Main Factors' ;
title3
'Calculation of Effects (Coefficients are half of the
                        effect of the contrasts)';

proc reg data = actselct ;
model activt = a b c d e f g h ;
model selectvt = activt a b c d e f g h ;

run;
```

177

Data from Daniel & Riblett (1954) and illustrated by Gnanadesikan et al.

Multivariate Test: ONLYMAIN

Multivariate Statistics and F Approximations

S=2   M=8.5   N=0

Statistic	Value	F	Num DF	Den DF	Pr > F
Wilks' Lambda	0.02063889	0.5961	40	4	0.8258
Pillai's Trace	1.66282174	0.7397	40	6	0.7425
Hotelling-Lawley Trace	14.33703301	0.3584	40	2	0.9266
Roy's Greatest Root	11.44314494	1.7165	20	3	0.3667

NOTE: F Statistic for Roy's Greatest Root is an upper bound.
NOTE: F Statistic for Wilks' Lambda is exact.

Data from Daniel & Riblett (1954) and illustrated by Gnanadesikan et al.

Multivariate Test: AG_EQ_0

Multivariate Statistics and Exact F Statistics

S=1   M=0   N=0

Statistic	Value	F	Num DF	Den DF	Pr > F
Wilks' Lambda	0.78244006	0.2781	2	2	0.7824
Pillai's Trace	0.21755994	0.2781	2	2	0.7824
Hotelling-Lawley Trace	0.27805317	0.2781	2	2	0.7824
Roy's Greatest Root	0.27805317	0.2781	2	2	0.7824

effects for Main Factors
Calculation of Effects (Coefficients are half of the effect of the contrasts)

OBS	_DEPVAR_	EFF_A	EFF_B	EFF_C	EFF_D
1	ACTIVT	0.03437	0.11563	-0.03437	0.024375
2	SELECTVT	0.71250	0.55000	0.85000	-0.062500

OBS	EFF_E	EFF_F	EFF_G	EFF_H
1	-0.17062	-0.02937	0.18813	0.08688
2	-1.00000	-1.11250	-0.53750	-0.48750

effects for Main Factors
Calculation of Effects (Coefficients are half of the effect of the contrasts)

Model: MODEL1
Dependent Variable: ACTIVT

Analysis of Variance

Source	DF	Sum of Squares	Mean Square	F Value	Prob>F
Model	8	0.71393	0.08924	3.551	0.0081
Error	23	0.57805	0.02513		
C Total	31	1.29197			

Root MSE	0.15853	R-square	0.5526
Dep Mean	5.02594	Adj R-sq	0.3970
C.V.	3.15428		

Parameter Estimates

Variable	DF	Parameter Estimate	Standard Error	T for H0: Parameter=0	Prob > |T|
INTERCEP	1	5.025938	0.02802481	179.339	0.0001
A	1	0.017187	0.02802481	0.613	0.5457
B	1	0.057813	0.02802481	2.063	0.0506
C	1	-0.017187	0.02802481	-0.613	0.5457
D	1	0.012188	0.02802481	0.435	0.6677
E	1	-0.085312	0.02802481	-3.044	0.0058
F	1	-0.014687	0.02802481	-0.524	0.6052
G	1	0.094063	0.02802481	3.356	0.0027
H	1	0.043438	0.02802481	1.550	0.1348

Output 4.6
effects for Main Factors
Calculation of Effects (Coefficients are half of the effect of the contrasts)

Model: MODEL2
Dependent Variable: SELECTVT

Analysis of Variance

Source	DF	Sum of Squares	Mean Square	F Value	Prob>F
Model	9	36.14596	4.01622	4.506	0.0019
Error	22	19.60904	0.89132		
C Total	31	55.75500			

Root MSE	0.94410	R-square	0.6483	
Dep Mean	92.91250	Adj R-sq	0.5044	
C.V.	1.01611			

Parameter Estimates

Variable	DF	Parameter Estimate	Standard Error	T for H0: Parameter=0	Prob > |T|
INTERCEP	1	101.631642	6.24320551	16.279	0.0001
ACTIVT	1	-1.734829	1.24175328	-1.397	0.1763
A	1	0.386067	0.16825356	2.295	0.0317
B	1	0.375295	0.18167937	2.066	0.0508
C	1	0.395183	0.16825356	2.349	0.0282
D	1	-0.010107	0.16757919	-0.060	0.9525
E	1	-0.648003	0.19767756	-3.278	0.0034
F	1	-0.581730	0.16788802	-3.465	0.0022
G	1	-0.105568	0.20370704	-0.518	0.6095
H	1	-0.168393	0.17539422	-0.960	0.3474

```
/* Program 4.7 */

options ls=78 ps=45 nodate nonumber;
title1 'Output 4.7';
title2 'Analysis of Covariance';

data heat ;
input foam $ fabric $ hr5 hr10 hr15 wt;
lines ;
foam_a fabric_x 9.2 18.3 20.4 10.3
foam_a fabric_x 9.5 17.8 21.1 10.1
foam_a fabric_y 10.2 15.9 18.9 10.5
foam_a fabric_y 9.9 16.4  19.2  9.7
foam_a fabric_z 7.1 12.8 16.7 9.8
foam_a fabric_z 7.3 12.6 16.9 9.9
foam_b fabric_x 8.2 12.3 15.9 9.5
foam_b fabric_x 8.0 13.4 15.4 9.3
foam_b fabric_y 9.4 17.7 21.4 11.0
foam_b fabric_y 9.9 16.9 21.6 10.8
foam_b fabric_z 8.8 14.7 20.1 9.3
foam_b fabric_z 8.1 14.1 17.4 7.7
foam_c fabric_x 7.7 12.5 17.3 10.0
foam_c fabric_x 7.4 13.3 18.1 10.5
foam_c fabric_y 8.7 13.9 18.4 9.8
foam_c fabric_y 8.8 13.5 19.1 9.8
foam_c fabric_z 7.7 14.4 18.7 8.5
foam_c fabric_z 7.8 15.2 18.1 9.0
;

proc glm data = heat;
class foam fabric ;
model hr5 hr10 hr15=wt foam fabric foam*fabric/ss1 nouni;
contrast '(a,z) vs. (c,x)'
intercept 0 foam 1 0 -1 fabric -1 0 1
                  foam*fabric  0 0 1 0 0 0 -1 0 0 ;
contrast 'Foam a vs b ' foam 1 -1 0 ;
manova h = foam fabric foam*fabric/ printe printh ;

/*
proc glm data = heat ;
class foam fabric ;
model hr5 hr10 hr15=wt foam fabric foam*fabric/ss3 nouni;
lsmeans foam fabric foam*fabric ;
contrast 'Foam a vs b ' foam 1 -1 0 ;
contrast '(a,z) vs. (c,x)'
        intercept 0 foam 1 0 -1 fabric -1 0 1
            foam*fabric  0 0 1 0 0 0 -1 0 0 ;
manova h = foam fabric foam*fabric/ printe printh ;
*/
run;
```

Output 4.7
Analysis of Covariance

General Linear Models Procedure
Multivariate Analysis of Variance

H = Type I SS&CP Matrix for FOAM*FABRIC

	HR5	HR10	HR15
HR5	4.2471325113	12.15109966	10.829644894
HR10	12.15109966	43.759660936	37.301538188
HR15	10.829644894	37.301538188	35.316721864

Characteristic Roots and Vectors of: E Inverse * H, where
H = Type I SS&CP Matrix for FOAM*FABRIC   E = Error SS&CP Matrix

Characteristic Root	Percent	Characteristic Vector V'EV=1		
		HR5	HR10	HR15
107.143996	97.32	1.83013721	0.94201413	0.10720385
2.336488	2.12	−1.48618484	−0.05890150	0.58324500
0.614490	0.56	0.39839071	−0.39388563	0.31410491

Manova Test Criteria and F Approximations for
the Hypothesis of no Overall FOAM*FABRIC Effect
H = Type I SS&CP Matrix for FOAM*FABRIC   E = Error SS&CP Matrix

S=3   M=0   N=2

Statistic	Value	F	Num DF	Den DF	Pr > F
Wilks' Lambda	0.00171661	13.6020	12	16.16601	0.0001
Pillai's Trace	2.07164591	4.4631	12	24	0.0009
Hotelling-Lawley Trace	110.09497331	42.8147	12	14	0.0001
Roy's Greatest Root	107.14399611	214.2880	4	8	0.0001

NOTE: F Statistic for Roy's Greatest Root is an upper bound.

184

Analysis of Covariance

General Linear Models Procedure
Multivariate Analysis of Variance

H = Contrast SS&CP Matrix for (a,z) vs. (c,x)

	HR5	HR10	HR15
HR5	0.048334471	0.0118010003	0.0992056057
HR10	0.0118010003	0.0028812482	0.0242213344
HR15	0.0992056057	0.0242213344	0.2036176665

Characteristic Roots and Vectors of: E Inverse * H, where
H = Contrast SS&CP Matrix for (a,z) vs. (c,x)   E = Error SS&CP Matrix

Characteristic Root	Percent	Characteristic Vector V'EV=1		
		HR5	HR10	HR15
0.29908902	100.00	2.01051973	0.72072806	0.14668199
0.00000000	0.00	−1.28334306	−0.24861955	0.65483868
0.00000000	0.00	−0.16644446	0.68172230	0.00000000

Manova Test Criteria and Exact F Statistics for
the Hypothesis of no Overall (a,z) vs. (c,x) Effect
H = Contrast SS&CP Matrix for (a,z) vs. (c,x)   E = Error SS&CP Matrix

S=1   M=0.5   N=2

Statistic	Value	F	Num DF	Den DF	Pr > F
Wilks' Lambda	0.76977019	0.5982	3	6	0.6392
Pillai's Trace	0.23022981	0.5982	3	6	0.6392
Hotelling-Lawley Trace	0.29908902	0.5982	3	6	0.6392
Roy's Greatest Root	0.29908902	0.5982	3	6	0.6392

CHAPTER 5: Analysis of Repeated Measures Data

5.1 Introduction
5.2 Single Population
    5.2.1 Profile Analysis
    5.2.2 Testing for Covariance Structures
    5.2.3 Univariate Analysis
    5.2.4 Fitting the Polynomial Curve
    5.2.5 Repeated Measure Designs for Treatment Combinations/Conditions
5.3 k Populations
    5.3.1 Comparison of Treatments
    5.3.2 Profile Analysis
    5.3.3 A Univariate Approach
    5.3.4 Study of Time Trends
5.4 Factorial Designs
5.5 Analysis in the Presence of Covariates
    5.5.1 A Multivariate Analysis of Covariance
    5.5.2 A Univariate Approach
5.6 Analysis Using Random Coefficient Models
5.7 The Growth Curve Models
    5.7.1 Polynomial Growth
    5.7.2 Rao-Khatri Reduction
    5.7.3 Test of Homogeneity of Regression Coefficients
    5.7.4 Growth as a Nonlinear Regression Model
5.8 Crossover Designs
    5.8.1 Analysis of Crossover Designs
    5.8.2 Construction of Crossover Designs

5.1 Introduction

In many experiments, several treatments are applied to the same experimental unit at different time points, or only a single treatment is applied to a subject but the measurements on the same characteristic or set of characteristics are taken on more than one occasion. The data collected under these or similar kinds of experimental setups are often referred to as *repeated measures data* and require extra care in their analyses.

A common reason for taking repeated measures on the same subject in many biological, medical, psychological, and sociological experiments is the fact that there is usually more variability in the measurements between the subjects than within a given subject. As a result, treatments applied to the same subject provide a more comparable set of measurements than several parallel groups subjected to different treatments. The analysis, however, is complicated by the fact that the measurements taken on the same subject will most likely be correlated. Therefore it is necessary to incorporate this special feature of the data in the modeling and analysis.

Within the domain of repeated measures, there are certain subtle differences in the analyses, depending on the design and the data collection scheme. For example, a situation in which three different drugs are all tried on a group of 30 patients at different time periods (and possibly in different sequences) is different in design and analysis from the one in which each of the three drugs is given to a different group of ten patients who are all observed over a certain period of time. These features are very important in choosing an appropriate model, in deciding the appropriate hypotheses to be tested, and in constructing of the corresponding statistical tests.

Repeated measures designs also arise naturally in many other research or industrial contexts. For example, an auto maker may be interested in the number of problems various models of cars may have over time. In order to study this, he may decide to follow up on a certain specific group of cars of these models for a given length of time. Similarly soft drink manufacturer may want to compare her drink with those from some of her competitors and to do so she may decide to conduct a double-blind taste test on a group of potential consumers. A psychologist may be interested in comparing the performance of students at various schools and may administer a battery of several tests to sample groups of students from these schools. The common aspect in all these problems is that the data are multivariate in nature: on each subject we have a vector of repeated measurements which are correlated within themselves but are independent for different subjects.

This chapter considers various experimental situations where repeated measures data may arise and concentrates on the analysis of such data. However an application to the generation of two particular crossover designs using SAS will also be included in Section 5.8.

5.2 Single Population

5.2.1 Profile Analysis

Example 1: Profile of Memory Data (Srivastava and Carter, 1983)

Srivastava and Carter (1983, p. 201) presented an example where a group of ten subjects was given a memory test three times. The purpose of the study was to test if there were any differences in the test scores for the three trials. In other words, if $\mu' = (\mu_1, \mu_2, \mu_3)$ is the vector of true mean scores at three occasions, then we wish to test $H_0 : \mu_1 = \mu_2 = \mu_3$. A graphical representation of the elements of μ (i.e., graph of μ_i versus i) is called a *profile of the vector* μ. Using this terminology, our null hypothesis represents the hypothesis of a horizontal profile. The sample profile, that is, a profile for the sample mean vector $\bar{Y}$ is given in Output 5.1 generated by Program 5.1.

The data can be thought of as collected under a randomized complete block design in which subjects are the blocks and the three trials are the treatments. Since the group of subjects is a random sample, the block effect is assumed to be random. If we can assume equal correlation between the three trials then the above data can be analyzed as the univariate randomized complete block design. This, however, may be a questionable assumption and its validity would need to be examined before any such analysis. We will come back to this analysis later. If no such assumption is made, it may be more appropriate to assume a general correlation structure for the three trials and analyze the data using multivariate techniques. The null hypothesis under consideration can be written as $\mathbf{C}\mu = \mathbf{0}$, where

$$\mathbf{C} = \begin{bmatrix} 1 & 0 & -1 \\ 0 & 1 & -1 \end{bmatrix}.$$

Since for the underlying multivariate linear model given in Equation 3.1, $\mathbf{B} = (\mu_1, \mu_2, \mu_3) = \mu'$, the above hypothesis can be written as $H_0 : \mathbf{BM} = \mathbf{0}$ with $\mathbf{M} = \mathbf{C}$ and can be tested using the multivariate approach presented in Chapters 3 and 4. Note that the multivariate linear model has only intercepts and no independent variables on the right-hand side. These kinds of models have already been examined in the previous chapters. To analyze these data, we use the SAS code given in Program 5.2. Selected parts of the corresponding output appear in Output 5.2. Note that the null hypothesis stated above will not be rejected (p values for all four tests are equal to 0.9639). In this case all four multivariate tests are exact and equivalent.

5.2.2 Testing for Covariance Structures

In the preceding section, we discussed the multivariate approach to comparison of components of the mean vector. An alternative, but not necessarily universally better, approach can be taken by interpreting each subject as a block and the memory test periods as the plots within blocks. This interpretation results in a complete block design structure for the experimental layout in which block (subject) effects are random. Remember, however, that since the plots are memory tests and hence of a temporal nature, they cannot be randomized within blocks. In addition, they may exhibit a certain dependence between the observations within a subject. If there were no such dependence, then assuming no SUBJECT*TEST interaction, a comparison of the memory tests could be made using the usual ANOVA F test. Unfortunately, this ideal situation rarely occurs in practice. There are, however, certain covariance structures modeling the dependence which would still admit the valid F tests for some comparisons. These possible covariance structures should therefore be formally tested for, before assuming them and applying the usual ANOVA F tests. We describe four tests for some of the covariance structures here.

A test for sphericity Let $\mathbf{y}_i$, $i = 1, ..., n$ be a random sample of size n from $N_p(\mu, \Sigma)$. To test the null hypothesis $H_0 : \Sigma = \sigma^2 \mathbf{I}$, σ^2 unknown, Mauchly (1940) derived the likelihood ratio test statistic $L^{n/2}$, where

$$L = |\mathbf{S}|/(p^{-1} tr\, \mathbf{S})^p, \tag{5.1}$$

and $\mathbf{S}$ is the sample variance-covariance matrix defined by

$$\mathbf{S} = \frac{1}{n-1}\sum_{i=1}^{n}(\mathbf{y}_i - \bar{\mathbf{y}})(\mathbf{y}_i - \bar{\mathbf{y}})', \quad \bar{\mathbf{y}} = \frac{1}{n}\sum_{i=1}^{n}\mathbf{y}_i.$$

For large samples, $-\{n - (2p^2 + p + 2)/6p\}\ln L$ has an approximate chi-square distribution with degrees of freedom $\frac{1}{2}p(p+1) - 1$.

Using the REPEATED statement in PROC GLM, we can perform the tests for sphericity on certain sets of contrasts but not on the original data. The use of the REPEATED statement included in Program 5.2 will be illustrated later in Section 5.2.3.

A test for compound symmetry Given a sample of size n from $N_p(\mu, \Sigma)$, for testing the null hypothesis $H_0 : \Sigma = \sigma^2 \mathbf{V}$, where

$$\mathbf{V} = \begin{bmatrix} 1 & \rho & . & . & . & \rho \\ \rho & 1 & . & . & . & \rho \\ . & . & . & . & . & . \\ \rho & \rho & . & . & . & 1 \end{bmatrix}, -(p-1)^{-1} \le \rho \le 1$$

and σ^2 unknown, the likelihood ratio test statistic is $L^{n/2}$, where

$$L = |\mathbf{S}|/[(s^2)^p(1-r)^{p-1}\{1 + (p-1)r\}],$$

$\mathbf{S} = (s_{ij})$ as defined before, $s^2 = p^{-1}\sum_{i=1}^{p} s_{ii}$, and

$$r = 2[p(p-1)s^2]^{-1}\sum_{i=1}^{p}\sum_{j=i+1}^{p} s_{ij}.$$

For large samples,

$$Q = -[n - \{p(p+1)^2(2p-3)\}/\{6(p-1)(p^2 + p - 4)\}]\ln L \tag{5.2}$$

follows approximate chi-square distribution with $\frac{1}{2}p(p+1) - 2$ degrees of freedom.

Example 1: Testing Compound Symmetry, Memory Data (continued)

To test if the variance-covariance matrix of the scores on the three memory tests possess compound symmetry, we use the likelihood ratio test described in Equation 5.2. The SAS/IML code to perform the calculations appears in Program 5.3. From Output 5.3,

$$s^2 = 8.9963, \; r = 0.9181$$

$$|\mathbf{S}| = 12.5091, \; L = 0.9025, \quad \text{and } Q = 0.9873.$$

Corresponding to the observed values 0.9873 of $Q \sim \chi^2_{\frac{1}{2}p(p+1)-2}$ (or χ^2_4) the p value is 0.9117. Therefore we accept the null hypothesis of compound symmetry.

The usual ANOVA F tests which traditionally assume sphericity for the variance-covariance matrix remain valid under compound symmetry as well. Thus an acceptance of the null hypothesis of compound symmetry may be helpful to researchers applying or wishing to apply the analysis of variance techniques in their data analysis.

A test for circular covariance A useful covariance structure which can naturally occur when repeated measures are taken with spatial and not time considerations is a circular pattern for the variance-covariance matrix. For example, for $p=5$ and 6, the variance-covariance matrix is

$$\begin{bmatrix} R_0 & R_1 & R_2 & R_2 & R_1 \\ R_1 & R_0 & R_1 & R_2 & R_2 \\ R_2 & R_1 & R_0 & R_1 & R_2 \\ R_2 & R_2 & R_1 & R_0 & R_1 \\ R_1 & R_2 & R_2 & R_1 & R_0 \end{bmatrix}, \begin{bmatrix} R_0 & R_1 & R_2 & R_3 & R_2 & R_1 \\ R_1 & R_0 & R_1 & R_2 & R_3 & R_2 \\ R_2 & R_1 & R_0 & R_1 & R_2 & R_3 \\ R_3 & R_2 & R_1 & R_0 & R_1 & R_2 \\ R_2 & R_3 & R_2 & R_1 & R_0 & R_1 \\ R_1 & R_2 & R_3 & R_2 & R_1 & R_0 \end{bmatrix}$$

Examples of the situations in which it is natural to assume such a covariance structure are spatial repeated measurements taken on the petals of a flower or on the tentacles of a starfish.

Although the assumption of circular covariance does not necessarily simplify the analysis of data, a test for it is important in its own right. A likelihood ratio test statistic for the null hypothesis of circular covariance structure given by Olkin and Press (1969) is

$$L^{2/n} = 2^{2(p-m-1)}|\mathbf{U}|/\prod_{j=1}^{p} \nu_j, \tag{5.3}$$

where m is such that $p = 2m$ or $p = 2m + 1$, $\mathbf{U} = (u_{ij}) = \Gamma'(n-1)\mathbf{S}\Gamma$, $\Gamma = (\gamma_{ij})$ is a p by p orthogonal (orthonormal) matrix with

$$\gamma_{ij} = p^{-1/2}[cos\, 2\pi\, p^{-1}\, (i-1)(j-1) + sin\, 2\pi\, p^{-1}\, (i-1)(j-1)], i,j = 1,...,p.$$

Further,

$$\nu_1 = u_{11},\ \nu_2 = u_{22} + u_{pp},...,\nu_m = u_{mm} + u_{m+2,m+2},\ \nu_{m+1} = u_{m+1,m+1},$$

for $p = 2m$ and

$$\nu_1 = u_{11},\ \nu_2 = u_{22} + u_{pp},...,\nu_{m+1} = u_{m+1,m+1} + u_{m+2,m+2},\ \text{ for } p = 2m + 1.$$

Also, $\nu_j = \nu_{p-j+2}$ for $j = 2,...,p$.

Under the null hypothesis, for L defined in Equation 5.3

$$-2(1 - \frac{2b}{n})ln\ L \tag{5.4}$$

follows an approximate chi-square distribution with f degrees of freedom, where for $p = 2m$, $f = (p^2 - 2)/2$ and $b = (2p^3 + 9p^2 - 2p - 18)/12(p^2 - 2)$; for $p = 2m + 1$, $f = (p^2 - 1)/2$ and for $b = (2p + 9)/12$. Hence the null hypothesis can be tested using the appropriate χ^2_f cutoff point.

The SAS/IML code to test for circular symmetry is given in Program 5.4 along with an illustrative analysis of cork data presented in Output 5.4.

Example 2: Testing Circular Covariance, Cork Boring Data (Rao, 1948)

For the data set of Rao (1948), extensively discussed in Chapters 1, 2, and 3 (cork boring in four directions: North, East, South, and West), we expect that the amount of correlation of a measurement, say taken at the north facing of the tree, with measurements at its immediate neighboring facings, east and west, may be the same while measurement on the opposite direction, south, may be different from these two. This assumption would lead to a circular structure for the 4 by 4 variance-covariance matrix for the cork measurements. Therefore, we want to statistically test the validity of this assumption. To perform the likelihood ratio test of Olkin and Press, we have, $L = 0.0000273$. Correspondingly, the observed value of the approximate chi-square statistic (Equation 5.4) with $df=7$ is 18.8204. This leads to a p value of 0.0088 and hence a rejection of the hypothesis of circular covariance structure.

Note that PROC MIXED uses, among many others, a Toeplitz structure in modeling and data analysis. The circular structure is a special case of the Toeplitz structure.

Covariance structures guaranteeing the sphericity of orthogonal contrasts
Huynh and Feldt (1970) and Rouanet and Le'pine (1970) derived a set of necessary and sufficient conditions on the covariance structures under which the usual F tests formed by the ratios of mean squares still follow the exact F distributions. As a result, in the repeated measures context despite the presence of correlation among the repeated measures on the same subject, the usual univariate ANOVA tests can still be used so long as these correlations can be assumed to have a particular structure. Specifically, the vector of all orthogonal contrasts would satisfy the sphericity requirement if for the original variance-covariance matrix $\Sigma = (\sigma_{ij})$, $\sigma_{ii} + \sigma_{jj} - 2\sigma_{ij}$ is a constant for all i, j. As in Huynh and Feldt (1970), we call this structure of a variance-covariance matrix a Type H structure and the condition of having a constant value for $\sigma_{ii} + \sigma_{jj} - 2\sigma_{ij}$ a Type H condition. This condition is automatically satisfied by the covariance matrices with compound symmetry, and hence the class of Type H structure covariance matrices form a slightly more general class. Note, however, that the circular covariance structure and many other important covariance structures including the autoregressive structure *do not* belong to this class.

To test if the variance-covariance matrix can be assumed to have this structure, Huynh and Feldt (1970) suggest applying the sphericity tests on the variance-covariance matrix of the set of $(p-1)$ orthogonal contrasts. If $\mathbf{S}$ is the sample variance-covariance matrix computed from the original data and $\mathbf{C}$ is the matrix defining $(p-1)$ orthogonal contrasts, then the likelihood ratio test is given by $L^{n/2}$, where

$$L = |\mathbf{C}\mathbf{S}\mathbf{C}'|/\{(p-1)^{-1}tr(\mathbf{C}\mathbf{S}\mathbf{C}')\}^{p-1}. \tag{5.5}$$

The value of L in Equation 5.5 does not depend on the choice of the suborthogonal matrix $\mathbf{C}$, and hence any of the several choices (such as HELMERT, or POLYNOMIAL, as specified in the REPEATED statement of PROC GLM) would serve the purpose. Under the null hypothesis of sphericity of the orthogonal contrasts,

$$-\{n - (2(p-1)^2 + (p-1) + 2)/(6(p-1))\}ln\,L$$

approximately follows a chi-square distribution with $p(p-1)/2 - 1\ df$. When we specify the PRINTE option on the REPEATED statement in PROC GLM, it produces this test and titles it

Applied to Orthogonal Components: Test for Sphericity: Mauchly's Criterion=

For the memory data, Mauchly's test on the orthogonal contrasts (see Output 5.2) strongly favors the null hypothesis (p value=0.9349).

This suggests, as will be seen later, that the analysis of these data using the univariate ANOVA may be deemed valid. Since certain orthogonal contrasts have meaningful and simple interpretations, accepting the independence of these contrasts and constant variances is very desirable.

5.2.3 Univariate Analysis

Repeated measures data can be analyzed using the univariate techniques applicable for split plot designs under certain assumptions on the covariance structures of within-subject measurements. These requirements on covariance structure are derived by the necessary and sufficient conditions for the usual F test to be valid and hence are rather artificial. It is hard to imagine repeated measures situations where such correlations would naturally occur due to practical considerations. Hence the validity of these assumptions should always be statistically tested before any univariate analysis based on these assumptions is used to draw conclusions about the significance of the effects. If the hypothesis of the validity of these assumptions is rejected, there may still be a way to draw meaningful conclusions from the univariate analysis after making certain adjustments to the degrees of freedom of the F test.

For example, consider the memory data discussed earlier in this chapter. In this experiment, each subject was given three memory tests. If we interpret each subject as a random block (whole plot) containing three treatments (memory tests), then the design resembles a complete block design, except that, within each block, the randomization of the treatments is not possible. In fact, from the very design of this experiment, such a randomization has no meaning. Since the scores on the three memory tests of a given subject are correlated, the design can be treated as a split plot design and can probably be analyzed using the standard univariate analysis of variance techniques for this particular design. However, there is still a subtle difference in that the split plot experiments assume that plots (tests) within a given block (subject) are equicorrelated with each other. This assumption we would seriously doubt for data collected over time, as in the present example. Hence it is necessary to formally test if such an assumption, usually referred to as the *assumption of compound symmetry*, can be made for the data at hand. The approximate likelihood ratio test for compound symmetry has been given in the previous pages, and we can use it for this purpose. If the data pass this test, univariate analysis of these data using the aforementioned techniques may be applicable, for most practical purposes.

Huynh and Feldt (1970) and Rouanet and Le'pine (1970) give a weaker requirement for the validity of the ANOVA F test in the split plot design. This requirement, already described in Section 5.2.2, amounts to a condition of sphericity of the variance-covariance matrix of all orthogonal contrasts of repeated measures and, hence, can be tested using Mauchly's sphericity test. Recall that the sphericity of the variance-covariance matrix implies a zero correlation as well as equality of the variances. Since, in the case of orthogonal contrasts, the zero correlation is ensured from the very definition of orthogonality, a rejection of the hypothesis points to unequal variances or to nonhomogeneity of the variances for the orthogonal contrasts.

When the homogeneity assumption is false, it is still possible to use the ANOVA F test by modifying its degrees of freedom. Box (1954) gave a measure defined as

$$\epsilon = \frac{[tr\,(\mathbf{C}'\Sigma\mathbf{C})]^2}{(p-1)tr\,(\mathbf{C}'\Sigma\mathbf{C})^2} = \frac{[\sum_j \theta_j]^2}{(p-1)\sum_j \theta_j^2},$$

where the θ_j are the $p-1$ eigenvalues of $\mathbf{C}'\Sigma\mathbf{C}$. From the above formula, it is evident that $(p-1)^{-1} \le \epsilon \le 1$, when p is the number of repeated measures. When the variance-covariance matrix is spherical, all the eigenvalues $\theta_1, ..., \theta_{p-1}$ are equal and hence $\epsilon = 1$. The smaller values of ϵ indicate a relatively high degree of departure from sphericity.

Box also suggests that in the case of departure from the sphericity, the conventional F test with degrees of freedom $(p-1)$ and $(p-1)(n-1)$ should be replaced by an approximate F test with degrees of freedom $\epsilon(p-1)$ and $\epsilon(p-1)(n-1)$. In practice, since ϵ is unknown, its estimate

$$\hat{\epsilon}_{GG} = \frac{[tr\,(\mathbf{C}'\mathbf{S}\mathbf{C})]^2}{(p-1)tr\,(\mathbf{C}'\mathbf{S}\mathbf{C})^2}$$

can be substituted to obtain the approximate degrees of freedom. This is known as the Greenhouse-Geisser procedure. See Greenhouse and Geisser (1959). As can be easily seen, the estimate $\hat{\epsilon}$ of ϵ is obtained by replacing the variances and covariances in the formula of ϵ given above by the corresponding elements of the sample variance-covariance matrix.

Huynh and Feldt (1976) have provided the following estimate of ϵ

$$\hat{\epsilon}_{HF} = \frac{n(p-1)\hat{\epsilon}_{GG} - 2}{(p-1)[n-1-(p-1)\hat{\epsilon}_{GG}]}.$$

Note that the value of this estimate may exceed one. In this case, its value is taken to be one.

Example 1: Testing Type H Structure, Memory Data (continued)

For the memory data discussed above, $n = 10$ and $p = 3$. Based on the p value in Output 5.3, we have accepted the null hypothesis of compound symmetry. This implies that the Type H conditions hold, since compound symmetry is a more restrictive condition. Hence the univariate split plot approach is justified. However, for the sake of illustration, let us consider these data again and formally test for the Type H structure. This task can be performed using the REPEATED statement.

Since the group of 10 subjects forms a random sample, SUBJECT is a random effect. The variable TEST, representing the variable with three memory tests as the treatments, is fixed and the interaction SUBJECT*TEST is random. The conventional F test statistic for the null hypothesis of no difference between the memory test is given by

$$F = \frac{MS_{TEST}}{MS_{SUBJECT*TEST}}$$

which under H_0 follows an F distribution with $(p-1) = 2$ and $(n-1)(p-1) = 18$ degrees of freedom. This test is automatically performed when a REPEATED statement is used for the variable TEST. The SAS code for this analysis is given in the latter part of Program 5.2. The resulting output is shown as part of the Output 5.2.

The statement

```
repeated test 3 profile/printe printm;
```

performs a repeated measures analysis, with the variable TEST as the within-subject effect. Both the univariate as well as multivariate analyses are performed. If desired, the multivariate output can be suppressed by using the NOM option. The matrix **E** is printed if we use the PRINTE option and, if we use PRINTM, the matrix defining the contrasts is printed. The contrasts do not necessarily have to be orthogonal. The default matrix of contrasts is the profile matrix (which corresponds to the option PROFILE) comparing the last treatment with all the previous ones. Specifically the profile matrix in this case is

$$\begin{bmatrix} 1 & 0 & -1 \\ 0 & 1 & -1 \end{bmatrix}$$

which is referred to as the M matrix in Output 5.2. The **E** matrix of the two transformed variables using the above profile matrix is

$$\begin{bmatrix} 14.9 & 7.9 \\ 7.9 & 12.9 \end{bmatrix}.$$

There are many other transformations such as HELMERT or POLYNOMIAL for **M** matrix. However in most situations, the main interest may be to compare the responses at various time points. This can be accomplished by choosing the default, PROFILE.

There are two sets of transformed variables on which Mauchly's sphericity test is performed. The first of these corresponds to the sphericity test on the variables obtained by using the transformation matrix **M** specified in the REPEATED statement (the default in this statement). As is the case in our example, this may correspond to a nonorthogonal transformation. In the present example, for the profiles Y1-Y3 and Y2-Y3, the Mauchly's criterion is 0.8374 with a corresponding observed value of an approximate χ_2^2 as 1.4196. The corresponding p value is 0.4917.

Recall that in general the validity of F test is subject to the Type H condition which is equivalent to the sphericity of orthogonal contrasts. The above test was conducted on a set of two nonorthogonal contrasts and is not applicable for this purpose.

The test applied to the orthogonal contrasts results in a value of 0.9833 for Mauchly's criterion with an observed approximate $\chi_2^2=0.1347$ and a corresponding p value $=0.9349$. This strongly supports the null hypothesis of Type H structure for the variance-covariance matrix. The choice of which orthogonal matrix to use is immaterial, as the test does not depend on any such choice. Thus it is not necessary to know the specific choices of orthogonal contrasts, nor are they printed as part of the SAS output.

Note that if a POLYNOMIAL transformation is selected in the repeated statement, for example as in the following;

```
repeated test 3 polynomial/printe printm;
```

there will be only one Mauchly's test printed. This is because the polynomial contrast is an *orthonormal transformation*. Although the HELMERT transformation serves as an orthogonal transformation, it is not an orthonormal transformation as it is adopted in SAS since the columns of the corresponding matrix may not have unit length. Hence there will be two Mauchly's tests printed.

The univariate F test is performed for the variable TEST. Since the design is balanced, all three types of sums of squares are identical and hence the default choice of Type III sums of squares is used. Under the null hypothesis of no difference between the three memory tests, and with the understanding that the error term is $MS_{SUBJECT*TEST}$,

$$F = \frac{MS_{TEST}}{MS_{SUBJECT*TEST}} = \frac{MS_{TEST}}{MS_{ERROR(TIME)}} = \frac{0.0333}{0.7370} \approx 0.05,$$

is an observed value of $F(2, 18)$. The corresponding p value=0.9559 is very high.

A few observations and checks need to be made before we decide to accept H_0 with such a high p value. First of all, the sphericity test resulted in the acceptance of a hypothesized Type H structure. This is confirmed by the values of $\hat{\epsilon}_{GG}$ (=0.9836) and $\hat{\epsilon}_{HF}$ (=1.2564 and truncated to 1) both of which are close to 1. Thus the adjustment in the degrees of freedom is not necessary, and the distribution of the F statistic indicated above can be safely assumed to be $F(2, 18)$. In view of the very high p value, we accept the null hypothesis of no treatment effect. However, comparable p values (0.9540 and 0.9559 respectively) would have been obtained had the degrees of freedom been adjusted using $\hat{\epsilon}_{GG}$ and $\hat{\epsilon}_{HF}$, resulting in the same conclusion.

5.2.4 Fitting the Polynomial Curve

When the measurements are repeated on the same subject or unit over several time points, we may want to model these responses as a function of time. The model may arise from some theoretical considerations or may be empirically chosen to be simple enough for inferential purposes but, at the same time, to provide sufficient flexibility in fitting the data reasonably well. As an empirical approximation, justified by the Taylor expansion of the function, a model can often be found by fitting polynomials to data.

Suppose n subjects or units receive a treatment and their responses are measured over p time points. The model can be written as

$$\mathbf{y}_j = \mu + \epsilon_j,$$

where $\mathbf{y}_j$ is the p by 1 vector of measurements on the jth subject and μ is the vector of the true means for these measurements.

To fit an rth order polynomial, we take $\mu = \mathbf{G}\beta$, where $\mathbf{G}$ is the known p by $(r+1)$ matrix

$$\mathbf{G} = \begin{bmatrix} 1 & t_1 & . & . & . & t_1^r \\ 1 & t_2 & . & . & . & t_2^r \\ . & . & . & . & . & . \\ 1 & t_p & . & . & . & t_p^r \end{bmatrix}$$

and $\beta' = (\beta_0, \beta_1, ..., \beta_r)$ is the vector of unknown coefficients in the rth degree polynomial.

To test if the rth order model may indeed be sufficient, we test the hypothesis

$$H_0 : \mu = \mathbf{G}\beta \text{ vs. } H_1 : \mu \neq \mathbf{G}\beta,$$

where $\mathbf{G}$ is as defined above. It is known that the rank of $\mathbf{G}$, $Rank(\mathbf{G}) = r + 1$. If $\mathbf{H}'$ is a p by $(p - (r+1))$ matrix orthogonal to $\mathbf{G}$, with $Rank(\mathbf{H}) = p - (r+1)$, then since $\mathbf{HG} = 0$, we must have under the null hypothesis $H_0 : \mathbf{H}\mu = \mathbf{HG}\beta = 0$, and hence the null hypothesis can be reduced to a linear hypothesis of the type $H_0 : \mathbf{L}\mu = 0$. The choice of

H is not unique but the resulting Wilks' Λ and other multivariate tests would, however, be invariant of the particular choice of **H**. The test requires us to reject H_0 if

$$\frac{(n-p+r+1)n}{(n-1)(p-r-1)}\bar{\mathbf{y}}'\mathbf{H}'(\mathbf{HSH}')^{-1}\mathbf{H}\bar{\mathbf{y}} > F_\alpha(p-r-1, n-p+r+1),$$

where $\bar{\mathbf{y}}$ is the sample mean vector and **S** is the sample variance-covariance matrix.

For data that are equally spaced in time, the matrix **H** can conveniently be chosen as a matrix corresponding to the orthogonal polynomials. This is especially helpful since such a matrix can be instantly created by using the function ORPOL in SAS/IML.

Example 3: Polynomial Fitting for Fish Data (Srivastava and Carter, 1983)

Consider the fish data discussed in Chapter 3 on the number of fish that were dead after 8, 14, 24, 36, and 48 hours in 25 tanks of 20 trout, after being given various doses of copper (in mg/liter). The objective of the study was to model the effects of copper dosage on fish mortality over time. The arcsine transformed data on the number of fish that were dead at various time points were used as the dependent variables. A natural question to ask is, for a fixed level of copper dose, what is the appropriate degree of polynomial in time which can be fitted to describe the death rate of the fish?

Suppose we are interested in fitting only the second-degree models. For a fixed dose, the second-degree model then would be

$$y_j(t) = \beta_0 + \beta_1 t + \beta_2 t^2 + \epsilon_j$$

while the biggest model that can be fit would be the fourth degree (since there are five time points), namely

$$y_j(t) = \beta_0 + \beta_1 t + \beta_2 t^2 + \beta_3 t^3 + \beta_4 t^4 + \epsilon_j.$$

Thus the null hypothesis $H_0 : \mu = \mathbf{G}\beta$ can be expressed as

$$H_0 : \mu = \begin{bmatrix} 1 & 1 & 1 & 1 & 1 \\ 8 & 14 & 24 & 36 & 48 \\ 8^2 & 14^2 & 24^2 & 36^2 & 48^2 \end{bmatrix}' \begin{bmatrix} \beta_0 \\ \beta_1 \\ \beta_2 \end{bmatrix}.$$

Since **G** is completely specified by the time points (second column of **G**), we could alternatively choose the 5 by 3 matrix of second-degree orthogonal polynomials. More specifically, if we transform the data on variables y_1, y_2, y_3, y_4, and y_5 to new variables z_1, z_2, z_3, z_4, and z_5 through a 5 by 5 matrix of fourth-degree orthogonal polynomials, then we only need to test that the last two variables z_4 and z_5 which respectively represent the third- and fourth-degree effects have zero means.

In Program 5.5, we used PROC/IML to first obtain the new variables z_i, $i = 1, ..., 5$, which are coded as Z1, Z2, Z3, Z4, and Z5. For the vector of time points (8, 14, 24, 36, 48), the matrix of fourth-degree orthogonal polynomials denoted as OPOLY is constructed using the IML function ORPOL. Subsequently the data on the transformed variables are obtained by using the matrix transformation

$$(Z1\ Z2\ Z3\ Z4\ Z5)_{n\times 5} = (Y1\ Y2\ Y3\ Y4\ Y5)_{n\times 5} * OPOLY_{5\times 5}$$

or $\mathbf{Z} = \mathbf{Z_0} * OPOLY$, where n is the number of data points. The columns of matrix $\mathbf{Z}$ are then assigned the variable names Z1, Z2, Z3, Z4, and Z5 respectively. The variable z_i thus represents the effect resulting from the terms corresponding to the $(i-1)^{th}$ or lower powers of time. Thus if an rth order polynomial is adequate, then $E(z_{r+2}) = ... = E(z_p) = 0$.

To test if the second-degree model is adequate for a given dose level, we have $r=2$, and hence the transformed variables corresponding to the higher degrees, namely Z4 and Z5, should have zero means. We thus use multivariate tests to see if the intercepts corresponding to Z4 and Z5 can be assumed to be zero. This is accomplished by first sorting the data by dose levels and then by using the code presented in Program 5.5.

```
proc glm data=newdata;
by dose;
model z4 z5= /nouni;
manova h=intercept;
```

Output 5.5 indicates that this hypothesis can be accepted for lower levels of doses. However as the doses increase, there is relatively stronger case against a second-degree model. This is not surprising as, at the higher doses, most of the fish died early in the experiment. A third-degree polynomial, however, seems to fit data for all the five doses. In this case, the corresponding MODEL and MANOVA statements are

```
model z5= /nouni;
manova h=intercept;
```

We have suppressed the output to save space. Having known that a third-degree polynomial may suffice in the case of all five doses, we ask if it is possible to fit a common third-degree polynomial. In other words, if DOSE is taken as a variable at five levels then does the variable Z5, when fitted as a function of DOSE, have a zero intercept? If the entire data set of 25 observations for Z5 is analyzed under the cubic polynomial model with DOSE as a variable, the value of Wilks' Λ for the null hypothesis of no intercept for Z5 is barely significant at $\alpha = 0.05$. If we are allowed to accept this null hypothesis, it suggests that a model of the type

$$y(t) = \beta_0 + \beta_1 t + \beta_2 t^2 + \beta_3 t^3 + \gamma x_1 + \epsilon_t,$$

where x_1 is the logarithm of the dose level can be fitted to this data set. In other words, acceptance of this null hypothesis implies that the cubic polynomial curves for the five dose levels are parallel in that they differ only in the intercepts which is determined by the corresponding value of the term $(\beta_0 + \gamma x_1)$. In this case, the number of fish that died over time can be described by cubic polynomials differing only in the intercept terms.

5.2.5 Repeated Measure Designs for Treatment Combinations/Conditions

When various treatment combinations of a factorial experiment with more than two variables are conducted on the same group of subjects, then it may not be appropriate to analyze the data from this factorial experiment using the univariate analysis of variance techniques. It is so since the conventional ANOVA assumes the independence of all the measurements (or the Type H covariance structure) as the minimum requirement for the distributional validity of the ANOVA F test. Obviously, if the same unit has been subjected to various treatments one after the other, the corresponding measurements cannot be assumed to be independent and are not guaranteed to have the Type H covariance structure. However, it is possible to formulate the comparison of treatments problem in the Hotelling's T^2 framework.

By appropriately numbering the treatments, say as $1, ..., p$, and denoting the measurements on the jth unit as $\mathbf{y}_j' = (y_{1j}, ..., y_{pj})$, $j = 1, ..., n$, we can write the model as

$$\mathbf{y}_j = \mu + \epsilon_j, \ j = 1, ..., n, \tag{5.6}$$

where μ is the p by 1 vector of true means of various treatment effects. The effects of individual variables can be expressed as the contrasts of the vector μ, say $\mathbf{c}_i'\mu$, by appropriately choosing the p by 1 vectors $\mathbf{c}_i$. Likewise a simultaneous comparison of several treatments can be accomplished by simultaneously testing for several, say r, linearly independent contrasts $\mathbf{C}\mu$, where $\mathbf{C}$ is an appropriately defined r by p matrix. To test the null hypothesis $H_0 : \mathbf{C}\mu = \mathbf{d}$, where $\mathbf{d}$ is a known vector of order r by 1, Hotelling's T^2 test can be used by defining

$$T^2 = n(\mathbf{C}\bar{\mathbf{y}} - \mathbf{d})'(\mathbf{C}\mathbf{S}\mathbf{C}')^{-1}(\mathbf{C}\bar{\mathbf{y}} - \mathbf{d}). \tag{5.7}$$

The null hypothesis then is rejected if

$$F = \frac{(n-r)}{(n-1)r}T^2 > F_\alpha(r, n-r).$$

The vector $\bar{\mathbf{y}}$ here is the vector of sample means for all treatments and $\mathbf{S}$ is the sample variance-covariance matrix. Chapter 4 showed that this hypothesis can be tested using the M= specification in the MANOVA statement of PROC GLM or PROC ANOVA.

Example 4: A Two-Way Factorial Experiment, Dog Data (Data Courtesy: J. Atlee)

Johnson and Wichern (1992) provided a very fitting example of such a study, where a two-way factorial experiment was conducted as a repeated measures design to explore the possibility of finding improved anesthetics. Two variables, carbon dioxide pressure and the presence or absence of halothane, each at two levels (namely, high, low, and absent, present) respectively were used. The four treatments here referred to as 1, 2, 3, and 4, were administered in the order (high, absent), (low, absent), (high, present) and (low, present) on each of the 19 dogs. The number of milliseconds between the heartbeats was taken as the response variable. These data were collected by Dr. J. Atlee, a physician at Veteran's Hospital, Madison, Wisconsin. If the mean response of the four treatments is represented by a 4 by 1 vector μ, then the effect of halothane is represented by the contrast $(\mu_1 + \mu_2) - (\mu_3 + \mu_4) = \mathbf{c}_1'\mu$ with $\mathbf{c}_1' = (1\ 1\ -1\ -1)$, the effect of carbon dioxide is represented by $(\mu_1 + \mu_3) - (\mu_2 + \mu_4) = \mathbf{c}_2'\mu$ with $\mathbf{c}_2' = (1\ -1\ 1\ -1)$, and the interaction effect by $(\mu_1 + \mu_4) - (\mu_2 + \mu_3) = \mathbf{c}_3'\mu$ with $\mathbf{c}_3' = (1\ -1\ -1\ 1)$. Also to test that there is no difference among any of the four means, that is, $H_0 : \mu_1 = \mu_2 = \mu_3 = \mu_4$, it is possible to simultaneously test that all the three contrasts described above are zero. This is so since the three equations

$$(\mu_1 + \mu_2) - (\mu_3 + \mu_4) = 0$$
$$(\mu_1 + \mu_3) - (\mu_2 + \mu_4) = 0 \qquad (5.8)$$
$$(\mu_1 + \mu_4) - (\mu_2 + \mu_3) = 0$$

imply and are implied by the null hypothesis $H_0 : \mu_1 = \mu_2 = \mu_3 = \mu_4$. Thus the null hypothesis can alternatively be expressed as $H_0 : \mathbf{C}\mu = \mathbf{0}$, where the 3 by 4 matrix $\mathbf{C}$ consists of $\mathbf{c}_1', \mathbf{c}_2'$, and $\mathbf{c}_3'$ as its three rows. It may be noted that there are many other choices of $\mathbf{C}$ to attain this equivalence. However, the value of T^2 and hence of the resulting F statistic remains invariant of the choice of $\mathbf{C}$ matrix.

To carry out these comparisons using SAS, we need to express the problem in the linear model setup. We denote the responses corresponding to four treatments as HIGH_NOH, LOW_NOH, HIGH_H, and LOW_H respectively and collectively represent the data on these responses as a 19 by 4 matrix $\mathbf{Y}$. Thus we have the linear model

$$\mathbf{Y}_{19\times4} = \mathbf{1}_{19\times1}\mu_{1\times4}' + \mathcal{E}_{19\times4}.$$

The linear model above has only the intercept term. The null hypothesis $H_0 : \mathbf{C}\mu = \mathbf{0}$ can be written as $H_0 : \mathbf{BM} = \mathbf{0}$, with $\mathbf{M} = \mathbf{C}'$. This hypothesis can be tested by specifying the MANOVA statement

```
manova h=intercept m=(1  1 -1 -1,
                      1 -1  1 -1,
                      1 -1 -1  1);
```

In Program 5.6, we have used the representation of the $\mathbf{M}$ matrix directly through Equations 5.8 only to illustrate that the two alternatives are equivalent. Also in Program 5.6, the PRINTE and PRINTH options are used to print the error and the hypothesis sums of squares and crossproduct matrices.

The output corresponding to this statement is given in the first part of Output 5.6. First the matrix $\mathbf{M} = \mathbf{C}'$ is printed, which is followed by the error SS&CP and the hypothesis

SS&CP matrices labeled **E** and **H** respectively for the three new variables defined as the linear combinations of the four measurements using the $\mathbf{M} = \mathbf{C}'$ matrix. SAS also prints the matrix of partial correlation coefficients between the three linear combinations as well as all the eigenvalues of $\mathbf{E}^{-1}\mathbf{H}$. We have suppressed certain parts of SAS output in Output 5.6 to save space. Since the design is balanced, all the three types of SS&CP matrices described in Chapter 4 are identical. We have therefore accepted the SAS default option of Type III matrices.

For the null hypothesis described in Equations 5.8, we observe that the value of Wilks' Λ is 0.1343, correspondingly giving the observed value of F(3, 16) as F=34.3752. This is highly significant with the corresponding p value=0.0001, indicating that at least one of the equations in Equations 5.8 is possibly not true. Incidentally, the other three multivariate tests are equivalent leading to the identical observed values of (exact) F(3, 16). This is so, since all four test statistics are the functions of

$$
\begin{aligned}
T^2 &= n(\mathbf{C}\bar{\mathbf{y}} - \mathbf{d})'(\mathbf{C}\mathbf{S}\mathbf{C}')^{-1}(\mathbf{C}\bar{\mathbf{y}} - \mathbf{d}) \\
&= n\, tr\, (\mathbf{C}\mathbf{S}\mathbf{C}')^{-1}(\mathbf{C}\bar{\mathbf{y}} - \mathbf{d})(\mathbf{C}\bar{\mathbf{y}} - \mathbf{d})' \\
&= tr\, \mathbf{E}^{-1}\mathbf{H}.
\end{aligned}
$$

Since T^2 is a 1 by 1 matrix, the matrix $\mathbf{E}^{-1}\mathbf{H}$ has rank 1 and hence only one nonzero eigenvalue. Consequently, all four multivariate test criteria, which are the functions of the eigenvalues of $\mathbf{E}^{-1}\mathbf{H}$, have a one-to-one correspondences between any pair of tests and hence are all equivalent. As remarked earlier, the Hotelling's T^2 statistic and hence also the four multivariate tests listed in the SAS output do not depend on the choice of **C** matrix. Another meaningful choice of **C** matrix is a profile matrix given by

$$
\begin{bmatrix}
1 & -1 & 0 & 0 \\
1 & 0 & -1 & 0 \\
1 & 0 & 0 & -1
\end{bmatrix}.
$$

Although the **E** and **H** matrices are different in this case, the four test statistics are all identical to those obtained in Output 5.6.

Having rejected the null hypothesis given in Equations 5.8, we want to know first if the interaction between carbon dioxide levels and the presence or absence of halothane is nonexistent; second, if halothane's presence has no effect on the response; and third, if the level of carbon dioxide has no effect on the response. The corresponding **M** matrices can respectively be defined by using the third, first, and the second equations in Equations 5.8, as shown in Program 5.6. The corresponding SAS output is not presented here. The hypothesis of no interaction is accepted with the corresponding p value of 0.5294. The other two null hypotheses are rejected with the respective p values as 0.0001 and 0.0019 concluding that halothane's presence has a strong effect on the response as does the level of carbon dioxide.

We could also analyze these data as a univariate two-way classification, provided that the Type H covariance structure can be assumed for the variance-covariance matrix $D(\mathbf{y}_j) = \Sigma$. Since the matrix $\mathbf{C}$ used in Hotelling's T^2 statistic in Equation 5.7 is, by construction, orthogonal, we need only to test for the sphericity of $\mathbf{C}\Sigma\mathbf{C}'$. Since the $\mathbf{E}$ matrix printed in the Output 5.6 is equal to $[n - (p-1)]\mathbf{CSC}'$ or $16\mathbf{CSC}'$, the estimated variance-covariance matrix $\mathbf{CSC}'$ for these orthogonal contrasts can be obtained as $\mathbf{E}/[n - (p-1)] = \mathbf{E}/16$, on which a sphericity test as given in Equation 5.1 can easily be performed. Alternatively, all these computations can be achieved with the use of REPEATED statement as described in the case of memory data. Specifically the REPEATED statement is

```
repeated trtment 4/ printe printm;
```

One can verify that the Type H structure can be assumed for these data as well, thereby validating the ANOVA F tests. Further, the same conclusions are reached by the univariate analysis. We stress, however, that to test the Type H structure, the transformations for which sphericity would be tested should be *orthonormal*. That is, the rows of $\mathbf{C}$ should be orthogonal to each other and should be of unit length. This was the case for the particular $\mathbf{C}$ we have considered but may not be true in several other possible choices such as in the case where $\mathbf{C}$ is a profile matrix as defined earlier.

Often, the data are collected over time by applying different treatments or are collected under different conditions, and the number of longitudinal observations under various conditions may be different. In those cases, we may want to compare the mean responses under various conditions. In this case, assuming no carryover effects, a simple way to compare of various treatments or conditions is to test for the suitable weighted linear combinations of the mean response at different time points. The approach is best illustrated by an example.

Example 5: Comparing Treatments, A Dietary Treatment Study (Crowder and Hand, 1990)

A group of 12 patients was subjected to a dietary regime treatment. Two observations before the treatment, three during and two after the conclusion of treatment, all at different time points, were made on a variable representing the level of plasma ascorbic acid. The problem is to compare the effectiveness of the treatments by comparing the three sets of responses.

As in the previous example, we have one group of repeated measures with an unequal number of time points for each of the three conditions. If μ_1, μ_2, ..., μ_7 are the mean responses at seven consecutive time points then we may want to test the hypothesis

$$H_0 : \frac{\mu_1 + \mu_2}{2} = \frac{\mu_3 + \mu_4 + \mu_5}{3} = \frac{\mu_6 + \mu_7}{2}$$

or

$$H_0 : 3(\mu_1 + \mu_2) = 2(\mu_3 + \mu_4 + \mu_5) = 3(\mu_6 + \mu_7).$$

In matrix form, it can be written as

$$H_0 : \begin{bmatrix} 3 & 3 & -2 & -2 & -2 & 0 & 0 \\ 0 & 0 & 2 & 2 & 2 & -3 & -3 \end{bmatrix} \begin{bmatrix} \mu_1 \\ \mu_2 \\ \mu_3 \\ \mu_4 \\ \mu_5 \\ \mu_6 \\ \mu_7 \end{bmatrix} = \begin{bmatrix} 0 \\ 0 \end{bmatrix}.$$

With $\mathbf{B} = \mu' = (\mu_1, ..., \mu_7)$, $\mathbf{X} = \mathbf{1}_{12}$, and

$$\mathbf{M}' = \begin{bmatrix} 3 & 3 & -2 & -2 & -2 & 0 & 0 \\ 0 & 0 & 2 & 2 & 2 & -3 & -3 \end{bmatrix}$$

and $\mathbf{Y}$ a 12 by 7 matrix of observed responses on twelve patients at seven time points, the above hypothesis testing problem can be formulated as

$$H_0 : \mathbf{BM} = \mathbf{0}$$

under the linear model setup

$$\mathbf{Y} = \mathbf{XB} + \mathcal{E} = \mathbf{1}\mu' + \mathcal{E}.$$

Taking normality as the underlying assumption, we can test the null hypothesis as in the previous example by appropriately defining the $\mathbf{M}$ matrix in MANOVA statement of PROC GLM.

The SAS code and the selected parts of the output are respectively presented in Program 5.7 and Output 5.7. The evidence is strongly against the null hypothesis (p value $=0.0001$) for all multivariate tests which are equivalent in this case and we consequently reject H_0. We thereby conclude that the dietary regime treatment is indeed effective. However, we may still want to know if the effect of the treatment lasts for the latter periods. This hypothesis can be tested by defining the new $\mathbf{M}$ matrix consisting only of the second column of the $\mathbf{M}$ matrix indicated above, that is, $(0\ 0\ 2\ 2\ 2\ \text{-3}\ \text{-3})'$. We can verify that this hypothesis is also rejected (p value$=0.0002$), leading us to accept the well-known fact that the effect of dietary treatment does not continue after the diet ends.

5.3 k Populations

Suppose there are k different treatments and the ith treatment, say A_i, is applied to a group of n_i subjects which are observed over time for p time points. In such a situation, the p dimensional observations on these groups can be thought of as the respective random samples from the k populations corresponding to various treatments. As a first step, we can look at the problem of comparing various treatments as a problem of multivariate one-way classification. Clearly, the p dependent variables, namely the observations taken over time, are correlated and may have different means for different time points as well as for the different treatments.

For the jth dependent variable $j = 1, ..., p$ the (univariate) one-way classification model is

$$y_{ijl} = \mu_j + \tau_{ij} + \epsilon_{ijl}, \ i = 1, ..., k; l = 1, ..., n_i,$$

which, by stacking $y_{1j}, ..., y_{nj}$ one below the other, can be written in matrix form as

$$\mathbf{y}_j = \mathbf{X}\beta_j + \epsilon_j, \tag{5.9}$$

with $\mathbf{X}$ and β_j respectively as

$$\mathbf{X} = \begin{bmatrix} 1 & 1 & 0 & . & . & . & 0 \\ 1 & 1 & 0 & . & . & . & 0 \\ . & . & . & . & . & . & . \\ 1 & 1 & 0 & . & . & . & 0 \\ 1 & 0 & 1 & . & . & . & 0 \\ . & . & . & . & . & . & . \\ 1 & 0 & 1 & . & . & . & 0 \\ . & . & . & . & . & . & . \\ . & . & . & . & . & . & . \\ 1 & 0 & 0 & . & . & . & 1 \\ . & . & . & . & . & . & . \\ 1 & 0 & 0 & . & . & . & 1 \end{bmatrix}_{n \times (k+1)} \qquad \beta_j = \begin{bmatrix} \mu_j \\ \tau_{1j} \\ \tau_{2j} \\ . \\ . \\ . \\ \tau_{kj} \end{bmatrix}_{(k+1) \times 1},$$

where $n = \sum_{i=1}^{k} n_i$. The vector ϵ_j has been arranged in essentially the same way as the vector $\mathbf{y}_j$, and ϵ_j has zero mean and the variance-covariance matrix $\sigma_{jj} \mathbf{I}_n$.

The multivariate model is obtained by arranging the linear models given in Equation 5.9 side by side as columns. That is,

$$(\mathbf{y}_1 : \mathbf{y}_2 : \cdots : \mathbf{y}_p) = (\mathbf{X}\beta_1 : \mathbf{X}\beta_2 : \cdots : \mathbf{X}\beta_p) + (\epsilon_1 : \epsilon_2 : \cdots : \epsilon_p)$$

or

$$\mathbf{Y} = \mathbf{XB} + \mathcal{E},$$

where the jth columns of $\mathbf{Y}$, $\mathcal{E}$, and $\mathbf{B}$ respectively are $\mathbf{y}_j$, ϵ_j, and β_j. Since the observations taken at different time points on the same subject may be correlated, we assume that each row of $\mathcal{E}$ has zero mean and a variance-covariance matrix Σ. On the other hand since the measurements on different subjects are uncorrelated, we assume, that for $j, j' = 1, ..., p$,

$$Cov(\mathbf{y}_j, \mathbf{y}_{j'}) = \sigma_{jj'} \mathbf{I}_n.$$

In other words, the variance-covariance matrix of the elements of $\mathbf{Y}$ stacked as a column vector by taking row after row is an np by np matrix

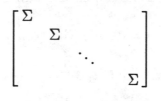

or $diag\ (\Sigma, \Sigma, ..., \Sigma)$.

The statistical problems of interest can be broadly classified into two classes: first, the comparison of various treatment groups and second, the comparison within the repeated measures. The hypothesis concerning the latter aspects are often referred to as *within-subject hypotheses*, while the former are termed *between-subject hypotheses*.

5.3.1 Comparison of Treatments

The multivariate approach to the analysis and the hypothesis testing for between-subject analysis has already been described in Chapter 4. Specifically, the hypothesis of interest is the comparison of the treatment mean vectors, namely $\mu_1,\ \mu_2, ..., \mu_k$, where $\mu_i = \mu + \tau_i,\ i = 1, ..., k$. This hypothesis is written as $H_0 : \mu_1 = \mu_2 = ... = \mu_k$ or $\tau_1 = \tau_2 = ... = \tau_k$, where $\tau_i' = (\tau_{i1},\ \tau_{i2}, ..., \tau_{ip}),\ i = 1, ..., k$. As discussed in Chapter 4, the testing of H_0 can be accomplished by MANOVA partitioning of the corrected total sums of squares and a crossproducts (SS&CP) matrix into the model SS&CP and error SS&CP matrices and then by using the appropriate Wilks' Λ or any other multivariate test statistic derived from these quantities. We will illustrate this using an example of drug comparison.

Example 6: A Three-Population Study, Heart Rate Data (Spector, 1987)

Spector (1987) presented a heart rate study which was carried out to compare the effects of two drugs on human heart rate. The twenty-four subjects were randomly assigned to one of the three groups (eight to each group): two receiving the experimental drugs and one receiving the control. The heart rate measurements were observed at four different time points five minutes apart after administering the drug. Consequently, for this data set $k = 3$, $n_1 = n_2 = n_3 = 8$, and $p = 4$. We test the null hypothesis of no differences between the three drugs, that is, $\tau_1 = \tau_2 = \tau_3$, by using the Wilks' Λ defined as

$$\Lambda = \frac{|\mathbf{E}|}{|\mathbf{E} + \mathbf{H}|}$$

or any of the other three multivariate tests defined in Chapters 3 and 4. Denoting the measurements at four time points as the variables y_1, y_2, y_3, and y_4 respectively, and the levels of variable DRUG as the three drug names AX23, BWW9, and CONTROL, the corresponding SAS statements are

```
proc glm;
class drug;
model y1 y2 y3 y4=drug/nouni;
manova h=drug;
```

These statements are specified in the beginning of Program 5.8. Correspondingly, Output 5.8 shows that there are significant differences between the three drugs, including placebo ($\Lambda = 0.0790$ leading to F = 11.5096 at (8, 36) degrees of freedom with a corresponding p value = 0.0001). All three types of analyses, namely Type I, II, and III, are identical in this case. Also, all multivariate test criteria lead to the same conclusions.

5.3.2 Profile Analysis

Profile analysis is a collection of statistical hypothesis testing procedures used to explore any possible similarities between the treatment effects. We have briefly touched upon the profile analysis of the population mean in Section 5.2. Profile analysis is especially relevant for the longitudinal data on a given response variable or in the situations where responses on several dependent variables are measured on the same experimental unit. A population profile is a plot of the components of the population mean vector versus the order in which these means are arranged. In such cases, the order usually represents the time, especially in cases such as longitudinal studies or clinical trials. Such an order may also occur when a battery of treatments is sequentially applied on a group of subjects. Since the population means are usually unknown, the sample profile plots in which the population means are replaced by the sample means are in some sense the graphical estimates of the population profile plots. A typical sample profile plot has already been shown in Output 5.1.

The hypothesis of equality of means $H_0 : \mu_1 = \mu_2 = \ldots = \mu_k$ implies that the treatments have the same average effects. Though useful, mere acceptance or rejection of such a hypothesis does not provide adequate insight into the type of similarities and dissimilarities that may exist among the treatments. In order to gain more understanding, we can formulate the above hypothesis as three hypotheses to be tested sequentially and subjected to the acceptance of the hypothesis at the previous stage. Specifically, we can ask: Are the profiles parallel? If so, are they coincidental? and finally, If so, are they all horizontal?

Are the k population profiles parallel? The question here is, for the k populations, are the profile curves all identical except for the constant shifts in the levels? In this case, the null hypothesis is

$$H_0^{(a)} : \mu_{11} - \mu_{21} = \mu_{12} - \mu_{22} = \ldots = \mu_{1p} - \mu_{2p}$$
$$\mu_{11} - \mu_{31} = \mu_{12} - \mu_{32} = \ldots = \mu_{1p} - \mu_{3p}$$
$$\vdots$$
$$\mu_{11} - \mu_{k1} = \mu_{12} - \mu_{k2} = \ldots = \mu_{1p} - \mu_{kp}.$$

The first equation in this set can be written as

$$\begin{bmatrix} 1 & -1 & 0 & \cdots & 0 \end{bmatrix} \begin{bmatrix} \mu_1' \\ \mu_2' \\ \vdots \\ \mu_k' \end{bmatrix}_{k \times p} \begin{bmatrix} 1 & 1 & \cdots & 1 \\ -1 & 0 & \cdots & 0 \\ 0 & -1 & \cdots & 0 \\ \vdots & & & \\ 0 & 0 & \cdots & -1 \end{bmatrix}_{p \times (p-1)} = \mathbf{0}.$$

Similarly for the jth equation, $j = 1, ..., k-1$, the left-most row vector would have 1 at the first place and -1 at the jth place. As a result, the system given in $H_0^{(a)}$ can be conveniently expressed as

$$\begin{bmatrix} 1 & -1 & 0 & \cdots & 0 \\ 1 & 0 & -1 & \cdots & 0 \\ \vdots & & & & \\ 1 & 0 & 0 & \cdots & -1 \end{bmatrix}_{(k-1) \times k} \begin{bmatrix} \mu_1' \\ \mu_2' \\ \vdots \\ \mu_k' \end{bmatrix}_{k \times p} \begin{bmatrix} 1 & 1 & \cdots & 1 \\ -1 & 0 & \cdots & 0 \\ 0 & -1 & \cdots & 0 \\ \vdots & & & \\ 0 & 0 & \cdots & -1 \end{bmatrix}_{p \times p-1} = \begin{bmatrix} \mathbf{0} \\ \mathbf{0} \\ \vdots \\ \mathbf{0} \end{bmatrix}$$

Since $\mu_i = \mu + \tau_i$, $i = 1, ..., k$, the above set of equations has an alternative representation as

$$\begin{bmatrix} 0 & 1 & -1 & 0 & \cdots & 0 \\ 0 & 1 & 0 & -1 & \cdots & 0 \\ \vdots & & & & & \\ 0 & 1 & 0 & 0 & \cdots & -1 \end{bmatrix}_{(k-1) \times (k+1)} \begin{bmatrix} \mu' \\ \tau_1' \\ \tau_2' \\ \vdots \\ \tau_k' \end{bmatrix}_{(k+1) \times p} \begin{bmatrix} 1 & 1 & \cdots & 1 \\ -1 & 0 & \cdots & 0 \\ 0 & -1 & \cdots & 0 \\ \vdots & & & \\ 0 & 0 & \cdots & -1 \end{bmatrix}_{p \times p} = \begin{bmatrix} \mathbf{0} \\ \mathbf{0} \\ \vdots \\ \mathbf{0} \end{bmatrix}.$$

or

$$H_0^{(a)} : \mathbf{LBM} = \mathbf{0}, \tag{5.10}$$

where the definitions of $\mathbf{L}$, $\mathbf{B}$, and $\mathbf{M}$ are obvious. Thus the hypothesis of parallel profiles can be formulated as a general linear hypothesis. As indicated in Section 3.4, the matrices $\mathbf{L}$ and $\mathbf{M}$ respectively have some special interpretations. The ith row of matrix $\mathbf{L}$ forms the appropriate linear functions of the regression coefficients (in matrix $\mathbf{B}$) within the ith model, $i = 1, ..., p$, whereas the jth column of the post-multiplied matrix $\mathbf{M}$ creates the desired linear combination of the coefficients from different models but corresponding to the same independent variable. In other words, in the present context, the specific comparisons between the population means are indicated by using the $\mathbf{L}$ matrix and the longitudinal comparisons (or the comparisons involving the parameters of the models for various dependent variables) for a fixed population are specified through the $\mathbf{M}$ matrix. Note however that although there are several equivalent choices of $\mathbf{L}$ and $\mathbf{M}$, the final test statistics and the conclusions do not depend on these choices.

The general linear hypothesis given in Equation 5.10 is tested using the appropriate multivariate test. All the tests described in Section 3.4 apply, with some specific modifications. This is so since the general linear model

$$\mathbf{Y} = \mathbf{XB} + \mathcal{E},$$

when post-multiplied by a p by s matrix $\mathbf{M}$, reduces to the model $\mathbf{YM} = \mathbf{XBM} + \mathcal{E}\mathbf{M}$ or $\mathbf{Y}^* = \mathbf{XB}^* + \mathcal{E}^*$ which is essentially the same model with p replaced by s. In the present context of the parallel profile hypothesis, the matrix $\mathbf{M}$ is of order p by $(p-1)$ and hence s is equal to $(p-1)$.

Example 6: Heart Rate Data (continued)

The sample profile plots for three drugs are given in part of Output 5.8. The SAS code used to obtain this plot is given in Program 5.8. Chapter 2 also discussed similar SAS code. Friendly (1991) provides an explanation as well. The sample profile plots reveal the differences between the drugs in several respects, and we consider some of them here.

First of all, we want to see if the three drugs have parallel profiles. Accepting such a hypothesis would mean that for the three drugs the changes in the heart rate measurements are in the same direction and have similar patterns. We call this the hypothesis of no interaction between the drug and time, if time itself is taken as a factor. In notation, we want to test

$$H_0^{(a)} : \mu_{11} - \mu_{21} = \mu_{12} - \mu_{22} = \mu_{13} - \mu_{23} = \mu_{14} - \mu_{24},$$
$$\mu_{11} - \mu_{31} = \mu_{12} - \mu_{32} = \mu_{13} - \mu_{33} = \mu_{14} - \mu_{34}$$

or equivalently,

$$\begin{bmatrix} 1 & -1 & 0 \\ 1 & 0 & -1 \end{bmatrix} \begin{bmatrix} \mu_{11} & \mu_{12} & \mu_{13} & \mu_{14} \\ \mu_{21} & \mu_{22} & \mu_{23} & \mu_{24} \\ \mu_{31} & \mu_{32} & \mu_{33} & \mu_{34} \end{bmatrix} \begin{bmatrix} 1 & 1 & 1 \\ -1 & 0 & 0 \\ 0 & -1 & 0 \\ 0 & 0 & -1 \end{bmatrix} = \begin{bmatrix} 0 \\ 0 \end{bmatrix}$$

or

$$\begin{bmatrix} 0 & 1 & -1 & 0 \\ 0 & 1 & 0 & -1 \end{bmatrix} \begin{bmatrix} \mu' \\ \tau_1' \\ \tau_2' \\ \tau_3' \end{bmatrix} \begin{bmatrix} 1 & 1 & 1 \\ -1 & 0 & 0 \\ 0 & -1 & 0 \\ 0 & 0 & -1 \end{bmatrix} = \begin{bmatrix} 0 \\ 0 \end{bmatrix}.$$

Thus, with

$$\mathbf{L} = \begin{bmatrix} 0 & 1 & -1 & 0 \\ 0 & 1 & 0 & -1 \end{bmatrix} \quad \text{and} \quad \mathbf{M} = \begin{bmatrix} 1 & 1 & 1 \\ -1 & 0 & 0 \\ 0 & -1 & 0 \\ 0 & 0 & -1 \end{bmatrix},$$

we have $H_0^{(a)} : \mathbf{LBM} = \mathbf{0}$. Note that another alternative choice (among many others) for the matrices $\mathbf{L}$ and $\mathbf{M}$ may be

$$\mathbf{L} = \begin{bmatrix} 0 & 1 & 0 & -1 \\ 0 & 0 & 1 & -1 \end{bmatrix} \text{ and } \mathbf{M} = \begin{bmatrix} 1 & 0 & 0 \\ -1 & 1 & 0 \\ 0 & -1 & 1 \\ 0 & 0 & -1 \end{bmatrix}.$$

In PROC GLM, the matrix $\mathbf{M}$ is specified by the M= specification on the MANOVA statement. The matrix $\mathbf{L}$, however, is specified in the CONTRAST statement which should appear before the MANOVA statement. The following statements (see Program 5.8) are used to test the hypothesis of parallel profiles.

```
proc glm;
class drug;
model y1 y2 y3 y4=drug;
contrast '"parallel?"' drug 1 0 -1,
                       drug 0 1 -1;
manova h=drug m=(1 -1 0 0,
                 1 0 -1 0,
                 1 0 0 -1)/printe printh;
```

A few comments are in order. As mentioned earlier, the matrix $\mathbf{L}$ is specified in the CONTRAST statement. Since the comparison involves μ_1, μ_2, and μ_3 or equivalently τ_1, τ_2, and τ_3 the coefficients for the intercept are zero and hence need not be specified. As a result, the matrix $\mathbf{L}$ is shortened in this SAS code by deleting the first column. Further, we have used the second of the two equivalent choices for $\mathbf{L}$. The $\mathbf{M}$ matrix is specified in the MANOVA statement, where the corresponding hypothesis is on the equality of the treatment effects for the variable DRUG. The specification of $\mathbf{M}$ is column by column, and hence it would resemble $\mathbf{M}'$ rather than $\mathbf{M}$. In the actual program, we have also used the NOUNI option to suppress the univariate analysis.

The selected pieces of the output resulting from these commands are given as part of Output 5.8. First the matrix $\mathbf{M}$ is printed. The transformed (by post-multiplication of $\mathbf{M}$) variables are referred to as MVAR1 MVAR2 MVAR3 (the output can be cosmetically improved by using the PREFIX option to assign the appropriate names to the transformed variables), and the error SS&CP matrix $\mathbf{E}$ as well as the corresponding hypothesis SS&CP matrix $\mathbf{H}$ are listed next. Based on these two matrices, the four multivariate test statistics are calculated for $H_0 : \mathbf{L}^*\mathbf{BM} = \mathbf{0}$ with $\mathbf{M}$ indicated above and $\mathbf{L}^* = (\mathbf{0} : \mathbf{I})$ with $\mathbf{0}$ as a vector of zeros. However the null hypothesis $H_0 : \mathbf{L}^*\mathbf{BM} = \mathbf{0}$ is not the null hypothesis of parallel profile. What we are testing is the null hypothesis that the vectors of differences between the mean responses for the three drugs are all equal.

The null hypothesis of parallel profiles gives the corresponding hypothesis SS&CP matrix **H** as

$$\mathbf{H} = \begin{bmatrix} 465.5833 & 593.5417 & 212.2500 \\ 593.5417 & 872.5833 & 308.2500 \\ 212.2500 & 308.2500 & 109.0000 \end{bmatrix},$$

and the error SS&CP matrix as

$$\mathbf{E} = \begin{bmatrix} 261.3750 & 119.5000 & 147.5000 \\ 119.5000 & 226.3750 & 235.0000 \\ 147.5000 & 235.0000 & 463.5000 \end{bmatrix}.$$

The value of Wilks' Λ is 0.1103 leading to the observed value of the (exact) $F(6, 38)$ random variable as 12.7376. This is highly significant with a very low p value of 0.0001. As a result, we reject the null hypothesis of parallel profiles. The other three multivariate tests are also in agreement with this conclusion.

Are the profiles coincidental, given that profiles are parallel? If the hypothesis of parallel profiles is accepted, the next thing to ask may be if they are all identical. Since parallelism of profiles guarantees that profiles do not intersect each other and are consistently one below the other, the profiles will all be identical only if sums of components in each profile vector μ_i are all equal. The corresponding null hypothesis is

$$H_0^{(b)} : \mathbf{1}_p'\mu_1 = \mathbf{1}_p'\mu_2 = \ldots = \mathbf{1}_p'\mu_k$$
$$\text{or } \mathbf{LBM} = \mathbf{0}$$

with the choice of **L** and **M** respectively as

$$\mathbf{L} = \begin{bmatrix} 0 & 1 & 0 & \cdots & 0 & -1 \\ 0 & 0 & 1 & \cdots & 0 & -1 \\ \vdots & & & & & \\ 0 & 0 & 0 & \cdots & 1 & -1 \end{bmatrix}_{(k-1)\times(k+1)} \quad \text{and } \mathbf{M} = \mathbf{1}_p.$$

The hypothesis of parallel profile was rejected for the heart data in Example 6. In view of this rejection, the null hypothesis of coincidental profiles has no meaning there. However, if such a hypothesis were to be tested for this data set, the following **L** and **M** matrices would need to be used.

$$\mathbf{L} = \begin{bmatrix} 0 & 1 & 0 & -1 \\ 0 & 0 & 1 & -1 \end{bmatrix} \quad \text{and } \mathbf{M}' = \begin{bmatrix} 1 & 1 & 1 & 1 \end{bmatrix}.$$

As earlier, omitting the first column of **L**, which corresponds to the coefficients of the intercepts, the corresponding SAS statements would be

```
contrast '"coincidental?"' drug 1 0 -1,
                          drug 0 1 -1;
manova h=drug m=(1 1 1 1)/printe printh;
```

Are the profiles horizontal? If we accepted the hypothesis of coincidental profiles, then the k populations supposedly have a common mean vector. It is natural to ask if the components in this common mean vector are also all equal. This amounts to testing the hypothesis $H_0^{(c)} : \mathbf{LBM} = \mathbf{0}$ with

$$
\mathbf{L} = (1,0,...,0) \text{ and } \mathbf{M} = \begin{bmatrix} 1 & 1 & \cdots & 1 \\ -1 & 0 & \cdots & 0 \\ 0 & -1 & \cdots & 0 \\ \vdots & \vdots & \vdots & \vdots \\ 0 & 0 & \cdots & -1 \end{bmatrix}.
$$

In this case, the coefficient of intercept vector in the $\mathbf{L}$ matrix is 1, while all other coefficients are zero. The $\mathbf{M}$ matrix is the same as that used to test the hypothesis of parallel profiles. If this hypothesis were to be tested for the heart data in Example 6, the corresponding part of the PROC GLM statements would be

```
contrast '"horizontal?"' drug 1 0 -1,
                         drug 0 1 -1;
manova h=drug m=(1 -1 0 0,
              1 0 -1 0,
              1 0 0 -1)/printe printh;
```

Example 6: Heart Rate Data (continued)

We recall that in Example 6, the hypothesis of parallel profiles was rejected. To gain further insight and identify the possible causes for nonparallelism, we may want to test for the significance of individual orthogonal contrasts. What we need to do first is to identify an appropriate $\mathbf{L}$ matrix in which rows are orthogonal to each other and then perform statistical tests for the significance of these individual contrasts.

The sample profile plots of the three drugs are given in the beginning of Output 5.8. It appears that the profile for the drug AX23 is very different from the other two and falls between the profiles for BWW9 and CONTROL. These observations seem to suggest that such comparisons should also be the part of the analysis. Specifically, we should first compare the profiles of the other two drugs, namely BWW9 and CONTROL, with each other and then their average profile with the profile of drug AX23. If the 2 by 4 matrix $\mathbf{L}$ is chosen as

$$
\mathbf{L} = \begin{bmatrix} 0 & 0 & 1 & -1 \\ 0 & 2 & -1 & -1 \end{bmatrix},
$$

the two rows of $\mathbf{L}$ are mutually orthogonal and the corresponding functions $\mathbf{LB}$ are estimable. This is an alternative choice of $\mathbf{L}$ in addition to the two nonorthogonal choices previously indicated (see $H_0^{(a)}$), namely

$$\begin{bmatrix} 0 & 1 & -1 & 0 \\ 0 & 1 & 0 & -1 \end{bmatrix} \text{ and } \begin{bmatrix} 0 & 1 & 0 & -1 \\ 0 & 0 & 1 & -1 \end{bmatrix}.$$

The rows of this new matrix $\mathbf{L}$, namely $\ell_1' = (0\ 0\ 1\ -1)$ and $\ell_2' = (0\ 2\ -1\ -1)$ respectively, can be used to test the hypotheses $H_0^{(a1)} : \ell_1'\mathbf{BM} = 0$, which tests for the parallelism of the profiles of drug BWW9 and CONTROL, and $H_0^{(a2)} : \ell_2'\mathbf{BM} = 0$, tests for the parallelism of the profiles of drug AX23 to the average profile of drugs BWW9 and CONTROL. These were the two hypotheses we have found to be of interest by looking at the profile plots given in Output 5.8.

The Wilks' Λ and other tests, all of which are exact and equivalent, support the hypothesis $H_0^{(a1)}$. The observed value of $F(3, 19)$ corresponding to all of these tests is 2.1841 with a p value of 0.1233. Thus, we conclude that, although it may be different and superior, drug BWW9 behaves similarly to CONTROL over time.

The null hypothesis given in $H_0^{(a2)}$ is rejected and in view of the very small p value (=0.0001), there is a strong argument for doing so. It indicates that as a function of time, the drug AX23 has a behavior very different from the other two. A look at the profile plots is visually convincing. Clearly, the major reason for the nonparallelism of profiles and hence the major component in the rejection of $H_0^{(a)}$ is the fact that drug AX23 acts very differently from the average of other two over time. CONTROL and drug BWW9 appear to be similar in their behavior.

5.3.3 A Univariate Approach

As in the one population case, a univariate approach to the analysis of repeated measure data for k populations can be devised by treating the experiments as a split plot design in which the units in the whole plots (whole plots are subjects in the present context) are correlated. By first testing for the Type H covariance structure and then accordingly taking the appropriate action (to adjust or not adjust the degrees of freedom for the test statistics), we can make inferences using the univariate approach as well. Of course each of the two approaches has its own shortcomings, and we should not think of these approaches as interchangeable. The split plot experiment leads to the linear model

$$y_{iju} = \mu + \alpha_i + \beta_j + (\alpha\beta)_{ij} + \delta_{iu} + \epsilon_{iju}, \tag{5.11}$$

$u = 1, ..., n_i$, $i = 1, ..., k$, $j = 1, ..., p$, in which μ represents the intercept or the general mean, α_i is the effect of the ith treatment, β_j is the effect of the jth time point, $(\alpha\beta)_{ij}$ is the interaction effect between the ith treatment and j^{th} time point, δ_{iu} represents the random error for the uth subject in the ith treatment group, and ϵ_{iju} is the random error corresponding to the uth subject in the ith treatment group at the jth time point. We assume that δ_{iu} and ϵ_{iju} are both independently and normally distributed with zero means and respective variances σ_δ^2 and σ^2. As a consequence of this assumption and the assumed split plot model, the repeated measurements on the subjects have the variance-covariance matrix possessing the property of compound symmetry. This is a mixed effect model in which the appropriate F tests for treatment effect, time effect, and their interaction can be constructed using ANOVA partitioning of the corrected total sum of squares. However, this model is seldom realistic. The assumption of compound symmetry of the variance-covariance matrix is artificial and should not be accepted on face value. If the appropriate statistical tests on the data suggest this assumption to be acceptable, then the usual split plot ANOVA F ratio tests for all the variables and the interaction are valid, exact F tests.

However, when the data do not conform to compound symmetry, only the test for the whole plot or between-subject treatment variable (DRUG) is a valid exact F test. As far as the other two tests, that is, for the time variable and the interaction between the drug and time, the F tests will be valid provided the Type H conditions, which are less stringent than compound symmetry on the covariance structure, are satisfied. These are discussed in Section 5.2.2 and also in Section 5.2.3. If Type H conditions do not hold, then, the distribution of usual F ratios for TIME and DRUG*TIME interaction can be approximated by an F distribution for which the degrees of freedom are appropriately adjusted. The two adjustments suggested by Greenhouse and Geisser (1959) and Huynh and Feldt (1976) have been discussed in Section 5.2.3. Huynh and Feldt's (1976) adjustment has been shown to maintain the desired level of significance to a higher degree than Greenhouse and Geisser's.

Example 6: Heart Rate Data (continued)

Let us analyze the heart rate data of Spector (1987) using the univariate approach. To fit the model in Equation 5.11, for the dependent variable heart rate (Y) on variables DRUG, TIME, and their interaction with SUBJECT as the whole plot using PROC GLM, we use the SAS statements

```
proc glm;
class subject drug time;
model y= drug subject (drug) time drug*time;
random subject (drug)/test;
```

In the MODEL statement we have specified the model given in Equation 5.11. The RANDOM statement indicates that subjects are a random sample and hence SUBJECT is a random effect *nested* within DRUG. It is necessary to account for such facts in constructing the appropriate F tests. The RANDOM command prints the table of expected values of various mean squares. The TEST option computes the values of the appropriate test statistics. Of course, since it is a univariate analysis, all values of Y1, Y2, Y3, and Y4 are to be stacked one below the other as Y with corresponding levels of the variable TIME appropriately identified. This is done in Program 5.9. The ANOVA part of the resulting output is presented in Output 5.9. The results are identical to certain parts of Output 5.10 that will be described later.

The analysis performed in Program 5.9 can be more efficiently achieved by using the REPEATED statement. It eliminates the need for arranging the data on Y1, Y2, Y3, and Y4 in a vector Y. The other added advantage is the availability of the test for sphericity for the prescribed contrasts and the Type H structure as well as the computation of the estimates of ϵ, to adjust the degrees of freedom, in case these conditions are not met. To indicate that the repeated measures are taken across TIME, which in this case has four levels, the SAS statement is

```
repeated time 4;
```

If we want, we can specify the levels of TIME (5, 10, 15, and 20 in our example) within parentheses following 4, the number of levels. Further, any other relevant variable name to represent the repeated measures is also applicable. For example, in spatial data the measurements may be named TRANSACT.

Tests on various contrasts of E(Y1),...,E(Y4) can also be performed. While the default choice is the difference between the means of the responses at various time points and the last time point, we can choose any other time point instead of the last for these contrasts. For example, to obtain the contrasts E(Y1)-E(Y2), E(Y1)-E(Y3) and E(Y1)-E(Y4) we specify the CONTRAST(1) transformation after TIME 4 in the REPEATED statement given above. The number 1 within parentheses ( ) indicates that time point 1 is taken as the base or reference point for CONTRAST comparisons. Many other values for contrasts may be used. For example, PROFILE can be used if we want the contrasts consisting of successive differences such as E(Y1)- E(Y2), E(Y2)-E(Y3), E(Y3)-E(Y4). The contrasts using the orthogonal polynomials (of degree $p-1$ if there are p time points) can be obtained by specifying the POLYNOMIAL transformation in the REPEATED statement. This choice is especially useful if we want to study time trends.

Returning to the univariate split plot analysis of heart rate data, suppose we want to fit the model in Equation 5.11 and examine if this split plot model is appropriate for the analysis. The statement

```
repeated time 4 profile/summary printm printe;
```

given in Program 5.10 first fits the split plot model given in Equation 5.11 and examines its appropriateness. If Σ is the p by p variance-covariance matrix of responses collected over time, then, program tests for the sphericity of $C\Sigma C'$, where C is the profile matrix given by

$$\mathbf{C} = \begin{bmatrix} 1 & -1 & 0 & \ldots & 0 & 0 \\ 0 & 1 & -1 & \ldots & 0 & 0 \\ \vdots & & & & & \\ 0 & 0 & 0 & \ldots & 1 & -1 \end{bmatrix}_{(p-1)\times p} .$$

In the case of heart rate data it simply is

$$\begin{bmatrix} 1 & -1 & 0 & 0 \\ 0 & 1 & -1 & 0 \\ 0 & 0 & 1 & -1 \end{bmatrix}.$$

In addition, the sphericity test is also applied on the matrix $\mathbf{D\Sigma D'}$, where $\mathbf{D}$ is the $(p-1)$ by p matrix of orthogonal contrasts. This test is invariant of the choice of orthogonal matrix and is used to test for the Type H condition. If the matrix $\mathbf{C}$ (specified in the REPEATED statement) itself is the matrix of orthogonal contrasts, then the two tests result in identical output and hence they are printed only once. Observe that PROFILE or CONTRAST(1) transformations are not the matrices of orthogonal contrasts. Therefore, we use Mauchly's test described in Section 5.2.2 to test the sphericity of $\mathbf{C\Sigma C'}$ and $\mathbf{D\Sigma D'}$.

Program 5.10 results in Output 5.10. With the choice of contrast matrix $\mathbf{C}$ as PROFILE matrix, we find that null hypothesis of the sphericity of $\mathbf{C\Sigma C'}$ is rejected. The observed value of approximate χ_5^2 is 32.7091 with a p value which is virtually zero. To test if the Type H structure can be assumed, we apply Mauchly's test to $\mathbf{D\Sigma D'}$ (see Section 5.2.2). In view of the observed value of approximate χ_5^2 =8.0703 with a p value of 0.1524, we accept this null hypothesis. This suggests that we can probably analyze these data using the split plot model, and we may not need to adjust the degrees of freedom for certain resulting F ratios, using $\hat{\epsilon}_{GG}$ or $\hat{\epsilon}_{HF}$.

Next, note that the remaining part of Output 5.10 essentially includes all the information provided by Output 5.9. The usual ANOVA F test for the interaction DRUG*TIME is significant (p value=0.0001). No adjustments are needed since the null hypothesis of Type H structure has been accepted, and hence we assume this structure. If we also want to conduct individual testing for certain specific contrasts, we can do it using the CONTRAST statement as shown in the Program 5.10. We have suppressed the corresponding output to save space.

5.3.4 Study of Time Trends

If the interaction between the treatment and time exists, we are interested in studying the time trends for individual treatments and in identifying the differences in such trends if any. The sample profile plots provide some visual insight about such trends and the differences between them, but we need a formal study. This can be done by partitioning the sum of squares corresponding to the variable TIME as well as the interaction TREAT-MENT*TIME into the independent sums of squares corresponding to various degrees of orthogonal polynomials up to $(p-1)^{th}$ degree. When orthogonal polynomial contrasts are used, the sums of squares corresponding to successive contrasts provide us with necessary information. In SAS, we can accomplish this by using the POLYNOMIAL transformation in the REPEATED statement as shown in Program 5.10.

Example 6: Heart Rate Data (continued)

Since $p = 4$, we can fit up to a third-degree polynomial and we can accordingly partition the sum of squares corresponding to the variable TIME as well as TIME*DRUG into three orthogonal components, namely linear, quadratic, and cubic. For the heart rate data in Output 5.10, these components are respectively labeled TIME.1, TIME.2, and TIME.3. The three sums of squares corresponding to the MEAN transformation provide the orthogonal partitioning of the sum of squares for the variable TIME, and the sums of squares corresponding to DRUG give the orthogonal decomposition of the sum of squares corresponding to the interaction TIME*DRUG (say, INT). We perform similar partitioning for the error sum of squares. The results are given in Table 5.1. The values are taken from Output 5.10.

Contrast	SS(TIME)	df	SS(INT)	df	SS(ERROR)	df
Linear	8.5333	1	85.4042	2	247.2625	21
Quadratic	234.3750	1	398.3125	2	106.3125	21
Cubic	36.3000	1	44.6375	2	108.8625	21
Total	279.2083	3	528.3542	6	462.4375	63

TABLE 5.1 PARTITIONING OF SS INTO ORTHO. POLY. CONTRASTS

The analysis of variance is carried out separately for each of the three contrasts. If $z^{(h)}$ represents the hth contrast, then the linear model for the hth contrast $h = 1, 2, 3$ is a one-way classification model in the drug effect $\alpha_i^{(h)}$, that is,

$$z_{ij}^{(h)} = \mu^{(h)} + \alpha_i^{(h)} + \epsilon_{ij}^{(h)}, \; i = 1, 2, 3, \; j = 1, ..., 8.$$

All the usual assumptions for this model are made. There are two questions that could be asked:

Are the contrast means zero? If all contrast means are zero, then it implies that there is no treatment effect.

Is there an interaction between the drug and trend? If there is no interaction between drug and trend, the situation corresponds to the case when all $\alpha_i^{(h)}$ are zero.

Thus we may individually test

$$H_0^{(a)} : \mu^{(h)} = 0$$
$$\text{and } H_0^{(b)} : \alpha_1^{(h)} = \alpha_2^{(h)} = \alpha_3^{(h)} = 0$$

for $h = 1, 2, 3$. We recall that in the split plot experiment, we rejected the null hypothesis of no DRUG effect and of no TIME*DRUG interaction. The tests performed here would provide the cause of rejection in each of the two cases. Output 5.10 shows that the DRUG for TIME.1 (linear contrast) is marginally significant (p value=0.0444). It is strongly significant (p value=0.0001) for TIME.2 (quadratic contrast) and is reasonable (p value=0.0271) in the case of TIME.3 (the cubic contrast). This indicates that there is sufficient evidence to assume that the response curves are quite different for the three drugs. Since the response curves are not the same for the three drugs, it is currently of no interest to test if the contrast means are all zero, because it is equivalent to saying that there is no treatment effect. These hypotheses would have been of interest if $H_0^{(b)}$ had been accepted for all the three contrasts.

A few comments are in order with respect to the analysis of contrasts outlined here. First of all, since two or more hypotheses are being tested to draw the simultaneous inference, we can use a Bonferroni approach to choose the appropriate levels of significance for each individual hypothesis. Secondly, the analysis on contrasts may be subject to serious error if the error variances for these contrasts are not nearly equal. Thus, we should be especially careful in the interpretation of these results if the Type H conditions are not met. Finally, the split plot analysis may be more useful than the present analysis of orthogonal contrasts. The reason for this is that when the Type H conditions are not met the degrees of freedom of the F tests in the former analysis can be adjusted to get approximate tests.

Given the two different approaches to the repeated measure data, namely multivariate and univariate, a natural question to ask is, which of the two approaches is superior? This question cannot be answered in a clear-cut way. Due to the data collection scheme and design, the problem is multivariate in nature and hence, theoretically, the multivariate approach is the "correct" approach for the problem. However, the multivariate tests usually have lower power than the corresponding univariate tests. This is more so when the sphericity assumptions are satisfied. Thus, the power of the tests can possibly be increased by following the univariate approach when the assumptions on the covariance structure (such as compound symmetry or Type H conditions) can be made.

Thus, although the multivariate approach is always a legitimate approach, we may be able to obtain more conclusive results and possibly gain more insight by using the univariate split plot models. Crowder and Hand (1990), however, state that in the absence of sphericity of orthogonal contrasts, there is little to choose between the multivariate tests and the univariate tests where the degrees of freedom of univariate F tests have been modified using either $\hat{\epsilon}_{GG}$ or $\hat{\epsilon}_{HF}$. Of course, in certain cases circumstances such as small sample size permit only univariate analysis of data.

There are certain cautions that we must take in analyzing the repeated measure data especially when using the univariate approach. A reason for this is the failure to appropriately identify the fixed and random effects in the model and form appropriate F ratios for the tests. Schaefer (1994) provides an excellent account, with special reference to SAS, of possible pitfalls in using the default packaged analysis: in PROC GLM, all the effects are by default considered fixed unless indicated otherwise by using a RANDOM statement and then using the TEST option to perform the appropriate test. Using simulation studies, he found that Type I and Type II errors in the testing of hypotheses can both be greatly affected if inappropriate tests are performed.

The univariate split plot analysis of repeated measures can be done in a somewhat more efficient and less error-prone way by using the PROC MIXED procedure, which makes available several alternative covariance structures in addition to compound symmetry. This is especially desirable in the context of repeated measures data where compound symmetry is assumed only as a convenience and no theoretical model-based justification for it can be given. The use of PROC MIXED facilitates a more powerful analysis in that the covariance structures other than compound symmetry can be assumed for the units within the whole plots, which are subjects in the repeated measures context. Some of the useful covariance structures other than compound symmetry for the repeated measure data are the first order autoregressive model, unstructured covariance, Toeplitz, and banded Toeplitz. PROC MIXED provides these covariance structures as options along with several other options.

The split plot model given in Equation 5.11 has two random effects, namely, δ_{iu} and ϵ_{iju}, corresponding to the whole plot and subplot errors. This in turn leads to the variance-covariance matrix of the repeated observations on the uth subject of the ith group, that is of $(y_{i1u}, y_{i2u}, ..., y_{ipu})'$ as

$$\Sigma_{subject} = \begin{bmatrix} \sigma_\delta^2 + \sigma^2 & \sigma_\delta^2 & \cdots & \sigma_\delta^2 \\ \sigma_\delta^2 & \sigma_\delta^2 + \delta^2 & \cdots & \sigma_\delta^2 \\ \vdots & \vdots & \cdots & \vdots \\ \sigma_\delta^2 & \sigma_\delta^2 & \cdots & \sigma_\delta^2 + \sigma^2 \end{bmatrix} = \frac{1}{\sigma_\delta^2 + \sigma^2} \begin{bmatrix} 1 & \rho & \cdots & \rho \\ \rho & 1 & \cdots & \rho \\ \vdots & \vdots & \cdots & \vdots \\ \rho & \rho & \cdots & 1 \end{bmatrix} \quad (5.12)$$

where $\rho = \sigma_\delta^2/(\sigma_\delta^2 + \sigma^2)$. The above matrix has a compound symmetry covariance structure. However since $(y_{i1u}, y_{i2u}, ..., y_{ipu})'$ are the measurements over time on the same subject, a more realistic covariance structure may be that of the first order autoregressive process, namely

$$\Sigma_{subject} = \frac{\sigma^2}{1 - \rho^2} \begin{bmatrix} 1 & \rho & \rho^2 & \cdots & \rho^{p-1} \\ \rho & 1 & \rho & \cdots & \rho^{p-2} \\ \vdots & \vdots & \vdots & \cdots & \vdots \\ \rho^{p-1} & \rho^{p-2} & \rho^{p-3} & \cdots & 1 \end{bmatrix} \quad (5.13)$$

or other suitable structures such as Toeplitz or even an unstructured covariance structure. Thus the model

$$y_{iju} = \mu + \alpha_i + \beta_j + (\alpha\beta)_{ij} + \epsilon_{iju}, \quad (5.14)$$

where ϵ_{iju} now represents the combined random error of whole as well as the subplot with an assumed suitable covariance structure, such as the first order autoregressive (AR(1)) structure is an improvement over the model in Equation 5.11.

Example 6: Heart Rate Data (continued)

To analyze the data using PROC MIXED, we first need to arrange all repeated measures as the values of a single dependent variable observed at various levels of the longitudinal variable TIME. This is done using the following code, included in Program 5.11.

```
data split;
set heart;
array t{4} y1-y4;
subject +1;
do time =1 to 4;
y=t{time};
output;
end;
drop y1-y4;
run;
```

The SET statement creates a new data set named SPLIT by reading observations from the data set HEART. The new single variable Y is defined as taking values Y1, Y2, Y3, and Y4 at the variables TIME 1, 2, 3, and 4 respectively. This is done by first defining a 4 by 1 array T containing Y1, Y2, Y3, and Y4 and then transferring the values in the array T to the variable Y within a DO loop which goes through TIME=4 iterations for every value of SUBJECT. We use the data set SPLIT in the univariate analysis.

Let us suppose that the analysis is to be done under the assumption of the first order autoregressive covariance structure (AR(1)). This means that for each subject the variance-covariance matrix of the measurement repeated over time is of AR(1) type given in Equation 5.13 and hence corresponds to the model in Equation 5.14

$$y_{iju} = \mu + \alpha_i + \beta_j + (\alpha\beta)_{ij} + \epsilon_{iju},$$

where α_i represents the treatment (drug) effect, β_j the time effect, $(\alpha\beta)_{ij}$ is the DRUG*TIME interaction, and for all i, u, the errors subvectors $(\epsilon_{i1u}, \epsilon_{i2u}, ..., \epsilon_{ipu})$ individually follow independent and identical AR(1) processes. The statements given in Program 5.11 fit the model and perform the analysis. The results appear in Output 5.11.

The MODEL statement for PROC MIXED is essentially similar to that in PROC GLM, except for the fact that only fixed effects are to be listed on the right-hand side of the MODEL statement and that it provides a very different set of options for the analysis. As the model given above shows, this statement should include, on the right-hand side, the variables DRUG, TIME, and their interaction DRUG*TIME. We have also used the CHISQ option, which specifies that all Type III Wald's chi-square tests be performed for all specified effects. These tests are asymptotically equivalent to the chi-square approximation of the likelihood ratio tests.

The covariance structure is specified in the REPEATED statement. By using the SUBJECT=option, we specify the way the block diagonal matrix for all the data are to be created. For example, in our heart rate data for each subject we have a 4 by 4 matrix $\Sigma_{subject}$ with an AR(1) covariance structure. As there is a total of 24 subjects, the 96 by 96 variance-covariance matrix of all 96 observations consists of 24 diagonal blocks of $\Sigma_{subject}$ and the nondiagonal blocks as 4 by 4 zero matrices. Of course, $\Sigma_{subject}$ is usually unknown, and hence for a given data set, SAS would provide an estimate of $\Sigma_{subject}$ using the estimation procedure indicated as the METHOD= option in PROC MIXED statement.

The REPEATED statement is also used to indicate the order of the repeated measurement. However, if the data are ordered similarly for each subject then there is no need to specify any effect in this statement. Program 5.11 takes advantage of this default. As shown in Output 5.11, the restricted maximum likelihood (REML) procedure converged in a single iteration. The corresponding estimate of $\Sigma_{subject}$ is $\hat{\Sigma}_{subject}$ (identified as the R matrix in SAS output) is given by

$$\hat{\Sigma}_{subject} = \begin{bmatrix} 40.1481 & 24.4572 & 14.8986 & 9.0759 \\ 24.4572 & 40.1481 & 24.4572 & 14.8986 \\ 14.8986 & 24.4572 & 40.1481 & 24.4572 \\ 9.0759 & 14.8986 & 24.4572 & 40.1481 \end{bmatrix}$$

The tests for fixed effects, namely the variables DRUG and TIME, and also TIME*DRUG, are shown next. The F test as well as Wald's chi-square test statistic both indicate that the DRUG effect is significant (p values=0.0184 and 0.0153 respectively) and hence the three drugs are possibly different in their effects on heart rate. The F test as well as the Wald's test are both approximate.

5.4 Factorial Designs

When the treatment combinations are made up of various levels of several variables, then both the multivariate and univariate approaches are generalized in a straightforward way. We illustrate this using a three-factor factorial experiment due to Box (1950).

Example 7: A Two-Way Factorial Experiment, Abrasion Data (Box, 1950)

Box (1950) presented data on fabric weight loss due to abrasion. Some of the fabrics were given the surface treatment (SURFTRT) and some were not, leading to two levels, YES and NO, for SURFTRT. Two fillers (FILL) A and B were used at three proportions (PROP), namely 25%, 50%, and 75%, and the weight losses were recorded at three successive periods, each after 1000, revolutions of the machine which tested the abrasion resistance. Two replicates for each treatment combination in this $2 \times 2 \times 3$ factorial experiment were obtained. The data are presented in Program 5.12, which performs the multivariate as well as the univariate analysis of the data.

The repeated measures are taken with respect to the increasing number of revolutions (REVOLUTN). The corresponding values of the dependent variable weight loss are denoted by Y1, Y2, and Y3. We first fit the multivariate model with all main variables and two- and three-factor interactions. The standard MANOVA (not shown) indicates that SURFTRT, FILL, SURFTRT*FILL, PROP, and FILL*PROP are all highly significant. For illustration we examine only the profiles corresponding to variable PROP. Thus all the comparisons are about the average weight losses due to various proportions of the fillers. The three sequential hypotheses to be tested are, are the PROP profiles parallel? given that they are parallel, are the PROP profiles coincidental? given that they are coincidental, are the PROP profiles horizontal?

Each of these three hypotheses is specified as $\mathbf{LBM} = \mathbf{0}$ in the linear model setup with the specific choices of matrices of $\mathbf{L}$ and $\mathbf{M}$ in the three hypotheses. Since the three hypotheses are about the variable PROP only, the $\mathbf{L}$ matrix is specified by using the CONTRAST statement with PROP as the variable of interest. The $\mathbf{M}$ matrices are appropriately defined with the M= specification on the MANOVA statement. Specifically, the SAS statements specifying $\mathbf{L}$ and $\mathbf{M}$, for the hypothesis

Are the PROP profiles parallel? are

```
contrast '"prop-parallel?"' prop 1 0 -1,
                            prop 0 1 -1;
manova h=prop m=(1 -1 0,
                 1 0 -1);
```

for the hypothesis

Given that they are parallel, are the PROP profiles coincidental? are

```
contrast '"prop-coincidental?"' prop 1 0 -1,
                                prop 0 1 -1;
manova h=prop m=(1 1 1);
```

and for the hypothesis

Given that they are coincidental, are the PROP profiles horizontal? are

```
contrast '"prop-horizontal?"' intercept 1;
manova h=prop m=(1 -1 0,
                 1 0 -1);
```

Output 5.12 shows that while the null hypothesis of parallel profiles for PROP is marginally accepted (with a p value for Wilks' Λ equal to 0.0701), the hypothesis of coincidental profiles is rejected with $\Lambda = 0.2161$ (leading to an observed value of F (2,12) as 21.7687 which corresponds to a very small p value of 0.0001).

To perform the univariate split plot analysis, we use the REPEATED statement. The corresponding time variable is defined here as REVOLUTN as the repeated measures are taken for the three increasing numbers of revolutions, namely 1,000, 2,000, and 3,000. If we are interested in studying the effects of various orthogonal polynomial contrasts, we must choose the POLYNOMIAL transformation for the type of orthogonal contrasts. The corresponding SAS statement is

```
repeated revolutn 3 polynomial;
```

In the Program 5.12 we have made certain other choices such as printing the corresponding $\mathbf{E}$ and $\mathbf{M}$ matrices and only summary output. The $\mathbf{M}$ matrix here is a 2 by 3 matrix of first- and second-degree orthogonal polynomial coefficients and the 2 by 2 matrix $\mathbf{E}$ is the matrix of the corresponding error SS&CP.

Output 5.12 shows that the interaction REVOLUTN*SURFTRT*FILL is highly significant (with a p value=.0070) and respective interactions of REVOLUTN with SURFTRT and FILL are very highly significant (both p values =0.0001). The interaction of REVOLUTN with PROP is only marginally significant (p value=0.0857). This indicates that the abrasion curves for various levels of the variables SURFTRT, FILL, and PROP are not parallel. The univariate F tests adjusted by using $\hat{\epsilon}_{GG}$ (=0.8384) or $\hat{\epsilon}_{HF}$ (=1.0, since it cannot exceed 1) for various interactions with REVOLUTN lead to the same conclusions. These adjustments, however, may not be necessary as Mauchly's test for the sphericity of orthogonal contrasts (in this case, since the contrast matrix itself is orthogonal, no separate output for orthogonal contrast is printed) provides sufficient evidence (p value =0.3079) to assume sphericity.

The tests on the linear and quadratic contrasts respectively denoted by REVOLUTN.1 and REVOLUTN.2 reveal that the quadratic contrast is not significant for any effect or interaction except FILL (p value=0.0001). However, the linear contrast is significant for all main variables and the SURFTRT*FILL interaction. The data can also be analyzed under various covariance structures, other than compound symmetry using PROC MIXED. While most of the output has been suppressed, the appropriate statements under AR(1) covariance structure and REML estimation procedure are included in Program 5.12. One especially interesting observation is that some of the off-diagonal elements of the estimates of the $\mathbf{R}$ matrix (referred to as $\Sigma_{subject}$ in the previous example), are negative. Normally we would not expect the negative correlations between the repeated measures of these weight losses. Lindsey (1993, p. 83) interprets such an occurrence as evidence of a situation where there is a greater variability within the experiment or subject than among the experiments or subjects.

Example 8: Two-Factor Experiment with Both Repeated Measures Factors

In a factorial design, if there are repeated measures on more than two variables then the analysis of the previous section can be applied in a straightforward manner. For example, consider this example: three participants in an experiment were given a large amount of a sleep-inducing drug on the day before the experiment. The next day, they were given placebos. The participants were tested in the morning (AM) and afternoon (PM) of the two different days. Each participant was given a stimulus, and his or her reaction (the response variable) was timed. See Cody and Smith (1991, p. 182). The problem considered here is to determine whether the drug had any effect on the reaction time and the effects are the same for AM and PM.

Since each subject is measured under two levels of TIME (AM, PM) and for two levels of DRUG (DRUG1 (Placebo), DRUG2), it is a 2 by 2 factorial experiment with both TIME and DRUG as *repeated measures variables* or *repeated measures factors*. The data are given below and the SAS code for analyzing these data is given in Program 5.13.

SUBJECT	DRUG1 AM	DRUG1 PM	DRUG2 AM	DRUG2 PM
1	77	67	82	72
2	84	76	90	80
3	102	92	109	97

Both the univariate and multivariate analysis are performed using the SAS statement

```
repeated drug 2, time 2;
```

One important thing to remember is that the order in which the variables are written in the REPEATED statement and the order in which data are presented in the INPUT statement must correspond. For every level of variable DRUG there are two levels of the variable TIME and the REPEATED statement given above reads exactly that way. That is, level 1 of variable DRUG and levels 1 and 2 of variable TIME are selected first, level 2 of variable DRUG and levels 1 and 2 of variable TIME are selected next, and so on. The logic behind writing the variables in the REPEATED statement is same as the logic behind nested DO loops!

An examination of Output 5.13 reveals that there is no interaction between the variables TIME and DRUG (p value=0.1835). However, the variable DRUG with a p value of 0.0039 and the variable TIME with a p value of 0.0033 are both highly significant.

Example 9: Three-Factor Experiment with Two Repeated Measures Factors (Cody and Smith, 1991)

In an educational testing program, students from two groups, namely those with relatively higher socioeconomic status (GP1) and with lower socioeconomic status (GP2), were tested and their scores in the tests recorded. See Cody and Smith (1991, pp. 194-195). The study was conducted for three years (denoted by 1, 2, and 3) during each of the two seasons, FALL and SPRING, for a group of 10 students. Each group consisted of five subjects. In this setup there are three variables, namely GROUP, YEAR, and SEASON. Repeated measures on each of the ten subjects are available for the variables YEAR and SEASON. In that sense, YEAR and SEASON are two repeated measures variables.

The three problems of interest are to test

- whether students do better on a reading comprehension test in the Spring than in the Fall,
- whether the differences in the mean scores become negligible as students get older,
- whether these differences in the mean scores are more prominent for one socio-economic group than the other.

In order to find answers to these problems, we first determine whether there are significant main effects and interactions. Once that is determined, if needed, we can perform an analysis of the means, applying multiple comparison techniques, to conduct pairwise differences between the variables. However, we restrict ourselves to the determination of the significance of the main effects and their interactions. The data and SAS code are given in Program 5.14 and the corresponding output in Output 5.14. The REPEATED statement is used to perform both the multivariate and univariate analyses.

The multivariate tests indicate that the YEAR*SEASON*GROUP and YEAR*GROUP interactions are not significant (p values are 0.7357 and 0.8724 respectively) whereas, YEAR and SEASON have significant effects with respective p values 0.0033 and 0.0001. Also significant are the interactions YEAR*SEASON (p value=0.0001) and SEASON*GROUP (p value=0.0003). The univariate tests also support these findings. Note from the output that there is a significant difference between the two socio-economic groups (p value=0.0062). Note also that the values of $\hat{\epsilon}_{GG}$ and $\hat{\epsilon}_{HF}$ are quite large, indicating that Type H structure for the covariance may be satisfied.

In order to understand the nature of the significant effect of the repeated measures variable YEAR, since the levels of it are quantitative (1, 2, 3), it may be useful to analyze the variables obtained by using the POLYNOMIAL transformation. The statement

```
repeated year 3 polynomial, season/summary nom nou;
```

can be used for this purpose. Both NOM and NOU options suppress redundant output. If the time points were not equidistant then the POLYNOMIAL transformation (t_1, t_2, t_3) can be used in the REPEATED statement to indicate the time points. The PRINTM option is used to print the contrast transformation. The output for this part of the analysis is shown in Output 5.14. The variable YEAR.N represents the nth degree orthogonal polynomial contrast for the variable YEAR as indicated in the output. Thus, in the output, YEAR.1 represents the first degree (linear) polynomial contrast and YEAR.2 represents the quadratic contrast. The line MEAN, listed under column SOURCE in the output, tests the hypothesis that the linear component of the variable YEAR is zero. Since the mean effect for YEAR.1 is significant (p value =0.0005), the linear component of YEAR is significantly different from zero. The variable GROUP listed under SOURCE is used to test the hypothesis that the first-order polynomial for the variable YEAR is the same for different levels of the variable GROUP. This hypothesis is accepted (p value=0.7855).

Similar interpretations are applicable for the contrast YEAR.2. Since the p value for the MEAN effect in this case is 0.0612 there is slight evidence that the quadratic component is different from zero. See Section 5.3.4 for a more detailed description and interpretation of the analysis of the orthogonal polynomial contrasts.

5.5 Analysis in the Presence of Covariates

When data contain covariates that might affect repeated measures tests, it is important to design the analysis to account for the covariate effects. Consider these examples. First, suppose the initial measurements on the subjects *before* the treatments are applied on the subjects provide the relevant information on the subsequent measurements. Second, suppose various blood pressure drugs are administered on groups of subjects, and blood pressure measurements are taken weekly. Also measured is the amount of sodium consumed by individuals the previous day. See Milliken (1989). Since the amount of sodium in the diet is known to affect blood pressure measurements, a better analysis may be possible by incorporating the sodium content in the previous day's diet as a covariate.

However, the two examples described above are different. In the first case, the value of the covariate is same for all time points and is specific only to the particular subject; in the second case, the values of covariates may be different for various time points for every subject. In other words, if the subjects are visualized as the whole plots with subplots represented by different time points, then the two situations differ in whether the value of the covariate is the same for all subplots within a whole plot or not. Unfortunately, only the first case can be expressed in terms of standard multivariate linear model. The second case, although quite common, requires that the matrix of regression coefficients corresponding to the covariates be block diagonal, thereby imposing restrictions on the matrix of unknown parameters.

5.5.1 A Multivariate Analysis of Covariance

If the values of covariates are the same for all time points for a given subject then the multivariate linear model can be written as

$$\mathbf{Y} = \mathbf{X}\mathbf{B} + \mathbf{Z}\Gamma + \mathcal{E},$$

where the matrix $\mathbf{Z}$ represents the matrix of the values of covariates and possibly interaction between the treatments and covariates. The matrix Γ stands for the corresponding unknown coefficients. This model has been described in Chapter 4 along with an appropriate approach to the analysis.

The effect of covariates may be different in various treatment groups. Also, they may influence the measurements taken at different time points very differently, and these two possibilities should be carefully investigated. The first of these possibilities can be examined by testing for the statistical significance of the interactions of the treatment with the covariates. The second possibility can be tested by examining the significance of the interaction between the covariates and time and also possibly that between treatment, covariates, and time. If the covariates have different effects on responses at various time points then the comparison of treatment profiles adjusted for the covariates does not have much meaning. If however, the covariate*time and the treatment*covariate*time interactions can be assumed to be zero, we can perform the profile analysis with only a slight modification. We will illustrate this in the following example.

Example 10: Subject-Specific Covariates, Diabetic Patients Study Data (Crowder and Hand, 1990)

Three groups of diabetic patients, without complications (DINOCOM), with hypertension (DIHYPER), and with postural hypotension (DIHYPOT) respectively and a control (CONTROL) of healthy subjects were asked to perform a small physical task at time zero. A particular response was observed at times -30, -1, 1, 2, 3, 4, 5, 6, 8, 10, 12, and 15 minutes. The corresponding variables are denoted by X1, X2, and Y1 through Y10 respectively and the pre-performance responses X1 and X2 are used as the covariates for the repeated measures Y1 through Y10. The data set has certain missing values and in such cases the entire row of the data set on the corresponding subjects is discarded in the SAS analysis. As a result, it is not possible to perform all the desirable analyses on this data set. Hence we illustrate the analysis only for variables Y1, Y2, Y3, and Y4.

The first step in the analysis is to examine if the effects of the two covariates are the same in all treatment groups. To do so, we need to include X1, X2 and their interactions with GROUP, namely GROUP*X1, and GROUP*X2, in the multivariate linear model. Thus the corresponding MODEL statement is

```
model y1-y4 =x1 x2 group group*x1 group*x2;
```

and the corresponding MANOVA statement is

```
manova h=group x1 x2 group*x1 group*x2;
```

The NOUNI option in Program 5.15 to suppresses the univariate output and the SS3 option produces the Type III SS&CP matrices. The PRINTE and PRINTH options in the MANOVA statement print the $\mathbf{E}$ and corresponding $\mathbf{H}$ matrices. The multivariate tests show that neither of the two interactions, GROUP*X1 and GROUP*X2, is significant (respective p values for Wilks' Λ are 0.9420 and 0.7343). Also, there is no overall GROUP effect. The corresponding Wilks' Λ test statistic has a value of 0.6131 with a p value of 0.9248. Further, X1 is not significant (p value =0.4753) but X2 appears to have a very significant effect ($\Lambda = 0.0609$ with a p value of 0.0001). This indicates that X2 should be included in the model for any treatment comparison. Also, since GROUP*X2 was found to be not significant, we can assume that the effect of covariate X2 is same in the four treatment groups.

Suppose we can assume that the covariates X1 and X2 do not influence the measurements taken at different time points differently (this assumption will be tested later). This assumption means that the covariates X1 and X2 affect the average of Y1, Y2, Y3, and Y4 for a given subject rather than the temporal changes in response. In that case, we want to perform the profile analysis for this data set. Under the assumption stated above, the hypotheses of parallel profiles and of coincidental profiles, given parallelism, will be unchanged. The SAS code for these hypotheses is given as part of Program 5.15. The two hypotheses are accepted in view of their large p values. These p values for Wilks' Λ are 0.7324 and 0.3776 respectively.

Given that the profiles are coincidental, the other hypothesis of interest is that all the profiles are horizontal. To test this hypothesis, we made a transformation by defining the variables YBAR=(Y1+Y2+Y3+Y4)/4, Z1=Y2-Y1, Z2=Y3-Y2, and Z3=Y4-Y3. The variable YBAR measures the average response for the subject and Z1, Z2, Z3 measure the changes in response from one time point to the next. For parallel profiles, the expected values of Z1, Z2, and Z3 are the same for all four groups. The hypothesis of horizontal profiles could be tested using the method described in the previous section. However, YBAR is correlated with Z1, Z2, and Z3 and hence these can be taken as the additional covariates in the model. In view of this, the hypothesis of horizontal profiles can be tested by testing the hypothesis of no GROUP effect in the univariate analysis of covariance model for YBAR given by the following statement

```
        model ybar =z1 z2 z3 x1 x2 group;
```

Output 5.15 indicates that the GROUP effect is marginally significant (p value =0.0498). Care must be taken to ensure that the sum of squares corresponding to GROUP have been corrected for all the covariates Z1, Z2, Z3, X1, and X2. Thus, we can either list GROUP last in the MODEL statement, if the sequential sums of squares (Type I) are used or alternatively specify the Type III sums of squares (SS3) as an option in the MODEL statement.

One assumption that was made in the profile analysis using YBAR presented above is that the covariates do not differently influence the measurements taken at different times. This hypothesis can be examined by testing for the significance of the covariate*time and treatment*covariate*time interaction in the corresponding univariate analysis. This can be easily achieved by using the REPEATED statement

```
        repeated time 4 (1 2 3 4) polynomial;
```

where the POLYNOMIAL option has often been chosen for further analyses (such as, to examine the polynomial trend etc.) in repeated measures data. The analysis presented in this section does not, however, depend on any such choice. The above REPEATED statement is included in Program 5.15 and the corresponding output appears in Output 5.15. Only the relevant parts of the output are presented. None of the multivariate tests for TIME*X1, TIME*X2, TIME*X1*GROUP, and TIME*X2*GROUP are significant. The respective p values for Wilks' Λ are 0.8369, 0.9411, 0.9802, and 0.7849. All other multivariate test statistics also confirm this conclusion. Thus the hypothesis that the covariates X1 and X2 do not differently affect the measurements taken at different time points, can be accepted.

5.5.2 A Univariate Approach

The alternative univariate approach of a split plot design with covariates can also be adopted. Specifically the observed value on the uth subject under the ith treatment at the jth time point y_{iju} can be modeled as (assuming only one covariate)

$$y_{iju} = \mu + \alpha_i + \beta_j + (\alpha\beta)_{ij} + \delta_{iu} + \beta_{ij} x_{iu} + \epsilon_{iju}, \tag{5.15}$$

where all the symbols except β_{ij} and x_{iu} have been defined in Equation 5.11. The covariate x_{iu} represents the value for the uth subject under the ith treatment and β_{ij} are the slope parameters for the jth time period and the ith treatment. The generalization of the above model for more than one covariate is straightforward.

Since for a given subject x_{iu} are same for all time points j, $j = 1, ..., p$, a *whole plot model* can be obtained by averaging the above model over suffix j. See Milliken and Johnson(1989). It leads to

$$\bar{y}_{i\cdot u} = \mu + \alpha_i + \bar{\beta}. + (\alpha\beta)_{i\cdot} + \delta_{iu} + \bar{\beta}_{i\cdot} x_{iu} + \epsilon_{i\cdot u}$$

or

$$\bar{y}_{i\cdot u} = \bar{\mu}_{i\cdot} + \bar{\beta}_{i\cdot} x_{iu} + \epsilon^*_{i\cdot u} \tag{5.16}$$

which is a one-way classification model with a covariate. We prefer to call it a *subject model* rather than a *whole plot model* to agree with our present context of repeated measures. Note that unlike the standard analysis of covariance model, "errors" $\epsilon^*_{i\cdot u}$ are not independently distributed but have a compound symmetry structure for the variance-covariance matrix. However, the analysis of variance tests are still valid under compound symmetry. The two hypotheses of interest are

$$H_0^{(1)} : \bar{\beta}_{1\cdot} = \ldots = \bar{\beta}_{k\cdot} = 0$$

and

$$H_0^{(2)} : \bar{\beta}_{1\cdot} = \ldots = \bar{\beta}_{k\cdot}$$

The null hypothesis $H_0^{(1)}$ tests if the average slopes are all zero, whereas, $H_0^{(2)}$ tests if the regression lines for various treatment groups are parallel. If $H_0^{(2)}$ is true then a common slope can be estimated.

Both of these hypotheses can be tested using the subject model in Equation 5.16 and its appropriate reduction under the corresponding null hypothesis. Specifically, if $H_0^{(1)}$ is true, then Equation 5.16 reduces to a one-way classification model. Although errors are not independent in view of their compound symmetric covariance structure, the usual partial F test can still be applied. The corresponding F statistic

$$F = \frac{(SSE_{Reduced} - SSE_{Full})/k}{SSE_{Full}/f} \qquad (5.17)$$

follows an F distribution with (k, f) df under the null hypothesis $H_0^{(1)}$. The quantity SSE_{Full} corresponds to the error sum of squares of the subject model given in Equation 5.16. Its degrees of freedom, for convenience, are denoted by f. We may add that the value of f is in part also determined by the number of missing values in the multivariate data. $SS_{Reduced}$ is the error sum of squares for the reduced model, that is, the model given in Equation 5.16 without $\bar{\beta}_{i\cdot}x_{iu}$ terms. To test $H_0^{(2)}$, we observe that under $H_0^{(2)}$, Equation 5.16 becomes

$$\bar{y}_{i\cdot u} = \bar{\mu}_{i\cdot} + \bar{\beta}x_{iu} + \epsilon^*_{i\cdot u}. \qquad (5.18)$$

A partial F test for $H_0^{(2)}$ can also be obtained using SSE_{Full} and $SSE_{Reduced}$ which now correspond to models in Equations 5.16 and 5.18 respectively. Since the null hypothesis $H_0^{(2)}$ specifies only $(k-1)$ linear restrictions, the divisor of the $(SSE_{Reduced} - SSE_{Full})$ is $(k-1)$ and not k. When there are two or more covariates, the hypothesis $H_0^{(1)}$ and $H_0^{(2)}$ can be generalized in a straightforward way. Also the corresponding F tests can be appropriately modified. All this can be best illustrated through the continuation of Example 10. Also see Example 15 in Section 5.7.3 for an alternative analysis of testing the homogeneity of regression coefficients and intercepts.

Example 10: Diabetic Patients Study Data (continued)

For the fitness data of Crowder and Hand, we first want to test if the covariates X1 and X2 have any effect on the average responses. Since $k = 4$ and there are two covariates, the quantity k in Equation 5.17 is replaced by $2k = 8$ here. The SSE_{Full} and $SSE_{Reduced}$ are the two sums of squares which can be respectively obtained by fitting the appropriate models using two MODEL statements

```
model y= group z11 z12 z13 z14 z21 z22 z23 z24;
```

and

```
model y=group;
```

While the second MODEL statement is straightforward, the first one needs further explanation, especially since Z11, Z12, etc., have not been introduced yet. Since x_{1iu} and x_{2iu} values are available only for the subjects in the ith group (CONTROL) and not others, and since the slopes for each group are different, we need to have (two covariates times four groups=) eight slope parameters in the model and correspondingly eight independent regression variables (apart from the treatment effect). The new regression variables are defined as z_{li^*}, $l = 1, 2$, $i^* = 1, .., 4$ where the value of z_{li^*} for u^{th} subject in the ith group, say z_{li^*u}, $l = 1, 2$, $i^* = 1, .., 4$, is

$$z_{li^*u} = \begin{cases} x_{liu} \ if \ i = i^* \\ 0 \ if \ i \neq i^* \end{cases}.$$

The hypotheses $H_0^{(1)}$ of no covariate effect is equivalent to testing that all z_{li}, $l = 1, 2$, $i = 1, 2, 3, 4$ are unimportant. Hence to assess their contribution, we use the corresponding hypothesis sum of squares which is computed as the difference between the SSE from two models indicated above in the MODEL statement.

The SAS program to calculate z_{li} and then to fit two models is given as the first part of Program 5.16. The output presented as Output 5.16 gives $SSE_{Reduced} = 243.3190$ and $SSE_{Full} = 11.9889$ and the value of f as the degree of freedom of SSE_{Full}, which is 14 for this data set. Note even though the covariates do not appear in the corresponding model, one observation with a missing X1 value was discarded for this calculation, to have the sum of squares comparable in the two models. Also $k = 8$, and hence the observed value of the F statistic with (8, 14) df is

$$F = \frac{(243.3190 - 11.9889)/8}{11.9889/14} = 33.7669$$

which is highly significant with a p value (calculated from an independent computation using the SAS function PROBF-not shown) almost zero. As a result, we reject the null hypothesis $H_0^{(1)}$ and conclude that the average response is indeed affected by the covariates.

Next, to test if the slopes in different groups for the covariate X1 are all equal and those for X2 are all equal, the MODEL statement for reduced model would be

```
model y=group x1 x2;
```

The corresponding SSE would be used as $SSE_{Reduced}$ while SSE_{Full} is the same as earlier. In Output 5.16, we have eliminated the corresponding calculations to save the space. We may verify that the hypothesis $H_0^{(2)}$ gets accepted (p value $= 0.1157$). Thus a common slope model can be used for all four groups. The estimated value of the two common slopes corresponding to X1 and X2 are -0.0322 and 1.0174 respectively.

Two other hypotheses of interest from the original model in Equation 5.15 are

$$H_0^{(3)} : \beta_{11} = \ldots = \beta_{1p} = \beta_{21} = \ldots = \beta_{2p} = \ldots = \beta_{k1} = \ldots = \beta_{kp} = 0$$

and

$$H_0^{(4)} : \beta_{11} = \ldots = \beta_{1p},$$
$$\beta_{21} = \ldots = \beta_{2p},$$
$$\vdots$$
$$\beta_{k1} = \ldots = \beta_{kp}.$$

The hypothesis $H_0^{(4)}$ can be tested using the model in Equation 5.15 but $H_0^{(3)}$ cannot be tested using the original model due to certain confounding difficulties. The alternative strategy to pursue may be that the acceptance of orthogonal hypotheses $H_0^{(1)}$ and $H_0^{(4)}$ would imply the acceptance of $H_0^{(3)}$, and hence reject $H_0^{(3)}$ only if either $H_0^{(1)}$ or $H_0^{(4)}$ is rejected. Milliken and Johnson (1989) provide an extensive discussion of the methodology involved and the related intricacies.

When the covariates are available for each subject and at every time point, the appropriate analysis using the univariate split plot design is given by Milliken (1990), who also warns that the use of the REPEATED statement does not provide the correct sums of squares for within-subject effects. See Milliken (1990) for more information.

5.6 Analysis Using Random Coefficient Models

Another approach to the modeling of repeated measures data is to use random coefficient models. This approach can be especially useful due to its capacity to provide a vast variety of covariance structures such as the autoregressive or the Toeplitz covariance structures. In SAS such models can be fitted using PROC MIXED.

A random coefficient model is mathematically represented by

$$\mathbf{y}_i = \mathbf{X}_i \beta + \mathbf{Z}_i \nu_i + \epsilon_i, \ i = 1, ..., n, \tag{5.19}$$

where $\mathbf{y}_i$ is an p_i by 1 vector of observations (e.g., in the repeated measures context, it is possibly collected over p_i time points on the ith subject, $i = 1, ..., n$), X_i and Z_i are the known matrices of orders p_i by q and p_i by r respectively, and β is the fixed q by 1 vector of unknown nonrandom regression coefficients. The r by 1 vectors ν_i are random with $E(\nu_i) = \mathbf{0}$, and $D(\nu_i) = \mathbf{G}_1$. Finally ϵ_i are the p_i by 1 vectors of random errors whose elements are no longer required to be uncorrelated. We assume that $E(\epsilon_i) = \mathbf{0}$, $D(\epsilon_i) = \mathbf{R}_i$, $Cov(\nu_i, \nu_{i'}) = \mathbf{0}$, $Cov(\epsilon_i, \epsilon_{i'}) = \mathbf{0}$ and $Cov(\nu_i, \epsilon_{i'}) = \mathbf{0}$ for all $i \neq i'$. Such assumptions seem to be reasonable in repeated measures data where subjects are assumed to be independent, yet the repeated data on a given subject may be correlated. An appropriate covariance structure can be assigned to the data by an appropriate choice of matrices $\mathbf{G}_1$ and $\mathbf{R}$. Note that since $\mathbf{y}_i$ is a p_i by 1 vector, $i = 1, ..., n$, the model can account for the unbalanced repeated measures data, that is, when data are such that all the subjects have not been observed at all time points.

The n submodels in Equation 5.19 can be stacked one below the other to give a single model

$$\begin{bmatrix} \mathbf{y}_1 \\ \mathbf{y}_2 \\ \vdots \\ \mathbf{y}_n \end{bmatrix} = \begin{bmatrix} \mathbf{X}_1 \\ \mathbf{X}_2 \\ \vdots \\ \mathbf{X}_n \end{bmatrix} \beta + \begin{bmatrix} \mathbf{Z}_1 & \mathbf{0} & \cdots & \mathbf{0} \\ \mathbf{0} & \mathbf{Z}_2 & \cdots & \mathbf{0} \\ \vdots & \vdots & \cdots & \vdots \\ \mathbf{0} & \mathbf{0} & \cdots & \mathbf{Z}_n \end{bmatrix} \begin{bmatrix} \nu_1 \\ \nu_2 \\ \vdots \\ \nu_n \end{bmatrix} + \begin{bmatrix} \epsilon_1 \\ \epsilon_2 \\ \vdots \\ \epsilon_n \end{bmatrix}$$

or

$$\mathbf{y}_{\Sigma p_i \times 1} = \mathbf{X}_{\Sigma p_i \times q} \beta + \mathbf{Z}_{\Sigma p_i \times r} \nu + \mathcal{E}_{\Sigma p_i \times 1}, \tag{5.20}$$

where the definitions of $\mathbf{y}$, $\mathbf{X}$, $\mathbf{Z}$, ν, and ϵ in terms of the matrices and vectors of submodels are self explanatory. In view of the assumptions made on Equation 5.19, we have $E(\nu) = \mathbf{0}$, $E(\epsilon) = \mathbf{0}$,

$$D(\nu) = \begin{bmatrix} \mathbf{G}_1 & \mathbf{0} & \ldots & \mathbf{0} \\ \mathbf{0} & \mathbf{G}_1 & \ldots & \mathbf{0} \\ \vdots & \vdots & \ldots & \vdots \\ \mathbf{0} & \mathbf{0} & \ldots & \mathbf{G}_1 \end{bmatrix} = \mathbf{I}_n \otimes \mathbf{G}_1 = \mathbf{G} \text{ and } D(\epsilon) = \begin{bmatrix} \mathbf{R}_1 & \mathbf{0} & \ldots & \mathbf{0} \\ \mathbf{0} & \mathbf{R}_2 & \ldots & \mathbf{0} \\ \vdots & \vdots & \ldots & \vdots \\ \mathbf{0} & \mathbf{0} & \ldots & \mathbf{R}_n \end{bmatrix} = \mathbf{R}.$$

The symbol $\otimes$ here stands for the Kronecker product defined for two matrices $\mathbf{U}_{s \times t} = (u_{ij})$ and $\mathbf{V}_{l \times m} = (v_{ij})$ as

$$\mathbf{U} \otimes \mathbf{V} = \begin{bmatrix} u_{11}\mathbf{V} & u_{12}\mathbf{V} & \ldots & u_{1t}\mathbf{V} \\ u_{21}\mathbf{V} & u_{22}\mathbf{V} & \ldots & u_{2t}\mathbf{V} \\ \vdots & \vdots & \ldots & \vdots \\ u_{s1}\mathbf{V} & u_{s2}\mathbf{V} & \ldots & u_{st}\mathbf{V} \end{bmatrix} = (u_{ij}\mathbf{V}).$$

It follows from Equation 5.20 that

$$D(\mathbf{y}) = \mathbf{Z}D(\nu)\mathbf{Z}' + D(\epsilon) = \mathbf{Z}\mathbf{G}\mathbf{Z}' + \mathbf{R}.$$

If in addition, multivariate normality can be assumed for ν_i and ϵ_i, $i = 1, ..., n$, then

$$\mathbf{y} \sim N_{\Sigma p_i}(\mathbf{X}\beta, \mathbf{Z}\mathbf{G}\mathbf{Z}' + \mathbf{R}).$$

If normality is assumed, the generalized least square estimator and also the maximum likelihood estimator of β is given by (assuming that it uniquely exists)

$$\hat{\beta} = [\mathbf{X}'(\mathbf{Z}\mathbf{G}\mathbf{Z}' + \mathbf{R})^{-1}\mathbf{X}]^{-1}\mathbf{X}'(\mathbf{Z}\mathbf{G}\mathbf{Z}' + \mathbf{R})^{-1}\mathbf{y}$$

$$= [\sum_{i=1}^{n} \mathbf{X}_i'(\mathbf{Z}_i\mathbf{G}_1\mathbf{Z}_i' + \mathbf{R}_i)^{-1}\mathbf{X}_i]^{-1}[\sum_{i=1}^{n} \mathbf{X}_i'(\mathbf{Z}_i\mathbf{G}_1\mathbf{Z}_i' + \mathbf{R}_i)^{-1}\mathbf{y}_i] \qquad (5.21)$$

provided the dispersion matrices $\mathbf{G}_1$ and $\mathbf{R}_i$, $i = 1, ..., n$ are all known. The dispersion matrix of $\hat{\beta}$ is

$$[\mathbf{X}'(\mathbf{Z}\mathbf{G}\mathbf{Z}' + \mathbf{R})^{-1}\mathbf{X}]^{-1} = [\sum_{i=1}^{n} \mathbf{X}_i'(\mathbf{Z}_i\mathbf{G}_1\mathbf{Z}_i' + \mathbf{R}_i)^{-1}\mathbf{X}_i]^{-1}.$$

Of course if the multivariate normality were an underlying assumption for model in Equation 5.19 then the resulting distribution of $\hat{\beta}$ would also be multivariate normal. Also, if

$\mathbf{X}'(\mathbf{ZGZ}' + \mathbf{R})^{-1}\mathbf{X}$ does not admit an inverse, for most estimation problems a generalized inverse would replace the inverse in Equation 5.21 provided estimability has been ensured.

The random coefficient models provide ample flexibility to deal with the repeated measures data. Within-subject variability is conveniently dealt with by modeling it through the random errors ϵ_i and the random slope coefficients ν_i for changes in repeated measures specific to the ith subject. The correlation structures such as compound symmetry and autoregressive or unstructured covariances can be assumed for $\mathbf{G}_1$ and $\mathbf{R}_i$.

Example 11: Random Coefficients, A Pharmaceutical Stability Study (Obenchain, 1990)

This example is adopted from *SAS Technical Report P-229, p. 354*. The pharmaceutical stability data (*used with permission from Glaxo Wellcome Inc.*) presents replicate assay results as the observed responses for the shelf life of various drugs (in months). The response variable is potency as the percentage claim on the label. There are three batches of products which may differ in initial potency represented by intercepts and in degradation rates represented by the slope parameters. Since the batches are taken randomly, these intercepts and slope parameters are assumed to be the random coefficients. Note that the values of p_i are not all the same.

Since there are two random coefficients, namely the batch intercept and the batch slope, both of which may not have zero means, we write their effects as $\beta + \nu_1, \beta + \nu_2, ...$, where β is the fixed effect part, representing the mean initial potency and mean degradation rate, and the vectors $\nu_1, \nu_2, ...$ are all 2 by 1 vectors with their variance-covariance matrix $\mathbf{G}_1$ a 2 by 2 matrix, which we assume to be unstructured. The three unknown parameters of $\mathbf{G}_1$, namely g_{11}, $g_{12} = g_{21}$, and g_{22}, need to be estimated, along with several other parameters. For errors, we assume the spherical covariance structure. We use the restricted maximum likelihood (REML) procedure for the estimation.

The subject effect is represented by three batches and on each batch, data are collected at 0, 1, 3, 6, 9, and 12 months. As mentioned earlier, the age of the drug in months represents a fixed effect factor as well, along with an intercept in the model which can be interpreted as the mean initial potency.

To analyze this data using PROC MIXED, we essentially need to spell out these facts in compact form with short SAS code. Specifically, we must indicate that BATCH plays the role of SUBJECT (SUBJECT=BATCH); that INTERCEPT and AGE are random effects (RANDOM=INT AGE); and we specify only the fixed part of the model, which includes an intercept, (which need not be specified) and the variable AGE. The SAS code is given as Program 5.17 and the output is presented in Output 5.17.

The output shows that the estimate of the matrix $\mathbf{G}_1$ is

$$\hat{\mathbf{G}}_1 = \begin{bmatrix} 0.9729 & -0.1019 \\ -0.1019 & 0.0365 \end{bmatrix}$$

and hence

$$\hat{\mathbf{G}} = \begin{bmatrix} \hat{\mathbf{G}}_1 & \mathbf{0} & \mathbf{0} \\ \mathbf{0} & \hat{\mathbf{G}}_1 & \mathbf{0} \\ \mathbf{0} & \mathbf{0} & \hat{\mathbf{G}}_1 \end{bmatrix}$$

which is a 6 by 6 block diagonal matrix. Since the covariance structure for error is assumed to be spherical, we do not need to specify that in the SAS code. It is the default in SAS. A REPEATED statement would be needed if any other covariance structure for error were to be specified. Under assumed sphericity, the estimated variance of the error component is $\hat{\sigma}^2 = 3.3023$.

The effects of the intercept and slope are in part fixed and in part random and may be represented as $(\beta_0 + \nu_0, \beta_1 + \nu_1)$, where β_0 and β_1 are the fixed parameters and ν_0 and ν_1 are the random coefficients, in each case respectively for the INTERCEPT and slope for AGE. The estimates of β and the predicted values of the random effects ν are presented in separate tables in Output 5.17. Specifically,

$$\hat{\beta}_0 = \begin{bmatrix} 102.7016 \\ -0.5242 \end{bmatrix} \text{ and } \hat{\nu}' = \begin{cases} (-0.9974, \ 0.1267) \ for \ Batch \ 1 \\ (0.3858, \ -0.2040) \ for \ Batch \ 2 \\ (0.6116, \ 0.0773) \ for \ Batch \ 3. \end{cases}$$

Also presented are the corresponding standard errors, the prediction errors, and corresponding tests for the significance.

Example 12: Modeling Linear Growth, Ramus Heights Data (Elston and Grizzle, 1962)

To further illustrate the use of PROC MIXED, we will analyze the ramus heights data of Elston and Grizzle (1962) where the heights of the ramus bone (in mm) for 20 boys were measured at 8, $8\frac{1}{2}$, 9, and $9\frac{1}{2}$ years of age. We may want to model the ramus height, say y_t, at age t as a polynomial growth function of their ages. Suppose we decide to fit an orthogonal linear growth function in u_t which represents the transformed age, so that the vector of the values of $\mathbf{u}$ is orthogonal to $\mathbf{1}_4$. Specifically, this vector is $(-3, -1, 1, 3)'$. Since each boy would have his own individual growth curve, we have for a given boy,

$$y_t = \beta_0 + \beta_1 u_t + \epsilon_t, \tag{5.22}$$

where $\epsilon_t \sim N(0, \sigma^2)$ are independent and the value of β_1 is specific to the boy. In other words, β_1 is a random coefficient. It may however not have a zero mean and so we partition β_1 into fixed and random parts as $\beta_1 = \beta_{1F} + \beta_{1R}$, where $E(\beta_{1R}) = 0$ and $var(\beta_{1R}) = \sigma^2_{\beta_1}$ which results in

$$y_t = \beta_0 + \beta_{1F} u_t + \beta_{1R} u_t + \epsilon_t. \tag{5.23}$$

Thus $\beta_0 + \beta_{1F} u_t$ represents the fixed part of the model, β_{1R} is a normally distributed random coefficient with zero mean, and $var(\beta_{1R}) = \sigma^2_{\beta_1}$. Normality is assumed since we intend to use REML as the method of estimation. Since the form of $\mathbf{G}_1$ here is $\sigma^2_{\beta_1} \mathbf{I}$ the default option, TYPE=SIM for the covariance structure of $\mathbf{G}_1$ can be used. Thus the appropriate MODEL, RANDOM, and REPEATED statements are

```
model y=u/s;
random boy/type=sim subject=boy;
repeated/type=sim subject=boy r;
```

where the option S in MODEL statement requests that the solution for the fixed effects be printed. The TYPE=SIM option in the RANDOM and REPEATED statements provides simple spherical covariance structure for the data on each subject. SUBJECT is specified by BOY in the above code. The option R in REPEATED statement is used to print a typical diagonal block (which is the variance-covariance matrix for the observations on a typical boy) of the block diagonal matrix $\mathbf{R}$. Also we have chosen to use the METHOD=REML option as the choice of estimation procedure. The complete code is given in Program 5.18. The corresponding output appears as Output 5.18. The SAS output provides $\hat{\sigma}^2 = 0.6629$ and $\hat{\sigma}^2_{\beta_1} = 6.1059$. Also since $E(y_t) = \beta_0 + \beta_{1F}u_t$, the estimate of average ramus height at time t is given by $\hat{E}(y_t) = \hat{\beta}_0 + \hat{\beta}_{1F}u_t$, where the estimated coefficients $\hat{\beta}_0$ and $\hat{\beta}_{1F}$ are also given in Output 5.18 as $\hat{\beta}_0 = 50.0713$ and $\hat{\beta}_{1F} = 0.4658$. Suppose instead of fitting Equation 5.23, we decide to fit Equation 5.22 with 4 by 1 vector of ϵ_t for each subject having a compound symmetric (CS) structure. In this case, there are no random effects in the model in Equation 5.22, but the covariance structure within each subject would need to be specified using the REPEATED statement

```
repeated/type=cs subject=boy r;
```

where SUBJECT=BOY indicates that repeated measures which are assumed to be independent are taken on boys. Option R in the REPEATED statement prints a typical diagonal block of the block diagonal matrix $\mathbf{R}$. The detailed program is included as part of Program 5.18 with the corresponding output included in Output 5.18. It may be observed that the estimates of $\sigma^2_{\beta_1}$ and σ^2 are exactly same. However, it could appear that the two codes fit the same model under identical assumptions. That it is not, follows from the fact that under the former model (fitted by using the RANDOM statement), $D(\mathbf{y}_{80 \times 1}) = \mathbf{Z}\mathbf{G}\mathbf{Z}' + \mathbf{R}$ with appropriate $\mathbf{Z}$ and $\mathbf{G}$, and with $\mathbf{R} = \sigma^2\mathbf{I}$, which may not have any simple covariance structure; however, under the latter model (fitted by using the REPEATED statement) $D(\mathbf{y}_{80 \times 1}) = \mathbf{R}$, where $\mathbf{R}$ has a compound symmetric structure.

5.7 The Growth Curve Models

Suppose a growth process is observed on a set of experimental subjects over a period of time. We want to build an appropriate growth function for this process. We may also want to compare the growth functions of groups of several sets of individuals or subjects. A generalization of MANOVA models can be used to fit certain polynomial growth curves to the growth process and hence, using the standard theory of multivariate analysis, we can compare the growths of several groups. We consider this model next.

5.7.1 Polynomial Growth

In Chapters 3 and 4 the linear model

$$\mathbf{Y} = \mathbf{XB} + \mathcal{E} \tag{5.24}$$

was considered and applications of this model to analyze various types of data were given. A slightly more general model than Equation 5.24 developed by Potthoff and Roy (1964), which is needed to analyze a certain types of measurements on growth curves, follows

$$\mathbf{Y}_{0_{n \times p}} = \mathbf{X}_{n \times k} \mathbf{B}_{k \times q} \mathbf{A}_{q \times p} + \mathcal{E}_{n \times p}, \tag{5.25}$$

where $\mathbf{X}$ and $\mathbf{A}$ are known full rank (as was also observed in the previous chapters, this assumption is really not needed) matrices of ranks k and q respectively. The matrix $\mathbf{B}$ is the matrix of unknown parameters. As in the previous discussion, p represents the number of time points at which the measurements are taken on each of the n experimental units. The degree of the polynomial curve that is being fit for the p measurements over time is $q - 1$. Accordingly $\mathbf{A}$ is a q by p matrix of the coefficients of the polynomials of various degrees up to $q - 1$. If the measurements are equidistant in time, the orthogonal polynomial term, k, represents the number of groups and accordingly $\mathbf{X}$ is the corresponding design matrix (with entries zeros and ones) to represent different groups. In general, the matrices $\mathbf{A}$ and $\mathbf{X}$ can be any matrices of known quantities. Assume that the rows of error matrix $\mathcal{E}$ are independently distributed as $N_p(\mathbf{0}, \Sigma)$, where Σ is a p by p positive definite matrix.

Consider the general linear hypothesis

$$H_0 : \mathbf{LBM} = \mathbf{0},$$

where $\mathbf{L}_{r \times k}$ and $\mathbf{M}_{q \times s}$ are full rank matrices with ranks r and s respectively. There are several approaches for testing H_0. However, we will adopt what is termed the Rao-Khatri approach (Seber, 1984, p. 480), since it reduces the present problem to a testing problem under the usual analysis of covariance model. Hence the standard SAS procedures, like PROC GLM, can be applied to test H_0 given above.

5.7.2 Rao-Khatri Reduction

Let $\mathbf{C}_1$ of order p by q and $\mathbf{C}_2$ of order p by $p - q$ be any two matrices such that $Rank$ $(\mathbf{C}_1) = q$, $Rank$ $(\mathbf{C}_2) = p - q$, $\mathbf{AC}_1 = \mathbf{I}_q$, and $\mathbf{AC}_2 = \mathbf{0}_{p-q}$ and that $\mathbf{C} = (\mathbf{C}_1 : \mathbf{C}_2)$ is a nonsingular matrix. For example, $\mathbf{C}_1$ and $\mathbf{C}_2$ can be taken as $\mathbf{A}'(\mathbf{AA}')^{-1}$ and any $p - q$ linearly independent columns of $\mathbf{I} - \mathbf{A}'(\mathbf{AA}')^{-1}\mathbf{A}$ respectively. An easy way of choosing $\mathbf{C}_1$ and $\mathbf{C}_2$ when $\mathbf{A}$ is the matrix of orthogonal polynomials is to take $\mathbf{C}_1 = \mathbf{A}'$ and $\mathbf{C}_2$ such that $\mathbf{C} = (\mathbf{C}_1 : \mathbf{C}_2)$ is an orthogonal matrix. Specifically, choose $\mathbf{C}_1$ to be the matrix of normalized orthogonal polynomials of degree 0 to $q - 1$ and $\mathbf{C}_2$ to be the similar matrix for degrees q to $p - 1$. Once $\mathbf{C}_1$ and $\mathbf{C}_2$ are selected, define $\mathbf{Y}_1 = \mathbf{Y}_0 \mathbf{C}_1$ and

$\mathbf{Y}_2 = \mathbf{Y}_0\mathbf{C}_2$ as the transformed data matrices of order n by q and n by $p - q$ respectively. This leads to $\mathbf{Y} = (\mathbf{Y}_1 : \mathbf{Y}_2) = \mathbf{Y}_0(\mathbf{C}_1 : \mathbf{C}_2) = \mathbf{Y}_0\mathbf{C}$. Also, $E(\mathbf{Y}_1) = \mathbf{XBAC}_1 = \mathbf{XB}$ and $E(\mathbf{Y}_2) = \mathbf{XBAC}_2 = \mathbf{0}$. Since $\mathbf{Y}_1$ and $\mathbf{Y}_2$ are correlated, even though $E(\mathbf{Y}_2)$ does not involve $\mathbf{B}$, the set of variables $\mathbf{Y}_2$ can be taken as covariates for estimating or testing the hypotheses about $\mathbf{B}$. That is, we consider the conditional model

$$E(\mathbf{Y}_1|\mathbf{Y}_2) = \mathbf{XB} + \mathbf{Y}_2\boldsymbol{\Gamma}, \tag{5.26}$$

where $(p - q)$ by q matrix $\boldsymbol{\Gamma}$ is the parameter matrix representing the effects of various covariates on the conditional mean of $\mathbf{Y}_1$ given $\mathbf{Y}_2$. The rows of $\mathbf{Y}_1$ are independent and are conditionally distributed as multivariate normal with the means as the rows of the right-hand side matrix of Equation 5.26 and a common variance-covariance matrix. Hence the method used in Section 4.7 can be used here. By writing Equation 5.26 as

$$\mathbf{Y}_1 = (\mathbf{X} \ \mathbf{Y}_2) \begin{bmatrix} \mathbf{B} \\ \boldsymbol{\Gamma} \end{bmatrix} + \mathcal{E},$$

it can be shown that the maximum likelihood estimate of $\mathbf{B}$ is given by

$$\hat{\mathbf{B}} = (\mathbf{X}'\mathbf{X})^{-1}\mathbf{X}'\mathbf{Y}_0\mathbf{S}^{-1}\mathbf{A}'(\mathbf{A}\mathbf{S}^{-1}\mathbf{A}')^{-1}$$

where

$$\mathbf{S} = \mathbf{Y}_0'[\mathbf{I} - \mathbf{X}(\mathbf{X}'\mathbf{X})^{-1}\mathbf{X}']\mathbf{Y}_0/(n - p).$$

Example 13: Modeling Cubic Growth, Dog Response Time Data (Grizzle and Allen, 1969)

Grizzle and Allen (1969) using the Rao-Khatri method analyzed this data set. Also see Seber (1984, p. 487). The data set includes observations on four groups of dogs showing the response of each dog at times 1, 3, 5, 7, 9, 11, and 13 minutes after a coronary occlusion. The four groups, the first being the control group, have respective sample sizes 9, 10, 8, and 9. The three experimental groups respectively include dogs with extrinsic cardiac denervation three weeks prior to coronary occlusion, with extrinsic cardiac denervation immediately prior to coronary occlusion, and with bilateral thoracic sympathectomy and stellectomy three weeks prior to coronary occlusion. The profile plots (not given) of the sample mean vectors for each group seem to suggest a third-degree polynomial growth curve. Since the times at which the observations are made are equidistant, a third-degree orthogonal polynomial may instead be used. The model then is

$$\mathbf{Y}_{0_{36 \times 7}} = \mathbf{X}_{36 \times 4}\mathbf{B}_{4 \times 4}\mathbf{A}_{4 \times 7} + \mathcal{E}_{36 \times 7},$$

where

$$\mathbf{X} = \begin{bmatrix} \mathbf{1}_9 & \mathbf{0} & \mathbf{0} & \mathbf{0} \\ \mathbf{0} & \mathbf{1}_{10} & \mathbf{0} & \mathbf{0} \\ \mathbf{0} & \mathbf{0} & \mathbf{1}_8 & \mathbf{0} \\ \mathbf{0} & \mathbf{0} & \mathbf{0} & \mathbf{1}_9 \end{bmatrix}$$

and $\mathbf{A}$ is the matrix with the first four columns of the 7 by 7 orthogonal polynomial matrix. In SAS the matrix of orthogonal coefficients, $\mathbf{C}$, is generated using the ORPOL function of PROC IML. Then

$$\mathbf{Y} = \mathbf{Y}_0\mathbf{C} = (\mathbf{Y}1 : \mathbf{Y}2 : \mathbf{Y}3 : \mathbf{Y}4 : \mathbf{Y}5 : \mathbf{Y}6 : \mathbf{Y}7).$$

A formal test for adequacy of the third-degree polynomial is performed by testing whether $E(Y5) = E(Y6) = E(Y7) = 0$. The SAS code is given in Program 5.19, and the output is presented in Output 5.19. The p value using Wilks' Λ is 0.4280. Hence we do not reject the null hypothesis that the third-degree polynomial is adequate.

The model for further analysis of the data can therefore be taken as the one in which $Y5$, $Y6$, and $Y7$ are covariates for the dependent variables $Y1$, $Y2$, $Y3$, $Y4$, and the basic independent variable is GROUP. For this, the null hypothesis of no difference between the groups can be written as $H_0 : \mathbf{LBM} = \mathbf{0}$ with $\mathbf{M} = \mathbf{I}_4$ and

$$\mathbf{L} = \begin{bmatrix} 1 & -1 & 0 & 0 \\ 0 & 1 & -1 & 0 \\ 0 & 0 & 1 & -1 \end{bmatrix}.$$

Wilks' Λ for this hypothesis is 0.4033 leading to an approximate F=2.3576 on 12 and 69 degrees of freedom. This yields a p value of 0.0132 thereby leading us to reject the null hypothesis that all the groups have the same third-degree polynomial curves. All the other three tests also lead to the same conclusion. Knowing that the groups may have different growth curves, we may want to estimate the matrix $\mathbf{B}$ consisting of parameters of these curves. To estimate $\mathbf{B}$ we use the ESTIMATE statement of PROC GLM. The columns of $\hat{\mathbf{B}}$, the estimate of $\mathbf{B}$, are obtained as the estimates of the regression parameter estimates from the individual outputs from the univariate analysis. The SAS code for finding the estimates is given at the end of Program 5.19 and the corresponding output is suppressed to save space. Another way to get these estimates is by using PROC REG. See Example 14.

The model in Equation 5.26 is applicable in many other designed experimental situations. For example, suppose data measured at p time points on n experimental units comes from a randomized block design. Then, by choosing the $\mathbf{X}$ matrix appropriately and including all the parameters of this model in $\mathbf{B}$ we can express the model as Equation 5.26.

It is not necessarily true that the inclusion of covariates would improve the efficiency of the estimates. In some instances, including only few covariates from $\mathbf{Y}_2$ (that is, only a few columns of $\mathbf{Y}_2$) may improve the efficiency of the estimates more than using the entire $\mathbf{Y}_2$. We illustrate a way of selecting a set of covariates from $\mathbf{Y}_2$ to improve the inference, using the mice data of Izenman and Williams (1989). Also see Williams and Izenman (1981).

Example 14: Choosing Covariates, Mice Data (Izenman and Williams, 1989)

The data, given in Program 5.20, are a part of those given in Izenman and Williams (1989). Complete details of data collection scheme is given in Izenman (1987). The observations represent the weights from birth until weaning of 14 male mice measured 2, 5,

8, 11, 14, 17, and 20 days after birth. We analyze this data set to illustrate how a set of covariates may increase the efficiency of the inference in growth curve modeling. Suppose that a second-degree polynomial is the correct model for these data. Rao (1987) has utilized a number of methods of selecting variables to arrive at this model.

A second degree polynomial model for these data can be written in matrix form as

$$\mathbf{Y}_{0_{14 \times 7}} = \mathbf{1}_{14 \times 1} \mathbf{B}_{1 \times 3} \mathbf{A}_{3 \times 7} + \mathcal{E}_{14 \times 7}.$$

As in the previous example, by transforming $\mathbf{Y}_0$ using an orthogonal polynomial matrix we obtain $\mathbf{Y} = \mathbf{Y}_0 \mathbf{C}$. Let $\mathbf{Y} = (\mathbf{Y}1 : \ldots : \mathbf{Y}7)$. The adequacy of the second-degree polynomial model is established by testing the null hypothesis $H_0 : E(Y4) = \ldots = E(Y7) = 0$. The variables $Y4, \ldots, Y7$ can thus be used as the covariates for the dependent variables $Y1$, $Y2$, and $Y3$. The problem is to estimate $\mathbf{B} = (\beta_0, \beta_1, \beta_2)'$, elements of which represent the expected values of $Y1$, $Y2$, and $Y3$ respectively. In Table 5.2 we present the standard errors (SE) of the least squares estimates of $\hat{\beta}_0$, $\hat{\beta}_1$, and $\hat{\beta}_2$ for the five models, namely with no covariates, only $Y4$ as a covariate, $Y4$ *and* $Y5$ as covariates,..., and $Y4, \ldots, Y7$ are all covariates. The standard errors presented in the table are taken from the outputs of PROC REG for each of the five models. For example, the values corresponding to the covariate $Y4$ in the table below respectively are the standard errors corresponding to intercepts for dependent variables Y1, Y2, and Y3 from the output of PROC REG when the code

```
proc reg;
model y1 y2 y3 = y4;
```

is used.

Covariates	$SE(\hat{\beta}_0)$	$SE(\hat{\beta}_1)$	$SE(\hat{\beta}_2)$
$None$	.0573	.0330	.0138
$Y4$	.0480	.0220	.0098
$Y4 \& Y5$	.0647	.0294	.0113
$Y4, Y5, Y6$	.0667	.0313	.0120
$Y4, Y5, Y6, Y7$	.0731	.0351	.0133

TABLE 5.2 STANDARD ERRORS FOR THE ESTIMATES

An examination of the values in the table suggests that including only Y4 in the model as a covariate may be the most beneficial. The complete SAS code for finding the estimates using PROC REG is given in Program 5.20. However, the corresponding output is suppressed to save space.

5.7.3 Test of Homogeneity of Regression Coefficients

It is a common practice in most of the growth studies in biological sciences to compare two or more groups by testing the equality of model parameters. First, we consider an example of a linear model and show how to use dummy variables to test the homogeneity of several regressions. The analysis is primarily univariate.

Suppose there are g groups with n_i, $i = 1, ..., g$ observations in each group. Let the dependent variable be denoted by y and the independent variable be x. Instead of a single independent variable we could have k independent variables. The linear model in this case can be written as

$$y_{ij} = \beta_{i0} + \beta_{i1} x_{ij} + \epsilon_{ij}, \quad j = 1, ..., n_i, \; i = 1, ..., g. \tag{5.27}$$

That is, each group has its own regression line possibly with different intercepts and regression parameters. Assume that ϵ_{ij}, $j = 1, ..., n_i$, $i = 1, ..., k$ are all independent $N(0, \sigma^2)$ random variables. In order to test the homogeneity of slopes or homogeneity of intercepts we may first express the above models as a single regression model using dummy variables for identifying the groups. We define

$$D_i = \begin{cases} 1 \text{ if the observation is from group } i, \\ 0 \text{ otherwise;} \end{cases}$$

$i = 1, ..., g$. Then Equation 5.27 can be written as

$$y_{ij} = D_1(\beta_{10} + \beta_{11} x_{ij}) + ... + D_g(\beta_{g0} + \beta_{g1} x_{ij}) + \epsilon_{ij},$$

or

$$y_{ij} = \beta_{10} D_1 + \beta_{11} D_1 x_{ij} + ... + \beta_{g0} D_g + \beta_{g1} D_g x_{ij} + \epsilon_{ij}. \tag{5.28}$$

It should be observed that the above model does not have an intercept term. Define $\mathbf{y} = (y_{11}, ..., y_{1n_1}, y_{21}, ..., y_{2n_2}, ..., y_{g1}, ..., y_{gn_g})'$, and define ϵ similarly. Also let

$$\mathbf{X} = \begin{bmatrix} 1 & x_{11} & 0 & 0 & ... & 0 & 0 \\ \vdots & \vdots & \vdots & \vdots & & \vdots & \vdots \\ 1 & x_{1n_1} & 0 & 0 & ... & 0 & 0 \\ 0 & 0 & 1 & x_{21} & ... & 0 & 0 \\ \vdots & \vdots & \vdots & \vdots & & \vdots & \vdots \\ 0 & 0 & 1 & x_{2n_2} & ... & 0 & 0 \\ \vdots & \vdots & \vdots & \vdots & & \vdots & \vdots \\ 0 & 0 & 0 & 0 & ... & 1 & x_{g1} \\ \vdots & \vdots & \vdots & \vdots & & \vdots & \vdots \\ 0 & 0 & 0 & 0 & ... & 1 & x_{gn_g} \end{bmatrix}, \quad \beta = \begin{bmatrix} \beta_{10} \\ \beta_{11} \\ \beta_{20} \\ \beta_{21} \\ \vdots \\ \beta_{g0} \\ \beta_{g1} \end{bmatrix}.$$

Then Equation 5.28 can be written in matrix form as

$$\mathbf{y}_{n \times 1} = \mathbf{X}_{n \times m} \beta_{m \times 1} + \epsilon_{n \times 1}, \quad \epsilon \sim N(\mathbf{0}, \sigma^2 \mathbf{I}),$$

where $n = \sum_{i=1}^{g} n_i$, and $m = 2g$. Here the matrix $\mathbf{X}$ is of full rank with rank $2g$. The hypotheses $H_0^{(1)} : \beta_{11} = \ldots = \beta_{g1}$ and $H_0^{(2)} : \beta_{10} = \ldots = \beta_{g0}$ can be tested using the standard tests from regression analysis.

Example 15: Homogeneity of Regression, Cabbage Data (Rawlings, 1988)

The problem is to compare ascorbic acid content (Y) in cabbage in two genetic lines (LINE) or cultivars planted on three different dates. A completely randomized design with ten experimental units for each combination of planting date and genetic line is used. Thus $g = 2 \times 3 = 6$, $n_i = 10$ for each of the six treatment groups and hence $n = \Sigma n_i = 60$. As the ascorbic acid content may also depend on the weight (X) of the cabbage, the weight of the cabbage head is taken as a covariate. A model for analyzing these data, taking $\bar{x}$ as the average head weight, is

$$y_{iju} = \mu_{ij} + \beta_{ij}(x_{iju} - \bar{x}) + \epsilon_{iju},$$

$u = 1, \ldots, 10$, $i = 1, 2$, $j = 1, 2, 3$. Here β_{ij} represent the slopes of different regression lines for each of the six groups. It is possible that μ_{ij} themselves may have a model, say of the type $\mu + \alpha_i + \delta_j + \gamma_{ij}$. The problem we consider here is to test for homogeneity of the regression coefficients β_{ij}. That is, we want to test the null hypothesis $H_0^{(1)} : \beta_{ij} = \beta$ for all i and j. The null hypothesis $H_0^{(2)}$ which is the hypothesis of the equality of intercepts can then be tested similarly. It is also possible to test the specific hypotheses on the individual components of μ_{ij}, such as α_i, δ_j or γ_{ij}, $i = 1, 2$; $j = 1, 2, 3$.

Since the main interest here is to test $H_0^{(1)} : \beta_{ij} = \beta$ we consider the alternative, yet equivalent, model

$$y_{iju} = \nu_{ij} + \beta_{ij}x_{iju} + \epsilon_{iju},$$

where $\nu_{ij} = \mu_{ij} + \beta_{ij}\bar{x}$. Of course both models will lead to the same test statistics for $H_0^{(1)}$. The SAS code for performing this test is provided in Program 5.21. Using the two levels (LIN1 and LIN2) of the genetic line variable LINE and three levels (DAT1, DAT2, and DAT3) of the variable DATE we first create six dummy variables D1-D6 to identify the six groups. The respective products of D1-D6 with the covariate X representing interactions are created as the variables XD1-XD6. Then we use the NOINT option in PROC REG to fit the model in Equation 5.28. The TEST statement is used to test the equality of regression parameters β_{ij}. From Output 5.21, the F statistic for testing $H_0 : \beta_{ij} = \beta$ has an observed value of 0.6643. Under $H_0^{(1)}$ it has an F distribution with $(5, 48)$ degrees of freedom thereby giving a p value of 0.6523. The high p value indicates that a common regression parameter can be used in the model. Thus a simplified model for the analysis of this data set is

$$y_{iju} = \mu_{ij} + \beta(x_{iju} - \bar{x}) + \epsilon_{iju},$$

with $\mu_{ij} = \mu + \alpha_i + \delta_j + \gamma_{ij}$.

For testing the equality of the intercepts ($H_0^{(2)}$) for the six groups the following SAS code could be utilized.

```
proc reg;
model y=d1-d6 xd1-xd6/noint;
test d1=d2=d3=d4=d5=d6;
run;
```

5.7.4 Growth as a Nonlinear Regression Model

There may be situations where the linear modeling of growth may not be appropriate. For more realistic applications, especially in fisheries and biological growths, we may need to use nonlinear functions for fitting the growth processes. Although there are several nonlinear models for growth curves, for illustration we will consider only a class of the most celebrated models. These models, called Von Bertalanffy models, are especially useful in fisheries and biological sciences.

The Von Bertalanffy model in its most general form can be written as

$$y_{ij} = l_{\infty i}[1 - exp\{-k_i(t_{ij} - t_{0i})\}] + \epsilon_{ij}, \tag{5.29}$$

$j = 1, ..., n_i$, $i = 1, ..., g$, where y_{ij} is the measurement, say, length of a fish, on the jth subject (j^{th} fish) from the ith group. Also, t_{ij} is the observed value of a covariate (for example, age of a fish) corresponding to y_{ij}, $l_{\infty i}$ for each group i is the unknown limiting value (as the time variable tends to infinity) of the expectation of y_{ij} (that is, the asymptote of the mean (expected value) as a function of the time variable). For example, $l_{\infty i}$ is the asymptotic length (or the expected length at maturity) of the fish from the ith group. The unknown constant k_i represents the rate at which the asymptotic value $l_{\infty i}$ is achieved, t_{0i} is the unknown hypothetical value of t_{ij} when the value of y_{ij} is zero, and ϵ_{ij} are independently distributed $N(0, \sigma^2)$ error variables.

As in the case of linear regression models, we define the dummy variables

$$D_i = \begin{cases} 1 \text{ if the observation is from group } i, \\ 0 \text{ otherwise;} \end{cases}$$

$i = 1, ..., g$. Then the model in Equation 5.29 can be written as

$$y_{ij} = \sum_{u=1}^{g} D_u l_{\infty u}[1 - exp\{-k_u(t_{ij} - t_{0u})\}] + \epsilon_{ij}, \quad j = 1, ..., n_i, \quad i = 1, ..., g.$$

The problem is to compare several of these groups. The likelihood ratio method may be used for such comparisons. The maximum likelihood estimates of the unknown parameters have been obtained using PROC NLIN (see Lakkis and Jones (1992)).

Rewrite the model Equation 5.29 as

$$y_{ij} = \mu(l_{\infty i}, k_i, t_{0i}, t_{ij}) + \epsilon_{ij},$$

where $\mu(l_{\infty i}, k_i, t_{0i}, t_{ij}) = l_{\infty i}[1 - exp\{-k_i(t_{ij} - t_{0i})\}]$. Then the likelihood function of the parameters given the data y_{ij}, $j = 1, ..., n_i$, $i = 1, ..., g$ is

$$f(\theta) = (\sqrt{(2\pi)})^{-n}(\sigma^2)^{-n/2} \; exp\{-\frac{1}{2\sigma^2} \sum_{i=1}^{g} \sum_{j=1}^{n_i} (y_{ij} - \mu(l_{\infty i}, k_i, t_{0i}, t_{ij}))^2\}, \; n = \sum_{i=1}^{g} n_i.$$

(5.30)

Here θ represents all the parameters $l_{\infty 1}, ..., l_{\infty g}, k_1, ..., k_g, t_{01}, ..., t_{0g}$ and σ^2. For a fixed σ^2 maximizing $f(\theta)$ in Equation 5.30 with respect to the parameters $l_{\infty i}, k_i, t_{0i}, i = 1, ..., g$ is same as minimizing

$$S(l_{\infty 1}, ..., l_{\infty g}, k_1, ..., k_g, t_{01}, ..., t_{0g}) = \sum_{i=1}^{g} \sum_{j=1}^{n_i} [y_{ij} - \mu(l_{\infty i}, k_i, t_{0i}, t_{ij})]^2$$

with respect to the corresponding parameters and this minimization will need to be done iteratively. Once have we obtained these estimates, the maximum likelihood estimate of σ^2 is given by

$$\hat{\sigma}^2 = \frac{1}{n} S(\hat{l}_{\infty 1}, ..., \hat{l}_{\infty g}, \hat{k}_1, ..., \hat{k}_g, \hat{t}_{01}, ..., \hat{t}_{0g}),$$

where $\hat{l}_{\infty 1}, ..., \hat{l}_{\infty g}, \hat{k}_1, ..., \hat{k}_g, \hat{t}_{01}, ..., \hat{t}_{0g}$ are the estimates obtained by the nonlinear least squares minimization described above.

Consider the general problem of testing a null hypothesis $H_0 : \theta \in \omega$ versus $H_1 : \theta \notin \omega$, where ω is a subset of Ω the parameter space. The likelihood ratio test statistic for this problem is

$$L = (\frac{\hat{\sigma}_{\Omega}^2}{\hat{\sigma}_{\omega}^2})^{n/2},$$

where $\hat{\sigma}_{\Omega}^2$ is the m.l.e. of σ^2 when no restrictions on the parameter space are placed and $\hat{\sigma}_{\omega}^2$ is the maximum likelihood estimate of σ^2 when the linear constraints prescribed by H_0 are put on the parameter space Ω. For large sample size n, the distribution of $-2 \ln L = -n \ln (\hat{\sigma}_{\Omega}^2/(\hat{\sigma}_{\omega}^2)$ is approximated by the chi-square distribution with ν degrees of freedom, where ν is the number of parameters estimated in Ω *minus* number of parameters estimated in ω.

We want to test the following hypotheses:

$H_0^{(1)} : l_{\infty 1} = ... = l_{\infty g}(= l_{\infty}, \; say)$ vs. not all $l_{\infty i}$ are equal

$H_0^{(2)} : k_1 = ... = k_g(= k)$ vs. not all k_i are equal

$H_0^{(3)} : t_{01} = ... = t_{0g}(= t_0)$ vs. not all t_{0i} are equal

$H_0^{(4)} : l_{\infty 1} = ... = l_{\infty g}(= l_{\infty}), \; t_{01} = ... = t_{0g}(= t_0)$ and $k_1 = ... = k_g(= k)$ vs. at least one inequality.

For testing $H_0^{(1)}$, $H_0^{(2)}$, $H_0^{(3)}$, and $H_0^{(4)}$ against the corresponding alternatives, the chi-square approximation of the likelihood ratio test statistics are $-n \ln(\hat{\sigma}_{\Omega}^2/\hat{\sigma}_{\omega_i}^2)$, $i = 1, 2, 3, 4$.

Each of these statistics has an approximate chi-square distribution with respective degrees of freedom $(g-1)$, $(g-1)$, $(g-1)$ and $3(g-1)$. The ω_i are the respective subsets of the parameter space Ω defined by the null hypotheses $H_0^{(i)}$, $i = 1, .., 4$. Given the initial estimates $\theta = \theta_0$ and the form of the function $\mu(\theta, x)$, PROC NLIN fits a model of the type $y = \mu(\theta, x) + \epsilon$ given the data (y_i, x_i), $i = 1, ..., n$ and obtains the least squares estimates of θ. This procedure can be adapted to the present case of having data on g groups with possibly different growth curves.

Example 16: Tests of Homogeneity, Fish Growth Data (Kimura, 1980)

This data set from Kimura (1980) and also analyzed by Lakkis and Jones (1992) using SAS programs contains observations on the average lengths at different ages for male and female fish (Pacific hake). The data in Program 5.22 are only a part of a data set. As $g = 2$, we introduce two more independent variables D_1 and D_2, respectively, identifying male and female fish. The model to analyze these data are

$$
\begin{aligned}
y_{ij} =& D_1 l_{\infty 1}[1 - exp\{-k_1(t_{ij} - t_{01})\}] \\
&+ D_2 l_{\infty 2}[1 - exp\{-k_2(t_{ij} - t_{02})\}] + \epsilon_{ij}
\end{aligned}
\tag{5.31}
$$

$j = 1, ..., n_i$, $i = 1, 2$; $n_1 = 11$, $n_2 = 13$, $n = n_1 + n_2 = 24$.

The objective of the study was to fit the separate Von Bertalanffy models to the data on male as well as female Pacific hakes. Interest was also in determining if a single model for the two groups could be considered adequate and if not, if there were certain parameters in the model that could be taken to be same for the two groups.

The SAS code for calculating the maximum likelihood estimates of the relevant parameters under Ω (no restriction on the parameter space), under ω_1 (linear constraint: $l_{\infty 1} = l_{\infty 2} = l_\infty$), ω_2 ($k_1 = k_2 = k$), ω_3 ($t_{01} = t_{02} = t_0$) and under ω_4 (all of the restrictions in ω_1, ω_2, and ω_3 together) is given in Program 5.22. In each case, PROC NLIN requires one to supply the initial estimates of the parameters with the PARMS= option. Following Lakkis and Jones (1992), we first plot for each group (male and female) the length as a function of age, and get the initial estimates for $(t_{0i}, l_{\infty i})$, $i = 1, 2$ by visually examining the graph. The initial estimates of k_i are obtained by substituting the corresponding initial estimates for $l_{\infty i}$, t_{0i} and by substituting the average, $\bar{y}_i$ for y_{ij}, the average, $\bar{t}_i$ for t_{ij}, $j = 1, ..., n_i$ in Equation 5.29 and then solving for k_i ignoring the error component. The initial estimates under the restricted models are obtained by appropriate simple averaging. For example, under ω_1 the average of initial estimates of $l_{\infty 1}$ and $l_{\infty 2}$ is used as an initial estimate of l_∞ since under $H_0^{(1)}$, we have the restriction $l_{\infty 1} = l_{\infty 2} = l_\infty$.

In the MODEL statement of PROC NLIN, the explicit form of the Equation 5.31 (barring error term) is provided. There are many iterative procedures available in PROC NLIN to fit the model some of which are derivative-based and require the explicit specification of partial derivatives. If no derivatives are provided, the procedure uses the default DUD (Doesn't Use Derivatives), where the derivatives are estimated by the program. The maximum number of iterations are specified in the MAXITER= option. In the output the estimates of each of the parameters and a regression type (ANOVA) summary table are provided. As in the ANOVA, we have partitioned the total sum of squares into sum of squares due to regression and the residual sum of squares. The maximum likelihood estimate of σ^2, say $\hat{\sigma}^2$, is obtained from the residual sum of squares by dividing it by n. Thus, by running the NLIN procedure under no restrictions and under various restrictions specified by $\omega_1 - \omega_4$ we obtain $\hat{\sigma}_\Omega^2$, $\hat{\sigma}_{\omega_1}^2$, .., $\hat{\sigma}_{\omega_4}^2$. These are used to obtain the test statistics for various hypotheses described above. In the following we present various parameter estimates, test statistics and the p values for the hypotheses $H_0^{(1)} - H_0^{(4)}$.

From Output 5.22 (part of which is provided), under no restrictions (Ω) on the parameters of the model in Equation 5.31 the estimates of various parameters are

$$\hat{l}_{\infty 1} = 55.9790, \ \hat{k}_1 = 0.3855, \ \hat{t}_{01} = 0.1711$$

$$\hat{l}_{\infty 2} = 61.2352, \ \hat{k}_2 = 0.2962, \ \hat{t}_{02} = -0.0575$$

and $n \hat{\sigma}_\Omega^2 = 48.2238$ (the residual sum of squares).

Under the restriction $l_{\infty 1} = l_{\infty 2} = l_\infty$ (ω_1), the estimates are $\hat{l}_\infty = 59.4037$, $\hat{k}_1 = 0.2968$, $\hat{t}_{01} = 0. - 0.1112$, $\hat{k}_2 = 0.3375$, $\hat{t}_{02} = 0.0873$, and $n \hat{\sigma}_{\omega_1}^2 = 71.6021$. The chi-square test statistic for testing $H_0^{(1)}$ is $-24 \, ln(\hat{\sigma}_\Omega^2 / \hat{\sigma}_{\omega_1}^2) = 9.4865$, which using the SAS PROBCHI function, yields a p value of 0.0021 based on a chi-square distribution with $g - 1 = 1$ degrees of freedom. Since the p value is small, a rejection of H_{01} occurs and we conclude that male and female fish have different asymptotic lengths upon maturity.

Similarly, under $H_{02} : k_1 = k_2 = k$, $n \, \hat{\sigma}_{\omega_2}^2 = 56.3368$ yielding the chi-square statistic $-24 \, ln(\hat{\sigma}_\Omega^2 / \hat{\sigma}_{\omega_2}^2) = 3.7319$. The p value based on the chi-square distribution with 1 df is 0.0534. There is some evidence for rejection of $H_0^{(2)}$ although this is only marginal. Output corresponding to $H_0^{(2)}$ is not presented here to save space. For the same reason we have also suppressed the output corresponding to $H_0^{(3)}$ and $H_0^{(4)}$.

Under $H_0^{(3)} : t_{01} = t_{02} = t_0$ $n \, \hat{\sigma}_{\omega_3}^2 = 50.7578$. Hence $-24 \, ln(\hat{\sigma}_\Omega^2 / \hat{\sigma}_{\omega_3}^2) = 1.2291$ yielding a p value of 0.2676 based on 1 df. We do not reject $H_0^{(3)}$. Finally, with all the three restrictions $n \, \hat{\sigma}_{\omega_4}^2 = 79.7645$ and $-24 \, ln(\hat{\sigma}_\Omega^2 / \hat{\sigma}_{\omega_4}^2) = 12.0774$ yielding a p value of 0.0071 based on the chi-square distribution with $3(g - 1) = 3$ degrees of freedom. Thus $H_0^{(4)}$ is rejected.

In summary, the analyses given above suggest that two different growth curves for male and female fish populations are needed with a common length at birth and possibly a common growth rate.

5.8 Crossover Designs

In crossover experiments, treatments are administered in a variety of sequences on various subjects. Thus each subject may get more than one treatment in the course of the experiment. One reason for doing so is that there is usually more variability across subjects than within subjects, and hence the subjects can be treated as random blocks for the purpose of increasing the precision by controlling experimental error variance. The problem, however, becomes complicated by the fact that the successive measurements on the subjects may be correlated. There is also the possible presence of carryover effect(s) at a given time point, of the treatment(s) applied at previous time point(s). This calls for a careful analysis of the data by incorporating these effects appropriately in the model.

5.8.1 Analysis of Crossover Designs

A linear model for crossover design for the response from the mth subject receiving the ith sequence and the kth treatment in the jth time point is

$$y_{ijkm} = \mu_{ijk} + \eta_{im} + \epsilon_{ijkm}$$

$i = 1, ..., s$, $j = 1, ..., p$, $k = 1, ..., a$, $m = 1, ..., n_i$, where μ_{ijk} is the average response of the kth treatment in sequence i at time point j, η_{im} is the error corresponding to the mth experimental unit in sequence i and ϵ_{ijkm} is the random error associated with time point j of the mth experimental unit in sequence i.

The mean response μ_{ijk} is, for convenience, assumed to be composed of several components as

$$\mu_{ijk} = \mu + \alpha_k + \pi_j + \sum_{r=0}^{j-1} \lambda_{jk_r},$$

where α_k is the treatment effect, π_j the time effect, and λ_{jk_r} is the carryover effect of k_r^{th} treatment administered in one or more times during time points $0, 1, ..., j-1$, on the observation at time point j. Initially, at the beginning of any sequence, there is not any carryover effect, so λ_{jk_0} is zero. To simplify the model, we also assume that any carryover effect lasts only up to next time point, and hence we take $\lambda_{jk_0} = \lambda_{jk_1} = ... = \lambda_{jk_{j-2}} = 0$. We also denote, for convenience, $\lambda_{jk_{j-1}}$ by $\lambda_{[k,j-1]}$. In view of this the model becomes

$$y_{ijkm} = \mu + \alpha_k + \pi_j + \lambda_{[k,j-1]} + \eta_{im} + \epsilon_{ijkm}. \tag{5.32}$$

It is further assumed that $\eta_{im} \sim N(0, \sigma_\eta^2)$ are all independent and are independent of $\epsilon_{i'jkm'}$ also for all i, i', j, m, m'. However, the assumption of independence of ϵ_{ijkm} and $\epsilon_{i'j'k'm'}$ may not be realistic. It is so because the observations taken over time on a given subject would most likely be correlated. For convenience the model in Equation 5.32 has been often analyzed as a split plot design, with an assumption of compound symmetric covariance structure for the observation on a given subject. The split plot analysis of Equation 5.32 is straightforward. We will illustrate it by an example adopted from Jones and Kenward (1989, p. 229).

Example 17: Univariate Analysis, Comparison of Drugs (Jones and Kenward, 1989)

Two drugs A and B and their combination termed drug C are to be compared for their effectiveness to control hypertension. Each subject was given three drugs in one of the six possible sequences ABC, ACB, BAC, BCA, CAB, and CBA and systolic blood pressure (Y) was measured at the conclusion of each of the three treatments, each of which lasted for four weeks. The data were collected at four different centers. However, we will not consider the variability due to centers in our analysis. The data are presented as part of Program 5.23 (the carryover effect for initial period is defined as zero). The objective of the study is to examine if there were significant differences between drugs, and to examine the period effect and the carryover effect. The model given in Equation 5.32 is the appropriate model and can be fitted using PROC GLM with the following MODEL statement

```
model y= subject period treat carry;
```

where all the variables on the right side are CLASS variables. Since SUBJECT forms a random sample, the variable SUBJECT is declared to be random. This instructs SAS to use the appropriate sums of squares in forming the F ratios for the tests.

The resulting output is presented in Output 5.23, which indicates a significant effect due to the differences in treatments (for Type I SS, the observed value of $F(2,40)$ is 13.80 and the corresponding p value is 0.0001). However the carryover effect and the period effect are both statistically insignificant. The same conclusions are reached when the analysis is done using Type III SS. Note that because of our convention of using 0 for the carryover effect at the initial period, the sum of squares due to the carryover effect is different from that reported by Jones and Kenward.

In view of the absence of the carryover effect and the period effect, it may be meaningful to compare the treatment means. The estimated difference between the mean effects of A and B, A and C, and B and C are respectively, 25.3971, 12.4140, and -12.9831, which are obtained by first obtaining the least squares solutions using the SOLUTION option in the MODEL statement and then by computing the appropriate differences $\hat{\alpha}_A - \hat{\alpha}_B$, $\hat{\alpha}_A - \hat{\alpha}_C$, and $\hat{\alpha}_B - \hat{\alpha}_C$. Using separate CONTRAST statements, we can perform tests for the significance of treatment differences. All three treatments are significantly different from each other (respective p values are 0.0001, 0.0297 and 0.0287), and A and B are especially markedly different from each other. Treatment C, being the combination of drugs A and B falls in between the two.

It must be remembered that the course of analysis in crossover designed data depends heavily on what the significant and insignificant effects are. The reason for this is that, depending on the particular design, certain effects may be confounded with each other, and if a sum of squares representing two or more confounded effects is found to be significant, it would require a further careful examination of data to decide which of the many confounded effects may have led to the statistical significance of the particular sum of squares. In fact, if each of the treatment sequences is tried on the groups of subjects, then the group*period interaction is composed of

- the treatment effect,
- carryover effect and treatment*period interaction, and

- other left over effects associated with group*period effects.

Since it is desirable that the effects listed above are all estimated, the choice of an appropriate crossover design becomes of great importance. This topic has been addressed at length in Jones and Kenward (1989) and Ratkowsky, Evans and Alldredge (1993). Later in this section we present the SAS code for generating suitable designs from two useful classes of crossover designs.

In some special cases, it may be possible to perform straightforward multivariate analysis of crossover data. One such case is the analysis of AB/BA designs, which are two-sequence (namely AB and BA) designs in two treatments A and B respectively applied to the groups of size, say n_1 and n_2. Since the analysis would follow a familiar pattern described earlier in great details, it can be best illustrated by an example.

Example 18: Multivariate Analysis, Effect of Onions in Diet (Dunsmore, 1981)

Dunsmore (1981) presents a case study which was initiated to investigate the effect of including onions in the diet on plasma triglyceride levels. A two-sequence crossover design with two treatments, namely breakfast without and with onions, to be referred to as A and B respectively, is used. Eight patients were assigned to sequence AB and six to BA. Increases in the plasma triglyceride levels at 1, 2, 3, 4, 5, and 6 hours after breakfast were measured. The analysis here is performed on 10,000 times the logarithm of the plasma triglyceride levels. In the SAS code the respective 12 responses are denoted as Y11,...,Y16 and Y21,...,Y26. While Dunsmore analyzed the data using the univariate technique, Grender and Johnson (1992) chose the multivariate route and listed a SAS approach using the 12 by 1 vectors of responses on each of the 14 subjects, which we will briefly present here. Multivariate normality has been assumed for the analysis. There are two groups, namely AB and BA. These are referred to as Group 1 and 2. Let us denote by μ_{ij}, the 6 by 1 vector of true mean responses on a subject in the ith group and under j^{th} treatment, $i, j=1,2$. This is displayed in Table 5.3:

Group	Treatment	Mean	Treatment	Mean
1	A	μ_{11}	B	μ_{12}
2	B	μ_{21}	A	μ_{22}

TABLE 5.3 A TWO SEQUENCE CROSSOVER DESIGN IN TWO TREATMENTS

where $\mu_{ij} = (\mu_{ij1},...,\mu_{ij6})'$, $i,j = 1,2$. Also, let $\mu_1' = (\mu_{11}' : \mu_{12}')$ and $\mu_2' = (\mu_{21}' : \mu_{22}')$ and let $\mu_i = \mu + \alpha_i$, $i = 1, 2$ for some μ and α_1, α_2. Then the linear model for these data can be written as

$$\mathbf{Y}_{14 \times 12} = [\mathbf{1}_{14}] \begin{bmatrix} \mathbf{1}_8 & \mathbf{0} \\ \mathbf{0} & \mathbf{1}_6 \end{bmatrix} \begin{bmatrix} \mu' \\ \alpha_1' \\ \alpha_2' \end{bmatrix} + \mathcal{E}$$

which is in the form of standard linear model

$$\mathbf{Y} = \mathbf{XB} + \mathcal{E}.$$

From Equation 5.32 we have

$$E(y_{ijkm}) = \mu + \alpha_k + \pi_j + \lambda_{[k,j-1]},$$
$$k = 1,2, \; j = 1,2, \; i = 1,2, \; m = 1,...,n_i; \; n_1 = 8, \; n_2 = 6.$$

Thus we have

$$E(y_{i11m}) = \mu + \alpha_1 + \pi_1,$$
$$E(y_{i21m}) = \mu + \alpha_2 + \pi_2 + \lambda_1,$$
$$E(y_{i12m}) = \mu + \alpha_2 + \pi_1,$$
$$\text{and } E(y_{i22m}) = \mu + \alpha_1 + \pi_2 + \lambda_2.$$

Hence

$$E(y_{111m} + y_{121m}) = 2\mu + (\alpha_1 + \alpha_2) + (\pi_1 + \pi_2) + \lambda_1,$$
$$E(y_{112m} + y_{122m}) = 2\mu + (\alpha_1 + \alpha_2) + (\pi_1 + \pi_2) + \lambda_2,$$
$$E(y_{111m} - y_{121m}) = (\alpha_1 - \alpha_2) + (\pi_1 - \pi_2) - \lambda_1,$$
$$\text{and } E(y_{112m} - y_{122m}) = (\alpha_2 - \alpha_1) + (\pi_1 - \pi_2) - \lambda_2.$$

These sums and differences can be calculated by pre- and post-multiplying $\mathbf{B} = (\mu, \alpha_1, \alpha_2)'$ by certain specific matrices, that is, as $\mathbf{LBM}$, where $\mathbf{L}$ and $\mathbf{M}$ are to be appropriately chosen. As a result, most of the relevant hypotheses can be expressed as $\mathbf{LBM} = \mathbf{0}$.

We adopt the following strategy for the analysis. The appropriate SAS code has been provided by Grender and Johnson (1992), which has been produced here with a few notational changes.

1. First test the null hypothesis that there is no group*time interaction. For this, use

$$\mathbf{L} = [0 \quad 1 \quad -1] \text{ and } \mathbf{M}' = \mathbf{I}_2 \otimes \begin{bmatrix} 1 & -1 & 0 & 0 & 0 & 0 \\ 0 & 1 & -1 & 0 & 0 & 0 \\ 0 & 0 & 1 & -1 & 0 & 0 \\ 0 & 0 & 0 & 1 & -1 & 0 \\ 0 & 0 & 0 & 0 & 1 & -1 \end{bmatrix} = \mathbf{M}_1, (\text{ say })$$

   where $\otimes$ stands for Kronecker product.
2. Test for the equal carryover effect, that is, $H_0 : \lambda_1 = \lambda_2$. For this, use $\mathbf{L} = (0 \; 1 \; -1)$ and, say, $\mathbf{M}' = (1\,1\,1\,1\,1\,1\,1\,1\,1\,1\,1\,1) = \mathbf{M}_2$.
3. If there are equal carryover effects, then test the hypothesis of no treatment*time interaction. For this, $\mathbf{L} = (0 \; 1 \; -1)$ and $\mathbf{M}' = \mathbf{M}_1$.
4. If there is no group*time interaction (that is, if H_0 in (i) is accepted), we may test the hypothesis of no period*time interaction. For this $\mathbf{L} = (1 \; 0 \; 0)$ and $\mathbf{M}' = \mathbf{M}_1$.

5. Test for the time effect by using $\mathbf{L} = (1\ 0\ 0)$ and $\mathbf{M'} = \mathbf{M}_1$.

6. Test for equal treatment effects using $\mathbf{L} = (1\ 0\ 0)$ and $\mathbf{M'} = (1\ 1\ 1\ 1\ 1\ 1\ -1\ -1\ -1\ -1\ -1\ -1) = \mathbf{M}_3$.

7. Test for equal treatment effects using $\mathbf{L} = (1\ 0\ 0)$ and $\mathbf{M'} = \mathbf{M}_3$.

Dunsmore's data are presented in Program 5.24 and the selected parts of the output are presented in Output 5.24. The interpretation of multivariate tests is straightforward and we do not cover it here.

5.8.2 Construction of Crossover Designs

There is a vast amount of literature available on the construction of p period crossover designs under various desirable criteria, such as the variance balance or the D-optimality criterion. These criteria have been discussed in detail in Jones and Kenward (1989). One common crossover design consists of augmenting various mutually orthogonal Latin squares one below the other. These designs are variance balanced in that the variances of the estimates of the treatment differences are minimum. The resulting design is a design in p periods, p treatments that requires $p(p-1)$ subjects (provided such a design exists).

A complete set of p by p mutually orthogonal Latin squares if it exists, is equivalent to a resolution III fractional factorial design for $p+1$, p level variables in p^2 runs that is a $p^{(p+1)-(p-1)}$ fractional factorial design. The problem can be approached by first generating the appropriate fractional factorial layout and then by extracting the elements to arrange $(p-1)$ Latin squares one below the other. The columns denote the period, and rows denote the subject number. The entry at the $(i,j)^{th}$ place indicates the particular treatment administered at the jth time point on the ith subject. The desired $p^{(p+1)-(p-1)}$ fractional factorial design is generated by using PROC FACTEX. A sample program to generate a 4 period, 4 treatment crossover arrangement requiring 12 subjects is given in Program 5.25. The output is given in Output 5.25. Crossover designs with $a = p$ treatments and $p_1 < p$ periods can be obtained by removing any $(p - p_1)$ columns from the above design.

Since the design obtained from the complete set of $p \times p$ mutually orthogonal Latin squares requires $p(p-1)$ subjects (and such a design may not even exist, e.g., when $p=6$), a smaller design may be desired. Williams' designs are possible candidates. These designs are obtained from a $p \times p$ cyclic Latin square (i.e., for which the ith row is i, $i+1, ..., p$, $1, ..., i-1$). When p is even, it requires only p subjects. However, when p is odd, the number of subjects required by the Williams' design is $2p$.

Given a cyclic Latin square, we first find its mirror image and interlace the columns of the two. That is, if $A_1, ..., A_p$ are columns of the cyclic Latin square and $B_p(= A_1), B_{p-1}(= A_2), ..., B_1(= A_p)$ are their respective mirror images (which appear in the order $B_1, ..., B_p$), then the resulting arrangement is

$$A_1 B_1\ A_2 B_2\ ...\ A_p B_p,$$

obtained by interlacing $B_1, ..., B_p$ with $A_1, ..., A_p$. This gives an arrangement with $2p$ columns. It can be generated by using Program 5.26 and is shown in Output 5.26 for $p = 5$. The desired design in p periods is obtained by taking either the first p or the last p columns of the above arrangement if p is even and by arranging the last p columns below the first p columns if p is odd. By virtue of being generated from a Latin square, all p treatments will appear in the design and every treatment will appear exactly once (if p is even) or twice (if p is odd) in every time period.

There are a number of alternative methods available to construct other crossover designs. See, for example, Jones and Kenward (1989) and John (1971). An extensive catalog of many useful designs is given in Ratkowsky, Evans and Alldredge (1993).

We may conclude this chapter with the following comments about missing values in repeated measures. One of the very frequent problems in conducting repeated measures experiments is the failure to follow the subject at all time points due to a variety of reasons. As a result, many repeated measures data sets are not balanced. This further complicates the problem in two ways. First, the standard multivariate methods may no longer be applicable. Second, most computer packages including SAS do not deal with the missing values in the multivariate data; for example, SAS ignores all the observations on a particular subject if it finds a missing value for any of the dependent variables in the MODEL statement. This not only reduces the sample size substantially but may also result in a sample that is biased due to this implicit self-selection.

A way to alleviate this problem would be to impute the missing values before analyzing the data. There are well-respected approaches, based on the EM algorithm, for imputing the missing values. Unfortunately, the EM algorithms by definition are very problem specific and often require the identification of appropriate sufficient statistics (for conditioning purposes) to even program the estimation procedure. However, it should be remembered that imputing the missing values and their substitution for further analysis may not necessarily be a desirable choice. This type of analysis would cause the variance terms to be underestimated. PROC MIXED provides some alternative modeling approaches for data sets of this kind.

```
/* Program  5.1 */

options ls = 78 ps=45 nodate nonumber;

*Memory data from Srivastava and Carter (1983, p. 201);

data memory ;
input y1 y2 y3 ;
lines ;
19 18 18
15 14 14
13 14 15
12 11 12
16 15 15
17 18 19
12 11 11
13 15 12
19 20 20
18 18 17
;
/* Source: Srivastava and Carter (1983, p. 201). */

Title1 'Output 5.1' ;
title2 'Profile for Memory Data: Srivastava and Carter
                              (1983, p. 201)' ;

filename gsasfile "prog51.graph";
goptions gaccess=gsasfile dev=pslmono;

proc summary data=memory;
var y1 y2 y3;
output out=new mean=my1-my3;
data plot;
set new;
array my{3} my1-my3;
do test =1 to 3;
Response=my(test);
output;
end;
drop my1-my3;

proc gplot data = plot;
plot response*test /vaxis=axis1 haxis=axis2 vminor=3
legend=legend1 ;
axis1  order =(14 to 16) label =(a=90 h=1.2 'Response');
axis2 offset=(2) label=(h=1.2 'Test');
symbol1 v=+ i = join;
legend1 across = 3;
run;
```

Output 5.1
Profile for Memory Data: Srivastava and Carter (1983, p. 201)

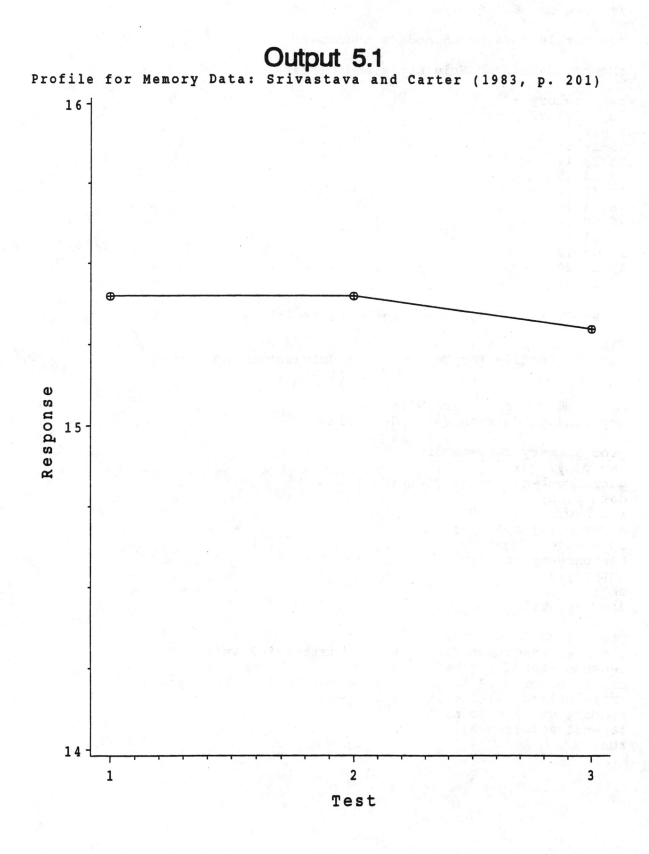

```
/* Program 5.2 */

options ls = 78 ps=45 nodate nonumber;

title1 'Output 5.2';
title2  'Memory data: Srivastava and Carter
                              (1983, p. 201)' ;

data memory ;
input y1 y2 y3 ;
lines ;
19 18 18
15 14 14
13 14 15
12 11 12
16 15 15
17 18 19
12 11 11
13 15 12
19 20 20
18 18 17
;

proc glm data = memory;
model y1 y2 y3 = /nouni ;
manova h = intercept m = ( 1 0 -1,
                           0 1 -1) /printe printh ;
proc glm data = memory ;
model y1 y2 y3 = /nouni ;
repeated test 3 profile/ printe printm ;

run;
```

Memory data: Srivastava and Carter (1983, p. 201)

General Linear Models Procedure
Multivariate Analysis of Variance

H = Type III SS&CP Matrix for INTERCEPT

	MVAR1	MVAR2
MVAR1	0.1	0.1
MVAR2	0.1	0.1

Characteristic Roots and Vectors of: E Inverse * H, where
H = Type III SS&CP Matrix for INTERCEPT   E = Error SS&CP Matrix

Variables have been transformed by the M Matrix

Characteristic Root	Percent	Characteristic Vector V'EV=1	
		MVAR1	MVAR2
0.00924499	100.00	0.12668991	0.17736588
0.00000000	0.00	-0.28867513	0.28867513

Manova Test Criteria and Exact F Statistics for
the Hypothesis of no Overall INTERCEPT Effect
on the variables defined by the M Matrix Transformation
H = Type III SS&CP Matrix for INTERCEPT   E = Error SS&CP Matrix

S=1   M=0   N=3

Statistic	Value	F	Num DF	Den DF	Pr > F
Wilks' Lambda	0.99083969	0.0370	2	8	0.9639
Pillai's Trace	0.00916031	0.0370	2	8	0.9639
Hotelling-Lawley Trace	0.00924499	0.0370	2	8	0.9639
Roy's Greatest Root	0.00924499	0.0370	2	8	0.9639

Memory data: Srivastava and Carter (1983, p. 201)

General Linear Models Procedure
Multivariate Analysis of Variance

M Matrix Describing Transformed Variables

	Y1	Y2	Y3
MVAR1	1	0	-1
MVAR2	0	1	-1

E = Error SS&CP Matrix

	MVAR1	MVAR2
MVAR1	14.9	7.9
MVAR2	7.9	12.9

Memory data: Srivastava and Carter (1983, p. 201)

General Linear Models Procedure
Repeated Measures Analysis of Variance

Partial Correlation Coefficients from the Error SS&CP Matrix
of the Variables Defined by the Specified Transformation / Prob > |r|

DF = 9	TEST.1	TEST.2
TEST.1	1.000000	-0.401869
	0.0001	0.2497
TEST.2	-0.401869	1.000000
	0.2497	0.0001

Test for Sphericity: Mauchly's Criterion = 0.8374058
Chisquare Approximation = 1.4195715 with 2 df   Prob > Chisquare = 0.4917

Applied to Orthogonal Components:
Test for Sphericity: Mauchly's Criterion = 0.9833085
Chisquare Approximation = 0.134659 with 2 df   Prob > Chisquare = 0.9349

Manova Test Criteria and Exact F Statistics for
the Hypothesis of no TEST Effect
H = Type III SS&CP Matrix for TEST   E = Error SS&CP Matrix

S=1   M=0   N=3

Statistic	Value	F	Num DF	Den DF	Pr > F
Wilks' Lambda	0.99083969	0.0370	2	8	0.9639
Pillai's Trace	0.00916031	0.0370	2	8	0.9639
Hotelling-Lawley Trace	0.00924499	0.0370	2	8	0.9639
Roy's Greatest Root	0.00924499	0.0370	2	8	0.9639

General Linear Models Procedure
Repeated Measures Analysis of Variance
Univariate Tests of Hypotheses for Within Subject Effects

Source: TEST

DF	Type III SS	Mean Square	F Value	Pr > F	Adj Pr > F G - G	Adj Pr > F H - F
2	0.06666667	0.03333333	0.05	0.9559	0.9540	0.9559

Source: Error(TEST)

DF	Type III SS	Mean Square
18	13.26666667	0.73703704

Greenhouse-Geisser Epsilon = 0.9836
Huynh-Feldt Epsilon = 1.2564

```
/* Program  5.3 */

options ls = 78 ps=45 nodate nonumber;

* Memory data from Srivastava and Carter (1983, p. 201) ;

proc iml;

y={
19 18 18,
15 14 14,
13 14 15,
12 11 12,
16 15 15,
17 18 19,
12 11 11,
13 15 12,
19 20 20,
18 18 17};

Title1 'Output 5.3' ;
Title2 'Test of Compound Symmetry for Memory Data' ;

p=ncol(y);
n=nrow(y);
s=y'*(I(n)-(1/n)*j(n,n))*y;
svar=s/(n-1);
/*
*Test for sphericity;
const1=-((n-1)-(2*p*p+p+2)/(6*p));
wlam=( det(svar)/((trace(svar)/p)**p) );
llam=wlam**(2/n);
print llam;
test=const1*log(wlam);
print const1 wlam test;
*/
* Test of Compound Symmetry;
detment=det(svar);
square=sum (diag(svar));
sumall=sum(svar);
ssquare=square/p;
correl=(sumall-square)/(p*(p-1)*ssquare);
lrlam=detment /( (ssquare**p)*((1-correl)**(p-1))
                              *(1+(p-1)*correl) );
correct=n- ( p*(p-1)**2*(2*p-3))/(6*(p-1)*(p*p+p-4));
lrstat=-correct*log(lrlam);

df=p*(p+1)/2-2;

pvalue=probchi(lrstat,df);
pvalue=1-pvalue;
print ssquare correl detment lrlam;

print lrstat pvalue;
run;
```

SSQUARE	CORREL	DETMENT	LRLAM
8.9962963	0.9180733	12.509053	0.9025129

LRSTAT	PVALUE
0.9872586	0.9117218

```
/* Program  5.4 */

options ls = 78 ps=45 nodate nonumber;

/* This program computes the LRT for testing circular
covariance structure vs. general cov. Ref. Olkin & Press,
                    AMS, 1969,40, 1358-1373.*/

proc iml;
options ls=76;
y={
72 66 76 77,
60 53 66 63,
56 57 64 58,
41 29 36 38,
32 32 35 36,
30 35 34 26,
39 39 31 27,
42 43 31 25,
37 40 31 25,
33 29 27 36,
32 30 34 28,
63 45 74 63,
54 46 60 52,
47 51 52 43,
91 79 100 75,
56 68 47 50,
79 65 70 61,
81 80 68 58,
78 55 67 60,
46 38 37 38,
39 35 34 37,
32 30 30 32,
60 50 67 54,
35 37 48 39,
39 36 39 31,
50 34 37 40,
43 37 39 50,
48 54 57 43};

Title1 'Output 5.4' ;
Title2 'Test of Circular Structure for Cork Data' ;

p=ncol(y);
n=nrow(y);
s=y'*(I(n)-(1/n)*j(n,n))*y;
svar=s/(n-1);

/* Test of Compound Symmetry;
detment=det(svar);
square=sum (diag(svar));
sumall=sum(svar);
ssquare=square/p;
correl=(sumall-square)/(p*(p-1)*ssquare);
lrlam=detment /(  (ssquare**p)*((1-correl)**(p-1))
                                *(1+(p-1)*correl) );
correct=n- ( p*(p-1)**2*(2*p-3))/(6*(p-1)*(p*p+p-4));
lrstat=-correct*log(lrlam);
print ssquare correl detment lrlam lrstat; */
```

```
/* Program 5.4 continued */

pi=3.1415927;
gam=I(p);
do k=1 to p;
 do l=1 to p;
 gam(|k,l|)=(p**(-0.5))*(cos(2*pi*(k-1)*(l-1)/p)+
 sin(2*pi*(k-1)*(l-1)/p));
 end;
end;
m=floor(p/2);

if(m = p/2) then b = (2*p**3+9*p**2-2*p-18)/
                                  (12*(p**2-2)) ;
else b = (2*p+9)/12 ;

if(m = p/2) then f = (p**2-2)/2 ;
else f = (p**2-1)/2 ;
 v=gam*s*gam';
x=j(p);
nu=x(|,1|);
 do k=1 to p;
 nu(|k|)=v(|k,k|);
 end;
 snu=x(|,1|);
 snu(|1|)=nu(|1|);
if (m=p/2) then
 snu(|m+1|)=nu(|m+1|);
 else
 snu(|m+1|)=nu(|m+1|)+nu(|m+2|);
  do k=2 to m;
  kp=p+2-k;
  snu(|k|)=nu(|k|)+nu(|kp|);
  end;
  do k=m+2 to p;
  snu(|k|)=snu(|p-k+2|);
  end;
 pdt=1.0;
  do k=1 to p;
  pdt=pdt*snu(|k|);
  end;

  wlamda=(2**(2*(p-m-1)))*det(v)/pdt;
  wlamda=wlamda**(n/2);
  test=-2*(1-2*b/n)*log(wlamda);

pvalue=probchi(test,f);
pvalue=1-pvalue;

print wlamda test pvalue;
run;
```

WLAMDA	TEST	PVALUE
0.0000273	18.820383	0.008769

```
/* Program 5.5 */

options ls=78 ps=45 nodate nonumber;

data fish;
infile 'fish.dat' firstobs = 1;
input p1 p2 p3 p4 p5 dose wt @@;
y1=arsin(sqrt(p1));
y2=arsin(sqrt(p2));
y3=arsin(sqrt(p3));
y4=arsin(sqrt(p4));
y5=arsin(sqrt(p5));
x1=log(dose);
x2=wt;

Title1 'Output 5.5' ;
title2 'Fish Data: Srivastava and Carter (1983)' ;

data growth;
set fish;
keep y1-y5;
proc iml;
use growth;
read all into z0;
vec={8 14 24 36 48};
opoly=orpol (vec,4);
z=z0*opoly;
varnames={z1 z2 z3 z4 z5};
create newdata from z (|colname=varnames|);
append from z;
close newdata;

data newdata;
set newdata fish;
merge newdata fish;
proc sort data=newdata;
by dose ;

proc glm data = newdata;
by dose;
model z4 z5 = /nouni;
manova h=intercept;

proc glm data = newdata;
by dose;
model  z5 = /nouni;
manova h=intercept;

run ;
```

Output 5.5
Fish Data: Srivastava and Carter (1983)

------------------------------- DOSE=270 -------------------------------

General Linear Models Procedure
Multivariate Analysis of Variance

Characteristic Roots and Vectors of: E Inverse * H, where
H = Type III SS&CP Matrix for INTERCEPT   E = Error SS&CP Matrix

Characteristic Root	Percent	Characteristic Vector V'EV=1	
		Z4	Z5
0.47322844	100.00	4.67067939	4.93219435
0.00000000	0.00	5.96378168	-2.56212053

Manova Test Criteria and Exact F Statistics for
the Hypothesis of no Overall INTERCEPT Effect
H = Type III SS&CP Matrix for INTERCEPT   E = Error SS&CP Matrix

S=1   M=0   N=0.5

Statistic	Value	F	Num DF	Den DF	Pr > F
Wilks' Lambda	0.67878136	0.7098	2	3	0.5592
Pillai's Trace	0.32121864	0.7098	2	3	0.5592
Hotelling-Lawley Trace	0.47322844	0.7098	2	3	0.5592
Roy's Greatest Root	0.47322844	0.7098	2	3	0.5592

-------------------------------- DOSE=410 --------------------------------

General Linear Models Procedure
Multivariate Analysis of Variance

Characteristic Roots and Vectors of: E Inverse * H, where
H = Type III SS&CP Matrix for INTERCEPT   E = Error SS&CP Matrix

Characteristic Root	Percent	Characteristic Vector V'EV=1	
		Z4	Z5
3.51618945	100.00	11.53372249	14.38455987
0.00000000	0.00	4.11871434	-3.80401964

Manova Test Criteria and Exact F Statistics for
the Hypothesis of no Overall INTERCEPT Effect
H = Type III SS&CP Matrix for INTERCEPT   E = Error SS&CP Matrix

S=1   M=0   N=0.5

Statistic	Value	F	Num DF	Den DF	Pr > F
Wilks' Lambda	0.22142561	5.2743	2	3	0.1042
Pillai's Trace	0.77857439	5.2743	2	3	0.1042
Hotelling-Lawley Trace	3.51618945	5.2743	2	3	0.1042
Roy's Greatest Root	3.51618945	5.2743	2	3	0.1042

------------------------------- DOSE=610 -------------------------------

General Linear Models Procedure
Multivariate Analysis of Variance

Characteristic Roots and Vectors of: E Inverse * H, where
H = Type III SS&CP Matrix for INTERCEPT   E = Error SS&CP Matrix

Characteristic Root	Percent	Characteristic Vector V'EV=1	
		Z4	Z5
11.8069168	100.00	11.87021950	3.38168215
0.0000000	0.00	-0.90283215	2.90498188

Manova Test Criteria and Exact F Statistics for
the Hypothesis of no Overall INTERCEPT Effect
H = Type III SS&CP Matrix for INTERCEPT   E = Error SS&CP Matrix

S=1   M=0   N=0.5

Statistic	Value	F	Num DF	Den DF	Pr > F
Wilks' Lambda	0.07808281	17.7104	2	3	0.0218
Pillai's Trace	0.92191719	17.7104	2	3	0.0218
Hotelling-Lawley Trace	11.80691676	17.7104	2	3	0.0218
Roy's Greatest Root	11.80691676	17.7104	2	3	0.0218

------------------------------ DOSE=940 ------------------------------

General Linear Models Procedure
Multivariate Analysis of Variance

Characteristic Roots and Vectors of: E Inverse * H, where
H = Type III SS&CP Matrix for INTERCEPT   E = Error SS&CP Matrix

Characteristic Root	Percent	Characteristic Vector V'EV=1	
		Z4	Z5
83.3784377	100.00	18.90718476	2.21041046
0.0000000	0.00	−0.83908494	7.22148922

Manova Test Criteria and Exact F Statistics for
the Hypothesis of no Overall INTERCEPT Effect
H = Type III SS&CP Matrix for INTERCEPT   E = Error SS&CP Matrix

S=1   M=0   N=0.5

Statistic	Value	F	Num DF	Den DF	Pr > F
Wilks' Lambda	0.01185137	125.0677	2	3	0.0013
Pillai's Trace	0.98814863	125.0677	2	3	0.0013
Hotelling-Lawley Trace	83.37843765	125.0677	2	3	0.0013
Roy's Greatest Root	83.37843765	125.0677	2	3	0.0013

----------------------------------- DOSE=1450 -----------------------------------

General Linear Models Procedure
Multivariate Analysis of Variance

Characteristic Roots and Vectors of: E Inverse * H, where
H = Type III SS&CP Matrix for INTERCEPT   E = Error SS&CP Matrix

Characteristic Root	Percent	Characteristic Vector V'EV=1	
		Z4	Z5
96.2710026	100.00	18.83635874	9.27855943
0.0000000	0.00	2.43082081	7.28957532

Manova Test Criteria and Exact F Statistics for
the Hypothesis of no Overall INTERCEPT Effect
H = Type III SS&CP Matrix for INTERCEPT   E = Error SS&CP Matrix

S=1   M=0   N=0.5

Statistic	Value	F	Num DF	Den DF	Pr > F
Wilks' Lambda	0.01028056	144.4065	2	3	0.0010
Pillai's Trace	0.98971944	144.4065	2	3	0.0010
Hotelling-Lawley Trace	96.27100255	144.4065	2	3	0.0010
Roy's Greatest Root	96.27100255	144.4065	2	3	0.0010

```
/* Program 5.6 */

options ls=78 ps=45 nodate nonumber;

* A two factor factorial as repeated measures experiment ;

data dog ;
input high_noh low_noh high_h low_h ;
y1 = high_noh;
y2 = low_noh ;
y3 = high_h;
y4 = low_h;
z=y1+y2-y3-y4;
lines ;
426 609 556 600
253 236 392 395
359 433 349 357
432 431 522 600
405 426 513 513
324 438 507 539
310 312 410 456
326 326 350 504
375 447 547 548
286 286 403 422
349 382 473 497
429 410 488 547
348 377 447 514
412 473 472 446
347 326 455 468
434 458 637 524
364 367 432 469
420 395 508 531
397 556 645 625
;
/* Original Data Source: Dr. J. Atlee, III, M.D.  Reproduced
   with permission from Dr. J. Altlee. */

title1 'Output 5.6 ';
title2 'Dog Data: Johnson and Wichern (1992, p. 228)';

proc glm data = dog ;
model high_noh low_noh high_h low_h = /nouni;
/* Test for Factor halothane;
manova h=intercept m=high_noh + low_noh -high_h -low_h
                                 /printe printh;
*Test for Factor Co2 ;
manova h=intercept m=high_noh - low_noh +high_h -low_h
                                  /printe printh;


*Test for interaction Co2*halothane;
manova h=intercept m=high_noh - low_noh -high_h +low_h
                                  /printe printh; */


*Testing Both factors and interaction simultaneously:
Comparing all treatments;
manova h=intercept m=high_noh+low_noh -high_h -low_h ,
                  high_noh - low_noh +high_h -low_h ,
                  high_noh - low_noh -high_h +low_h
                                  /printe printh ;
run;
```

General Linear Models Procedure
Multivariate Analysis of Variance

H = Type III SS&CP Matrix for INTERCEPT

	MVAR1	MVAR2	MVAR3
MVAR1	832448.89474	238829.31579	50863.736842
MVAR2	238829.31579	68520.052632	14592.789474
MVAR3	50863.736842	14592.789474	3107.8421053

Characteristic Roots and Vectors of: E Inverse * H, where
H = Type III SS&CP Matrix for INTERCEPT   E = Error SS&CP Matrix

Variables have been transformed by the M Matrix

Characteristic Root	Percent	Characteristic Vector V′EV=1		
		MVAR1	MVAR2	MVAR3
6.44535118	100.00	0.00232259	0.00154805	0.00025916
0.00000000	0.00	0.00000083	−0.00058630	0.00273933
0.00000000	0.00	−0.00083221	0.00290069	0.00000000

Manova Test Criteria and Exact F Statistics for
the Hypothesis of no Overall INTERCEPT Effect
on the variables defined by the M Matrix Transformation
H = Type III SS&CP Matrix for INTERCEPT   E = Error SS&CP Matrix

S=1   M=0.5   N=7

Statistic	Value	F	Num DF	Den DF	Pr > F
Wilks' Lambda	0.13431200	34.3752	3	16	0.0001
Pillai's Trace	0.86568800	34.3752	3	16	0.0001
Hotelling-Lawley Trace	6.44535118	34.3752	3	16	0.0001
Roy's Greatest Root	6.44535118	34.3752	3	16	0.0001

```
/* Program 5.7 */

*This data from Crowder and Hand (1990, p. 32) shows the
reaction of 12 patients to dietary regime treatment.
Observations were made on each of seven occasions:
(weeks: 1, 2, 6, 10, 14, 15, and 16) twice before, thrice
during, and twice after the treatment regime.;

options ls=78 ps=45 nodate nonumber;

title1 'Output 5.7';

 data react;
 input patient y1-y7;
lines;
1    0.22 0.00 1.03 0.67 0.75 0.65 0.59
2    0.18 0.00 0.96 0.96 0.98 1.03 0.70
3    0.73 0.37 1.18 0.76 1.07 0.80 1.10
4    0.30 0.25 0.74 1.10 1.48 0.39 0.36
5    0.54 0.42 1.33 1.32 1.30 0.74 0.56
6    0.16 0.30 1.27 1.06 1.39 0.63 0.40
7    0.30 1.09 1.17 0.90 1.17 0.75 0.88
8    0.70 1.30 1.80 1.80 1.60 1.23 0.41
9    0.31 0.54 1.24 0.56 0.77 0.28 0.40
10 1.40 1.40 1.64 1.28 1.12 0.66 0.77
11 0.60 0.80 1.02 1.28 1.16 1.01 0.67
12 0.73 0.50 1.08 1.26 1.17 0.91 0.87
;
/* Source: Crowder and Hand (1990, p. 32). */

proc glm data = react;
model y1-y7= /nouni;
manova
h=intercept
m=3*y1+3*y2-2*y3-2*y4-2*y5, 2*y3+2*y4+2*y5-3*y6-3*y7;
title2 'Dietary Regime Treatment Data: Crowder & Hand
                                    (1990, p. 32)';

run;
```

Dietary Regime Treatment Data: Crowder & Hand (1990, p. 32)

General Linear Models Procedure
Multivariate Analysis of Variance

Characteristic Roots and Vectors of: E Inverse * H, where
H = Type III SS&CP Matrix for INTERCEPT   E = Error SS&CP Matrix

Variables have been transformed by the M Matrix

Characteristic Root	Percent	Characteristic Vector V'EV=1	
		MVAR1	MVAR2
6.34076809	100.00	0.13205067	-0.09275497
0.00000000	0.00	0.11594649	0.15516843

Manova Test Criteria and Exact F Statistics for
the Hypothesis of no Overall INTERCEPT Effect
on the variables defined by the M Matrix Transformation
H = Type III SS&CP Matrix for INTERCEPT   E = Error SS&CP Matrix

S=1   M=0   N=4

Statistic	Value	F	Num DF	Den DF	Pr > F
Wilks' Lambda	0.13622553	31.7038	2	10	0.0001
Pillai's Trace	0.86377447	31.7038	2	10	0.0001
Hotelling-Lawley Trace	6.34076809	31.7038	2	10	0.0001
Roy's Greatest Root	6.34076809	31.7038	2	10	0.0001

```
/* Program 5.8 */

* Data from "Strategies for Repeated Measures Analysis of
Variance", Phil Spector, 1174-1177, SUGI 1987. ;

options ls=78 ps=45 nodate nonumber;
data heart;
infile 'heart.dat';
input drug $ y1 y2 y3 y4;

title1 ' Output 5.8';
title2 'Drug Study: Ref: Phil Spector, SUGI, 1987,
                                    pp. 1174-1177';
proc glm data = heart;
class drug;
model y1 y2 y3 y4 = drug/nouni;
manova h = drug/printe printh ;

filename gsasfile "prog58.graph";
goptions gaccess=gsasfile dev=pslmono;
goptions horigin=1in vorigin=2in;
   goptions hsize=6in vsize=8in;
proc summary nway data=heart;
class drug;
var y1 y2 y3 y4;
output out=new mean=my1-my4;
data plot;
set new;
array my{4} my1-my4;
do test =1 to 4;
Response=my(test);
output;
end;
drop my1-my4;

proc gplot data = plot;
plot response*test=drug /vaxis=axis1 haxis=axis2 vminor=3
legend=legend1 ;
axis1 label =(a=90 h=1.2 'Response');
axis2 offset=(2) label=(h=1.2 'Test');
symbol1 v=+ i = join;
symbol2 v=x i=join;
symbol3 v=* i=join;
legend1 across = 3;

proc glm data = heart ;
class drug;
model y1 y2 y3 y4 =drug/nouni;
contrast ' "bww9 vs. control" ' drug 0 1  -1 ;
contrast ' "ax23 vs. the rest" '  drug 2 -1 -1  ;
contrast ' "parallel?" ' drug 1 0 -1,
             drug  0 1 -1;
contrast ' "horizontal?" ' intercept 1 ;
manova h=drug
m= (1 -1 0 0,   1 0 -1 0, 1 0 0 -1)/printe printh ;
contrast ' "coincidental?" '  drug  1 0 -1,
                              drug  0 1 -1 ;
manova h = drug m=(1 1  1 1) /printe printh;
run;
```

A Drug Study

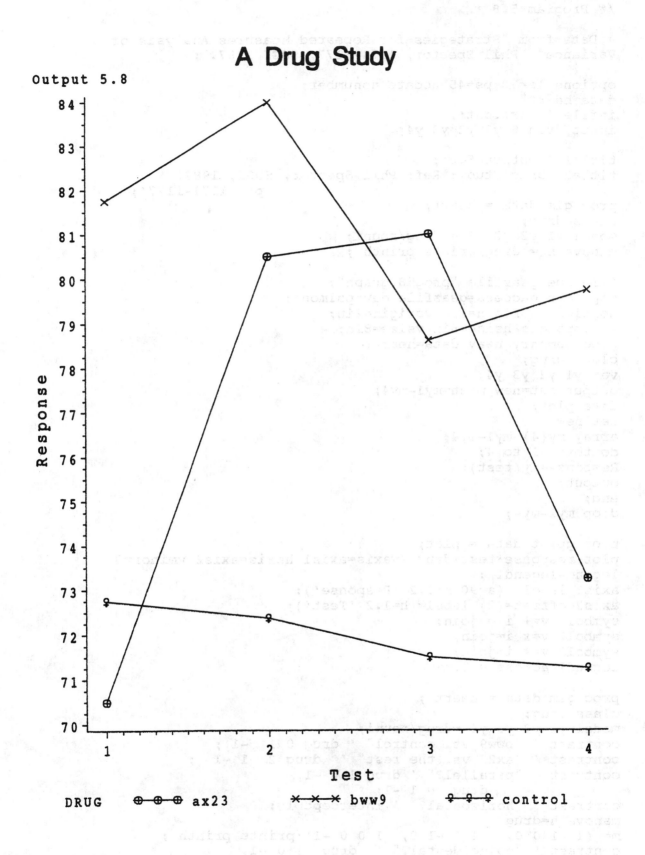

Output 5.8

General Linear Models Procedure
Multivariate Analysis of Variance

Manova Test Criteria and F Approximations for
the Hypothesis of no Overall DRUG Effect
H = Type III SS&CP Matrix for DRUG   E = Error SS&CP Matrix

S=2   M=0.5   N=8

Statistic	Value	F	Num DF	Den DF	Pr > F
Wilks' Lambda	0.07900691	11.5096	8	36	0.0001
Pillai's Trace	1.28345595	8.5081	8	38	0.0001
Hotelling-Lawley Trace	7.06938412	15.0224	8	34	0.0001
Roy's Greatest Root	6.34650854	30.1459	4	19	0.0001

NOTE: F Statistic for Roy's Greatest Root is an upper bound.
NOTE: F Statistic for Wilks' Lambda is exact.

Drug Study: Ref: Phil Spector, SUGI, 1987, pp. 1174-1177

General Linear Models Procedure
Multivariate Analysis of Variance

M Matrix Describing Transformed Variables

	Y1	Y2	Y3	Y4
MVAR1	1	-1	0	0
MVAR2	1	0	-1	0
MVAR3	1	0	0	-1

E = Error SS&CP Matrix

	MVAR1	MVAR2	MVAR3
MVAR1	261.375	119.5	147.5
MVAR2	119.5	226.375	235
MVAR3	147.5	235	463.5

Drug Study: Ref: Phil Spector, SUGI, 1987, pp. 1174-1177

General Linear Models Procedure
Multivariate Analysis of Variance

H = Type III SS&CP Matrix for DRUG

	MVAR1	MVAR2	MVAR3
MVAR1	465.58333333	593.54166667	212.25
MVAR2	593.54166667	872.58333333	308.25
MVAR3	212.25	308.25	109

Characteristic Roots and Vectors of: E Inverse * H, where
H = Type III SS&CP Matrix for DRUG   E = Error SS&CP Matrix

Variables have been transformed by the M Matrix

Characteristic Root	Percent	Characteristic Vector V'EV=1		
		MVAR1	MVAR2	MVAR3
5.95508874	95.15	0.01461289	0.08646881	-0.03926112
0.30369649	4.85	-0.06991922	0.04912790	-0.00222979
0.00000000	0.00	-0.00230526	-0.01799476	0.05537774

H = Contrast SS&CP Matrix for "parallel?"

	MVAR1	MVAR2	MVAR3
MVAR1	465.58333333	593.54166667	212.25
MVAR2	593.54166667	872.58333333	308.25
MVAR3	212.25	308.25	109

Characteristic Roots and Vectors of: E Inverse * H, where
H = Contrast SS&CP Matrix for "parallel?"   E = Error SS&CP Matrix

Variables have been transformed by the M Matrix

Characteristic Root	Percent	Characteristic Vector V'EV=1		
		MVAR1	MVAR2	MVAR3
5.95508874	95.15	0.01461289	0.08646881	-0.03926112
0.30369649	4.85	-0.06991922	0.04912790	-0.00222979
0.00000000	0.00	-0.00230526	-0.01799476	0.05537774

Output 5.8
Drug Study: Ref: Phil Spector, SUGI, 1987, pp. 1174-1177

General Linear Models Procedure
Multivariate Analysis of Variance

Manova Test Criteria and F Approximations for
the Hypothesis of no Overall "parallel?" Effect
on the variables defined by the M Matrix Transformation
H = Contrast SS&CP Matrix for "parallel?"   E = Error SS&CP Matrix

S=2   M=0   N=8.5

Statistic	Value	F	Num DF	Den DF	Pr > F
Wilks' Lambda	0.11028611	12.7376	6	38	0.0001
Pillai's Trace	1.08917068	7.9720	6	40	0.0001
Hotelling-Lawley Trace	6.25878523	18.7764	6	36	0.0001
Roy's Greatest Root	5.95508874	39.7006	3	20	0.0001

NOTE: F Statistic for Roy's Greatest Root is an upper bound.
NOTE: F Statistic for Wilks' Lambda is exact.

H = Contrast SS&CP Matrix for "bww9 vs. control"

	MVAR1	MVAR2	MVAR3
MVAR1	27.5625	-19.6875	-5.25
MVAR2	-19.6875	14.0625	3.75
MVAR3	-5.25	3.75	1

Characteristic Roots and Vectors of: E Inverse * H, where
H = Contrast SS&CP Matrix for "bww9 vs. control"   E = Error SS&CP Matrix

Variables have been transformed by the M Matrix

Characteristic Root	Percent	Characteristic Vector V'EV=1		
		MVAR1	MVAR2	MVAR3
0.34486444	100.00	0.06019122	-0.07660192	0.01600949
0.00000000	0.00	-0.02286312	-0.04960997	0.06600604
0.00000000	0.00	0.03101360	0.04341905	0.00000000

280

General Linear Models Procedure
Multivariate Analysis of Variance

Manova Test Criteria and Exact F Statistics for
the Hypothesis of no Overall "bww9 vs. control" Effect
on the variables defined by the M Matrix Transformation
H = Contrast SS&CP Matrix for "bww9 vs. control"   E = Error SS&CP Matrix

S=1   M=0.5   N=8.5

Statistic	Value	F	Num DF	Den DF	Pr > F
Wilks' Lambda	0.74356937	2.1841	3	19	0.1233
Pillai's Trace	0.25643063	2.1841	3	19	0.1233
Hotelling-Lawley Trace	0.34486444	2.1841	3	19	0.1233
Roy's Greatest Root	0.34486444	2.1841	3	19	0.1233

H = Contrast SS&CP Matrix for "ax23 vs. the rest"

	MVAR1	MVAR2	MVAR3
MVAR1	438.02083333	613.22916667	217.5
MVAR2	613.22916667	858.52083333	304.5
MVAR3	217.5	304.5	108

Characteristic Roots and Vectors of: E Inverse * H, where
H = Contrast SS&CP Matrix for "ax23 vs. the rest"   E = Error SS&CP Matrix

Variables have been transformed by the M Matrix

Characteristic Root	Percent	Characteristic Vector V'EV=1		
		MVAR1	MVAR2	MVAR3
5.91392079	100.00	0.01596248	0.08550244	-0.03921064
0.00000000	0.00	0.00145020	-0.02070581	0.05545833
0.00000000	0.00	-0.06964657	0.04974755	0.00000000

General Linear Models Procedure
Multivariate Analysis of Variance

Manova Test Criteria and Exact F Statistics for
the Hypothesis of no Overall "ax23 vs. the rest" Effect
on the variables defined by the M Matrix Transformation
H = Contrast SS&CP Matrix for "ax23 vs. the rest"   E = Error SS&CP Matrix

S=1   M=0.5   N=8.5

Statistic	Value	F	Num DF	Den DF	Pr > F
Wilks' Lambda	0.14463573	37.4548	3	19	0.0001
Pillai's Trace	0.85536427	37.4548	3	19	0.0001
Hotelling-Lawley Trace	5.91392079	37.4548	3	19	0.0001
Roy's Greatest Root	5.91392079	37.4548	3	19	0.0001

```
/* heart.dat */

ax23      72 86 81 77
ax23      78 83 88 82
ax23      71 82 81 75
ax23      72 83 83 69
ax23      66 79 77 66
ax23      74 83 84 77
ax23      62 73 78 70
ax23      69 75 76 70
bww9      85 86 83 80
bww9      82 86 80 84
bww9      71 78 70 75
bww9      83 88 79 81
bww9      86 85 76 76
bww9      85 82 83 80
bww9      79 83 80 81
bww9      83 84 78 81
control 69 73 72 74
control 66 62 67 73
control 84 90 88 87
control 80 81 77 72
control 72 72 69 70
control 65 62 65 61
control 75 69 69 68
control 71 70 65 65

/* Source: Spector (1987, pp. 1174-1177).  "Strategies for
   Repeated Measures Analysis of Variance", SUGI 1987. */
```

```
/* Program 5.9 */

* Data from "Strategies for Repeated Measures Analysis of
Variance", Phil Spector, 1174-1177, SUGI 1987. ;
title1 'Output 5.9';
title2 'Univaraite Analysis of Heart Rate Data';

options ls=78 ps=45 nodate nonumber;

data heart;
infile 'heart.dat';
input drug $ y1 y2 y3 y4;

data split;
set heart ;
array t{4} y1-y4;
subject+1;
do time=1 to 4;
y=t{time};
output;
end;
drop y1-y4;

proc glm data = split;
class subject drug time ;
model y = drug subject(drug) time time*drug;
random subject(drug)/test;

run;
```

General Linear Models Procedure
Tests of Hypotheses for Mixed Model Analysis of Variance

Dependent Variable: Y

Source: DRUG *
Error: MS(SUBJECT(DRUG))

DF	Type III MS	Denominator DF	Denominator MS	F Value	Pr > F
2	657.40625	21	111.08630952	5.9180	0.0092

* - This test assumes one or more other fixed effects are zero.

Source: SUBJECT(DRUG)
Error: MS(Error)

DF	Type III MS	Denominator DF	Denominator MS	F Value	Pr > F
21	111.08630952	63	7.3402777778	15.1338	0.0001

Source: TIME *
Error: MS(Error)

DF	Type III MS	Denominator DF	Denominator MS	F Value	Pr > F
3	93.069444444	63	7.3402777778	12.6793	0.0001

* - This test assumes one or more other fixed effects are zero.

Source: DRUG*TIME
Error: MS(Error)

DF	Type III MS	Denominator DF	Denominator MS	F Value	Pr > F
6	88.059027778	63	7.3402777778	11.9967	0.0001

```
/* Program 5.10 */

* Data from "Strategies for Repeated Measures Analysis of
Variance", Phil Spector, 1174-1177, SUGI 1987. ;
title1 'Output 5.10';

options ls=78 ps=45 nodate nonumber;
data heart;
infile 'heart.dat';
input drug $ y1 y2 y3 y4;

proc glm data = heart;
class drug ;
model y1 y2 y3 y4 = drug/ nouni ;
repeated time 4 / printe;

proc glm data = heart;
class drug ;
model y1 y2 y3 y4 = drug/ nouni ;
repeated time 4 polynomial/summary printm printe;
title2 'Drug Study: Ref: Phil Spector, SUGI, 1987,
                                    pp. 1174-1177';

/*
repeated time 4 contrast(1);
repeated time 4 contrast(2);
*/
run;
```

Output 5.10

General Linear Models Procedure
Repeated Measures Analysis of Variance

Partial Correlation Coefficients from the Error SS&CP Matrix
of the Variables Defined by the Specified Transformation / Prob > |r|

DF = 21	TIME.1	TIME.2	TIME.3
TIME.1	1.000000	0.707931	0.715770
	0.0001	0.0002	0.0002
TIME.2	0.707931	1.000000	0.652162
	0.0002	0.0001	0.0010
TIME.3	0.715770	0.652162	1.000000
	0.0002	0.0010	0.0001

Test for Sphericity: Mauchly's Criterion = 0.1904267
Chisquare Approximation = 32.709065 with 5 df   Prob > Chisquare = 0.0000

Applied to Orthogonal Components:
Test for Sphericity: Mauchly's Criterion = 0.6641817
Chisquare Approximation = 8.0703245 with 5 df   Prob > Chisquare = 0.1524

Manova Test Criteria and Exact F Statistics for
the Hypothesis of no TIME Effect
H = Type III SS&CP Matrix for TIME   E = Error SS&CP Matrix

S=1   M=0.5   N=8.5

Statistic	Value	F	Num DF	Den DF	Pr > F
Wilks' Lambda	0.30680870	14.3093	3	19	0.0001
Pillai's Trace	0.69319130	14.3093	3	19	0.0001
Hotelling-Lawley Trace	2.25935995	14.3093	3	19	0.0001
Roy's Greatest Root	2.25935995	14.3093	3	19	0.0001

Output 5.10

General Linear Models Procedure
Repeated Measures Analysis of Variance
Tests of Hypotheses for Between Subjects Effects

Source	DF	Type III SS	Mean Square	F Value	Pr > F
DRUG	2	1314.81250	657.40625	5.92	0.0092
Error	21	2332.81250	111.08631		

Output 5.10
General Linear Models Procedure
Repeated Measures Analysis of Variance
Univariate Tests of Hypotheses for Within Subject Effects

Source: TIME

DF	Type III SS	Mean Square	F Value	Pr > F	Adj Pr > F G - G	Adj Pr > F H - F
3	279.20833333	93.06944444	12.68	0.0001	0.0001	0.0001

Source: TIME*DRUG

DF	Type III SS	Mean Square	F Value	Pr > F	Adj Pr > F G - G	Adj Pr > F H - F
6	528.35416667	88.05902778	12.00	0.0001	0.0001	0.0001

Source: Error(TIME)

DF	Type III SS	Mean Square
63	462.43750000	7.34027778

Greenhouse-Geisser Epsilon = 0.7947
Huynh-Feldt Epsilon = 0.9887

Drug Study: Ref: Phil Spector, SUGI, 1987, pp. 1174-1177

General Linear Models Procedure
Repeated Measures Analysis of Variance
Analysis of Variance of Contrast Variables

TIME.N represents the nth degree polynomial contrast for TIME

Contrast Variable: TIME.1

Source	DF	Type III SS	Mean Square	F Value	Pr > F
MEAN	1	8.53333333	8.53333333	0.72	0.4042
DRUG	2	85.40416667	42.70208333	3.63	0.0444
Error	21	247.26250000	11.77440476		

Contrast Variable: TIME.2

Source	DF	Type III SS	Mean Square	F Value	Pr > F
MEAN	1	234.37500000	234.37500000	46.30	0.0001
DRUG	2	398.31250000	199.15625000	39.34	0.0001
Error	21	106.31250000	5.06250000		

Contrast Variable: TIME.3

Source	DF	Type III SS	Mean Square	F Value	Pr > F
MEAN	1	36.30000000	36.30000000	7.00	0.0151
DRUG	2	44.63750000	22.31875000	4.31	0.0271
Error	21	108.86250000	5.18392857		

```
/* Program 5.11 */

options ls=78 ps=45 nodate nonumber;

title1 ' Output 5.11';
* Data from "Strategies for Repeated Measures Analysis of
Variance", Phil Spector, 1174-1177, SUGI 1987. ;

data heart;
infile 'heart.dat';
input drug $ y1 y2 y3 y4; lines;

data split;
set heart ;
array t{4} y1-y4;
subject+1;
do time=1 to 4;
y=t{time};
output;
end;
drop y1-y4;

proc mixed data = split  method = reml mmeq;
class drug subject;
model y =  drug time time*drug /chisq e3 s;
repeated /type = ar(1) subject = subject r ;
title2 'Analysis of Heart Rate Data (Spector, 1987)
                              using PROC MIXED';

run;
```

Analysis of Heart Rate Data (Spector, 1987) using PROC MIXED

The MIXED Procedure

Class Level Information

Class	Levels	Values
DRUG	3	ax23 bww9 control
SUBJECT	24	1 2 3 4 5 6 7 8 9 10 11 12 13 14 15 16 17 18 19 20 21 22 23 24

The MIXED Procedure

REML Estimation Iteration History

Iteration	Evaluations	Objective	Criterion
0	1	441.15554344	
1	2	408.34489656	0.00000001

Convergence criteria met.

The MIXED Procedure

R Matrix for SUBJECT 1

Row	COL1	COL2	COL3	COL4
1	40.14814025	24.45715953	14.89863910	9.07584737
2	24.45715953	40.14814025	24.45715953	14.89863910
3	14.89863910	24.45715953	40.14814025	24.45715953
4	9.07584737	14.89863910	24.45715953	40.14814025

The MIXED Procedure

Type III Coefficients for TIME

Parameter	Row 1
INTERCEPT	0
DRUG ax23	0
DRUG bww9	0
DRUG control	0
TIME	1
TIME*DRUG ax23	0.3333333333
TIME*DRUG bww9	0.3333333333
TIME*DRUG control	0.3333333333

The MIXED Procedure

Type III Coefficients for TIME*DRUG

Parameter	Row 1	Row 2
INTERCEPT	0	0
DRUG ax23	0	0
DRUG bww9	0	0
DRUG control	0	0
TIME	0	0
TIME*DRUG ax23	1	0
TIME*DRUG bww9	0	1
TIME*DRUG control	-1	-1

The MIXED Procedure

Tests of Fixed Effects

Source	NDF	DDF	Type III ChiSq	Type III F	Pr > ChiSq	Pr > F
DRUG	2	90	8.36	4.18	0.0153	0.0184
TIME	1	90	0.05	0.05	0.8206	0.8211
TIME*DRUG	2	90	1.88	0.94	0.3900	0.3938

```
/* Program 5.12 */

options ls=78 ps=45 nodate nonumber;

title1 ' Output 5.12';
data box;
input surftrt $ fill $ prop y1 y2 y3 ;
lines;
yes a 25 194 192 141
yes a 25 208 188 165
yes a 50 233 217 171
yes a 50 241 222 201
yes a 75 265 252 207
yes a 75 269 283 191

yes b 25 239 127 90
yes b 25  187 105 85
yes b 50 224 123 79
yes b 50 243 123 110
yes b 75 243 117 100
yes b 75 226 125 75

no a 25 155 169 151
no a 25  173 152 141
no a 50 198 187 176
no a 50 177 196 167
no a 75 235 225 166
no a 75 229 270 183

no b 25 137 82 77
no b 25  160 82 83
no b 50 129 94 78
no b 50 98 89 48
no b 75 155 76 91
no b 75 132 105 67
;
/* Source: Box (1950).  Reproduced by permission of the
   International Biometric Society. */

title2 'Repeated Measures in Factorials: Tire Wear Data,
                                 G. E. P. Box (1950)';

proc glm data = box;
class surftrt fill prop;
model y1 y2 y3 =surftrt|fill|prop/nouni;
contrast ' "prop-parallel?" ' prop 1 0 -1,
                    prop  0 1 -1;
contrast ' "prop-horizontal?" ' intercept 1 ;
manova h=prop
        m= (1 -1  0,   1 0 -1)/printe printh ;

contrast ' "prop-concidental?" '  prop  1 0 -1,
                                   prop 0 1 -1 ;
manova h = prop m=(1 1 1) /printe printh;

proc glm data = box ;
class surftrt fill prop ;
model y1 y2 y3  = surftrt|fill|prop/ nouni ;
repeated revolutn 3 polynomial/summary printm printe ;
```

```
/* Program 5.12 continued */

title2 'Univariate Split Plot Analysis of Tire Wear Data,
                                        Box (1950)';
data boxsplit;
set box;
array yy{3} y1-y3;
subject+1;
do time=1 to 3;
y=yy(time);
output;
end;

proc mixed data = boxsplit  method = reml ;
class surftrt fill prop subject;
model y =  surftrt fill prop surftrt*fill surftrt*prop
fill*prop  surftrt*time  fill*time  prop*time
surftrt*fill*time surftrt*prop*time fill*prop*time/chisq;
repeated /type = ar(1) subject = subject r ;
title2 'Analysis of Tire Wear Data (Box, 1950) using
                                        PROC MIXED';

run;
```

Repeated Measures in Factorials: Tire Wear Data, G. E. P. Box (1950)

General Linear Models Procedure
Multivariate Analysis of Variance

H = Contrast SS&CP Matrix for "prop-parallel?"

	MVAR1	MVAR2
MVAR1	300.08333333	-273.875
MVAR2	-273.875	2070.25

Characteristic Roots and Vectors of: E Inverse * H, where
H = Contrast SS&CP Matrix for "prop-parallel?"   E = Error SS&CP Matrix

Variables have been transformed by the M Matrix

Characteristic Root	Percent	Characteristic Vector V'EV=1	
		MVAR1	MVAR2
1.04243414	96.15	-0.00698997	0.02137559
0.04176050	3.85	0.01250260	0.00215344

Manova Test Criteria and F Approximations for
the Hypothesis of no Overall "prop-parallel?" Effect
on the variables defined by the M Matrix Transformation
H = Contrast SS&CP Matrix for "prop-parallel?"   E = Error SS&CP Matrix

S=2   M=-0.5   N=4.5

Statistic	Value	F	Num DF	Den DF	Pr > F
Wilks' Lambda	0.46998506	2.5227	4	22	0.0701
Pillai's Trace	0.55047459	2.2786	4	24	0.0904
Hotelling-Lawley Trace	1.08419463	2.7105	4	20	0.0594
Roy's Greatest Root	1.04243414	6.2546	2	12	0.0138

NOTE: F Statistic for Roy's Greatest Root is an upper bound.
NOTE: F Statistic for Wilks' Lambda is exact.

General Linear Models Procedure
Multivariate Analysis of Variance

H = Contrast SS&CP Matrix for "prop-concidental?"

MVAR1

	MVAR1	40711.083333

Characteristic Roots and Vectors of: E Inverse * H, where
H = Contrast SS&CP Matrix for "prop-concidental?"   E = Error SS&CP Matrix

Variables have been transformed by the M Matrix

Characteristic Root	Percent	Characteristic Vector V'EV=1
		MVAR1
3.62811544	100.00	0.00944027

Manova Test Criteria and Exact F Statistics for
the Hypothesis of no Overall "prop-concidental?" Effect
on the variables defined by the M Matrix Transformation
H = Contrast SS&CP Matrix for "prop-concidental?"   E = Error SS&CP Matrix

S=1   M=0   N=5

Statistic	Value	F	Num DF	Den DF	Pr > F
Wilks' Lambda	0.21607067	21.7687	2	12	0.0001
Pillai's Trace	0.78392933	21.7687	2	12	0.0001
Hotelling-Lawley Trace	3.62811544	21.7687	2	12	0.0001
Roy's Greatest Root	3.62811544	21.7687	2	12	0.0001

Output 5.12
Univariate Split Plot Analysis of Tire Wear Data, Box (1950)

General Linear Models Procedure
Repeated Measures Analysis of Variance

Partial Correlation Coefficients from the Error SS&CP Matrix
of the Variables Defined by the Specified Transformation / Prob > |r|

DF = 12	REVOLU.1	REVOLU.2
REVOLU.1	1.000000	-0.070331
	0.0001	0.8194
REVOLU.2	-0.070331	1.000000
	0.8194	0.0001

Test for Sphericity: Mauchly's Criterion = 0.8071909
Chisquare Approximation = 2.3561456 with 2 df   Prob > Chisquare = 0.3079

Manova Test Criteria and Exact F Statistics for
the Hypothesis of no REVOLUTN Effect
H = Type III SS&CP Matrix for REVOLUTN   E = Error SS&CP Matrix

S=1   M=0   N=4.5

Statistic	Value	F	Num DF	Den DF	Pr > F
Wilks' Lambda	0.02074653	259.6045	2	11	0.0001
Pillai's Trace	0.97925347	259.6045	2	11	0.0001
Hotelling-Lawley Trace	47.20082034	259.6045	2	11	0.0001
Roy's Greatest Root	47.20082034	259.6045	2	11	0.0001

Output 5.12
Univariate Split Plot Analysis of Tire Wear Data, Box (1950)

General Linear Models Procedure
Repeated Measures Analysis of Variance
Univariate Tests of Hypotheses for Within Subject Effects

Source: REVOLUTN

					Adj Pr > F	
DF	Type III SS	Mean Square	F Value	Pr > F	G – G	H – F
2	60958.52777778	30479.26388889	160.68	0.0001	0.0001	0.0001

Source: REVOLUTN*SURFTRT

					Adj Pr > F	
DF	Type III SS	Mean Square	F Value	Pr > F	G – G	H – F
2	8248.02777778	4124.01388889	21.74	0.0001	0.0001	0.0001

Source: REVOLUTN*FILL

					Adj Pr > F	
DF	Type III SS	Mean Square	F Value	Pr > F	G – G	H – F
2	18287.69444444	9143.84722222	48.20	0.0001	0.0001	0.0001

Source: REVOLUTN*SURFTRT*FILL

					Adj Pr > F	
DF	Type III SS	Mean Square	F Value	Pr > F	G – G	H – F
2	2328.08333333	1164.04166667	6.14	0.0070	0.0111	0.0070

Source: REVOLUTN*PROP

					Adj Pr > F	
DF	Type III SS	Mean Square	F Value	Pr > F	G – G	H – F
4	1762.80555556	440.70138889	2.32	0.0857	0.1002	0.0857

Source: REVOLUTN*SURFTRT*PROP

					Adj Pr > F	
DF	Type III SS	Mean Square	F Value	Pr > F	G – G	H – F
4	685.97222222	171.49305556	0.90	0.4772	0.4658	0.4772

Source: REVOLUTN*FILL*PROP

					Adj Pr > F	
DF	Type III SS	Mean Square	F Value	Pr > F	G – G	H – F
4	1415.63888889	353.90972222	1.87	0.1493	0.1633	0.1493

General Linear Models Procedure
Repeated Measures Analysis of Variance
Univariate Tests of Hypotheses for Within Subject Effects

Source: REVOLUTN*SURFTRT*FILL*PROP

					Adj Pr > F	
DF	Type III SS	Mean Square	F Value	Pr > F	G - G	H - F
4	465.91666667	116.47916667	0.61	0.6566	0.6308	0.6566

Source: Error(REVOLUTN)

DF	Type III SS	Mean Square
24	4552.66666667	189.69444444

Greenhouse-Geisser Epsilon = 0.8384
Huynh-Feldt Epsilon = 1.8522

Univariate Split Plot Analysis of Tire Wear Data, Box (1950)

General Linear Models Procedure
Repeated Measures Analysis of Variance
Analysis of Variance of Contrast Variables

REVOLU.N represents the nth degree polynomial contrast for REVOLUTN

Contrast Variable: REVOLU.1

Source	DF	Type III SS	Mean Square	F Value	Pr > F
MEAN	1	60705.187500	60705.187500	565.91	0.0001
SURFTRT	1	7676.020833	7676.020833	71.56	0.0001
FILL	1	9436.020833	9436.020833	87.96	0.0001
SURFTRT*FILL	1	1938.020833	1938.020833	18.07	0.0011
PROP	2	1035.125000	517.562500	4.82	0.0290
SURFTRT*PROP	2	191.541667	95.770833	0.89	0.4350
FILL*PROP	2	260.541667	130.270833	1.21	0.3309
SURFTRT*FILL*PROP	2	255.791667	127.895833	1.19	0.3371
Error	12	1287.250000	107.270833		

Contrast Variable: REVOLU.2

Source	DF	Type III SS	Mean Square	F Value	Pr > F
MEAN	1	253.3402778	253.3402778	0.93	0.3536
SURFTRT	1	572.0069444	572.0069444	2.10	0.1727
FILL	1	8851.6736111	8851.6736111	32.53	0.0001
SURFTRT*FILL	1	390.0625000	390.0625000	1.43	0.2543
PROP	2	727.6805556	363.8402778	1.34	0.2991
SURFTRT*PROP	2	494.4305556	247.2152778	0.91	0.4292
FILL*PROP	2	1155.0972222	577.5486111	2.12	0.1625
SURFTRT*FILL*PROP	2	210.1250000	105.0625000	0.39	0.6879
Error	12	3265.4166667	272.1180556		

The MIXED Procedure

Class Level Information

Class	Levels	Values
SURFTRT	2	no yes
FILL	2	a b
PROP	3	25 50 75
SUBJECT	24	1 2 3 4 5 6 7 8 9 10 11 12 13 14 15 16 17 18 19 20 21 22 23 24

The MIXED Procedure

REML Estimation Iteration History

Iteration	Evaluations	Objective	Criterion
0	1	404.80623949	
1	2	397.58072226	0.00000000

Convergence criteria met.

The MIXED Procedure

R Matrix for SUBJECT 1

Row	COL1	COL2	COL3
1	368.56581667	-166.1922475	74.93875414
2	-166.1922475	368.56581667	-166.1922475
3	74.93875414	-166.1922475	368.56581667

```
/*  Program 5.13 */

option ls=78 ps=45 nodate nonumber;
title1 'Output 5.13';

data react;
input y1 y2 y3 y4;
lines;
77 67 82 72
84 76 90 80
102 92 109 97
;
proc glm;
model y1-y4= /nouni;
repeated drug 2, time 2;

run;
```

General Linear Models Procedure
Repeated Measures Analysis of Variance
Repeated Measures Level Information

Dependent Variable	Y1	Y2	Y3	Y4
Level of DRUG	1	1	2	2
Level of TIME	1	2	1	2

Manova Test Criteria and Exact F Statistics for
the Hypothesis of no DRUG Effect
H = Type III SS&CP Matrix for DRUG   E = Error SS&CP Matrix

S=1   M=-0.5   N=0

Statistic	Value	F	Num DF	Den DF	Pr > F
Wilks' Lambda	0.00775194	256.0000	1	2	0.0039
Pillai's Trace	0.99224806	256.0000	1	2	0.0039
Hotelling-Lawley Trace	128.00000000	256.0000	1	2	0.0039
Roy's Greatest Root	128.00000000	256.0000	1	2	0.0039

Manova Test Criteria and Exact F Statistics for
the Hypothesis of no TIME Effect
H = Type III SS&CP Matrix for TIME   E = Error SS&CP Matrix

S=1   M=-0.5   N=0

Statistic	Value	F	Num DF	Den DF	Pr > F
Wilks' Lambda	0.00662252	300.0000	1	2	0.0033
Pillai's Trace	0.99337748	300.0000	1	2	0.0033
Hotelling-Lawley Trace	150.00000000	300.0000	1	2	0.0033
Roy's Greatest Root	150.00000000	300.0000	1	2	0.0033

General Linear Models Procedure
Repeated Measures Analysis of Variance

Manova Test Criteria and Exact F Statistics for
the Hypothesis of no DRUG*TIME Effect
H = Type III SS&CP Matrix for DRUG*TIME   E = Error SS&CP Matrix

S=1   M=-0.5   N=0

Statistic	Value	F	Num DF	Den DF	Pr > F
Wilks' Lambda	0.33333333	4.0000	1	2	0.1835
Pillai's Trace	0.66666667	4.0000	1	2	0.1835
Hotelling-Lawley Trace	2.00000000	4.0000	1	2	0.1835
Roy's Greatest Root	2.00000000	4.0000	1	2	0.1835

```
/* Program 5.14 */

options ls=64 ps=45 nodate nonumber;
title1 'Output 5.14';

data read;
input group y1-y6;
lines;
1 61 50 60 55 59 62
1 64 55 62 57 63 63
1 59 49 58 52 60 58
1 63 59 65 64 67 70
1 62 51 61 56 60 63
2 57 42 56 46 54 50
2 61 47 58 48 59 55
2 55 40 55 46 57 52
2 59 44 61 50 63 60
2 58 44 56 49 55 49
;
/* Source: Cody, R. P./Smith, J. K. APPLIED STATISTICS AND SAS
PROGRAMMING LANGUAGE, 3/E, 1991, p. 194.  Reprinted by permission of
Prentice-Hall, Inc. Englewood Cliffs, N.J. */

proc glm data=read;
class group;
model y1-y6=group/nouni;
repeated year 3, season 2;

proc glm data=read;
class group;
model y1-y6=group/nouni;
repeated year 3(1 2 3) polynomial,
                season 2/summary nom nou;

run;
```

General Linear Models Procedure
Repeated Measures Analysis of Variance
Repeated Measures Level Information

Dependent Variable	Y1	Y2	Y3	Y4	Y5	Y6
Level of YEAR	1	1	2	2	3	3
Level of SEASON	1	2	1	2	1	2

Manova Test Criteria and Exact F Statistics for
the Hypothesis of no YEAR Effect
H = Type III SS&CP Matrix for YEAR   E = Error SS&CP Matrix

S=1   M=0   N=2.5

Statistic	Value	F	Num DF	Den DF	Pr > F
Wilks' Lambda	0.19558215	14.3953	2	7	0.0033
Pillai's Trace	0.80441785	14.3953	2	7	0.0033
Hotelling-Lawley Trace	4.11294094	14.3953	2	7	0.0033
Roy's Greatest Root	4.11294094	14.3953	2	7	0.0033

Manova Test Criteria and Exact F Statistics for
the Hypothesis of no YEAR*GROUP Effect
H = Type III SS&CP Matrix for YEAR*GROUP   E = Error SS&CP Matrix

S=1   M=0   N=2.5

Statistic	Value	F	Num DF	Den DF	Pr > F
Wilks' Lambda	0.96176044	0.1392	2	7	0.8724
Pillai's Trace	0.03823956	0.1392	2	7	0.8724
Hotelling-Lawley Trace	0.03975996	0.1392	2	7	0.8724
Roy's Greatest Root	0.03975996	0.1392	2	7	0.8724

General Linear Models Procedure
Repeated Measures Analysis of Variance

Manova Test Criteria and Exact F Statistics for
the Hypothesis of no SEASON Effect
H = Type III SS&CP Matrix for SEASON   E = Error SS&CP Matrix

S=1   M=-0.5   N=3

Statistic	Value	F	Num DF	Den DF	Pr > F
Wilks' Lambda	0.03436198	224.8154	1	8	0.0001
Pillai's Trace	0.96563802	224.8154	1	8	0.0001
Hotelling-Lawley Trace	28.10192837	224.8154	1	8	0.0001
Roy's Greatest Root	28.10192837	224.8154	1	8	0.0001

Manova Test Criteria and Exact F Statistics for
the Hypothesis of no SEASON*GROUP Effect
H = Type III SS&CP Matrix for SEASON*GROUP   E = Error SS&CP Matrix

S=1   M=-0.5   N=3

Statistic	Value	F	Num DF	Den DF	Pr > F
Wilks' Lambda	0.17759295	37.0468	1	8	0.0003
Pillai's Trace	0.82240705	37.0468	1	8	0.0003
Hotelling-Lawley Trace	4.63085399	37.0468	1	8	0.0003
Roy's Greatest Root	4.63085399	37.0468	1	8	0.0003

Manova Test Criteria and Exact F Statistics for
the Hypothesis of no YEAR*SEASON Effect
H = Type III SS&CP Matrix for YEAR*SEASON   E = Error SS&CP Matrix

S=1   M=0   N=2.5

Statistic	Value	F	Num DF	Den DF	Pr > F
Wilks' Lambda	0.03714436	90.7270	2	7	0.0001
Pillai's Trace	0.96285564	90.7270	2	7	0.0001
Hotelling-Lawley Trace	25.92198764	90.7270	2	7	0.0001
Roy's Greatest Root	25.92198764	90.7270	2	7	0.0001

Output 5.14
General Linear Models Procedure
Repeated Measures Analysis of Variance

Manova Test Criteria and Exact F Statistics for
the Hypothesis of no YEAR*SEASON*GROUP Effect
H = Type III SS&CP Matrix for YEAR*SEASON*GROUP   E = Error SS&CP Matrix

S=1   M=0   N=2.5

Statistic	Value	F	Num DF	Den DF	Pr > F
Wilks' Lambda	0.91603774	0.3208	2	7	0.7357
Pillai's Trace	0.08396226	0.3208	2	7	0.7357
Hotelling-Lawley Trace	0.09165808	0.3208	2	7	0.7357
Roy's Greatest Root	0.09165808	0.3208	2	7	0.7357

General Linear Models Procedure
Repeated Measures Analysis of Variance
Tests of Hypotheses for Between Subjects Effects

Source	DF	Type III SS	Mean Square	F Value	Pr > F
GROUP	1	680.06667	680.06667	13.54	0.0062
Error	8	401.66667	50.20833		

Output 5.14

General Linear Models Procedure
Repeated Measures Analysis of Variance
Univariate Tests of Hypotheses for Within Subject Effects

Source: YEAR

DF	Type III SS	Mean Square	F Value	Pr > F	Adj Pr > F G - G	Adj Pr > F H - F
2	252.03333333	126.01666667	26.91	0.0001	0.0002	0.0001

Source: YEAR*GROUP

DF	Type III SS	Mean Square	F Value	Pr > F	Adj Pr > F G - G	Adj Pr > F H - F
2	1.03333333	0.51666667	0.11	0.8962	0.8186	0.8700

Source: Error(YEAR)

DF	Type III SS	Mean Square
16	74.93333333	4.68333333

Greenhouse-Geisser Epsilon = 0.6757
Huynh-Feldt Epsilon = 0.8658

Source: SEASON

DF	Type III SS	Mean Square	F Value	Pr > F	Adj Pr > F G - G	Adj Pr > F H - F
1	680.06666667	680.06666667	224.82	0.0001	.	.

Source: SEASON*GROUP

DF	Type III SS	Mean Square	F Value	Pr > F	Adj Pr > F G - G	Adj Pr > F H - F
1	112.06666667	112.06666667	37.05	0.0003	.	.

Source: Error(SEASON)

DF	Type III SS	Mean Square
8	24.20000000	3.02500000

General Linear Models Procedure
Repeated Measures Analysis of Variance
Univariate Tests of Hypotheses for Within Subject Effects

Source: YEAR*SEASON

| | | | | | Adj | Pr > F |
DF	Type III SS	Mean Square	F Value	Pr > F	G - G	H - F
2	265.43333333	132.71666667	112.95	0.0001	0.0001	0.0001

Source: YEAR*SEASON*GROUP

| | | | | | Adj | Pr > F |
DF	Type III SS	Mean Square	F Value	Pr > F	G - G	H - F
2	0.43333333	0.21666667	0.18	0.8333	0.7592	0.8168

Source: Error(YEAR*SEASON)

DF	Type III SS	Mean Square
16	18.80000000	1.17500000

Greenhouse-Geisser Epsilon = 0.7073
Huynh-Feldt Epsilon = 0.9221

General Linear Models Procedure
Repeated Measures Analysis of Variance
Analysis of Variance of Contrast Variables

YEAR.N represents the nth degree polynomial contrast for YEAR

Contrast Variable: YEAR.1

Source	DF	Type III SS	Mean Square	F Value	Pr > F
MEAN	1	490.05000000	490.05000000	31.06	0.0005
GROUP	1	1.25000000	1.25000000	0.08	0.7855
Error	8	126.20000000	15.77500000		

Contrast Variable: YEAR.2

Source	DF	Type III SS	Mean Square	F Value	Pr > F
MEAN	1	14.01666667	14.01666667	4.74	0.0612
GROUP	1	0.81666667	0.81666667	0.28	0.6135
Error	8	23.66666667	2.95833333		

SEASON.N represents the contrast between the nth level of SEASON and the last

Contrast Variable: SEASON.1

Source	DF	Type III SS	Mean Square	F Value	Pr > F
MEAN	1	4080.4000000	4080.4000000	224.82	0.0001
GROUP	1	672.4000000	672.4000000	37.05	0.0003
Error	8	145.2000000	18.1500000		

YEAR.N represents the nth degree polynomial contrast for YEAR
SEASON.N represents the contrast between the nth level of SEASON and the last

Contrast Variable: YEAR.1*SEASON.1

```
/* Program 5.15 */

/* Data from Crowder and Hand (1990, p. 8)*/

options ls=78 ps=45 nodate nonumber;

title1 'Output 5.15';

data task;
infile 'task.dat';
input group$ x1 x2 y1-y10;

proc glm data=task;
class group;
model y1-y4=x1 x2 group group*x1 group*x2/nouni ss3;
manova  h=group x1 x2 group*x1 group*x2/printe printh;
title2 'Interactions of Covariates and Treatment Factor';

title2 'MANCOVA: Profile Analysis';
proc glm data = task ;
class group;
model y1-y4  = x1 x2 group/nouni;
contrast ' "parallel?" ' group 1  -1 0 0, group 1 0 -1 0,
                                          group 1 0 0 -1;
*contrast ' "horizontal?" ' intercept 1 ;
manova h=group
        m= y1-y2,y1-y3,y1-y4 /printe printh ;

proc glm data = task;
class group;
model y1-y4  = group/nouni;
contrast ' "coincidental?" '   group 1 -1 0 0,
                group 1 0 -1 0, group 1 0 0 -1;
manova h = group m=(1 1 1 1 ) /printe printh;

title2 'Analysis as in Carter and Srivastava';
data task;
set task;
z1=y2-y1;
z2=y3-y2;
z3=y4-y3;
ybar = (y1+y2+y3+y4)/4;
proc glm data = task;
class group;
model ybar = z1 z2 z3 x1 x2 group;

title2 'MANCOVA with Repeated Measures:
                        Using repeated statement';
proc glm data=task;
class group;
model y1-y4=x1 x2 group x1*group x2*group/nouni ss3;
repeated time 4 (1 2 3 4) polynomial/printe ;

run;
```

MANCOVA: Profile Analysis

General Linear Models Procedure
Multivariate Analysis of Variance

Manova Test Criteria and F Approximations for
the Hypothesis of no Overall GROUP Effect
H = Type III SS&CP Matrix for GROUP   E = Error SS&CP Matrix

S=3   M=0   N=4

Statistic	Value	F	Num DF	Den DF	Pr > F
Wilks' Lambda	0.61307592	0.4528	12	26.74902	0.9248
Pillai's Trace	0.44028566	0.5160	12	36	0.8903
Hotelling-Lawley Trace	0.54665445	0.3948	12	26	0.9529
Roy's Greatest Root	0.30771562	0.9231	4	12	0.4822

NOTE: F Statistic for Roy's Greatest Root is an upper bound.

H = Type III SS&CP Matrix for X1

	Y1	Y2	Y3	Y4
Y1	1.2118878517	1.5930389908	2.1374741086	1.5420368584
Y2	1.5930389908	2.094066066	2.8097316034	2.0270232407
Y3	2.1374741086	2.8097316034	3.7699821468	2.7197763016
Y4	1.5420368584	2.0270232407	2.7197763016	1.9621268331

Characteristic Roots and Vectors of: E Inverse * H, where
H = Type III SS&CP Matrix for X1   E = Error SS&CP Matrix

Characteristic Root	Percent	Characteristic Vector V'EV=1		
		Y1 Y4	Y2	Y3
0.37969698	100.00	0.10271570 -0.08311973	-0.08176403	0.38002367

Output 5.15
MANCOVA: Profile Analysis

General Linear Models Procedure
Multivariate Analysis of Variance

Characteristic Roots and Vectors of: E Inverse * H, where
H = Type III SS&CP Matrix for X1   E = Error SS&CP Matrix

Characteristic Root	Percent	Characteristic Vector V'EV=1		
		Y1 Y4	Y2	Y3
0.00000000	0.00	-0.22581512 0.42370709	0.06418893	-0.22548335
0.00000000	0.00	-0.41659806 0.00000000	0.40659944	-0.06683526
0.00000000	0.00	0.24499254 0.00000000	0.11743912	-0.22643015

Manova Test Criteria and Exact F Statistics for
the Hypothesis of no Overall X1 Effect
H = Type III SS&CP Matrix for X1   E = Error SS&CP Matrix

S=1   M=1   N=4

Statistic	Value	F	Num DF	Den DF	Pr > F
Wilks' Lambda	0.72479683	0.9492	4	10	0.4753
Pillai's Trace	0.27520317	0.9492	4	10	0.4753
Hotelling-Lawley Trace	0.37969698	0.9492	4	10	0.4753
Roy's Greatest Root	0.37969698	0.9492	4	10	0.4753

Output 5.15
MANCOVA: Profile Analysis

General Linear Models Procedure
Multivariate Analysis of Variance

Manova Test Criteria and Exact F Statistics for
the Hypothesis of no Overall X2 Effect
H = Type III SS&CP Matrix for X2   E = Error SS&CP Matrix

S=1   M=1   N=4

Statistic	Value	F	Num DF	Den DF	Pr > F
Wilks' Lambda	0.06086373	38.5754	4	10	0.0001
Pillai's Trace	0.93913627	38.5754	4	10	0.0001
Hotelling-Lawley Trace	15.43014730	38.5754	4	10	0.0001
Roy's Greatest Root	15.43014730	38.5754	4	10	0.0001

H = Type III SS&CP Matrix for X1*GROUP

	Y1	Y2	Y3	Y4
Y1	2.2225037317	2.3828845246	2.254449755	2.9446076048
Y2	2.3828845246	2.8001859929	2.7947427603	3.2904437757
Y3	2.254449755	2.7947427603	3.1941140289	3.0787618934
Y4	2.9446076048	3.2904437757	3.0787618934	4.0132372658

Characteristic Roots and Vectors of: E Inverse * H, where
H = Type III SS&CP Matrix for X1*GROUP   E = Error SS&CP Matrix

Characteristic Root	Percent	Characteristic Vector V'EV=1		
		Y1 Y4	Y2	Y3
0.32612367	63.76	0.09915243 0.07406831	-0.04557557	0.20995786
0.15535059	30.37	0.02286385 0.31847001	0.07169701	-0.43369212

Output 5.15
MANCOVA: Profile Analysis

General Linear Models Procedure
Multivariate Analysis of Variance

Characteristic Roots and Vectors of: E Inverse * H, where
H = Type III SS&CP Matrix for X1*GROUP   E = Error SS&CP Matrix

Characteristic Root	Percent	Characteristic Vector V'EV=1		
		Y1 Y4	Y2	Y3
0.02998196	5.86	-0.52161605 0.18118179	0.35827412	-0.11480183
0.00000000	0.00	-0.11260994 0.21610295	-0.23311517	0.07515100

Manova Test Criteria and F Approximations for
the Hypothesis of no Overall X1*GROUP Effect
H = Type III SS&CP Matrix for X1*GROUP   E = Error SS&CP Matrix

S=3   M=0   N=4

Statistic	Value	F	Num DF	Den DF	Pr > F
Wilks' Lambda	0.63368374	0.4195	12	26.74902	0.9420
Pillai's Trace	0.40949358	0.4742	12	36	0.9167
Hotelling-Lawley Trace	0.51145622	0.3694	12	26	0.9631
Roy's Greatest Root	0.32612367	0.9784	4	12	0.4552

NOTE: F Statistic for Roy's Greatest Root is an upper bound.

318

Output 5.15
MANCOVA: Profile Analysis

General Linear Models Procedure
Multivariate Analysis of Variance

Manova Test Criteria and F Approximations for
the Hypothesis of no Overall X2*GROUP Effect
H = Type III SS&CP Matrix for X2*GROUP   E = Error SS&CP Matrix

S=3   M=0   N=4

Statistic	Value	F	Num DF	Den DF	Pr > F
Wilks' Lambda	0.48389631	0.7037	12	26.74902	0.7343
Pillai's Trace	0.58755986	0.7307	12	36	0.7126
Hotelling-Lawley Trace	0.92069157	0.6649	12	26	0.7680
Roy's Greatest Root	0.72555470	2.1767	4	12	0.1335

NOTE: F Statistic for Roy's Greatest Root is an upper bound.

Output 5.15
MANCOVA: Profile Analysis

General Linear Models Procedure
Multivariate Analysis of Variance

H = Contrast SS&CP Matrix for "parallel?"

	MVAR1	MVAR2	MVAR3
MVAR1	1.9016949767	1.6899235845	1.1059308158
MVAR2	1.6899235845	1.9664206875	0.816691484
MVAR3	1.1059308158	0.816691484	0.7413593136

Characteristic Roots and Vectors of: E Inverse * H, where
H = Contrast SS&CP Matrix for "parallel?"   E = Error SS&CP Matrix

Variables have been transformed by the M Matrix

Characteristic Root	Percent	Characteristic Vector V'EV=1		
		MVAR1	MVAR2	MVAR3
0.24675499	68.30	0.24455118	0.05251991	0.11789561
0.11269629	31.19	0.15209379	−0.37308380	0.31085418
0.00184041	0.51	−0.20390236	0.08785825	0.21376719

Manova Test Criteria and F Approximations for
the Hypothesis of no Overall "parallel?" Effect
on the variables defined by the M Matrix Transformation
H = Contrast SS&CP Matrix for "parallel?"   E = Error SS&CP Matrix

S=3   M=−0.5   N=7.5

Statistic	Value	F	Num DF	Den DF	Pr > F
Wilks' Lambda	0.71952138	0.6682	9	41.52414	0.7324
Pillai's Trace	0.30103698	0.7064	9	57	0.7005
Hotelling-Lawley Trace	0.36129169	0.6289	9	47	0.7665
Roy's Greatest Root	0.24675499	1.5628	3	19	0.2312

NOTE: F Statistic for Roy's Greatest Root is an upper bound.

Analysis as in Carter and Srivastava

General Linear Models Procedure
Multivariate Analysis of Variance

H = Contrast SS&CP Matrix for "coincidental?"

MVAR1

MVAR1   621.26621703

Characteristic Roots and Vectors of: E Inverse * H, where
H = Contrast SS&CP Matrix for "coincidental?"   E = Error SS&CP Matrix

Variables have been transformed by the M Matrix

Characteristic Root	Percent	Characteristic Vector V'EV=1
		MVAR1
0.14745078	100.00	0.01540581

Manova Test Criteria and Exact F Statistics for
the Hypothesis of no Overall "coincidental?" Effect
on the variables defined by the M Matrix Transformation
H = Contrast SS&CP Matrix for "coincidental?"   E = Error SS&CP Matrix

S=1   M=0.5   N=10

Statistic	Value	F	Num DF	Den DF	Pr > F
Wilks' Lambda	0.87149708	1.0813	3	22	0.3776
Pillai's Trace	0.12850292	1.0813	3	22	0.3776
Hotelling-Lawley Trace	0.14745078	1.0813	3	22	0.3776
Roy's Greatest Root	0.14745078	1.0813	3	22	0.3776

MANCOVA with Repeated Measures:Using repeated statement

General Linear Models Procedure

Dependent Variable: YBAR

Source	DF	Sum of Squares	Mean Square	F Value	Pr > F
Model	8	254.2986412	31.7873302	37.00	0.0001
Error	16	13.7457588	0.8591099		
Corrected Total	24	268.0444000			

R-Square	C.V.	Root MSE	YBAR Mean
0.948718	14.46671	0.926882	6.407000

Source	DF	Type I SS	Mean Square	F Value	Pr > F
Z1	1	0.4150309	0.4150309	0.48	0.4970
Z2	1	4.0302115	4.0302115	4.69	0.0458
Z3	1	0.6699834	0.6699834	0.78	0.3903
X1	1	63.7302037	63.7302037	74.18	0.0001
X2	1	177.0953839	177.0953839	206.14	0.0001
GROUP	3	8.3578278	2.7859426	3.24	0.0498

Source	DF	Type III SS	Mean Square	F Value	Pr > F
Z1	1	3.0630137	3.0630137	3.57	0.0773
Z2	1	0.2959040	0.2959040	0.34	0.5655
Z3	1	1.1301653	1.1301653	1.32	0.2683
X1	1	0.3895503	0.3895503	0.45	0.5103
X2	1	177.8589388	177.8589388	207.03	0.0001
GROUP	3	8.3578278	2.7859426	3.24	0.0498

MANCOVA with Repeated Measures:Using repeated statement

General Linear Models Procedure
Repeated Measures Analysis of Variance

Manova Test Criteria and Exact F Statistics for
the Hypothesis of no TIME*X1 Effect
H = Type III SS&CP Matrix for TIME*X1   E = Error SS&CP Matrix

S=1   M=0.5   N=4.5

Statistic	Value	F	Num DF	Den DF	Pr > F
Wilks' Lambda	0.92842547	0.2827	3	11	0.8369
Pillai's Trace	0.07157453	0.2827	3	11	0.8369
Hotelling-Lawley Trace	0.07709238	0.2827	3	11	0.8369
Roy's Greatest Root	0.07709238	0.2827	3	11	0.8369

Manova Test Criteria and Exact F Statistics for
the Hypothesis of no TIME*X2 Effect
H = Type III SS&CP Matrix for TIME*X2   E = Error SS&CP Matrix

S=1   M=0.5   N=4.5

Statistic	Value	F	Num DF	Den DF	Pr > F
Wilks' Lambda	0.96610027	0.1287	3	11	0.9411
Pillai's Trace	0.03389973	0.1287	3	11	0.9411
Hotelling-Lawley Trace	0.03508924	0.1287	3	11	0.9411
Roy's Greatest Root	0.03508924	0.1287	3	11	0.9411

Output 5.15
MANCOVA with Repeated Measures:Using repeated statement

General Linear Models Procedure
Repeated Measures Analysis of Variance

S=3   M=-0.5   N=4.5

Statistic	Value	F	Num DF	Den DF	Pr > F
Wilks' Lambda	0.67564015	0.5229	9	26.92172	0.8449
Pillai's Trace	0.35785791	0.5869	9	39	0.7996
Hotelling-Lawley Trace	0.43147146	0.4634	9	29	0.8870
Roy's Greatest Root	0.26636350	1.1542	3	13	0.3644

NOTE: F Statistic for Roy's Greatest Root is an upper bound.

Manova Test Criteria and F Approximations for
the Hypothesis of no TIME*X1*GROUP Effect
H = Type III SS&CP Matrix for TIME*X1*GROUP   E = Error SS&CP Matrix

S=3   M=-0.5   N=4.5

Statistic	Value	F	Num DF	Den DF	Pr > F
Wilks' Lambda	0.81629982	0.2602	9	26.92172	0.9802
Pillai's Trace	0.19151428	0.2955	9	39	0.9718
Hotelling-Lawley Trace	0.21550306	0.2315	9	29	0.9869
Roy's Greatest Root	0.15609074	0.6764	3	13	0.5818

NOTE: F Statistic for Roy's Greatest Root is an upper bound.

MANCOVA with Repeated Measures:Using repeated statement

General Linear Models Procedure
Repeated Measures Analysis of Variance

Manova Test Criteria and F Approximations for
the Hypothesis of no TIME*X2*GROUP Effect
H = Type III SS&CP Matrix for TIME*X2*GROUP   E = Error SS&CP Matrix

S=3   M=-0.5   N=4.5

Statistic	Value	F	Num DF	Den DF	Pr > F
Wilks' Lambda	0.64048700	0.6009	9	26.92172	0.7849
Pillai's Trace	0.37654996	0.6220	9	39	0.7710
Hotelling-Lawley Trace	0.53495609	0.5746	9	29	0.8066
Roy's Greatest Root	0.48181329	2.0879	3	13	0.1513

NOTE: F Statistic for Roy's Greatest Root is an upper bound.

```
/* task.dat */

control  4.1  6.1  7.6  7.5  8.9  9.5  8.7  8.8    .   7.0    .   6.5
control  5.8  7.5 10.1 10.4 10.4  8.9  8.9  8.4  9.9  8.6    .   6.9
control  7.0  8.4 11.2 12.8 10.0 10.3  9.5  9.2  9.0  9.4    .   8.4
control  9.0  7.8 10.8 10.3  9.3 10.3 11.5 12.3 10.0 11.4    .   5.9
control  3.6  4.3  3.9  3.9  4.5  3.2  4.1  4.0  3.5  3.7  3.0  2.8
control  7.7  7.0  6.7  7.0  7.9  7.4  7.3  7.2  6.6  6.6  8.3  7.9
control  3.4  2.1  2.2  2.0  2.2  2.2  2.5  2.3  2.5  2.4  2.0  2.2
control  1.8  1.4  2.1  2.4  2.5  2.3  2.0  2.0  1.9  2.0  2.0  1.4
dinocom  7.6  8.9  8.5  8.4  8.5  8.2  5.6  8.8  8.8  8.4  8.0  8.2
dinocom  4.2  6.5  7.5  7.1  7.2  7.0  5.0  4.2  6.9  9.5    .    .
dinocom  6.9 13.3 12.9 13.5 13.4 13.1 13.6 13.1 14.8 15.3 16.1 16.9
dinocom  8.1  7.4  8.8  9.2  8.4  9.2  7.9  7.9  7.9  7.3    .   7.2
dinocom  4.5  4.9  5.5  5.6  5.2  5.3  6.4  6.0  6.4  6.4    .   6.9
dinocom  4.2  3.2  3.2  4.0  3.2  3.4  3.4  3.2  3.2  3.2  2.8  2.8
dihypot  5.9  5.5  5.5  5.5  5.3  5.0  4.5  4.1  4.3  3.9  3.7  3.5
dihypot   .   0.8  0.4  0.6  0.4  0.4  0.5  0.6  0.5  0.5  0.8  0.7
dihypot 10.1  6.5  6.2  6.3  6.6  5.9  6.5  5.5  5.7  5.1  4.4  4.9
dihypot  5.7  4.3  4.6  3.8  3.9  3.6  3.0  3.7  3.2  3.1  2.7  2.4
dihypot  2.1  2.9  3.2  3.2  2.7  2.7  2.4  2.2  1.8  1.7  1.7  1.5
dihypot  5.5 11.1 10.8  8.7  9.3 10.5 12.7 11.3 19.1 18.9 37.0 39.0
dihypot  0.9  4.9  5.7  7.0  7.0  5.8  6.9  7.7  7.5  8.8  8.1  9.9
dihyper  5.0  5.2  3.4  3.0  3.1  3.6  3.2  2.6  4.6  3.8  4.9  2.7
dihyper  4.2  4.3  4.1  3.5  2.8  2.8  4.7  3.7  3.7  4.2    .   4.4
dihyper  3.2  3.0  3.3  3.5  3.4  3.3  3.3  3.3  3.4  3.2  3.1  3.2
dihyper  5.0  6.9  7.5  5.9    .   7.7  7.3  7.6  7.5  7.5  7.0  7.5
dihyper  2.5 12.0 12.2 11.4 11.6 11.7 12.6 10.1 11.4 12.8 11.5 10.7
dihyper  1.6  1.6  2.1  1.9  1.7  2.5  1.6  1.3  3.5  0.6    .    .

/* Source: Crowder and Hand (1990, p. 8). */
```

```
/* Program 5.16 */

/* Data from Crowder and Hand (1990, p. 8)*/

options ls=78 ps=45 nodate nonumber;

title1 'Output 5.16';

data task;
infile 'task.dat';
input group$ x1 x2 y1-y10;
data task;
set task;
ybar = mean(y1,y2,y3,y4);

if group = 'control'  then  z11=x1;
if group = 'control'  then  z12 =0;
if group = 'control'  then  z13 =0 ;
if group = 'control'  then  z14 =0;
if group = 'control'  then  z21 = x2 ;
if group = 'control'  then  z22=0 ;
if group = 'control'  then z23 = 0 ;
if group = 'control'  then  z24 =0;

if group = 'dinocom' then  z11=0;
if group = 'dinocom' then z12 =x1;
if group = 'dinocom' then z13 =0 ;
if group = 'dinocom' then z14 =0;
if group = 'dinocom' then z21 = 0 ;
if group = 'dinocom' then z22=x2 ;
if group = 'dinocom' then z23 = 0 ;
if group = 'dinocom' then z24 =0;

if group = 'dihypot' then  z11=0;
if group = 'dihypot' then z12 =0;
if group = 'dihypot' then z13 =x1 ;
if group = 'dihypot' then z14 =0;
if group = 'dihypot' then z21 = 0 ;
if group = 'dihypot' then z22=0 ;
if group = 'dihypot' then z23 = x2 ;
if group = 'dihypot' then z24 =0;

if group = 'dihyper' then  z11=0;
if group = 'dihyper' then  z12 =0;
if group = 'dihyper' then  z13 =0 ;
if group = 'dihyper' then  z14 =x1;
if group = 'dihyper' then  z21 = 0 ;
if group = 'dihyper' then  z22=0 ;
if group = 'dihyper' then  z23 = 0 ;
if group = 'dihyper' then  z24 =x2;

data nomiss;
set task ;
if x1 > 0;
title2 'Subject Model';
proc glm data =nomiss;
classes group ;
model ybar = group z11 z12 z13 z14 z21 z22 z23 z24 ;
```

```
/* Program 5.16 continued */

proc glm data =nomiss;
classes group ;
model ybar = group ;

proc glm data =nomiss;
classes group ;
model ybar = group x1 x2 /solution;

run;
```

Output 5.16
Subject Model

General Linear Models Procedure

Dependent Variable: YBAR

Source	DF	Sum of Squares	Mean Square	F Value	Pr > F
Model	11	256.4327219	23.3120656	27.22	0.0001
Error	14	11.9888833	0.8563488		
Corrected Total	25	268.4216052			

R-Square	C.V.	Root MSE	YBAR Mean
0.955336	14.38934	0.925391	6.431090

Source	DF	Type I SS	Mean Square	F Value	Pr > F
GROUP	3	25.10256299	8.36752100	9.77	0.0010
Z11	1	58.41514960	58.41514960	68.21	0.0001
Z12	1	25.87781079	25.87781079	30.22	0.0001
Z13	1	1.37336113	1.37336113	1.60	0.2260
Z14	1	0.20993081	0.20993081	0.25	0.6282
Z21	1	28.45105991	28.45105991	33.22	0.0001
Z22	1	28.24970738	28.24970738	32.99	0.0001
Z23	1	25.18912634	25.18912634	29.41	0.0001
Z24	1	63.56401299	63.56401299	74.23	0.0001

Source	DF	Type III SS	Mean Square	F Value	Pr > F
GROUP	3	1.47949170	0.49316390	0.58	0.6403
Z11	1	0.69358869	0.69358869	0.81	0.3834
Z12	1	0.19611204	0.19611204	0.23	0.6396
Z13	1	0.58344468	0.58344468	0.68	0.4230
Z14	1	1.51142271	1.51142271	1.76	0.2053
Z21	1	28.45105991	28.45105991	33.22	0.0001
Z22	1	28.24970738	28.24970738	32.99	0.0001
Z23	1	25.18912634	25.18912634	29.41	0.0001
Z24	1	63.56401299	63.56401299	74.23	0.0001

General Linear Models Procedure

Dependent Variable: YBAR

Source	DF	Sum of Squares	Mean Square	F Value	Pr > F
Model	3	25.10256299	8.36752100	0.76	0.5304
Error	22	243.31904225	11.05995647		
Corrected Total	25	268.42160524			

	R-Square	C.V.	Root MSE	YBAR Mean
	0.093519	51.71210	3.325651	6.431090

Source	DF	Type I SS	Mean Square	F Value	Pr > F
GROUP	3	25.10256299	8.36752100	0.76	0.5304

Source	DF	Type III SS	Mean Square	F Value	Pr > F
GROUP	3	25.10256299	8.36752100	0.76	0.5304

General Linear Models Procedure

Dependent Variable: YBAR

Source	DF	Sum of Squares	Mean Square	F Value	Pr > F
Model	5	246.7939993	49.3587999	45.64	0.0001
Error	20	21.6276059	1.0813803		
Corrected Total	25	268.4216052			

R-Square	C.V.	Root MSE	YBAR Mean
0.919427	16.16980	1.039894	6.431090

Source	DF	Type I SS	Mean Square	F Value	Pr > F
GROUP	3	25.1025630	8.3675210	7.74	0.0013
X1	1	49.6507184	49.6507184	45.91	0.0001
X2	1	172.0407179	172.0407179	159.09	0.0001

Source	DF	Type III SS	Mean Square	F Value	Pr > F
GROUP	3	11.5623064	3.8541021	3.56	0.0325
X1	1	0.0958549	0.0958549	0.09	0.7690
X2	1	172.0407179	172.0407179	159.09	0.0001

Parameter		Estimate	T for H0: Parameter=0	Pr > |T|	Std Error of Estimate
INTERCEPT		0.458447572 B	0.61	0.5503	0.75461427
GROUP	control	0.937316398 B	1.63	0.1191	0.57555302
	dihyper	-0.812192361 B	-1.27	0.2190	0.63995925
	dihypot	-0.481557175 B	-0.79	0.4396	0.61063120
	dinocom	0.000000000 B	.	.	.
X1		-0.032229071	-0.30	0.7690	0.10825051
X2		1.017385670	12.61	0.0001	0.08066019

Subject Model

General Linear Models Procedure

NOTE: The X'X matrix has been found to be singular and a generalized inverse was used to solve the normal equations. Estimates followed by the letter 'B' are biased, and are not unique estimators of the parameters.

```
/* Program 5.17*/

/* This data is from SAS Tech. Report No. P-229, p. 354
                                (in Proc Mixed)*/

options ls=78 ps=45 nodate nonumber;
title1 'Output 5.17';
title2 'A Pharmaceutical Stability Study: Obenchain (1990)';

data rc;
input batch age@;

do i=1 to 6;
input y@;
output;
end;
cards;
1 0 101.2 103.3 103.3 102.1 104.4 102.4
1 1 98.8 99.4 99.7 99.5 . .
1 3 98.4 99.0 97.3 99.8 . .
1 6 101.5 100.2 101.7 102.7 . .
1 9 96.3 97.2 97.2 96.3 . .
1 12 97.3 97.9 96.8 97.7 97.7 96.7
2 0 102.6 102.7 102.4 102.1 102.9 102.6
2 1 99.1 99.0 99.9 100.6 . .
2 3 105.7 103.3 103.4 104.0 . .
2 6 101.3 101.5 100.9 101.4 . .
2 9 94.1 96.5 97.2 95.6 . .
2 12 93.1 92.8 95.4 92.5 92.2 93.0
3 0 105.1 103.9 106.1 104.1 103.7 104.6
3 1 102.2 102.0 100.8 99.8 . .
3 3 101.2 101.8 100.8 102.6 . .
3 6 101.1 102.0 100.1 100.2 . .
3 9 100.9 99.5 102.5 100.8 . .
3 12 97.8 98.3 96.9 98.4 96.9 96.5
;
/* Source: Obenchain (1990).  Data Courtesy of R. L. Obenchain */

proc mixed data=rc;
class batch;
model y=age/s;
random int age/type=un sub=batch s;

run;
```

A Pharmaceutical Stability Study: Obenchain (1990)

The MIXED Procedure

Class Level Information

Class	Levels	Values
BATCH	3	1 2 3

The MIXED Procedure

REML Estimation Iteration History

Iteration	Evaluations	Objective	Criterion
0	1	216.36501995	
1	1	199.81975606	0.00000000

Convergence criteria met.

The MIXED Procedure

Covariance Parameter Estimates (REML)

Cov Parm		Ratio	Estimate	Std Error	Z	Pr > |Z|
INTERCEPT	UN(1,1)	0.29462159	0.97292750	1.24809244	0.78	0.4357
	UN(2,1)	−0.03086542	−0.10192674	0.18687848	−0.55	0.5855
	UN(2,2)	0.01105080	0.03649300	0.04210237	0.87	0.3861
Residual		1.00000000	3.30229533	0.52879045	6.24	0.0000

The MIXED Procedure

Model Fitting Information for Y

Description	Value
Observations	84.0000
Variance Estimate	3.3023

A Pharmaceutical Stability Study: Obenchain (1990)

The MIXED Procedure

Model Fitting Information for Y

Description	Value
Standard Deviation Estimate	1.8172
REML Log Likelihood	-175.263
Akaike's Information Criterion	-179.263
Schwarz's Bayesian Criterion	-184.076
-2 REML Log Likelihood	350.5257
Null Model LRT Chi-Square	16.5453
Null Model LRT DF	3.0000
Null Model LRT P-Value	0.0009

The MIXED Procedure

Solution for Fixed Effects

Parameter	Estimate	Std Error	DDF	T	Pr > |T|
INTERCEPT	102.70159884	0.64480457	78	159.28	0.0000
AGE	-0.52417636	0.11845227	78	-4.43	0.0000

The MIXED Procedure

Solution for Random Effects

Parameter	Subject	Estimate	Std Error	DDF	T	Pr > |T|
INTERCEPT	BATCH 1	-0.99744294	0.68336297	78	-1.46	0.1484
AGE	BATCH 1	0.12668799	0.12362914	78	1.02	0.3087
INTERCEPT	BATCH 2	0.38582987	0.68336297	78	0.56	0.5740
AGE	BATCH 2	-0.20397070	0.12362914	78	-1.65	0.1030
INTERCEPT	BATCH 3	0.61161307	0.68336297	78	0.90	0.3735
AGE	BATCH 3	0.07728271	0.12362914	78	0.63	0.5337

```
/* Program 5.18 */

options ls = 78 ps=45 nodate nonumber;
Title1 'Output 5.18';

data ramus;
input boy y1 y2 y3 y4;
y=y1;
age=8;
u=-3;
output;
y=y2;
age=8.5;
u=-1;
output;
y=y3;
age=9;
u=1;
output;
y=y4;
age=9.5;
u=3;
output;
lines;
1 47.8 48.8 49. 49.7
2 46.4 47.3 47.7 48.4
3 46.3 46.8 47.8 48.5
4 45.1 45.3 46.1 47.2
5 47.6 48.5 48.9 49.3
6 52.5 53.2 53.3 53.7
7 51.2 53. 54.3 54.5
8 49.8 50. 50.3 52.7
9 48.1 50.8 52.3 54.4
10 45. 47. 47.3 48.3
11 51.2 51.4 51.6 51.9
12 48.5 49.2 53. 55.5
13 52.1 52.8 53.7 55.
14 48.2 48.9 49.3 49.8
15 49.6 50.4 51.2 51.8
16 50.7 51.7 52.7 53.3
17 47.2 47.7 48.4 49.5
18 53.3 54.6 55.1 55.3
19 46.2 47.5 48.1 48.4
20 46.3 47.6 51.0 51.8
;
/* Source: Elsten and Grizzle (1962).  Reproduced by permission
of the International Biometric Society. */

proc mixed data=ramus;
class boy;
model y= u/s;
random boy/type = sim subject = boy;
repeated /type=sim subject = boy r;
title2' Random Effect Model, Linear Growth with
                        Random Slope: Ramus Data' ;
proc mixed data=ramus;
class boy;
model y= u/s;
repeated /type=cs subject = boy r;
title2' Repated Measures Model with Compound Symmetry: Ramus Data' ;
run;
```

The MIXED Procedure

Class Level Information

Class	Levels	Values
BOY	20	1 2 3 4 5 6 7 8 9 10 11 12 13 14 15 16 17 18 19 20

The MIXED Procedure

REML Estimation Iteration History

Iteration	Evaluations	Objective	Criterion
0	1	235.70943380	
1	1	125.34421797	0.00000000

Convergence criteria met.

The MIXED Procedure

R Matrix for BOY 1

Row	COL1	COL2	COL3	COL4
1	0.66293686			
2		0.66293686		
3			0.66293686	
4				0.66293686

The MIXED Procedure

Covariance Parameter Estimates (REML)

Cov Parm	Estimate	Std Error	Z	Pr > |Z|
BOY	6.10586282	2.03500356	3.00	0.0027

Output 5.18
Random Effect Model, Linear Growth with Random Slope: Ramus Data

The MIXED Procedure

Covariance Parameter Estimates (REML)

Cov Parm	Estimate	Std Error	Z	Pr > |Z|
DIAG	0.66293686	0.12205657	5.43	0.0000
Residual	1.00000000	.	.	.

The MIXED Procedure

Model Fitting Information for Y

Description	Value
Observations	80.0000
Variance Estimate	1.0000
Standard Deviation Estimate	1.0000
REML Log Likelihood	−134.349
Akaike's Information Criterion	−136.349
Schwarz's Bayesian Criterion	−138.706
−2 REML Log Likelihood	268.6986

The MIXED Procedure

Solution for Fixed Effects

Parameter	Estimate	Std Error	DDF	T	Pr > |T|
INTERCEPT	50.07125000	0.55998201	78	89.42	0.0000
U	0.46575000	0.04071047	78	11.44	0.0000

The MIXED Procedure

Class Level Information

Class	Levels	Values
BOY	20	1 2 3 4 5 6 7 8 9 10 11 12 13 14 15 16 17 18 19 20

The MIXED Procedure

REML Estimation Iteration History

Iteration	Evaluations	Objective	Criterion
0	1	235.70943380	
1	1	125.34421797	0.00000000

Convergence criteria met.

The MIXED Procedure

R Matrix for BOY 1

Row	COL1	COL2	COL3	COL4
1	6.76879969	6.10586282	6.10586282	6.10586282
2	6.10586282	6.76879969	6.10586282	6.10586282
3	6.10586282	6.10586282	6.76879969	6.10586282
4	6.10586282	6.10586282	6.10586282	6.76879969

The MIXED Procedure

Covariance Parameter Estimates (REML)

Cov Parm	Ratio	Estimate	Std Error	Z	Pr > |Z|
DIAG CS	9.21032326	6.10586282	2.03500356	3.00	0.0027

```
/* Program 5.19 */

/* This is a growth curve anlysis program where
        dog data is used (Grizzle and Allen (1969))*/

options ls=78 ps=45 nodate nonumber;
title1 ' Output 5.19 ';
title2 ' Growth Curves Analysis of Dog Data';

data dog;
 infile "dog.dat";
 input d1 d2 d3 d4 d5 d6 d7;
proc iml;
 use dog;
  read all into y0;

/* Here we generate the Ortho Poly of degree p-1=6*/
vec1={1 3 5 7 9 11 13};
c=orpol(vec1,6);
y=y0*c;

/* Here we convert Y matrix to a data set Trandata*/
varnames={y1 y2 y3 y4 y5 y6 y7};
create trandata from y (|colname=varnames|);
append from y;
close trandata;

/* Creating the independent variables named group*/
data trandata;
set trandata;
 dog+1;
if (dog<10 and dog>0) then group='control';
if (dog<19 and dog>9) then group='treat1';
if (dog<28 and dog>18) then group='treat2';
if (dog<37 and dog>27) then group='treat3';
 output;

/* Here we test the adequacy of the 3rd deg. poly.
                                        by choosing*/
proc glm data=trandata;
model y5 y6 y7= /nouni;
manova h=intercept;

/* In the following we fit a 3rd degree polynomial
                        using Rao-Khatri method*/
/* Contrast defines a 3 by 4 L matrix.*/
proc glm data=trandata;
classes group;
model y1 y2 y3 y4=group y5 y6 y7/nouni;
contrast 'growth curves' group 1 -1 0 0,
                         group 1 0 -1 0,
                         group 1 0 0 -1/E;
manova h=group;
```

```
/* Program 5.19 continued */

*To obtain the estimates one of the following two
                                  programs can be used;

proc glm data=trandata;
classes group;
model y1 y2 y3 y4=group y5 y6 y7;
estimate 'est' intercept 1 group 1 0 0 0 ;
estimate 'es2' intercept 1 group 0 1 0 0 ;
estimate 'es3' intercept 1 group 0 0 1 0 ;
estimate 'es4' intercept 1 group 0 0 0 1 ;

proc glm data=trandata;
classes group;
model y1 y2 y3 y4=group y5 y6 y7/noint;
estimate 'es1' group 1 0 0 0 ;
estimate 'es2' group 0 1 0 0 ;
estimate 'es3' group 0 0 1 0 ;
estimate 'es4' group 0 0 0 1 ;

run;
```

Growth Curves Analysis of Dog Data

General Linear Models Procedure
Multivariate Analysis of Variance

Characteristic Roots and Vectors of: E Inverse * H, where
H = Type III SS&CP Matrix for INTERCEPT   E = Error SS&CP Matrix

Characteristic Root	Percent	Characteristic Vector V'EV=1		
		Y5	Y6	Y7
0.08631005	100.00	-0.01994746	-0.17722343	0.87970901
0.00000000	0.00	0.51778825	-0.00251837	0.01250080
0.00000000	0.00	0.05698109	0.59848846	0.20344776

Manova Test Criteria and Exact F Statistics for
the Hypothesis of no Overall INTERCEPT Effect
H = Type III SS&CP Matrix for INTERCEPT   E = Error SS&CP Matrix

S=1   M=0.5   N=15.5

Statistic	Value	F	Num DF	Den DF	Pr > F
Wilks' Lambda	0.92054750	0.9494	3	33	0.4280
Pillai's Trace	0.07945250	0.9494	3	33	0.4280
Hotelling-Lawley Trace	0.08631005	0.9494	3	33	0.4280
Roy's Greatest Root	0.08631005	0.9494	3	33	0.4280

General Linear Models Procedure
Multivariate Analysis of Variance

Characteristic Roots and Vectors of: E Inverse * H, where
H = Type III SS&CP Matrix for GROUP   E = Error SS&CP Matrix

Characteristic Root	Percent	Characteristic Vector V'EV=1		
		Y1 Y4	Y2	Y3
1.13181551	87.71	0.09314829 -0.22264520	0.04324263	-0.12633871
0.12039579	9.33	0.02983311 0.59189705	0.25307413	0.05889421
0.03823867	2.96	-0.13096523 -0.41097034	0.23724594	0.07691560
0.00000000	0.00	0.03679986 -0.35099038	-0.11403991	0.52424164

Manova Test Criteria and F Approximations for
the Hypothesis of no Overall GROUP Effect
H = Type III SS&CP Matrix for GROUP   E = Error SS&CP Matrix

S=3   M=0   N=12

Statistic	Value	F	Num DF	Den DF	Pr > F
Wilks' Lambda	0.40325681	2.3576	12	69.08104	0.0132
Pillai's Trace	0.67520485	2.0331	12	84	0.0309
Hotelling-Lawley Trace	1.29044997	2.6526	12	74	0.0052
Roy's Greatest Root	1.13181551	7.9227	4	28	0.0002

NOTE: F Statistic for Roy's Greatest Root is an upper bound.

```
/* dog.dat */

4.  4.  4.1 3.6 3.6 3.8 3.1
4.2 4.3 3.7 3.7 4.8 5.0 5.2
4.3 4.2 4.3 4.3 4.5 5.8 5.4
4.2 4.4 4.6 4.9 5.3 5.6 4.9
4.6 4.4 5.3 5.6 5.9 5.9 5.3
3.1 3.6 4.9 5.2 5.3 4.2 4.1
3.7 3.9 3.9 4.8 5.2 5.4 4.2
4.3 4.2 4.4 5.2 5.6 5.4 4.7
4.6 4.6 4.4 4.6 5.4 5.9 5.6
3.4 3.4 3.5 3.1 3.1 3.7 3.3
3.0 3.2 3.0 3.0 3.1 3.2 3.1
3.0 3.1 3.2 3.0 3.3 3.0 3.0
3.1 3.2 3.2 3.2 3.3 3.1 3.1
3.8 3.9 4.0 2.9 3.5 3.5 3.4
3.0 3.6 3.2 3.1 3.0 3.0 3.0
3.3 3.3 3.3 3.4 3.6 3.1 3.1
4.2 4.0 4.2 4.1 4.2 4.0 4.0
4.1 4.2 4.3 4.3 4.2 4.0 4.2
4.5 4.4 4.3 4.5 5.3 4.4 4.4
3.2 3.3 3.8 3.8 4.4 4.2 3.7
3.3 3.4 3.4 3.7 3.7 3.6 3.7
3.1 3.3 3.2 3.1 3.2 3.1 3.1
3.6 3.4 3.5 4.6 4.9 5.2 4.4
4.5 4.5 5.4 5.7 4.9 4.0 4.0
3.7 4.0 4.4 4.2 4.6 4.8 5.4
3.5 3.9 5.8 5.4 4.9 5.3 5.6
3.9 4.0 4.1 5.0 5.4 4.4 3.9
3.1 3.5 3.5 3.2 3.0 3.0 3.2
3.3 3.2 3.6 3.7 3.7 4.2 4.4
3.5 3.9 4.7 4.3 3.9 3.4 3.5
3.4 3.4 3.5 3.3 3.4 3.2 3.4
3.7 3.8 4.2 4.3 3.6 3.8 3.7
4.0 4.6 4.8 4.9 5.4 5.6 4.8
4.2 3.9 4.5 4.7 3.9 3.8 3.7
4.1 4.1 3.7 4.0 4.1 4.6 4.7
3.5 3.6 3.6 4.2 4.8 4.9 5.0

/* Source: Grizzle and Allen (1969).  Reproduced by permission
of the International Biometric Society. */
```

```
/* Program 5.20 */

options ls=78 ps=45 nodate nonumber;
title1 'Output 5.20';
title2 'Mice Data';

data mice;
input d1 d2 d3 d4 d5 d6 d7;
lines;
0.190 0.388 0.621 0.823 1.078 1.132 1.191
0.218 0.393 0.568 0.729 0.839 0.852 1.004
0.141 0.260 0.472 0.662 0.760 0.885 0.878
0.211 0.394 0.549 0.700 0.783 0.870 0.925
0.209 0.419 0.645 0.850 1.001 1.026 1.069
0.193 0.362 0.520 0.530 0.641 0.640 0.751
0.201 0.361 0.502 0.530 0.657 0.762 0.888
0.202 0.370 0.498 0.650 0.795 0.858 0.910
0.190 0.350 0.510 0.666 0.819 0.879 0.929
0.219 0.399 0.578 0.699 0.709 0.822 0.953
0.225 0.400 0.545 0.690 0.796 0.825 0.836
0.224 0.381 0.577 0.756 0.869 0.929 0.999
0.187 0.329 0.441 0.525 0.589 0.621 0.796
0.278 0.471 0.606 0.770 0.888 1.001 1.105
;
/* Source: Izenman and Williams (1989).  Reproduced by
permission of the International Biometric Society. */

proc iml;
 use mice;
   read all into y0;
   print y0;

/* Here we generate the Ortho Poly of degree p-1=6*/
vec1={2 5 8 11 14 17 20};
c=orpol(vec1,6);
y=y0*c;
/* Here we convert Y matrix to a data set Trandata*/
varnames={y1 y2 y3 y4 y5 y6 y7};
create trandata from y (|colname=varnames|);
append from y;
close trandata;

proc glm data=trandata;
 model y1 y2 y3=y4 y5 y6 y7/nouni;
 manova h=intercept/printe;


proc reg data=trandata;
model y1 y2 y3= ;
model y1 y2 y3=y4;
model y1 y2 y3=y4 y5;
model y1 y2 y3=y4 y5 y6;
model y1 y2 y3=y4 y5 y6 y7;

 run;
```

```
/* Program 5.21 */

option ls=78 ps=45 nodate nonumber;
/* Cabbage Data: Rawlings (1988, p. 219)*/
title1 ' Output 5.21 ';

data a;
input line $ date $ @;
 do i=1 to 5;
   input x y@;
   output;
drop i;
   end;
lines;
lin1 dat1 2.5 51 2.2 55 3.1 45 4.3 42 2.5 53
lin1 dat1 4.3 50 3.8 50 4.3 52 1.7 56 3.1 49
lin1 dat2 3.0 65 2.8 52 2.8 41 2.7 51 2.6 41
lin1 dat2 2.8 45 2.6 51 2.6 45 2.6 61 3.5 42
lin1 dat3 2.2 54 1.8 59 1.6 66 2.1 54 3.3 45
lin1 dat3 3.8 49 3.2 49 3.6 55 4.2 49 1.6 68
lin2 dat1 2.0 58 2.4 55 1.9 67 2.8 61 1.7 67
lin2 dat1 3.2 68 2.0 58 2.2 63 2.2 56 2.2 72
lin2 dat2 4.0 52 2.8 70 3.1 57 4.2 58 3.7 47
lin2 dat2 3.0 56 2.2 72 2.3 63 3.8 54 2.0 60
lin2 dat3 1.5 78 1.4 75 1.7 70 1.3 84 1.7 71
lin2 dat3 1.6 72 1.4 62 1.0 68 1.5 66 1.6 72
;
/* Source: Rawlings (1988, p. 219).  Reprinted by permission
   of the Wadsworth Publishing Company. */

proc print data=a;
data cabbage;
set a;
if (line='lin1' and date='dat1') then d1=1;
   else d1=0;
if (line='lin1' and date='dat2') then d2=1;
   else d2=0;
if (line='lin1' and date='dat3') then d3=1;
   else d3=0;
if (line='lin2' and date='dat1') then d4=1;
   else d4=0;
if (line='lin2' and date='dat2') then d5=1;
   else d5=0;
if (line='lin2' and date='dat3') then d6=1;
   else d6=0;
 output;
data cabbage;
set cabbage;
   xd1=x*d1;
xd2=x*d2;
xd3=x*d3;
   xd4=x*d4;
xd5=x*d5;
xd6=x*d6;
title2 'Homogeneity of Regression';

proc reg data=cabbage;
   model y=d1-d6 xd1-xd6/noint;
   test xd1=xd2=xd3=xd4=xd5=xd6;
run;
```

Dependent Variable: Y
Test: Numerator: 25.5634 DF: 5   F value: 0.6643
               Denominator: 38.48409 DF: 48 Prob>F: 0.6523

```
/* Program 5.22*/

options ls=78 ps=45 nodate nonumber;
title1 'Output 5.22';
title2 'Nonlinear Growth Curve Analysis';

data fish;
input length d1 d2 age@@;
lines;
15.40 1 0 1.0 26.93 1 0 2.0 42.23 1 0 3.3
44.59 1 0 4.3 47.63 1 0 5.3
49.67 1 0 6.3 50.87 1 0 7.3 52.30 1 0 8.3
54.77 1 0 9.3 56.43 1 0 10.3
55.88 1 0 11.3
15.40 0 1 1.0 28.03 0 1 2.0 41.18 0 1 3.3
46.20 0 1 4.3 48.23 0 1 5.3
50.26 0 1 6.3 51.82 0 1 7.3 54.27 0 1 8.3
56.98 0 1 9.3 58.93 0 1 10.3
59.00 0 1 11.3 60.91 0 1 12.3 61.83 0 1 13.3
;
/* Source: Kimura (1980).  U. S. Fishery Bulletin. */

/* The following code fits von Bertalanffy model
                              under Omega*/
proc nlin data=fish maxiter=100;
parms l1=55 k1=.276 t1=0 l2=60 k2=.23 t2=0;
model length= l1*d1*(1-exp(-k1*(age-t1)))+
                l2*d2*(1-exp(-k2*(age-t2)));
/* The following code fits von Bertalanffy model
                       under omega 1:l1=l2=l*/
/* The initial estimate of l is taken as the average
                          of that of l1 and l2*/
proc nlin data=fish maxiter=100;
parms l=57.5 k1=.276 t1=0 k2=.23 t2=0;
model length= l*d1*(1-exp(-k1*(age-t1)))+
                l*d2*(1-exp(-k2*(age-t2)));
/* The following code fits von Bertalanffy model
                       under omega 2:k1=k2=k*/
/* The initial estimate of k is taken as the average
                          of that of k1 and k2*/
proc nlin data=fish maxiter=100;
parms l1=55 k=.253 t1=0 l2=60 t2=0;
model length= l1*d1*(1-exp(-k*(age-t1)))+
                l2*d2*(1-exp(-k*(age-t2)));
/* The following code fits von Bertalanffy model
                       under omega 3:t1=t2=t*/
/* The initial estimate of t is taken as the average
                          of that of t1 and t2*/
proc nlin data=fish maxiter=100;
parms l1=55 k1=.276 t=0 l2=60 k2=.23;
model length= l1*d1*(1-exp(-k1*(age-t)))+
                l2*d2*(1-exp(-k2*(age-t)));
/* The following code fits von Bertalanffy model
                       under omega 4:
l1=l2 ,k1=k2 and t1=t2*/
proc nlin data=fish maxiter=100;
parms l=57.5 k=.253 t=0 ;
model length= l*d1*(1-exp(-k*(age-t)))+
                l*d2*(1-exp(-k*(age-t)));
run;
```

Output 5.22
Nonlinear Growth Curve Analysis

Non-Linear Least Squares Iterative Phase
Dependent Variable LENGTH   Method: DUD

Iter	L1 L2	K1 K2	T1 T2	Sum of Squares
14	55.980733 61.253551	0.385754 0.295754	0.172331 -0.059130	48.224936
15	55.979016 61.234451	0.385520 0.296236	0.170992 -0.057328	48.223783
16	55.978717 61.235343	0.385530 0.296214	0.171068 -0.057420	48.223782
17	55.979031 61.235229	0.385535 0.296206	0.171084 -0.057508	48.223781
18	55.979001 61.235208	0.385535 0.296206	0.171082 -0.057500	48.223781

NOTE: Convergence criterion met.

Non-Linear Least Squares Summary Statistics   Dependent Variable LENGTH

Source	DF	Sum of Squares	Mean Square
Regression	6	57120.508419	9520.084736
Residual	18	48.223781	2.679099
Uncorrected Total	24	57168.732200	
(Corrected Total)	23	3989.046050	

Output 5.22
Nonlinear Growth Curve Analysis

Parameter	Estimate	Asymptotic Std. Error	Asymptotic 95 % Confidence Interval	
			Lower	Upper
L1	55.97900061	1.1377098402	53.588776726	58.369224496
K1	0.38553509	0.0409808068	0.299438177	0.471631999
T1	0.17108151	0.1489629380	-0.141875940	0.484038963
L2	61.23520817	1.1742185799	58.768282773	63.702133561
K2	0.29620606	0.0276983316	0.238014405	0.354397706
T2	-0.05750014	0.1693572920	-0.413304257	0.298303976

Asymptotic Correlation Matrix

Corr	L1	K1	T1	L2	K2	T2
L1	1	-0.815556	-0.510785	0.0024887	0.0008766	-0.001379
K1	-0.815556	1	0.810093	-0.003034	-0.000867	0.002127
T1	-0.510785	0.810093	1	-0.003786	-0.000958	0.0024494
L2	0.0024887	-0.003034	-0.003786	1	-0.842916	-0.544549
K2	0.0008766	-0.000867	-0.000958	-0.842916	1	0.8213017
T2	-0.001379	0.002127	0.0024494	-0.544549	0.8213017	1

Output 5.22
Nonlinear Growth Curve Analysis

Non-Linear Least Squares Iterative Phase
Dependent Variable LENGTH   Method: DUD

Iter	L	K1	T1	Sum of Squares
	K2	T2		
10	59.397471	0.296899	-0.110987	71.602334
	0.337586	0.087862		
11	59.398164	0.296912	-0.110774	71.602306
	0.337539	0.087526		
12	59.398772	0.296920	-0.110545	71.602250
	0.337574	0.087718		
13	59.404853	0.296727	-0.111360	71.602119
	0.337434	0.087195		
14	59.404104	0.296747	-0.111306	71.602118
	0.337456	0.087224		
15	59.404115	0.296757	-0.111227	71.602117
	0.337453	0.087282		
16	59.403863	0.296760	-0.111183	71.602116
	0.337458	0.087293		
17	59.403748	0.296758	-0.111221	71.602116
	0.337466	0.087349		

NOTE: Convergence criterion met.

Non-Linear Least Squares Summary Statistics   Dependent Variable LENGTH

Source	DF	Sum of Squares	Mean Square
Regression	5	57097.130084	11419.426017
Residual	19	71.602116	3.768532
Uncorrected Total	24	57168.732200	
(Corrected Total)	23	3989.046050	

Parameter	Estimate	Asymptotic Std. Error	Asymptotic 95 % Confidence Interval Lower	Upper
L	59.40374844	1.0078652240	57.294277355	61.513219524
K1	0.29675802	0.0270878745	0.240062848	0.353453184
T1	-0.11122113	0.1952531103	-0.519887664	0.297445409
K2	0.33746601	0.0327766644	0.268864156	0.406067870
T2	0.08734880	0.1719614976	-0.272568178	0.447265780

Asymptotic Correlation Matrix

Corr	L	K1	T1	K2	T2
L	1	−0.717798456	−0.37993007	−0.7520929	−0.432873298
K1	−0.717798456	1	0.7956667488	0.5376751597	0.3091189868
T1	−0.37993007	0.7956667488	1	0.2849128661	0.1643346708
K2	−0.7520929	0.5376751597	0.2849128661	1	0.7963760045
T2	−0.432873298	0.3091189868	0.1643346708	0.7963760045	1

```
/* Program 5.23 */

options ls= 78 ps=45 nodate nonumber;
title1 'Output 5.23';

*Systolic  BP Data from Jones and Kenward (1989, p. 230);

data  bp;
input patient $ y treat $ carry $ period center subject;
lines;
1 206 c 0 1 1 1
1 220 a c 2 1 1
1 210 b a 3 1 1
2 174 a 0 1 1 2
2 146 b a 2 1 2
2 164 c b 3 1 2
3 192 a 0 1 1 3
3 150 c a 2 1 3
3 160 b c 3 1 3
4 184 b 0 1 1 4
4 192 a b 2 1 4
4 176 c a 3 1 4
5 136 b 0 1 1 5
5 132 c b 2 1 5
5 138 a c 3 1 5
1 190 c 0 1 4 6
1 145 b c 2 4 6
1 160 a b 3 4 6
1 145 a 0 1 2 7
1 125 b a 2 2 7
1 130 c b 3 2 7
2 160 c 0 1 2 8
2 180 a c 2 2 8
2 145 b a 3 2 8
3 145 b 0 1 2 9
3 154 c b 2 2 9
3 166 a c 3 2 9
1 230 a 0 1 3 10
1 174 b a 2 3 10
1 200 c b 3 3 10
2 194 b 0 1 3 11
2 210 c b 2 3 11
2 190 a c 3 3 11
3 180 c 0 1 3 12
3 180 b c 2 3 12
3 208 a a 3 3 12
4 140 b 0 1 3 13
4 150 a b 2 3 13
4 150 c a 3 3 13
5 194 a 0 1 3 14
5 208 c a 2 3 14
5 160 b c 3 3 14
6 188 c 0 1 3 15
6 200 a c 2 3 15
6 190 b a 3 3 15
7 240 a 0 1 3 16
7 130 b a 2 3 16
7 195 c b 3 3 16
```

```
/* Program 5.23 continued */

8 180 b 0 1 3 17
8 180 c b 2 3 17
8 190 a c 3 3 17
9 210 c 0 1 3 18
9 160 b c 2 3 18
9 226 a b 3 3 18
10 175 a 0 1 3 19
10 152 c a 2 3 19
10 175 b c 3 3 19
11 155 b 0 1 3 20
11 230 a b 2 3 20
11 226 c a 3 3 20
12 202 a 0 1 3 21
12 160 c a 2 3 21
12 180 b c 3 3 21
13 180 b 0 1 3 22
13 185 a b 2 3 22
13 190 c a 3 3 22
14 185 c 0 1 3 23
14 180 b c 2 3 23
14 200 a b 3 3 23
;
/* Source: Jones and Kenward (1989, p. 230).  Reprinted
   by permission of the  Chapman and Hall, Andover, England. */

proc glm data = bp ;
class treat carry period subject;
model y = subject period treat carry/ ss1 ;
random subject/test ;
contrast 'a vs. b' treat 1 -1 0;
contrast ' a vs. c' treat 1 0 -1;
contrast ' b vs. c' treat 0 1 -1;

proc glm data = bp ;
class treat carry period subject;
model y = subject period treat carry/ ss3 ;
random subject/test ;
contrast 'a vs. b' treat 1 -1 0;
contrast ' a vs. c' treat 1 0 -1;
contrast ' b vs. c' treat 0 1 -1;

run;
```

Output 5.23

General Linear Models Procedure

Dependent Variable: Y

Source	DF	Sum of Squares	Mean Square	F Value	Pr > F
Model	28	40095.95607	1431.99843	4.95	0.0001
Error	40	11573.98596	289.34965		
Corrected Total	68	51669.94203			

	R-Square	C.V.	Root MSE	Y Mean
	0.776002	9.575829	17.01028	177.6377

Source	DF	Type I SS	Mean Square	F Value	Pr > F
SUBJECT	22	30646.60870	1393.02767	4.81	0.0001
PERIOD	2	1395.59420	697.79710	2.41	0.1026
TREAT	2	7983.87171	3991.93585	13.80	0.0001
CARRY	2	69.88147	34.94073	0.12	0.8866

General Linear Models Procedure

Dependent Variable: Y

Contrast	DF	Contrast SS	Mean Square	F Value	Pr > F
a vs. b	1	6303.024031	6303.024031	21.78	0.0001
a vs. c	1	1471.222649	1471.222649	5.08	0.0297
b vs. c	1	1491.202625	1491.202625	5.15	0.0287

```
/* Program 5.24*/

options ls= 78 ps=45 nodate nonumber;
title1 'Output 5.24';
/* Effect of Onion in Diet: data from Dunsmore (1981, App. Stat.,
   30, 223-229).  Program illustrated in Grender & Johnson
(1992, SUGI 17th Annual Conference, 1355-1360) */

data onion;
input patient meal $
y11 y12 y13 y14 y15 y16 group  patient2  meal2 $
y21 y22 y23 y24 y25 y26 group2;
lines;
1 a 0146 3756 2172 3956 3806 4990 1
1 b 9666 8496 12056 8216 5076 -1568 1
2 a 5767 12321 16440 15736 12760 8504 1
2 b 2784 9668 9138 8096 9286 7413  1
3 a 2723 3177 3427 3549 4084 4754 1
3 b 2595 4959 6993 5614 5108 2690 1
4 a 3365 3567 3646 5120 5390 5051 1
4 b -2191 1281 1184 1750 0532 1328 1
5 a 3238 8804 6480 7221 5680 4439 1
5 b 1872 3655 4810 4737 3776 0682 1
6 a 3567 2820 5878 4410 6988 7962 1
6 b -1640 1063 0430 0476 0145 -3326 1
7 a 1878 3832 3459 4300 3010 2541 1
7 b 2126 2041 0771 1985 -1914 -0537 1
8 a -0408 0392 1310 -0619 0770 1310 1
8 b 2412 0000 3102 3953 3536 1671 1
9 a 3933 5674 5878 9235 8089 7676 2
9 b -0119 -3483 0000 2208 0791 5132 2
10 a 6373 5902 7357 7357 5021 4888 2
10 b -1424 0601 0546 3289 2284 0000 2
11 a  0426 0834 8285 7357 6022 6101 2
11 b 1773 8579 6931 6473 4774 2839 2
12 a 8249 12011 13649 15364 14803 9191 2
12 b 2800 6698 8755 8228 6737 -1947 2
13 a 5623 7302 7482 0370 -1861 0370 2
13 b 3716 4055 9555 15041 11151 2231 2
14 a -0089 4361 4893 5001 7493 6025 2
14 b 0517 0785 4068 3931 4776 2918 2
;
/* Source: Dunsmore (1981).  Reprinted by permission of the
   Royal Statistical Society. */

proc glm data = onion ;
class group ;
model y11 y12 y13 y14 y15 y16 y21 y22 y23 y24 y25 y26=
                                      group / nouni;
 contrast 'groupxtime  interaction' group 1 -1 ;
manova h = group
m = y11-y12+y21-y22,
    y12-y13+y22-y23,
    y13-y14+y23-y24,
    y14-y15+y24-y25,
    y15-y16+y25-y26;
title2 'Test for Group*Time Interaction';
proc glm data = onion ;
class group ;
model y11 y12 y13 y14 y15 y16 y21 y22 y23 y24 y25 y26=
                                      group / nouni;
```

356

```
/* Program 5.24 continued */

   contrast 'Carryover  Effect' group 1 -1 ;
   manova h = group
   m = y11+y12+y13+y14+y15+y16+y21+y22+y23+y24+y25+y26;
title2 'Test for Equality of Carryover Effects';
proc glm data = onion ;
class group ;
model y11 y12 y13 y14 y15 y16 y21 y22 y23 y24 y25 y26=
                                      group / nouni;
   contrast 'Teatment*Time  Interaction' group 1 -1 ;
    manova h = group
   m = y11-y12+y21-y22,
       y12-y13+y22-y23,
       y13-y14+y23-y24,
       y14-y15+y24-y25,
       y15-y16+y25-y26;
title2 'Test for Treatment*Time Interaction
               (Assuming equal Carryover Effects)';
proc glm data = onion ;
class group ;
model y11 y12 y13 y14 y15 y16 y21 y22 y23 y24 y25 y26=
                                      group / nouni;
manova h = intercept  m = y11-y12+y21-y22,
                          y12-y13+y22-y23,
                          y13-y14+y23-y24,
                          y14-y15+y24-y25,
                          y15-y16+y25-y26;
title2 'Test for Period*Time Interaction
         (assuming no Group*Time Interaction)';
proc glm data = onion ;
class group ;
model y11 y12 y13 y14 y15 y16 y21 y22 y23 y24 y25 y26=
group / nouni;
manova h = intercept
   m = y11-y12+y21-y22,
       y12-y13+y22-y23,
       y13-y14+y23-y24,
       y14-y15+y24-y25,
       y15-y16+y25-y26;

title2 'Test for Time Effect';

proc glm data = onion ;
class group ;
model y11 y12 y13 y14 y15 y16 y21 y22 y23 y24 y25 y26=
                                      group / nouni;
  contrast 'Treatment  Effect' group 1 -1 ;
manova h = group
m = y11+y12+y13+y14+y15+y16-y21-y22-y23-y24-y25-y26;
title2 'Test for Equality of Treatment Effects';

proc glm data = onion ;
class group ;
model y11 y12 y13 y14 y15 y16 y21 y22 y23 y24 y25 y26=
                                      group / nouni;
manova h = intercept
m = y11+y12+y13+y14+y15+y16+y21+y22+y23+y24+y25+y26;
title2 'Test for Equality of Period Effects';
run;
```

Output 5.24
Test for Group*Time Interaction

General Linear Models Procedure
Multivariate Analysis of Variance

Manova Test Criteria and Exact F Statistics for
the Hypothesis of no Overall groupxtime interact Effect
on the variables defined by the M Matrix Transformation
H = Contrast SS&CP Matrix for groupxtime   interact   E = Error SS&CP Matrix

S=1   M=1.5   N=3

Statistic	Value	F	Num DF	Den DF	Pr > F
Wilks' Lambda	0.25706306	4.6242	5	8	0.0279
Pillai's Trace	0.74293694	4.6242	5	8	0.0279
Hotelling-Lawley Trace	2.89009605	4.6242	5	8	0.0279
Roy's Greatest Root	2.89009605	4.6242	5	8	0.0279

Test for Equality of Carryover Effects

General Linear Models Procedure
Multivariate Analysis of Variance

M Matrix Describing Transformed Variables

	Y11	Y12	Y13	Y14	Y15	Y16
MVAR1	1	1	1	1	1	1

	Y21	Y22	Y23	Y24	Y25	Y26
MVAR1	1	1	1	1	1	1

Output 5.24
Test for Equality of Carryover Effects

General Linear Models Procedure
Multivariate Analysis of Variance

Manova Test Criteria and Exact F Statistics for
the Hypothesis of no Overall Carryover Effect Effect
on the variables defined by the M Matrix Transformation
H = Contrast SS&CP Matrix for Carryover Effect   E = Error SS&CP Matrix

S=1   M=-0.5   N=5

Statistic	Value	F	Num DF	Den DF	Pr > F
Wilks' Lambda	0.95067566	0.6226	1	12	0.4454
Pillai's Trace	0.04932434	0.6226	1	12	0.4454
Hotelling-Lawley Trace	0.05188346	0.6226	1	12	0.4454
Roy's Greatest Root	0.05188346	0.6226	1	12	0.4454

Test for Treatment*Time Interaction (Assuming equal Carryover Effects)

General Linear Models Procedure
Multivariate Analysis of Variance

M Matrix Describing Transformed Variables

	Y11	Y12	Y13	Y14	Y15	Y16
MVAR1	1	-1	0	0	0	0
MVAR2	0	1	-1	0	0	0
MVAR3	0	0	1	-1	0	0
MVAR4	0	0	0	1	-1	0
MVAR5	0	0	0	0	1	-1

	Y21	Y22	Y23	Y24	Y25	Y26
MVAR1	1	-1	0	0	0	0
MVAR2	0	1	-1	0	0	0
MVAR3	0	0	1	-1	0	0
MVAR4	0	0	0	1	-1	0
MVAR5	0	0	0	0	1	-1

Test for Treatment*Time Interaction (Assuming equal Carryover Effects)

General Linear Models Procedure
Multivariate Analysis of Variance

Manova Test Criteria and Exact F Statistics for
the Hypothesis of no Overall Teatment*Time Inter Effect
on the variables defined by the M Matrix Transformation
H = Contrast SS&CP Matrix for Teatment*Time Inter   E = Error SS&CP Matrix

S=1   M=1.5   N=3

Statistic	Value	F	Num DF	Den DF	Pr > F
Wilks' Lambda	0.25706306	4.6242	5	8	0.0279
Pillai's Trace	0.74293694	4.6242	5	8	0.0279
Hotelling-Lawley Trace	2.89009605	4.6242	5	8	0.0279
Roy's Greatest Root	2.89009605	4.6242	5	8	0.0279

General Linear Models Procedure
Multivariate Analysis of Variance

M Matrix Describing Transformed Variables

	Y11	Y12	Y13	Y14	Y15	Y16
MVAR1	1	-1	0	0	0	0
MVAR2	0	1	-1	0	0	0
MVAR3	0	0	1	-1	0	0
MVAR4	0	0	0	1	-1	0
MVAR5	0	0	0	0	1	-1

	Y21	Y22	Y23	Y24	Y25	Y26
MVAR1	1	-1	0	0	0	0
MVAR2	0	1	-1	0	0	0
MVAR3	0	0	1	-1	0	0
MVAR4	0	0	0	1	-1	0
MVAR5	0	0	0	0	1	-1

Test for Period*Time Interaction (assuming no Group*Time Interaction)

General Linear Models Procedure
Multivariate Analysis of Variance

Manova Test Criteria and Exact F Statistics for
the Hypothesis of no Overall INTERCEPT Effect
on the variables defined by the M Matrix Transformation
H = Type III SS&CP Matrix for INTERCEPT   E = Error SS&CP Matrix

S=1   M=1.5   N=3

Statistic	Value	F	Num DF	Den DF	Pr > F
Wilks' Lambda	0.08495154	17.2343	5	8	0.0004
Pillai's Trace	0.91504846	17.2343	5	8	0.0004
Hotelling-Lawley Trace	10.77141700	17.2343	5	8	0.0004
Roy's Greatest Root	10.77141700	17.2343	5	8	0.0004

General Linear Models Procedure
Multivariate Analysis of Variance

M Matrix Describing Transformed Variables

	Y11	Y12	Y13	Y14	Y15	Y16
MVAR1	1	-1	0	0	0	0
MVAR2	0	1	-1	0	0	0
MVAR3	0	0	1	-1	0	0
MVAR4	0	0	0	1	-1	0
MVAR5	0	0	0	0	1	-1

	Y21	Y22	Y23	Y24	Y25	Y26
MVAR1	1	-1	0	0	0	0
MVAR2	0	1	-1	0	0	0
MVAR3	0	0	1	-1	0	0
MVAR4	0	0	0	1	-1	0
MVAR5	0	0	0	0	1	-1

General Linear Models Procedure
Multivariate Analysis of Variance

Manova Test Criteria and Exact F Statistics for
the Hypothesis of no Overall INTERCEPT Effect
on the variables defined by the M Matrix Transformation
H = Type III SS&CP Matrix for INTERCEPT   E = Error SS&CP Matrix

S=1   M=1.5   N=3

Statistic	Value	F	Num DF	Den DF	Pr > F
Wilks' Lambda	0.08495154	17.2343	5	8	0.0004
Pillai's Trace	0.91504846	17.2343	5	8	0.0004
Hotelling-Lawley Trace	10.77141700	17.2343	5	8	0.0004
Roy's Greatest Root	10.77141700	17.2343	5	8	0.0004

Test for Equality of Treatment Effects

General Linear Models Procedure
Multivariate Analysis of Variance

M Matrix Describing Transformed Variables

	Y11	Y12	Y13	Y14	Y15	Y16
MVAR1	1	1	1	1	1	1

	Y21	Y22	Y23	Y24	Y25	Y26
MVAR1	-1	-1	-1	-1	-1	-1

Test for Equality of Treatment Effects

General Linear Models Procedure
Multivariate Analysis of Variance

Manova Test Criteria and Exact F Statistics for
the Hypothesis of no Overall Treatment Effect Effect
on the variables defined by the M Matrix Transformation
H = Contrast SS&CP Matrix for Treatment Effect   E = Error SS&CP Matrix

S=1   M=-0.5   N=5

Statistic	Value	F	Num DF	Den DF	Pr > F
Wilks' Lambda	0.97899573	0.2575	1	12	0.6211
Pillai's Trace	0.02100427	0.2575	1	12	0.6211
Hotelling-Lawley Trace	0.02145491	0.2575	1	12	0.6211
Roy's Greatest Root	0.02145491	0.2575	1	12	0.6211

Test for Equality of Period Effects

General Linear Models Procedure
Multivariate Analysis of Variance

M Matrix Describing Transformed Variables

	Y11	Y12	Y13	Y14	Y15	Y16
MVAR1	1	1	1	1	1	1

	Y21	Y22	Y23	Y24	Y25	Y26
MVAR1	1	1	1	1	1	1

Output 5.24
Test for Equality of Period Effects

General Linear Models Procedure
Multivariate Analysis of Variance

Characteristic Roots and Vectors of: E Inverse * H, where
H = Type III SS&CP Matrix for INTERCEPT   E = Error SS&CP Matrix

Variables have been transformed by the M Matrix

Characteristic Root	Percent	Characteristic Vector V'EV=1
		MVAR1
3.96889585	100.00	0.00000994

Manova Test Criteria and Exact F Statistics for
the Hypothesis of no Overall INTERCEPT Effect
on the variables defined by the M Matrix Transformation
H = Type III SS&CP Matrix for INTERCEPT   E = Error SS&CP Matrix

S=1   M=-0.5   N=5

Statistic	Value	F	Num DF	Den DF	Pr > F
Wilks' Lambda	0.20125195	47.6268	1	12	0.0001
Pillai's Trace	0.79874805	47.6268	1	12	0.0001
Hotelling-Lawley Trace	3.96889585	47.6268	1	12	0.0001
Roy's Greatest Root	3.96889585	47.6268	1	12	0.0001

Test for Group*Time Interaction

General Linear Models Procedure
Multivariate Analysis of Variance

M Matrix Describing Transformed Variables

	Y11	Y12	Y13	Y14	Y15	Y16
MVAR1	1	-1	0	0	0	0
MVAR2	0	1	-1	0	0	0
MVAR3	0	0	1	-1	0	0
MVAR4	0	0	0	1	-1	0
MVAR5	0	0	0	0	1	-1

	Y21	Y22	Y23	Y24	Y25	Y26
MVAR1	1	-1	0	0	0	0
MVAR2	0	1	-1	0	0	0
MVAR3	0	0	1	-1	0	0
MVAR4	0	0	0	1	-1	0
MVAR5	0	0	0	0	1	-1

```
/* Program 5.25 */

title1 'Output 5.25';
options ls=78 ps=45 nodate nonumber;

proc factex;
factors row col t1-t3/nlev=4;
size design=16;
model resolution=3;
output out=latinsq  ;
run;

data latinsq1;
set latinsq;
keep t1-t3;
proc iml;
use latinsq1;
read all into z0;
p=4;
latin1 = i(p);
latin2 = i(p);
latin3 = i(p);
do i = 1 to p;
do j = 1 to p;
ij = (i-1)*p +j ;
latin1[i,j] = z0[ij,1];
latin2[i,j] = z0[ij,2];
latin3[i,j] = z0[ij,3];
end;
end;
title2
'A Latin Square Cross Over Design: 4 Treatments,
               4 Time Points in 12 Subjects';
print latin1 latin2 latin3;

run;
```

```
LATIN1
        0           3           1           2
        3           0           2           1
        1           2           0           3
        2           1           3           0


LATIN2
        0           3           1           2
        2           1           3           0
        3           0           2           1
        1           2           0           3


LATIN3
        0           3           1           2
        1           2           0           3
        2           1           3           0
        3           0           2           1
```

```
/* Program 5.26 */

options ls=78 ps=45 nodate nonumber;
title 'Output 5.26';
proc iml;
p=4;
p2=p*2;
/*
Initialize the matrices;
* a is the circular p by p Latin Lquare, b is
                    its mirror image and the specific;
* colums of Williams as indicate in the output
                    provide the William's Design.*/
a=i(p);
b=i(p);
Williams=j(p,p2);
*Create the matrix a;

do i = 1 to p;
i1=i-1;
do j = 1 to p;
if (i = 1) then  a[i,j] =j;
if (i >1) then do;
 if (j < p) then do ;
jmod = j+1;
a[i,j] = a[i1,jmod] ;
end ;
 if (j = p) then do ;
jmod = 1 ;
  a[i,j] = a[i1,jmod] ;
end ;
end ;
end ;
end ;

* Create b, the mirror image of a;

do i = 1 to p;
do j = 1 to p;
jj=(p+1-j);
b[i,j] = a[i,jj];
end ;

*Interlace the Circular Latin Square and its
                    mirror image;

do k = 1 to p2;
kby2 =k/2;
if  kby2=floor(kby2) then do;
Williams[i,k] = b[i,kby2];
end;
if  kby2>floor(kby2) then do;
kk= floor(kby2)+1;
Williams[i,k] = a[i,kk];
end;
end;
end;
print a b ;
```

```
/* Program 5.26 continued */

print 'Williams Design: p Treatments in p Time points ';
print 'with p subjects (if p even) or
                            2p subjects (if p odd)';
print 'If p is even take either first p or
                    last p colums as the Design.';
print
'If p is odd slice after first p colums and augment
                    last p columns below it.';

print 'p is equal to ' p;
print '   ' ;
print Williams;

run;
```

```
           A
           1        2        3        4
           2        3        4        1
           3        4        1        2
           4        1        2        3

           B
           4        3        2        1
           1        4        3        2
           2        1        4        3
           3        2        1        4
```

Williams Design: p Treatments in p Time points

with p subjects (if p even) or 2p subjects (if p odd)

If p is even take either first p or last p colums as the Design.

If p is odd slice after first p colums and augment last p columns below it.

p is equal to   P
                         4

WILLIAMS
         1   4   2   3   3   2   4
:   1

         2   1   3   4   4   3   1
:   2

         3   2   4   1   1   4   2
:   3

         4   3   1   2   2   1   3
:   4

References

Anderson, T. W. (1984), *An Introduction to Multivariate Statistical Analysis,* New York: John Wiley & Sons, Inc.

Andrews, D. F. (1972), "Plots of High-Dimensional Data", *Biometrics,* 28, 125-136.

Bose, R. C. (1951), *Least Square Aspects of the Analysis of Variance,* Mimeograph Series No. 9, University of North Carolina, Chapel Hill.

Box, G. E. P. (1950), "Problems in the Analysis of Growth and Wear Curves", *Biometrics,* 6, 362-389.

Box, G. E. P. (1954), "Some Theorems on Quadratic Forms Applied in the Study of Analysis of Variance Problems II. Effect of Inequality of Variance and Correlations Between Errors in the Two Way Classification", *Ann. Math. Statist.,* 25, 484-498.

Christensen, R. and Blackwood, L. G. (1993), "Tests for Precision and Accuracy of Multiple Measuring Devices", *Technometrics,* 35, 411-420.

Cody, R. P. and Smith, J. K. (1991), *Applied Statistics and the SAS Programming Language, Third Edition,* New York: Prentice-Hall, Inc.

Crowder, M. J. and Hand, D. J. (1990), *Analysis of Repeated Measures,* New York: Chapman Hall.

Dallal, G. E. (1992), "The Computer Analysis of Factorial Experiments with Nested Factors", *Amer. Statist.,* 46, 240.

Daniel, C. and Riblett, E. W. (1954), "A Multifactor Experiment", *Industrial and Engineering Chemistry,* 46, 1465-1468.

Das, R. and Sinha, B. K. (1986), "Detection of Multivariate Outliers with Dispersion Slippage in Elliptically Symmetric Distributions", *Ann. Statist.,*14, 1619-1624.

De Long, D. (1994), "Invited Response to Dallal, G. E. (1992)", *Amer. Statist.,* 48, 141.

Dunsmore, I. R. (1981), "Growth Curves in Two Period Changeover Models", *Jour. of Royal Statist. Soc., Ser. C,* 30, 223-229.

Elston, R. C. and Grizzle, J.E. (1962), "Estimation of Time Response Curves and Their Confidence Bands", *Biometrics,* 18, 148-159.

Friendly, M. (1991), *SAS System for Statistical Graphics, First Edition,* Cary, NC: SAS Institute Inc.

Gabriel, K. R. (1971), "The Biplot Graphic Display of Matrices with Application to Principal Component Analysis", *Biometrika,* 58, 453-467.

Giri, N. C. (1977), *Multivariate Statistical Inference,* New York: Academic Press.

Gnanadesikan, R. (1980), "Graphical Methods for Internal Comparisons in ANOVA and MANOVA", In *Handbook of Statistics, Vol. 1: Analysis of Variance,* Ed. P. R. Krishnaiah, 133-177, Amsterdam: North Holland.

Goldstein, R. (1994), "Editor's Notes", *Amer. Statist.,* 48, 138-139.

Goodnight, J. H. (1976), "General Linear Model Procedure", *SAS.ONE, Proceedings of the First International Users Conference,* 1-39.

Greenhouse, S. W. and Geisser, S. (1959), "On Methods in the Analysis of Profile Data", *Psychometrika,* 24, 95-112.

Grender, J. M. and Johnson, W. D. (1992), "Using the GLM Procedure to Analyze Multivariate Response in Crossover Designs", *Proceedings of the Seventeenth Annual SAS Users Group International Conference,* Cary, NC: SAS Institute Inc., 17, 1355-1360.

Grizzle, J. E. and Allen, D. M. (1969), "Analysis of Growth and Dose Response Curves", *Biometrics,* 25, 357-381.

Guo, R. S. and Sachs E. (1993), "Modelling Optimization and Control of Spatial Uniformity in Manufacturing Processes", *IEEE Transactions on Semiconductor Manufacturing,* 6, 41-57.

Gupta, R. D. and Richards, D. S. P. (1983), "Application of Results of Kotz, Johnson and Boyd to the Null Distribution of Wilks' Criterion", *Contributions to Statistics : Essays in Honor of Norman Lloyd Johnson,* Ed. P. K. Sen, 205- 210, Amsterdam: North Holland.

Hartigan J. A. (1975), *Clustering Algorithms,* New York: John Wiley & Sons, Inc.

Huynh, H. and Feldt, L. S. (1970), "Conditions Under Which Mean Square Ratios in Repeated Measure Designs Have Exact F-Distribution", *Jour. Amer. Statist. Assoc.,* 65, 1582-1589.

Huynh, H. and Feldt, L. S. (1976), "Estimation of Box Correction for Degrees of Freedom from the Sample Data in the Randomized Block and Split-Plot Designs", *Jour. Educ. Statist.,* 1, 69-82.

Izenman, A. J. (1987), "Comments on C. R. Rao (1987)", Statist. Sci., 2, 416-463.

Izenman, A. J. and Williams, J. S. (1989), "A Class of Linear Spectral Models and Analyses for the Study of Longitudinal Data", *Biometrics*, 45, 831-849.

Jackson, J. E. (1991), *A User's Guide to Principal Component Analysis*, New York: John Wiley & Sons, Inc.

Jobson, J. D. (1992), *Applied Multivariate Data Analysis, Vol. 2*, New York: Springer-Verlag.

Jones, B. and Kenward, M. G.(1989), *Design and Analysis of Cross-over Trials*, London: Chapman and Hall.

John, P. W. M. (1971), *Statistical Designs and Analysis of Experiments*, New York: MacMillan.

Johnson, R. A. and Wichern, D. W. (1992), *Applied Multivariate Statistical Analysis*, Englewood Cliffs, NJ: Prentice Hall.

Kennedy, W. J. and Gentle, J. E. (1980), *Statistical Computing*, New York: Dekker.

Kimura, D. K. (1980), "Likelihood Methods for the Von Bertalanffy Growth Curve", *U. S. Fishery Bulletin*, 77, 765-776.

Kshirsager, A. M. (1972), *Multivariate Analysis*, New York: Marcel Dekker.

Lakkis, H. D. and Jones, C. M. (1992), "Comparing Von Bertalanffy Growth Curves with SAS Using the Likelihood Methods Developed by Kimura", *Preprint*.

Lindsey, J. K. (1993), *Models for Repeated Measurements*, New York: Oxford University Press.

Littell, R. C., Freund, R. J. and Spector, P. C. (1991), *SAS System for Linear Models, Third Edition*, Cary, NC: SAS Institute Inc.

Mahalanobis, P. S. (1936), "On the Generalized Distance in Statistics", *Proc. Nat. Inst. Sci. India*, 12, 49-55.

Mardia, K. V. (1970), "Measures of Multivariate Skewness and Kurtosis with Applications", *Biometrika*, 519-530.

Mardia, K. V. (1974), "Applications of Some Measures of Multivariate Skewness and Kurtosis for Testing Normality and Robustness Studies", *Sankhyā*, A 36, 115-128.

Mardia, K. V. (1980), "Tests for Univariate and Multivariate Normality", *Handbook of Statistics, Vol. 1: Analysis of Variance*, Ed. P. R. Krishnaiah, 279-320, Amsterdam: North Holland.

Mardia, K. V., Kent, J. J. and Bibby, J. M. (1979), *Multivariate Analysis*, New York: Academic Press.

Mauchly, J. W. (1940), "Significance Test for Sphericity of a Normal *n*-Variate Distribution", *Ann. Math. Statist.*, 29, 204-209.

Milliken, G. A. (1990), "Analysis of Covariance: Repeated Measures and Split Plot Designs", *Proceedings of the Fifteenth Annual SAS Users Group International Conference*, 1268-1277.

Milliken, G. A. (1989), "Analysis of Covariance: Multiple Covariates", *Proceedings of the Fourteenth Annual SAS Users Group International Conference*, 51-60.

Milliken, G. A. and Johnson, D. E. (1989), *Analysis of Messy Data: Analysis of Covariance*, The Institute of Professional Education, Arlington, VA.

Milliken, G. A. and Johnson, D. E. (1991), *Analysis of Messy Data, Vol. 1*, New York: Von Nostrand Reinhold.

Montgomery, D. C. (1991), *Design and Analysis of Experiments*, New York: John Wiley & Sons, Inc.

Morrison, D. F. (1976), *Multivariate Statistical Methods*, New York: McGraw Hill.

Muirhead, R. J. (1982), *Aspects of Multivariate Statistical Theory*, New York: John Wiley & Sons, Inc.

Naik, D. N. (1989), "Detection of Outliers in the Multivariate Linear Regression Model", *Commun. Statist.*, Ser. A, 18, 2225-2232.

Obenchain, R. L. (1990), *STATBLSIM.EXE Version 9010*, Unpublished C Code, Eli Lilly & Company, Indianapolis, IN.

Olkin, I. and Press, S. J. (1969), "Testing and Estimation for a Circular Stationary Model", *Ann. Math. Statist.*, 40, 1358-1373.

Pillai, K. C. S. (1960), *"Statistical Tables for Tests of Multivariate Hypotheses"*, Manila: Statistical Center, University of Phillipines.

Pillai K. C. S. and Jayachandran, K. (1967), "Power Comparison of Tests of Two Multivariate Hypotheses Based on Four Criteria", *Biometrika*, 54, 195-210.

Pillai, K. C. S. and Jayachandran, K. (1968), "Power Comparison of Tests of Equality of Two Covariance Matrices Based on Four Criteria", *Biometrika*, 55, 335-342.

Potthoff, R. F. and Roy, S. N. (1964), "A Generalized Multivariate Analysis of Variance Model Useful Especially for Growth Curve Problems", *Biometrika*, 51, 313-326.

Rao, C. R. (1948), "Tests of Significance in Multivariate Analysis", *Biometrika*, 35, 58-79.

Rao, C. R. (1964), "The Use and Interpretation of Principal Components in Applied Research", *Sankhyā*, A, 26, 329-358.

Rao, C. R. (1973), *Linear Statistical Inference and Its Applications*, New York: John Wiley & Sons, Inc.

Rao, C. R. (1987), "Prediction of Future Observations in Growth Curve Models", *Statist. Sci.*, 2, 434-471.

Ratkowsky, D., Evans, M. and Alldredge, J. (1993), *Cross-over Experiments*, New York: Marcel Decker, Inc.

Rawlings, J. O. (1988), *Applied Regression Analysis: A Research Tool*, Pacific Grove CA: Wadsworth & Brooks.

Rouanet, H. and Le'pine, D. (1970), "Comparison Between Treatments in a Repeated Measures Designs: ANOVA and Multivariate Methods", *British Jour. of Math. and Stat. Psych.*, 23, 147-163.

Roy, S. N., Gnanadesikan, R. and Srivastava, J. N. (1971), *Analysis and Design of Certain Quantitative Multiresponse Experiments*, New York: Oxford University Press.

SAS Institute Inc. (1989), *SAS/IML Software: Usage and Reference, Version 6, First Edition*, Cary NC: SAS Institute Inc.

SAS Institute Inc. (1993), *SAS/INSIGHT User's Guide, Version 6, Second Edition*, Cary NC: SAS Institute Inc.

SAS Institute Inc. (1990), *SAS Language: Reference, Version 6, First Edition,* Cary NC: SAS Institute Inc.

SAS Institute Inc. (1990), *SAS Procedure Guide, Version 6, Third Edition,* Cary NC: SAS Institute Inc.

SAS Institute Inc. (1989), *SAS/QC Software: Reference, Version 6, First Edition,* Cary NC: SAS Institute Inc.

SAS Institute Inc. (1989), *SAS/STAT User's Guide, Version 6, Fourth Edition, Volume 1,* Cary NC: SAS Institute Inc.

SAS Institute Inc. (1989), *SAS/STAT User's Guide, Version 6, Fourth Edition, Volume 2,* Cary NC: SAS Institute Inc.

SAS Institute Inc. (1992), SAS Technical Report P-229, *SAS/STAT Software: Changes and Enhancements, Release 6.07,* Cary NC: SAS Institute Inc.

Schaefer, R. L. (1994), "Using Default Tests in Repeated Measures: How Bad Can It Get?", *Commun. Statist.,* Ser. B, 23, 109-127.

Schwager, J. J. and Margolin, B. H.(1982), "Detection of Multivariate Normal Outliers", *Ann. Statist.,* 10, 943-954.

Searle, S. R. (1971), *Linear Models,* New York: John Wiley & Sons, Inc.

Searle, S. R. (1987), *Linear Models for Unbalanced Data,* New York: John Wiley & Sons, Inc.

Searle, S. R. (1994), "Analysis of Variance Computing Package Output for Unbalanced Data from Fixed-Effects Models with Nested Factors", *Amer. Statist.,* 48, 148-153.

Seber, G. A. F. (1984), *Multivariate Observations,* New York: John Wiley & Sons, Inc.

Smith, W. B. and Hocking, R. R. (1972), "Wishart Variate Generator", *Appl. Statist.,* 21, 341-345.

Spector, P. (1987), "Strategies for Repeated Measures Analysis of Variance", *Proceedings of the Twelfth Annual SAS Users Group International Conference,* 1174-1177.

Srivastava, M. S. and Carter, E. M. (1983), *An Introduction to Applied Multivariate Statistics,* New York: North Holland.

Tatsuoka, M.M. (1988), *Multivariate Analysis: Techniques for Education and Psychological Research,* New York: John Wiley & Sons, Inc.

Timm, N. (1975), *Multivariate Analysis with Applications in Education and Psychology,* California: Brooks/Cole.

Tseo, C. L., Deng, J. C., Cornell, J. A., Khuri, A. I. and Schmidt, R. H. (1983), "Effect of Washing Treatment on Quality of Minced Mullet Flesh", *Jour. Food Sci.,* 48, 163-167.

Tong, Y. L. (1990), *Multivariate Normal Distribution,* New York: Springer Verlag.

Williams, J. S. and Izenman, A. J. (1981), "A Class of Linear Spectral Models and Analyses for the Study of Longitudinal Data." *Technical Report,* Dept. of Statistics, Colorado State University.

Index

A

analysis of covariance 149–153
  flammability study, example 150–153,
    183–185
  model for analyzing data 149–150
Andrews function plots 26–27
  effect of order of elements in vector 27
  example 47–48
ANOVA F test
  See F test/statistic
ANOVA partitioning 70–72
ANOVA procedure 146
ARRAY statement 26
assumption of compound symmetry 194
autoregressive covariance structure, first
    order
  factorial design analysis 223
  time trend analysis 219, 220

B

balanced and unbalanced data 130–134
  analysis of covariance, example 151
  sums of squares and crossproducts (SS&CP)
    matrices 132–134
  two-way classification models 132–133
  Type I and Type II SS&CP matrices 133
  Type I through Type IV sums of squares
    131–132
  Type III SS&CP matrices 132–133
  unbalanced one-way classification, example
    136–139, 158–161
banded Toeplitz structure 219
Bartlett-Hotelling-Lawley trace 73
Bartlett Nanda-Pillai's trace 73
Best Linear Unbiased Estimator (BLUE) 70
Beta (Type I) matrix variate distribution 7
Beta matrices, generating 13–14, 21–22
between-subject hypotheses 206
biplots 27–30
  choices for coordinates 28–29
  correlation of variables 30
  dimension 1 (horizontal axis) output 29–30
  dimension 1 (horizontal axis) output,
    example 53–54
  dimension 2 (vertical axis) output 30
  dimension 2 (vertical axis) output, example
    53–54
  macro BIPLOT 29
  macro BIPLOT, example 49–52
  plotting observations and variables together
    27–30
bivariate normal distribution 33–34
  contour plot of density 33–34
  contour plot of density, example 65
  definition 33

probability density function plotting 33
probability density function plotting, example
  63–64
block design structure
  testing for covariance structures 189
  univariate analysis of repeated measure
    data 194
blocking 144–145
  comparison of corn varieties, example
    144–145, 173–174
blocking effects 76
Bonferroni intervals 85, 218

C

calibration problems 91–94
  example 123–126
CALIS procedure
  computing multivariate kurtosis 10
  computing multivariate kurtosis, example
    11, 15–17
canonical correlation coefficients 4
CAPABILITY procedure 31
carryover effects in crossover designs 247
chi-square distributions
  approximation of Wilks' lambda 75
  nonlinear regression model of growth
    244–245
  Q-Q plots 30
chi-square tests
  nonlinear regression growth model,
    example 246
  Type III Wald's chi-square tests 221, 291
CHISQ option, MODEL statement 220, 291
CINV function 31
  example 56
circular covariance test
  cork boring data, example 192, 262–264
  covariance structures 191–192
CLASS statement, example 136, 155
coefficients
  See also correlation coefficients
  population coefficient of determination 4
  slope coefficient for regression 93
common slope model, univariate analysis of
    covariates 231
comparison of treatments
  See treatment comparisons in k populations
compound symmetry assumption 194
compound symmetry test
  covariance structures 190
  memory data, example 190–191, 260–261
confidence intervals
  bark deposits in cork data, example 84–85,
    111–112

confidence intervals *(continued)*
    cutoff point 83
    simultaneous, example 83–85, 111–112
confounded effects
    definition 146
    univariate analysis of crossover design
        248–249
contour plot of density 33–34
    example 65–66
contours
    bivariate probability density function 34
    bivariate probability density function,
        example 66
    definition 33
CONTRAST statement
    pairwise comparison in analysis of
        covariance, example 152–153, 183
    pairwise comparison in two-way blocking,
        example 145
    profile analysis of k populations, example
        210, 212, 275
    testing general linear hypotheses 90
    two-way factorial experiment, example 222,
        294
    univariate analysis of crossover design,
        example 248, 353
    univariate analysis of k populations 215,
        216
    univariate analysis of k populations,
        example 286
contrasts
    contrast means of zero in time trend studies
        217–218
    covariance structures guaranteeing sphericity,
        example 192–193, 255
    factorial design analysis 223
    factorial design analysis, example 301
    first degree (linear) polynomial contrast 225
    matrix of orthogonal contrasts 216
    matrix of orthogonal contrasts, example 290
    orthogonal polynomial contrasts 215, 216
    profile analysis of k populations 212
    profile as default matrix of contrasts
        195–196
    quadratic contrasts 225
    testing 12
    univariate analysis of k populations 215
correlation, multiple 3–4
correlation coefficient matrix 3
correlation coefficients
    canonical correlation coefficients 4
    multiple correlation coefficient 4
    partial correlation coefficient 3
    Pearson's correlation coefficient 2–3
covariables 76
covariance analysis 149–153
    flammability study, example 150–153,
        183–185
    model for analyzing data 149–150
covariance structures
    specifying in REPEATED statement,
        example 221
    specifying in SUBJECT= option, example
        221, 291
    time trend studies 219

covariance structures, testing 189–193
    circular covariance 191–192
    circular covariance, example 192, 262–264
    compound symmetry 190
    compound symmetry, example 190–191,
        260–261
    guaranteeing sphericity of orthogonal
        contrasts 192–193
    guaranteeing sphericity of orthogonal
        contrasts, example 255
    sphericity test 189–190
    sphericity test, example 255
covariances 1–4
    denoting covariances 1–2
    variance-covariance matrix 2–3
covariates 226–232
    increasing efficiency of inference in growth
        curve modeling, example 240
    multivariate analysis of covariance 226–229
    repeated measures analysis 226–232
    subject-specific covariates, example 227–229,
        314–326
    univariate approach to split plot design
        229–232
    univariate approach to split plot design,
        example 230–231, 327–331
crossover designs 246–252
    analysis 247–251
    construction 251–252
    construction, example 372–376
    multivariate analysis, example 249–251,
        356–371
    univariate analysis, example 247–249,
        352–355
curve fitting, polynomial
    See polynomial curve fitting
curves for displaying multivariate data
    See Andrews function plots

D

diagonal matrix 3
DISCRIM procedure 153
dispersion matrices 2–3
distributions
    See also normal distribution, multivariate
    bivariate normal distribution 33–34
    bivariate normal distribution, example
        63–64
    important sample statistics and their
        distributions 8–9
    matrix variate Beta (Type I) distribution 7
    probability distribution 3
    Wishart distribution 5, 6–7
DROP statement 33
    example 63

E

EM algorithm for imputing missing values
    252
empty cells 132

error sums of squares and crossproducts
  See also sums of squares and crossproducts (SS&CP)
  multivariate regression for fish data, example 79, 102–107
  partitioning for time trend studies, example 217
  profile analysis of *k* populations 210–211
  profile analysis of *k* populations, example 278–281
  univariate analysis of covariates 230
estimable functions 70
ESTIMATE statement
  fractional factorial experiments, example 148
  modeling cubic growth, example 239, 340
estimation, least squares
  See least squares estimation
estimation method, specifying in METHOD= option 221, 291
experimental data analysis, multivariate 127–185
  analysis of covariance 149–153
  analysis of covariance, example 150–153, 183–185
  balanced and unbalanced data 130–134
  blocking 144–145
  blocking, example 144–145, 173–174
  checking estimability, example 128–130
  fractional factorial experiments 146–149
  fractional factorial experiments, example 147–149, 175–182
  generalized theory 127
  one-way classification 134–139
  one-way classification, example 135–139, 155–161
  two-way classification 140–144
  two-way classification, example 140–144, 162–172

F

F test/statistic
  adjusting degrees of freedom for repeated measures data 194
  applicability to covariance structures 192
  approximations, table 74
  compound symmetry 191
  exact transformation to Wilks' lambda 136
  exact transformation to Wilks' lambda, table 75
  factorial design analysis 223
  factorial design analysis, example 296–298
  multivariate hypothesis testing 77
  testing Type H structure for memory data, example 195, 196–197
  time trend studies 221
  univariate analysis of covariates 230
  univariate analysis of *k* populations 214
  validity in split plot design 194, 196
FACTEX procedure
  construction of crossover design, example 251, 373
  fractional factorial experiments 146

factorial designs 221–226
  See also fractional factorial experiments
  coincidental profiles 222
  horizontal profiles 222
  parallel profiles 222
  repeated measure designs for treatment combinations, example 200–203, 271–272
  three-factor experiment with both repeated measures factors, example 224–226, 306–313
  two-factor experiment with both repeated measures factors, example 223–224, 303–305
  two-way factorial experiment, example 221–223, 294–302
first order autoregressive covariance structure
  factorial design analysis 223
  time trend analysis 219, 220
fixed effects
  identifying in time trend studies 218
  tests for fixed effects, example 221, 293
FOOTNOTE statement
  JUSTIFY=LEFT option 25
  JUSTIFY=RIGHT option 25
Fourier series expansion 27
fractional factorial experiments 146–149
  construction and analysis 146
  modeling of chemical process, example 147–149, 175–182

G

GCONTOUR procedure 33
  example 65
general linear hypotheses
  See linear hypotheses, testing
GLM procedure
  See also MODEL statement, GLM procedure
  analysis of covariance, example 150, 183
  compared with REG procedure 76, 80, 147
  fractional factorial experiments 146, 147
  fractional factorial experiments, example 148
  multivariate regression for fish data, example 79
  multivariate tests available as options 76
  one-way classification model 135
  one-way classification, example 136, 155
  polynomial curve fitting, example 199, 265
  profile analysis of *k* populations, example 210, 275
  testing equality of variances in calibration of thermocouples, example 93, 124
  testing hypotheses, example 78, 97
  time trend studies 218
  treatment comparisons in *k* populations, example 207, 275
  two-factor experiment with both repeated measures factors, example 303
  Type IV hypotheses for designs with missing observations 134

GLM procedure *(continued)*
  univariate analysis of crossover design,
      example 248, 353
  univariate analysis of *k* populations,
      example 214, 284
GPLOT procedure
  Andrews function plots 27
  Andrews function plots, example 47
  biplots 29
  biplots, example 49
graphical representation of multivariate data
    23–66
  Andrews function plots 26–27
  Andrews function plots, example 48
  biplots for plotting observations and variables
      together 27–30
  biplots for plotting observations and variables
      together, example 49–54
  bivariate normal distribution 33–34
  contour plot of density 33–34
  contour plot of density, example 65
  plots for detecting multivariate outliers 32
  plots for detecting multivariate outliers,
      example 60–62
  probability density function plotting 33
  probability density function plotting, example
      63–64
  profile plots 26
  profile plots, example 44–46
  Q-Q plots for assessing multivariate
      normality 30–31
  Q-Q plots for assessing multivariate
      normality, example 56–59
  scatter plots 24–26
  scatter plots, example 35–43
Greenhouse-Geisser procedure 194
growth curve models 236–246
  growth as nonlinear regression model
      243–246
  growth as nonlinear regression model,
      example 245–246, 347–351
  polynomial growth 237
  Rao-Khatri reduction 237–240
  Rao-Khatri reduction, example 238–240,
      339–344
  test of homogeneity of regression coefficients
      240–243
  test of homogeneity of regression coefficients,
      example 242–243, 245–246
G3D procedure
  drawing three-dimensional scatter plots 25
  plotting pdf of bivariate normal distribution
      33
  plotting pdf of bivariate normal distribution,
      example 63

H

H= specification, MANOVA statement
  hypothesis testing in laboratories comparison
      data, example 136, 138

  two-way factorial experiment, example 222,
      294
  unbalanced one-way classification, example
      155, 158
HELMERT option, REPEATED statement 193,
    196
homogeneity of regression coefficients, testing
    240–243
  cabbage data, example 242–243, 345–346
  linear model 241–242
Hotelling-Lawley trace criterion
  approximation to F statistic, table 74
  testing linear hypotheses 73
Hotelling's T^2 statistic
  basic concepts 8–9
  calculating confidence intervals 84–85
  obtaining from Wilks' lambda 77
  repeated measure designs for treatment
      combinations 200
  test for cork data, example 76–78, 95–98
hypotheses
  between-subject 206
  within-subject 206
hypotheses, testing
  See linear hypotheses, testing
  See multivariate tests

I

IML procedure
  calculating confidence intervals, example
      83, 111–112
  calculating skewness, example 11, 18–20
  generating Wishart random matrix, example
      13–14, 21–22
  plotting Q-Q plots 31
  plotting Q-Q plots, example 56
  polynomial curve fitting, example 198–199,
      265
  testing circular covariance, example 192,
      262
  testing compound symmetry, example 190,
      260–261
INPUT statement 303
INTERCEPT keyword, MTEST statement
  excluding for testing intercept differences
      91
  specifying for null hypothesis 80

J

JUSTIFY=LEFT option 25
JUSTIFY=RIGHT option 25

K

k populations 204–221
  comparison of treatments 206
  comparison of treatments, example 206–207,
      275–283
  multivariate model 205–206
  one-way classification model 205

profile analysis 207–213

profile analysis, example 209–212, 275–283

time trend studies 216–221

time trend studies, example 217, 220–221, 291–293

univariate analysis 213–216

univariate analysis, example 214–216, 284–290

KEEP statement 33

example 63

kurtosis, multivariate

computing with CALIS procedure, example 11, 15–17

Mardia's multivariate skewness and kurtosis measures 9–10

L

Latin square design

construction of crossover designs 251

two-way blocking 144

least squares estimation 69–70

checking estimability for experimental data, example 128–130

experimental data 127

growth curve models 240

iterative reweighted 81

univariate analysis of crossover design, example 248

LEVELS option, PLOT statement 34

example 65

likelihood ratio test statistic

nonlinear regression model of growth 244

testing sphericity 189–190

testing sphericity of orthogonal contrasts 193

linear hypotheses, testing 72–83

general linear hypotheses 87–91

general linear hypotheses, example 88–91, 117–122

general linear hypothesis of parallel profiles 208–209

multivariate tests 73–81

multivariate tests, example 95–107

one-way classification model, example 135–136, 155–157

spatial uniformity in semiconductor processes, example 88–91, 117–122

stepdown analysis 81–83

stepdown analysis, example 82–83, 109–110

testability in experimental data 130

linear regression model 67

LINESIZE= option 24

LSMEANS statement 151, 183

M

M matrix column as alternative to M= specification 78

M= specification, MANOVA statement

Hotelling's T^2 test for cork data, example 77–78, 97–98

hypothesis testing in laboratories comparison data, example 139, 158

M matrix column as alternative 78

profile analysis of k populations, example 210, 275

two-way factorial experiment, example 222, 294

Mahalanobis distance, squared

assessing multivariate normality 30

sample version 10

MANOVA partitioning

blocking, example 144

corrected total SS&CP matrix 132

MANOVA statement

See also M= specification, MANOVA statement

See also PRINTE option, MANOVA statement

See also PRINTH option, MANOVA statement

compared with MTEST statement 80

comparing dietary treatments, example 204, 273

H= specification 136, 138, 155, 158, 222, 294

MNAMES= specification 78, 97

multivariate analysis of covariance, example 237, 314

multivariate hypothesis testing of cork data, example 77, 78, 95, 97

multivariate hypothesis testing of fish data, example 79, 99

one-way classification, example 136, 155

polynomial curve fitting, example 199, 265

profile analysis of k populations, example 210, 212, 275

requesting Types I, II, and III SS&CP, example 142, 167

testing equality of variances in calibration of thermocouples, example 93, 124

testing general linear hypotheses 90

treatment comparisons in k populations, example 207, 275

two-way classification, example 140, 162

two-way factorial experiment of treatment combinations, example 201, 271

unbalanced one-way classification, example 138–139, 158

MANOVA table 71

Mardia's multivariate skewness and kurtosis measures 9–10

defining 9–10

value for kurtosis, example 11, 16–17

matrices

See also sums of squares and crossproducts (SS&CP)

correlation coefficient matrix 3

diagonal matrix 3

dispersion matrices 2–3

factorial design analysis, example 223, 296–302

generating Wishart random matrix 13–14

generating Wishart random matrix, example 21–22

matrices *(continued)*
matrix of all partial correlation coefficients 3
matrix of orthogonal coefficients, generating 239
matrix of orthogonal contrasts 216
profile analysis of *k* populations, example 210, 278–281
sample variance-covariance matrix 5–7
scatter plot matrix 25–26
scatter plot matrix, example 42–43
testing equality of variance-covariance matrices 153
variance-covariance matrix 2–3
matrix variate Beta (Type I) distribution 7
Mauchly's sphericity test
factorial design analysis, example 223, 298
likelihood ratio test statistic 189–190
restricted to one test by POLYNOMIAL option 196
testing sphericity of orthogonal contrasts, example 193, 258
univariate analysis of *k* populations, example 216, 287
univariate analysis of repeated measures data 194
MAXITER= option, NLIN procedure 245, 347
MEAN= option, STANDARD procedure 86
MEAN transformation 217
means 1–4
MEANS procedure
Q-Q plots 31
Q-Q plots, example 58
METHOD= option, MIXED procedure 221, 291
missing values
EM algorithm for imputing missing values 252
ignored or deleted by SAS software 134, 252
repeated measures analysis 252
Type IV sums of squares and crossproducts 132, 134
MIXED procedure
See also MODEL statement, MIXED procedure
factorial design analysis 223
METHOD= option 221, 291
modeling approach for data with missing values 252
modeling linear growth, example 235, 335
random coefficients analysis, example 234, 332
time trend studies, example 218, 220, 291
Toeplitz structure for modeling and data analysis 12
MNAMES= specification 78, 97
MODEL statement, GLM procedure
analysis of covariance, example 151, 183
multivariate analysis of covariance, example 227, 314
multivariate regression for fish data, example 79
NOUNI option 210, 227

NOUNI option, example 77, 78, 95, 314
polynomial curve fitting, example 199, 265
profile analysis of *k* populations, example 210, 275
profile analysis of subject-specific covariates, example 228, 314
SOLUTION option 248
SS1 option 145
SS3 option 144–145, 227, 314
testing equality of variances in calibration of thermocouples, example 93, 124
treatment comparisons in *k* populations, example 207, 275
two-way blocking, example 144–145, 173
univariate analysis of covariates, example 230–231, 327–328
univariate analysis of crossover design, example 248, 353
univariate analysis of *k* populations, example 214, 284
MODEL statement, MIXED procedure
CHISQ option 220, 291
modeling linear growth, example 236
random coefficients analysis, example 335
time trend studies, example 220, 291
MODEL statement, NLIN procedure 245, 347
MODEL statement, REG procedure
fractional factorial experiment, example 147
homogeneity of regression, example 243, 345
NOINT option 90
spatial uniformity in semiconductor processes, example 88, 90, 117
stepdown analysis for fish data, example 82, 109
testing equality of variances in calibration of thermocouples, example 93, 124
Type I sums of squares 131
Type II sums of squares 131–132
Type III sums of squares 132
MTEST statement, REG procedure 80
compared with MANOVA statement 80
computing Wilks' lambda test, example 80, 99
excluding INTERCEPT keyword 91
fractional factorial experiment, example 147–148, 176
INTERCEPT keyword 80
multiple response surface modeling, example 85–86, 113–116
performing partial tests 80
PRINT option 80
PRINT option, example 99
spatial uniformity in semiconductor processes, example 90–91, 117
testing equality of device variances and biases, example 94, 126
testing individual hypotheses 80
multiple correlation 3–4
multiple correlation coefficient 4
multiple response surface modeling 85–87
quality improvement of mullet flesh, example 85–87, 114–116
two-way classification, example 143

multivariate analysis concepts 1–22
  covariances 1–4
  important sample statistics and their
      distributions 8–9
  means 1–4
  multivariate normal distribution 4–5
  normal distribution 4–5
  random vector and matrix generation 12–14
  random vectors 1–2
  sampling from multivariate normal
      populations 5–7
  tests for multivariate normality 9–12
  variances 1–4
multivariate analysis of experimental data
  See experimental data analysis,
      multivariate
multivariate analysis of variance (MANOVA)
      table 71
multivariate data, representing graphically
  See graphical representation of multivariate
      data
multivariate normal distribution
  See normal distribution, multivariate
multivariate normal populations, sampling 5–7
multivariate regression 67–126
  ANOVA partitioning 70–72
  general linear hypotheses 87–91
  general linear hypotheses, example 88–91,
      117–122
  least squares estimation 69–70
  models 67–68
  multiple response surface modeling 85–87
  multiple response surface modeling, example
      85–87, 114–116
  multivariate tests 73–81
  multivariate tests, example 95–107
  simultaneous confidence intervals 83–85
  simultaneous confidence intervals, example
      84–85, 111–112
  statistical background 68–69
  stepdown analysis 81–83
  stepdown analysis, example 109–110
  testing linear hypotheses 72–83
  variance and bias analyses for calibration
      problems 91–94
  variance and bias analyses for calibration
      problems, example 92–94, 123–126
multivariate tests 73–81
  analysis of covariance, example 153
  examples 95–107
  general recommendations for selecting
      75–76
  Hotelling's T^2 test for cork data, example
      76–78, 95–98
  multivariate regression for fish data, example
      78–81, 99–107
  one-way classification model 135

N

_N_ automatic variable 31
negatively correlated variables in biplots 30
nested random effect 214

NLIN procedure
  See also MODEL statement, NLIN
      procedure
  DUD (doesn't use derivatives) as default
      245
  MAXITER= option 245, 347
  obtaining maximum likelihood estimates for
      growth model 243, 245–246
  PARMS= option 245, 347
  tests of homogeneity in growth models,
      example 245–246, 347
NOINT option
  MODEL statement 90
  REG procedure 242, 345
NOM option, REPEATED statement 195, 225,
      306
nonlinear regression model of growth 243–246
  tests of homogeneity, example 245–246,
      347–351
normal distribution, multivariate 4–5
  See also bivariate normal distribution
  properties 4–5
  Q-Q plots for assessing 30–31
  Q-Q plots for assessing, example 56–59
  sensitivity of multivariate regression to
      assumption of normality 94
  testing for contrasts, example 12
  testing for normality, example 10–12
  tests for multivariate normality 9–12
normal multivariate populations, sampling 5–7
normal random number generator 14
NOU option, REPEATED statement 225, 306
NOUNI option, MODEL statement
  example 95
  suppressing output from univariate analysis
      78, 210, 227, 314
  suppressing univariate analysis of individual
      variables 77
null hypothesis
  identifying before determining significance of
      effects 133

O

observations
  See also missing values
  Andrews function plots for identifying
      clusters 27
  profile plots for identifying clusters 26
one-way classification 134–139
  hypothesis testing, example 135–136,
      155–157
  unbalanced design, example 136–139,
      158–161
ORPOL function
  creation of orthogonal polynomial matrix
      198
  generating matrix of orthogonal coefficients
      239
  polynomial curve fitting, example 199, 265
orthogonal coefficients matrix, generating 239
orthogonal contrasts
  See contrasts
orthogonal polynomial, third degree 238

orthonormal transformation 196, 203
outliers
   See also tests for multivariate normality
   Andrews function plots for identifying 27
   plots for detecting 32
   plots for detecting, example 60–62
   profile plots for identifying 26
   sensitivity of multivariate regression to
      outliers 94
OUTPUT statement
   Andrews function plots 27
   Andrews function plots, example 47
OVERLAY option, PLOT statement 31
   example 56

P

PAGESIZE= option 24
pairwise comparison
   analysis of covariance, example 151–152,
      183
   two-way blocking, example 145
PARMS= option, NLIN procedure 245, 347
partial correlation coefficient
   definition 3
   matrix of all partial correlation coefficients
      3
partial sums of squares 132
partial tests, performing 80
Pearson's correlation coefficient 2–3
percentile plot, drawing with PROBPLOT
      statement 31
Pillai's trace criterion/statistic
   approximation to F statistic, table 74
   definition 72
   quality improvement of mullet flesh, example
      86–87
   testing for nonnormality in multivariate
      regression 94
   testing linear hypotheses 73
PLOT procedure 24
   example 35–37
PLOT statement
   LEVELS option 34, 65
   OVERLAY option 31, 56
   profile plots 26
   two-dimensional scatter plots 24
   two-dimensional scatter plots, example
      35–37
plotting symbol, specifying 24
polynomial curve fitting 197–200
   fish data, example 198–200, 265–270
polynomial growth 237
POLYNOMIAL option, REPEATED statement
   multivariate analysis of covariates, example
      228, 314
   restriction on Mauchly's sphericity test 196
   testing sphericity of orthogonal contrasts
      193
   three-factor experiment with both repeated
      measures factors, example 225, 306
   time trend analysis 216
   univariate analysis of k populations,
      example 215, 286

polynomials
   second degree 240
   third degree 238
population coefficient of determination 4
populations
   See also k populations
   See also single population analysis
   sampling from multivariate normal
      populations 5–7
positively correlated variables in biplots 30
PREFIX option 210
principal component representation, biplots 29
PRINCOMP procedure
   plotting Q-Q plots 31
   plotting Q-Q plots, example 56
   STD option 31, 56
PRINT option, MTEST statement 80, 99
PRINTE option, MANOVA statement
   multivariate analysis of covariance,
      example 227, 314
   multivariate regression, example 79, 99
   one-way classification, example 136, 155
   two-way classification, example 140, 162
   two-way factorial experiment of treatment
      combinations, example 201, 271
PRINTE option, REPEATED statement
   testing sphericity of orthogonal contrasts,
      example 193, 255
   testing Type H structure, example 195, 255
PRINTH option, MANOVA statement
   multivariate analysis of covariance,
      example 227, 314
   multivariate regression, example 79, 99
   one-way classification, example 136, 155
   two-way classification, example 140, 162
   two-way factorial experiment of treatment
      combinations, example 201, 271
PRINTM option, REPEATED statement
   testing Type H structure, example 195, 255
   three-factor experiment with both repeated
      measures factors, example 225, 306
probability density function (pdf)
   contour plot of density 33–34
   contour plot of density, example 65–66
   plotting 33
   plotting, example 63–64
probability distribution 3
PROBCHI function 246
PROBF function 231
PROBPLOT statement 31
profile analysis
   multivariate analysis of covariance 228
   single populations, example 188–189,
      253–259
profile analysis of k populations 207–213
   coincidental profiles 211–212
   heart rate data, example 209–213, 275–283
   horizontal profiles 212–213
   parallel profiles 207–211
profile matrix
   default for contrasts 195–196
   two-way factorial experiment of treatment
      combinations, example 202
   univariate analysis of k populations 215–216

PROFILE option, REPEATED statement 195, 196, 215
profile plots 26
  examples 44–46

Q

Q-Q plots 30–31
  assessing multivariate normality 30–31
  plotting, example 56–59
QQPLOT statement, CAPABILITY procedure 31
quadratic contrasts 225
quantile-quantile plots
  See Q-Q plots

R

R option, REPEATED statement 236, 335
random coefficient models 232–236
  linear growth example 235–236, 335–338
  mathematical representation 232–234
  pharmaceutical stability study, example 234–235, 332–334
random effect, nested 214
random matrix
  generating, example 13–14, 21–22
RANDOM statement
  random coefficients analysis, example 236, 335
  TEST option 214, 218, 284
  time trend studies 218
  TYPE=SIM option 235, 236, 335
  univariate analysis of *k* populations, example 214, 284
random vectors 1–2
  basic concepts 1–4
  generating 12–14
Rao-Khatri reduction 237–240
  choosing covariates, example 239–240, 344
  modeling cubic growth, example 238–239, 339–343
REG procedure
  See also MODEL statement, REG procedure
  See also MTEST statement, REG procedure
  compared with GLM procedure 76, 80, 147
  computing Wilks' lambda test 80
  computing Wilks' lambda test, example 99
  fractional factorial experiments 146, 147
  homogeneity of regression, example 243, 345
  multivariate tests available as options 76
  NOINT option 242, 345
  obtaining estimates for growth curves 239
  spatial uniformity in semiconductor processes, example 88, 117
  standard errors for least squares estimates, example 240, 344
  stepdown analysis for fish data, example 82, 109
  testing equality of variances in calibration of thermocouples, example 93, 124

regression, multivariate
  See multivariate regression
regression, nonlinear
  See nonlinear regression model of growth
regression coefficients, comparing 87–88
REML procedure
  See restricted maximum likelihood (REML) procedure
REPEAT function 14
repeated measure variables 224
repeated measures analysis 187–376
  analysis in presence of covariates 226–232
  analysis in presence of covariates, example 314–331
  crossover designs 246–252
  crossover designs, example 352–376
  definition 187
  factorial designs 221–226
  factorial designs, example 294–313
  growth curve models 236–246
  growth curve models, example 339–351
  k populations 204–221
  k populations, example 275–293
  random coefficient models 232–236
  random coefficient models, example 332–338
  single population 188–204
  single population, example 253–274
  when to use 187–188
REPEATED statement
  See also POLYNOMIAL option, REPEATED statement
  HELMERT option 193, 196
  incorrect sums of squares in covariate analysis 232
  indicating order of repeated measures 221
  multivariate analysis of covariance, example 228, 314
  NOM option 195, 225
  NOU option 225
  PRINTE option 193
  PRINTM option 225, 306
  PROFILE option 195, 196, 215
  R option 236, 335
  random coefficients analysis, example 236, 335
  specifying covariance structure, example 221, 291
  testing for sphericity 190
  testing for sphericity, example 255
  testing sphericity of orthogonal contrasts, example 193, 255
  testing Type H structure for memory data, example 195–196, 255
  three-factor experiment with both repeated measures factors, example 225, 306
  two-factor experiment with both repeated measures factors, example 224, 303
  two-way factorial experiment of treatment combinations 203
  univariate analysis of *k* populations 215
  univariate analysis of *k* populations, example 286
  univariate split plot analysis, example 223, 294

response surface modeling
  See multiple response surface modeling
restricted maximum likelihood (REML)
    procedure
  factorial design analysis 223
  random coefficients analysis, example 235,
    335
  time trend studies, example 221, 292
ROOT function 14
Roy's maximum root criterion
  approximation to F statistic, table 74
  testing linear hypotheses 74
R^2 (R-squared) value 71–72

S

sample statistics
  See test statistics
sample variance-covariance matrix 5–7
  obtaining 6
  properties 6–7
  writing 6
SAS/INSIGHT software 34
  features 34
  invoking 42
SAS/QC software 146
scatter plot matrix 25–26
  example 42–43
scatter plots 24–26
  three-dimensional scatter plots 25
  three-dimensional scatter plots, example 38
  two-dimensional scatter plots 24–25
  two-dimensional scatter plots, example
    35–37
SCATTER statement 25
  example 38
second degree polynomial model 240
sequential sums of squares 142, 151
SET statement, example 220, 291
simultaneous confidence intervals
  See confidence intervals
single population analysis 188–204
  circular covariance test 191–192
  circular covariance test, example 192,
    262–264
  compound symmetry test 190
  compound symmetry test, example 190–191,
    260–261
  compounding treatments, example 203–204,
    273–274
  covariance structures guaranteeing sphericity
    192–193
  covariance structures guaranteeing sphericity,
    example 255
  fitting polynomial curve 197–200
  fitting polynomial curve, example 198–200,
    265–270
  profile analysis, example 188–189, 253–259
  repeated measure designs for treatment
    combinations/conditions 200–204
  sphericity test 189–190
  testing for covariance structures 189–193
  testing for covariance structures, example
    190–191, 192, 255

testing type H structure, example 195–197,
  255–259
two-way factorial experiment, example
  200–203, 271–272
univariate analysis 193–197
singular value decomposition (SVD) 28
skewness
  calculating with IML procedure, example
    11, 18–20
  Mardia's multivariate skewness and kurtosis
    measures 9–10
slope coefficient for regression 93
SOLUTION option, MODEL statement 248
sphericity of orthogonal contrasts
  covariance structures guaranteeing 192–193
  covariance structures guaranteeing,
    example 255
sphericity test
  testing for covariance structures 189–190
  testing for covariance structures, example
    255
  univariate analysis of k populations 215,
    216
  univariate analysis of k populations,
    example 287
split plot design
  factorial design analysis 223
  time trend analysis 218, 219
  validity of F test 194
split plot design with univariate analysis
  covariates 229–232
  crossover design, example 247–249,
    352–355
  k populations 213–216
  k populations, example 286–290
  repeated measure data 194
square of multiple correlation coefficient 4
squared Mahalanobis distance
  assessing multivariate normality 30
  sample version 10
SS&CP
  See sums of squares and crossproducts
    (SS&CP)
SS1 option, MODEL statement 131, 145
SS3 option, MODEL statement 144–145, 227,
  314
standard errors for least squares estimates
  240
STANDARD procedure
  MEAN= option 86
  obtaining response surfaces 86
  standardization of variables 26
  STD= option 86
standardized variables, plotting 26
STD option, PRINCOMP procedure 31, 56
STD= option, STANDARD procedure 86
stepdown analysis 81–83
  examples 82–83, 109–110
  fractional factorial experiments 148–149
Student-Newman-Keuls test 93
subject model 229
SUBJECT= option, covariance structures 221,
  291

sums of squares and crossproducts (SS&CP)
  See also error sums of squares and
      crossproducts
  adjusting for block effects 144
  correcting for multivariate analysis of
      covariance 228
  experimental data analysis 131–134
  one-way classification, example 136
  partial 132
  partitioning for nonlinear regression growth
      models 246
  partitioning for time trend studies, example
      217
  profile analysis of k populations 210–211
  profile analysis of k populations, example
      278–281
  sequential 131, 151
  spatial uniformity in semiconductor
      processes, example 91, 118–122
  total sum of squares in ANOVA 70
  two-way classification 140, 141
  two-way factorial experiment of treatment
      combinations, example 202, 272
  Type I 131
  Type I, example 167
  Type II 131–132
  Type III 79, 132
  Type III, example 103–105
  Type IV 132
  uniformity and selectivity in etching process,
      example 142–144, 167–172
  univariate analysis of covariates, example
      231, 329–331
  univariate analysis of crossover design,
      example 248, 354–355

T

Taylor expansion 197
TEST option, RANDOM statement
  time trend studies 218
  univariate analysis of repeated measures,
      example 214, 284
TEST statement
  homogeneity of regression, example 242,
      243, 345
  stepdown analysis for fish data, example 83,
      109
test statistics
  Hotelling's T^2 statistic 8–9
  important sample statistics and their
      distributions 8–9
  Wilks' lambda 9
testing hypotheses
  See linear hypotheses, testing
  See multivariate tests
tests for covariance structures 189–193
  circular covariance 191–192
  circular covariance, example 192, 262–264
  compound symmetry 190
  compound symmetry, example 190–191,
      260–261
  covariance structures guaranteeing sphericity
      192–193

covariance structures guaranteeing sphericity,
    example 255
  sphericity test 189–190
  sphericity test, example 255
tests for multivariate normality 9–12
  Mardia's multivariate skewness and kurtosis
      measures 9–10
  testing cork data, example 10–12
  testing for contrasts in cork data, example
      12
three-dimensional scatter plots 25
  examples 38–41
time trend studies 216–221
  contrast means of zero 217
  covariance structures 219
  heart rate data, example 217, 220–221,
      291–293
  identifying fixed and random effects 218
  interaction between drug and trend 217–218
  multivariate vs. univariate analysis 218
  univariate split plot analysis 219
TITLE statement
  JUSTIFY=LEFT option 25
  JUSTIFY=RIGHT option 25
Toeplitz structure 192, 219
TRANSPOSE procedure 26
  example 44
treatment combinations/conditions
  comparing dietary treatments, example
      203–204, 273–274
  repeated measures designs 200–204
  two-way factorial experiment, example
      200–203, 271–272
  univariate analysis of crossover design,
      example 248
treatment comparisons in k populations
    206–207
  three population study of heart rate data,
      example 206–207, 275–283
two-dimensional scatter plots
  drawing 24–25
  drawing, example 35–37
  negative correlation between variables 25
  positive correlation between variables 24–25
two-way classification 140–144
  analysis of covariance, example 151, 152
  balanced two-way classification, example
      140–141, 162–166
  sums of squares estimation 132–133
  two-way factorial experiment of treatment
      combinations 203
  unbalanced design, example 131
  uniformity and selectivity in etching process,
      example 141–144, 167–172
Type H conditions
  definition 192
  time trend analysis 218
  univariate analysis of k populations 214,
      216
Type H structure
  class of covariance matrices 192
  definition 192
  testing for memory data, example 195–197,
      255–259

Type H structure *(continued)*
two-way factorial experiment of treatment
combinations 203
univariate analysis of *k* populations 215,
216
Type I sums of squares and crossproducts 131
two-way classification models 133
two-way classification models, example
142–144, 168–172
when to use 131
Type II sums of squares and crossproducts
131–132
Type III sums of squares and crossproducts
132
default for multivariate regression 79
example 103–105
two-way blocking, example 145
two-way classification models 132–133
when to use 132
Type III Wald's chi-square tests 291
Type IV sums of squares and crossproducts
definition 132
effect of reordered data 134
when to use 134
TYPE=SIM option, RANDOM statement 235,
236, 335

U

unbalanced data
See balanced and unbalanced data
univariate analysis
crossover design, example 247–249,
352–355
k populations 213–216
k populations, example 214–216, 284–290
R^2 (R-squared) value 71–72
single population analysis 193–197
split plot design with covariates 229–232
split plot design with covariates, example
230–232, 327–331
suppressing output corresponding to
univariate models 78
unstructured covariance model 219
USS function 31
example 56

V

variables
negatively correlated in biplots 30
positively correlated in biplots 30
standardizing 26
variance and bias analyses for calibration
problems 91–94
equality of variances in calibration of
thermocouples, example 92–94
reducing testing to MANOVA problem
91–92
variance-covariance matrix
basic concepts 2–3
testing 153
variances 1–4

Von Bertalanffy model 243, 245

W

Wald's chi-square tests
time trend studies 221
Type III Wald's chi-square tests 291
whole plot model 229
Wilks' lambda
approximation to F statistic, table 74
approximations 75
computing with MTEST statement 80
computing with MTEST statement, example
99
definition 9
exact transformation to F statistic 136
exact transformation to F statistic, table 75
obtaining value of Hotelling's T^2 77
testing linear hypotheses 73
unavailable with GLM procedure 79
Wilks' ratio 72
Williams' designs for crossover analysis 251
Wishart distribution
definition 5
distribution of sample variance-covariance
matrix 6–7
Wishart random matrix
generating 13–14
generating, example 21–22
within-subject hypotheses 206

Call your local SAS® office to order these other books and tapes available through the Books by Users℠ program:

Applied Statistics and the SAS® Programming Language, Third Edition
by **Ronald P. Cody**
and **Jeffrey K. Smith** ....Order #A56191

Beyond the Obvious with SAS® Screen Control Language
by **Don Stanley** ....Order #A55073

The Cartoon Guide to Statistics
by **Larry Gonick**
and **Woollcott Smith** ....Order #A55153

Categorical Data Analysis Using the SAS® System
by **Maura E. Stokes, Charles S. Davis,**
and **Gary G. Koch** ....Order #A55320

Essential Client/Server Survival Guide
by **Robert Orfali, Dan Harkey,**
and **Jeri Edwards** ....Order #A55305

The How-To Book for SAS/GRAPH® Software
by **Thomas Miron** ....Order #A55203

Learning SAS® in the Computer Lab
by **Rebecca J. Elliott** ....Order #A55273

The Little SAS® Book: A Primer
by **Lora D. Delwiche**
and **Susan J. Slaughter** ....Order #A55200

Mastering the SAS® System, Second Edition
by **Jay A. Jaffe** ....Order #A55123

Professional SAS® Programmer's Pocket Reference
by **Rick Aster** ....Order #A56198

Professional SAS® Programming Secrets
by **Rick Aster**
and **Rhena Seidman** ....Order #A56192

Professional SAS® User Interfaces
by **Rick Aster** ....Order #A56197

Quick Results with SAS/GRAPH® Software
by **Arthur L. Carpenter**
and **Charles E. Shipp** ....Order #A55127

Reporting from the Field: SAS® Software Experts Present Real-World Report-Writing Applications ....Order #A55135

SAS® Applications Programming: A Gentle Introduction
by **Frank C. Dilorio** ....Order #A56193

SAS® Foundations: From Installation to Operation
by **Rick Aster** ....Order #A55093

SAS® Programming by Example
by **Ron Cody**
and **Ray Pass** ....Order #A55126

SAS® Programming for Researchers and Social Scientists
by **Paul E. Spector** ....Order #A56199

SAS® Software Roadmaps: Your Guide to Discovering the SAS® System
by **Laurie Burch**
and **SherriJoyce King** ....Order #A56195

SAS® Software Solutions
by **Thomas Miron** ....Order #A56196

SAS® System for Elementary Statistical Analysis
by **Sandra D. Schlotzhauer**
and **Ramon C. Littell** ....Order #A5619

SAS® System for Forecasting Time Series, 1986 Edition
by **John C. Brocklebank**
and **David A. Dickey** ....Order #A5612

SAS® System for Linear Models,
Third Edition
by **Ramon C. Littell, Rudolf J. Freund,**
and **Philip C. Spector**...Order #A56140

SAS® System for Regression,
Second Edition
by **Rudolf J. Freund**
and **Ramon C. Littell** ....Order #A56141

SAS® System for Statistical Graphics,
First Edition
by **Michael Friendly** ....Order #A56143

A Step-by-Step Approach to Using the SAS®
System for Factor Analysis and Structural
Equation Modeling
by **Larry Hatcher** ....Order #A55129

A Step-by-Step Approach to Using the SAS®
System for Univariate and Multivariate Statistics
by **Larry Hatcher**
and **Edward Stepanski** ....Order #A55072

Table-Driven Strategies for Rapid SAS®
Applications Development
by **Tanya Kolosova**
and **Samuel Berestizhevsky** ....Order #A55198

Working with the SAS® System
by **Erik W. Tilanus**...Order #A55190

Audio Tapes

100 Essential SAS® Software Concepts (set of two)
by **Rick Aster** ....Order #A55309

A Look At SAS® Files (set of two)
by **Rick Aster** ....Order #A55207